Economists in Government

The text of this book was originally published without preface or index as Volume 13, No. 3 (Fall 1981) of the journal *History of Political Economy*.

Economists in Government

An international comparative study

Edited by A. W. Coats

Duke University Press

Durham, North Carolina   1981

Library of Congress Cataloging in Publication Data

Economists in Government

   Outgrowth of two conferences, the first held April
2–7, 1977 at the Villa Serbelloni, Bellagio, Italy and
the second held March 25–31, 1979 at the Inter-University
Centre for Postgraduate Studies, Dubrovnik, Yugoslavia.
   Originally published without preface or index as vol.
13:3 of the journal History of Political Economy.
   Bibliography: p.
   Includes index.
   Contents: Introduction / A. W. Coats — Britain, the
rise of the specialists / A. W. Coats — Australia,
economists in a federal system / A. Petridis — [etc.]
   1. Government economists—Congresses.
   I. Coats, A. W. (Alfred William), 1924–
HB21.E25   331.11′913300973   81-9858
ISBN 0-8223-0459-7   AACR2

Contents

Preface

The process of modernisation—a loose term that both embraces and transcends the more timeworn concepts of industrialisation and urbanisation—has been accompanied by a remarkable expansion in the size and functions of government, and this has necessarily led to an unprecedented growth in the number of specialists and other professionals employed in the public service throughout the world. The essays in this volume are concerned with one significant category of specialists, the economists, who, since World War II, have come to play an increasingly prominent and not infrequently controversial role at all levels of government—as technicians, administrators, advisers, legislators, and ministers.

The nature and objectives of these essays are explained more fully in the editorial introduction. At this stage it is sufficient to record that they represent the outcome of two conferences: the first, a planning meeting held at the Villa Serbelloni, Bellagio, Italy, from April 2–7, 1977; the second, at the Inter-University Centre for Postgraduate Studies, Dubrovnik, Yugoslavia, from March 25–31, 1979, where the draft chapters were examined critically by the assembled authors and two expert discussants. During the period since the second conference the draft papers have been substantially revised, and in some cases extended, with the aim of providing as much uniformity of treatment as seemed attainable, given the variety of experiences and situations to which they refer.

The subject matter of this volume cuts across several well-established disciplines, consequently there was no ready-made category of specialists available at the outset. Most of the authors would describe themselves as economists with a special interest in the history of the discipline and its applications to public policy; several have served as government advisers or civil servants; and all are fully aware that in this project we have been "learning by doing", as is unavoidable in all processes of innovation, intellectual or otherwise. If this venture stimulates others to improve on or supplement the accounts herein, whether by extending the period, adding to the present unrepresentative roster of countries, or applying a similar approach to other major disciplinary professions in modern government, our efforts will have been adequately rewarded.

The successful completion of a lengthy and complex project of this kind is necessarily dependent on the cooperation and expertise of many individuals, not all of whom can be mentioned here. This includes, for example, those public officials who must remain anonymous, and the many scholars and government economists, both past and present, who have been consulted or interviewed in the course of this research. Nevertheless, on behalf of all the participants in this undertaking, I would especially like to thank the following persons and organisations for their indispensable contributions: Professor Craufurd D. Goodwin, of Duke University, who was partly responsible for the initial conception and who subsequently played an essential role as participant and adviser; the Ford Foundation, for financial support and advice; the Rockefeller Foundation and staff at the Villa Serbelloni, Bellagio, Italy; the Director-General and staff of the Inter-University Centre for Postgraduate Studies, Dubrovnik, Yugoslavia; and a series of secretaries—at Nottingham: especially Gillian Deave, Gwen Parker, and Jane Smullen—and at the University of Texas at Austin, Emory University, Atlanta, Georgia, and the University of Western Australia, Perth, where I was a visitor while the project was under way.

University of Nottingham   A. W. Coats

Contributors

S. Ambirajan   Department of Economics, Indian Institute of Economics, Madras.

William J. Barber   Department of Economics, Wesleyan University, Middletown, Connecticut.

Trond Bergh   Historisk Institutt, Universitetet i Oslo, Blindern, Oslo.

A. W. Coats   Department of Economic and Social History, University of Nottingham, Nottingham.

Franco Ferraresi   Fondazione Olivetti, Rome, and Università degli Studi di Torino.

Giuseppe Ferrari   Università degli Studi di Torino.

Paulo Roberto Haddad   Planning Secretary, Minas Gerais State, and Fundação Joso, Av. João Pinheiro, Belo Horizonte.

Egon Kemenes   Institute for World Economics of the Hungarian Academy of Sciences, Budapest.

Ephraim Kleiman   Hebrew University, and the Falk Institute for Economic Research, Jerusalem.

Ryutaro Komiya   Faculty of Economics, University of Tokyo, Bunkyo-Ku, Tokyo.

A. Petridis   Department of Economics, University of Western Australia, Nedlands, Perth.

Kozo Yamamoto   Ministry of Finance, Government of Japan.

Economists in Government

Introduction

A. W. Coats

I

The essays collected here represent a preliminary effort to open up a new field of comparative social science research—the systematic study of the activities and influence of professional economists in modern government. This introduction is designed to provide a general background to the individual country studies that follow, and to highlight some of the themes and problems which recur in the subsequent chapters.[1]

It is important at the outset to stress the exploratory character of these studies which, in a number of countries, have involved opening up hitherto uncharted territory that cuts across several distinct academic disciplines. The unevenness of the essays, of which the authors are only too well aware, is largely attributable to the impossibility of adequately covering so extensive and multifaceted a subject within a limited space. In several cases the inaccessibility or absence of relevant evidence (e.g. government documents bearing directly on economic policy decisions) and the unwillingness of officials and policymakers to discuss their experiences, have precluded the investigation of certain topics, while in other cases the contributors have deliberately examined in detail certain aspects that were of special relevance in their chosen country. Greater comprehensiveness and uniformity of treatment, with some concomitant risk of forcing the material into a preconceived mould, could undoubtedly have been achieved by means of a more elaborate and lengthy research undertaking. On the other hand, there is much to be said in favour of presenting preliminary findings as early as possible in a field which holds out so much promise for future researchers. Admittedly the studies published here go only part of the way towards filling the vast gaps in our knowledge of the context in which and the methods by which the government economist applies his expertise. Nevertheless we are confident that the

1. Several readers of earlier versions of this introduction, whose constructive comments and criticisms are hereby acknowledged, have remarked that the underlying preconceptions are Western (i.e. Anglo-American). This bias is admitted, and remains, despite efforts to compensate for it. It is to be hoped that others can be persuaded to present an alternative perspective on the subject.

results will not only be of interest to students of recent economic history and policy, public administration, and the sociology of the professions and bureaucracy, but will also provide important new insights into recent developments in economics of value to those responsible for the training of economists and their recruitment and deployment in the public service.

Needless to say, the selection of countries included here is by no means representative. As is not unusual in collaborative research exercises, the final choice is attributable partly to design, partly to chance. Nevertheless the range and variety of case studies will suffice to provide a basis for provisional generalisations and an inducement to others to explore the rich potentialities for future research both in the countries represented here and elsewhere.

II. *Historical Background*

Although 'economists' of one sort or another have tendered advice to governments from time immemorial, the practice of employing any significant number of professional economists in government did not become widespread until World War II. This was a watershed in many countries, both in official economic and social policy, and in the development of economics as an academic discipline and as a policy science. The subsequent expanding demand for government economists is but one manifestation of an increasingly complex social division of labour which characterises modern industrial society,[2] and it has been directly encouraged by the adoption of more interventionist economic and social programmes by a wide spectrum of political regimes, all of which require skilled officials to undertake the increased functions and responsibilities involved.[3]

These trends are apparent in all the countries examined here, though the timing and pace of change have not been uniform. Thus in Italy, Japan, Norway and, for different reasons, Israel, war or the transition to peacetime conditions brought a sharp break with the past. In Hungary the economists' position was directly affected by events of the mid-1950s, while in Brazil the turning point was delayed for roughly another decade. Even where there was no radical change in the political and economic system, as in Australia, Britain, and the United States, or where the bureaucracy remained essentially intact, as in India, the role of economists expanded markedly under the influence of

2. As William Goode has observed, "an industrializing society is a professionalizing society." Cf. "Encroachment, Charlatanism, and the Emerging Professions: Psychology, Sociology, Medicine," *American Sociological Review* 25 (1960): 902.

3. For a broad multi-country survey of these developments see, for example, Andrew Shonfield, *Modern Capitalism* (London, 1965).

Keynesian ideas, with or without a mild dose of socialist planning. There was a widespread belief in the possibility of achieving a much higher and more sustained level of activity than in the 1930s, and it seemed probable that economists could contribute to the fulfilment of this objective.

III. *The Supply of 'Economists'*

(a) *Definitions, numbers, and academic qualifications*

The definition of 'economist,' and the calculation of the numbers of persons to be included under this heading, constitute the most fundamental and intractable problems encountered in this research. There is no generally accepted definition and no internationally recognised set of standards by which to measure unambiguously the number of qualified professional economists. The relevant conditions vary from country to country, and during the postwar period there have been considerable, sometimes rapid changes in the content and quality of economics teaching and research. Variations in undergraduate requirements are especially significant in those countries where there are few graduate economists available for government employment. At the level of graduate training, especially with respect to 'core' courses, there has been a measure of standardisation, and local cultural traditions are at least partly offset by the desire to emulate the international standards set by American or western European institutions—though these obviously do not apply with equal force in Communist countries.

After considerable discussion among the contributors it became clear that there was no simple satisfactory solution to this problem. Consequently each participant in the project has made an independent judgement of the appropriate definition of 'economist' and the minimum entry qualifications for the profession on the basis of his personal knowledge and experience. In certain countries where the educational conditions are likely to be less familiar to most readers (e.g. Brazil, Hungary, Italy) somewhat more information on student numbers and academic courses is provided. However, it should be noted that course titles which appear similar on paper may in fact be quite dissimilar in practice, as is apparent from a recent comparative study of economics curricula in European countries.[4] In the case of Japan and Italy the specific content of university training is irrelevant, since it plays no part in the placing of new entrants into the civil service.

When all the appropriate qualifications have been made, certain general features of the educational background are apparent. In the

4. J. F. H. Roper, *The Teaching of Economics at University Level* (London, 1970).

early postwar years some countries' educational institutions were much better equipped than others to provide a supply of qualified economists for the public service, and there has been a fairly general long-run rise in the levels of analytical rigour and technical skill involved in their training, albeit with some concomitant losses resulting from excessive specialisation. Once a significant growth of demand occurred, the supply usually responded fairly rapidly, especially where substantial public funds were available. Brazil and Hungary provide especially striking examples of this process, which has also occurred in some less developed countries (e.g. India), where the role of foreign-born and foreign-trained native-born economists has been particularly significant. There has, however, been no precise correlation between the quality and extent of educational provision, the reputation of the economics profession, and the growth in the numbers and importance of a country's economists in postwar government. (The United Kingdom affords a noteworthy illustration of the divergencies between these variables.)

Here, as elsewhere in economics, mere numbers are deceptive. A tiny handful of strategically placed individuals with direct access to powerful decisionmakers may, of course, be far more influential than a mighty host of trained economists located in the middle and lower bureaucratic ranks. Nevertheless, in the following chapters considerable attention has been paid to these modest toilers in the vineyards, for they have been unduly neglected in the published literature, much of which emanates from senior ex-government economists who have concentrated on the higher-level advisory functions. There is, moreover, a general tendency among academic economists to underestimate the extent to which the formulation as well as the implementation of policy is undertaken in the middle levels of the government machine. A study of the tasks performed at these levels, where most of the employment opportunities for economists occur, provides a more representative impression of the economists' contributions to the expanding economic and social functions of government.

(b) Functions

All governments perform economic 'functions.' But they do not all recognise 'economists' as a distinct category of personnel, nor do they all designate certain positions as economist 'posts,' to be occupied only by those with recognised academic qualifications. Moreover, while the categories of personnel, functions, and posts may be conceptually distinct, they are not necessarily so in practice. Qualified 'economists' may be appointed or promoted into general administrative or executive posts which call for little or no economic expertise.

Furthermore, it is virtually impossible to define economic 'functions' precisely: at the margin they shade imperceptibly into other types of work (general administration, routine collection of economic intelligence and statistics, etc.); and an individual economist's activities may change over time according to his experience, the development of his knowledge and skills, and the demands imposed on him.

Economics may be termed a vocationally non-specific subject; its relations with other disciplinary professions and the division of labour between them are not static. They will depend, among other things, on the structure and style of the bureaucracy, on the objectives and methods of government policies, and—a point unduly neglected—on the prevailing perceptions of the professional economist's potential contributions on the part of political leaders and those responsible for civil service personnel management.

Needless to say, while all these aspects are touched on in the following country studies, they have not all been examined in detail. It will be obvious to readers that certain tasks reserved for economists in some bureaucracies are performed in others by personnel with few or no formal qualifications, and one of the most basic questions motivating this enquiry is this: Why do governments employ any professional economists? What are their special skills, knowledge, and claims to expertise—if any? Well before the end of the volume it will become clear that the answers to these questions are by no means as clear as some economics textbook writers suggest. Economics is not so esoteric a subject as to be wholly inaccessible and incomprehensible to the layman. Many intelligent civil servants without formal training in the subject have proved themselves capable of 'learning by doing' ('sitting by Nellie' is the appropriate British civil service colloquialism), and it is a well-known cliché that most government economic work requires no more than sophomore (i.e. second-year American undergraduate) economics—with the added proviso that the individual may require several additional years' study and practice before he has fully assimilated this intermediate-level analysis.[5] Many economic problems call for general intellectual qualities, judgement, and experience, rather than advanced technical or professional knowledge. Hence economic specialists have no claim to monopoly privileges, particularly in the field of decisionmaking or policy advice, one of the central issues in several of the following studies.

5. Cf. the widely quoted remarks by Alain Enthoven reproduced in William R. Allen, "Economics, Economists, and Economic Policy: Modern American Experiences," *History of Political Economy* 9 (1977): 73. There are, of course, some exceptions to this general dictum, but Allen's article provides a highly stimulating compendium of views on the matter.

(c) *The market for economists*

In the market for the professional economist's services the central government is seldom, if ever, a monopsonist. At least until the early 1970s, and in some cases beyond that period, there has been a high and sustained postwar demand for economists on the part of academic institutions, business, and non-governmental public agencies at home and abroad. More recently, when certain segments of the market have been less buoyant, the demand from provincial and municipal governments has been expanding in some countries. Hence in considering the availability of economists for central government employment or other official posts some attention must be paid to their alternative employment opportunities.

Unfortunately there is a serious dearth of reliable data on relevant market conditions, especially in the business sector, and bewildering complexities arise in any attempt to make intergovernmental comparisons, partly because of marked differences in official personnel practices. In some countries bureaucratic standards and procedures are lax, appointments are politicised, and competitive bidding occurs. In other instances established personnel policies are carefully managed by officials and monitored by civil service trade unions with the aim of preventing inequities between different individuals or categorie; of staff. These obstacles can often be overcome or circumvented by strong ministers, especially in emergency conditions; and even in normal times it is usually possible, without corrupt practices, to create occasional or short-term posts for consultants or 'special advisers' attached to a minister, committee, or commission of enquiry—although such appointments usually constitute a very small proportion of the total.

Given the severe limitations of the available evidence, the variety and changeability of market conditions, and the lack of uniformity of bureaucratic procedures, the contributors to these studies have usually been forced to rely on impressionistic judgements based on their personal experience or, in some cases, on interviews with civil servants and past or present government economists. Nevertheless one or two preliminary general observations may be helpful at this stage.

In the British and American cases there have been substantial numbers of short-term government economists, primarily at the upper levels in the United States, but also at the middle levels in Whitehall, whereas in most of the other countries the great majority of such personnel have been permanent officials. The relative attractiveness of government and non-government (primarily academic) employment for economists has varied over time and is determined by a subtle combination of pecuniary and non-pecuniary considerations—including the opportunities for promotion, personal and intellectual independence, freedom to publish and mix with other professionals, and the prospect of exerting an influence on public policy. Over the long run the gap between government and academic economists has narrowed, owing to a combination of developments within the discipline, changes in the nature and scope of government responsibilities in the economic and social spheres, and the increasing feedback effects of government work, and ex-government economists, on the academic community's and general public's conception of the civil service. References to all these matters will be found in the following studies.

(d) *General social and cultural attitudes towards intellectuals, professionals, and experts*

In any international comparative study of this kind some attention must be paid to national social and cultural attitudes towards economists and other experts, specialists, or disciplinary professionals. In some countries economists and other social scientists are regarded as a strange new breed, to be considered alongside natural scientists and technologists. In traditional humanistic cultures the educational system may be ill-equipped to provide the necessary resources and training facilities for social scientists, and those who obtain the requisite qualifications may find that their rewards, roles, and status are inferior to those of personnel trained in more traditional subjects.[6] In such situations the influence of economists trained in Europe or the U.S.A. has often been crucial prior to the development of an indigenous economics profession.

In the British civil service, which left a strong imprint on the Indian bureaucracy, the traditional preference for the 'all rounder' over the specialist inevitably restricted the latter's career opportunities and may have discouraged some men of exceptional ability, ambition, or energy from seeking a civil service career, thereby confirming the generalists' preconceptions that most specialists were of an inferior intellectual calibre. In Australia, by contrast, a deep-rooted anti-elitist attitude imposed barriers to the recruitment of graduates into the civil service during the interwar period, but did not discourage specialisation within the organisation. Indeed, those with specialist post-entry academic

6. There are stimulating reflections on the influence of cultural factors on the organisation of top-level economic advisory functions in Henry C. Wallich, "The American Council of Economic Advisers and the German Sachsverstaendigenrat: A Study in the Economics of Advice," *Quarterly Journal of Economics* 82 (Aug. 1968): 349–79.

qualifications often rose more rapidly through the ranks. Generally speaking, in northern and western Europe and the United States, unlike Britain, expertise was fully recognised, and special qualifications were an asset in securing senior posts; while in Brazil, the relative position of economists and technocrats in the public service, as in society at large, improved rapidly as a result of powerful support from an authoritarian government, a situation not uncommon under such regimes.[7]

Bureaucratic procedures and styles usually reflect the national culture, as do higher educational institutions, for it can be said of them, as of governments, that the nation gets the universities it deserves. However, as subsequent chapters reveal, an inhospitable cultural climate can be overcome, given sufficient determination and resources.

IV. *Professionalism and Bureaucracy*

(a) *General issues*

Economists in government are necessarily members of a large organisation and must accordingly to some extent work in cooperation with, though not invariably in close proximity to, other public servants (some of whom may be professionals) and politicians. They may, of course, be employed in specialist research units where they are comparatively uninhibited by the customary constraints of organisational life, but in such cases they will usually be away from the centres of power and unlikely to be able to exert much influence on the organisation's policies or its day-to-day activities. By contrast, the higher the professional rises in the bureaucratic hierarchy the more likely he is to be drawn into its operations and to be working in direct contact with senior bureaucrats and/or politicians. In such circumstances conflicts of loyalty and interest are more likely to arise.

Whereas a professional in a bureaucracy has a dual loyalty, to his profession and to his employer, the bureaucrat has no such problem. In the interests of his career, if for no more laudable motive, he will naturally tend to identify himself with the organisation's goals, accept its conventions, and acquire a mastery of its procedures.[8] To the profes-

7. Unfortunately the studies that follow do not include a genuinely underdeveloped country. For a relevant, and exceptional, study of this type see B. D. Giles, "Economists in Government: The Case of Malawi," *Journal of Development Studies* 15 (Jan. 1979): 216–22.

8. Of course, bureaucrats are heterogeneous. See, for example, Robert Putnam's useful distinction between the 'classical' and the 'political' types and comments on the decline of the former in Germany, Sweden (also Norway), and Italy in the postwar period. Cf. his essay in Mattei Dogan, ed., *The Mandarins of Western Europe: The Political Role of Top Civil Servants* (New York, 1975), pp. 87–126. As Reinhart Bendix has

sional, however, adaptation or socialisation into the bureaucracy poses certain dangers, including the loss of professional independence and initiative, intellectual obsolescence resulting from total immersion in day-to-day routines, with the consequent inability to keep in touch with new developments in his specialist field, and possibly even the corrupting influence of bribery, power seeking, and politicisation.

In this section some indication of the relevance of these issues to the following case studies will be provided, though once again it is necessary to forewarn the reader that it has proved neither possible nor desirable to aim at complete uniformity of content and structure.

(b) *Economics as a profession*

Economics is one among a number of modern professions which, unlike their traditional predecessors—law, medicine, and the church —do not have strict controls on entry, formal codes of ethics, or effective methods for disciplining their members. Nevertheless they possess the essential internal and external requirements[9]—namely, that their members are subjectively aware of themselves as professionals and are recognised as such by those who use their services and by the public at large. As in other cases this recognition is based on the possession of degrees and other qualifications which are not readily accessible to laymen; and it takes the form of specialised appointments, high remuneration, delegation of responsibility or authority, and a measure of social esteem.

The professionalisation of economics has not hitherto been subjected to detailed comparative study,[10] but it would be generally agreed that a recognisable corps of professional economists emerged within the academic community in Britain and the United States around the

---

noted, the element of 'trust' involved in professional judgements is, at least in principle, at odds with the requirement of 'accountability' in administrative actions, which implies distrust. A modern government relies on both professional and administrative skills, "but to be responsible it must necessarily check on the discretionary judgements that are indispensable for both professional work and good government." Cf. "Bureaucracy," *International Encyclopedia of the Social Sciences*, 2 (New York, 1968): 214.

9. On professions and professionalisation see, for example, Talcott Parsons, "Professions," *International Encyclopedia of the Social Sciences* (New York, 1968), 12: 536–46; H. M. Vollmer and Donald L. Mills, *Professionalization* (New Jersey, 1966); and Phillip Elliott, *Sociology of the Professions* (London, 1972).

10. See, however, my "The Development of the Economics Profession: A Preliminary Review," in L. Houmanidis, ed., *International Congress of Economic History and History of Economic Theories* (Piraeus: The Piraeus Graduate School of Industrial Studies, 1975), pp. 277–90; "The Development of the Agricultural Economics Profession in England," *Journal of Agricultural Economics* 27 (Sept. 1976): 381–92; and "Reflections on the Professionalization of Economics" (Newcastle University, New South Wales, 1980).

turn of the century, but somewhat later in many other countries.[11] The usual indications are the appearance of specialist learned societies, scholarly periodicals, and academic degrees. Government employment, with its hierarchical gradations of title, status, responsibility, and emoluments, has markedly accelerated the process and has also helped to arouse a sense of professional self-consciousness and *esprit de corps* among economists, both in the public service and in the academic world, where the postwar expansion has led to increasing specialisation and division of labour within the discipline.

While professional economists may be said to share a common culture which is circumscribed by certain accepted conventions, ideas, and methodological rules, they do not constitute a tightly organised or homogeneous community. On the whole, academic training in economics has not been so rigorous, nor the socialisation process so effective, as to engender a sharp differentiation between economists and other social scientists, statisticians, operations researchers, mathematicians, etc. Nor are they immune from lay judgement on technical matters on the grounds that the laity is presumed incompetent to comprehend their arcane knowledge or evaluate their performance, although some more technical branches of the discipline (e.g. mathematical and econometric model building) possess this character.

In fact the professional economists' relations with the public —including non-economist bureaucrats and politicians—have often been uneasy, for many laymen have firm preconceived ideas about economic affairs and unwarranted confidence in their own ability to prescribe solutions to current economic problems. Some of those most outspokenly hostile or sceptical towards economists' expertise have also been inclined to exaggerate their influence on public policy. When economic affairs have been proceeding smoothly and prosperously, economists have generally been in popular favour, and they have usually been willing to take at least some of the credit for the situation. By contrast, when economic conditions have deteriorated, they have correspondingly received undeserved blame.

Several of the studies in this volume (e.g. those of the U.S.A., Australia, Brazil, and Israel) provide clear indications of the postwar rise and subsequent deflation—whether mild or serious—of the professional economists' public reputation. In some instances the initial upswing was directly associated with the prestige or influence of a partic-

11. This is not the place to discuss whether economists of earlier periods, such as the exponents of *Kameralwissenschaft*, should be regarded as professionals. It is, however, appropriate to note the parallels between contemporary government economists and the "consultant administrators of the mercantilist era." Cf. Joseph A. Schumpeter, *History of Economic Analysis* (New York, 1954), part II, ch. 3.

ular individual or 'school' of economics (e.g. J. M. Keynes in Britain, Australia, India, the United States and also Canada; Don Patinkin in Israel; Jan Tinbergen in the Netherlands; and Ragnar Frisch in Norway, where the Oslo School's reputation has remained remarkably high throughout the postwar era). In the case of Brazil (as to a lesser extent with Greece under the so-called Colonels' Regime) the economists' rise to power and influence occurred under a military government determined to use its powers to improve the country's economic performance. Similar experiences can be recorded in other South American countries (e.g. Mexico), where authoritarian regimes have been favourably disposed to economists and other technocrats.[12] But here, as in more democratic societies, exaggerated expectations which carry the economics profession on the crest of a wave of public enthusiasm (as in the United States and, to a lesser extent in Britain during the 1960s) are all too often followed by a reaction when the high hopes are dashed—with obvious consequences for those involved. This, indeed, is one of the reasons for the much discussed 'crisis' in economics in the late 1960s and early 1970s,[13] a state of affairs that has not yet been fully resolved.

(c) *Some relevant features of modern bureaucracy*

According to Max Weber's classic analysis, bureaucratic organisations involve specialised and differentiated administrative roles; recruitment, transfer, and promotion by universalistic criteria of achievement, rather than by ascription; reliance on full-time salaried officials; and administrative decisionmaking within a context of hierarchy, responsibility, and discipline.[14] Needless to say, practice often diverges substantially from this 'ideal type,' for example in the extent to which the organisation functions smoothly and efficiently, and is free from political interference, corruption, nepotism, etc. One of the principal aims of this series of studies is, while acknowledging the differences between Weber's model and the complex realities of

12. There is a suggestive analysis of the differences in economists' roles between an authoritarian and a democratic regime in Roderic Ai Camp, *The Role of Economists in Policy-Making: A Comparative Case Study of Mexico and the United States* (Tucson, Ariz., 1977).

13. For general reviews of this episode see, for example, Walter W. Heller, "What's Right with Economics?" *American Economic Review* 65 (March 1965): 1–26; and A. W. Coats, "The Current Crisis in Economics in Historical Perspective," *Nebraska Journal of Economics and Business* 16 (Summer 1977): 3–16. For evidence that the discussion is not yet closed see the special issue of *The Public Interest* (1980) in which a dozen authors, including several leading economists, examine "The Crisis in Economic Theory."

14. See Weber's classic essay on "Bureaucracy" in H. H. Gerth and C. Wright Mills, *From Max Weber, Essays in Sociology* (New York, 1946), pp. 196–244.

twentieth-century government, to examine how and with what effects economists function within modern bureaucracies.

As might be expected, the studies included here reveal a wide variety of experiences. In Britain, India, and to a lesser extent Australia, the advent of professional economists into government encountered some resistance from a stable, politically neutral, and well-entrenched traditional body of 'intelligent laymen' generalist administrators; and strong exogenous forces (e.g. depression, war, or the pressure of a determinedly innovative government) were sometimes required before any significant number of economists rose to positions of influence within the bureaucratic hierarchy. In Norway, where the traditional nineteenth-century European 'juristenmonopol' prevailed until World War II,[15] the subsequent rise of professional economists was so remarkably frictionless that a 'harmony model' has been found applicable. Numbers are important here, for while one or two influential advisers (e.g. in a European-style ministerial 'cabinet') may be added to an existing organisation without much affecting its main operations or internal structure, more significant changes may be required when, as in the United States and Britain, considerable numbers of short-service or temporary specialist professionals are added. In the British case the reliance on short-term economists was due both to shortages of suitably qualified personnel and to the politicians' and established bureaucrats' unwillingness to create sufficient attractive niches for the professionals. It was not until the numbers reached a critical minimum size that it became necessary to provide formal procedures for the recruitment, deployment, and promotion of economists, a development that was accompanied by an increased measure of professional autonomy and self-control. In the United States, where, by long-established convention, a sizeable number of senior posts have been reserved for political appointees, most of whom come and go with changes in the political leadership, it was easy to find suitable slots for professional economists right up to and including cabinet rank.[16] These outsiders were, of course, obliged to collaborate with the corps of lower-level permanent officials, some of whom were certainly qualified to be regarded as professional economists;[17] but this does not seem to

15. For general background see John A. Armstrong, *The European Administrative Elite* (Princeton, 1973).

16. More extensive research would, of course, reveal many examples of political influences on the appointment of economists and other civil servants. For a fascinating example, not included among the studies in this volume, see Georges Stienlet, *Economists and the Civil Service System: The Belgian Case* (Centrum voor Economischen Studien, Katolieke Universiteit te Leuven, 1978).

17. In recent years the growing demand for technical and professional expertise has led to some changes in the boundaries between political and established posts in

have generated much friction. Some of the effects of these short-term arrangements on the relationships between academic and government economists will be noted later in this introduction.

At this point it is appropriate to refer to the situation in those countries where the bureaucracy makes no provision whatever for specialist posts for professional economists. In Japan this deficiency is offset by a regular system of in-service training and secondment for selected officials, whereas in Italy the problem is handled on an *ad hoc* basis by calling upon outside advisers, usually university professors, and utilizing the resources of specialist research institutes and agencies. Whether these arrangements are sufficient to meet the need for economic expertise is a matter for conjecture. It would, indeed, be ironic if the research embodied in these studies were to suggest that the vastly increased employment of economists in postwar governments was in fact an unnecessary luxury. The performance of the Japanese economy may be cited by some, superficially, as supporting evidence; but few observers are likely to argue that the same applies to Italy. There is, in fact, no necessary or observed correlation between the number of professional economists in a government and that country's growth rate, notwithstanding some cynics' contention that the relationship is an inverse one!

In-service training both for professionals and for generalist administrators has become increasingly fashionable in recent years. The elaborate preparation provided for senior French civil servants at the Ecole Nationale d'Administration has been much admired in Europe and elsewhere. In Britain determined efforts were made in the 1960s, especially in connection with the work of the Fulton Committee, to modernise the public bureaucracy, with somewhat mixed success;[18] and in the U.S.A. there have been many experiments with graduate instruction in public administration and, more recently, policy analysis and other supposedly relevant disciplines. With respect to economics, the value of in-service training for generalist administrators dealing

Washington. Cf. Hugh Heclo, *A Government of Strangers* (Brookings Institution, Washington, D.C., 1977).

18. The critics' major contention was that Britain's senior civil servants were inadequately equipped "to tackle the political, scientific, social, economic and technical problems of our time." *The Civil Service: Report of the Committee, 1966–68: Chairman, Lord Fulton* Cmnd. 3638 (London: H.M.S.O., 1968), vol. 1, paras. 31–2. As the Head of the Civil Service conceded in 1970, since the war it was "not so much that 'generalism' has been found inadequate, as that the particular skills covered by that description have either been overtaken by events or seem to require a great deal more formal training as well as experience, and to be supplemented by the skills and experience of people formally dubbed 'specialists.' " William (Lord) Armstrong, *Personnel Management in the Civil Service* (London: H.M.S.O., 1971), p. 2.; also his *Professionals and Professionalism in the Civil Service* (Welwyn Garden City, 1970), pp. 5–19.

with economic and social problems and needing to communicate with social scientists has been widely recognised; and the mounting volume of statistical information and analysis has put an increasing premium on numeracy as well as the traditional verbal and literary skills. In all these respects economists have proved themselves valuable both as 'new generalists' and as specialists; and in many governments (as illustrated in the cases of Norway and Hungary in these studies) they have been supplementing and even competing for positions with traditional jurists, who for so long enjoyed a monopoly of the highest positions in European bureaucracies.

As the role of professionals and experts increases in modern government, economists, like other categories of staff, find themselves dealing and occasionally competing with other professionals, often in so-called 'mixed divisions.' In the more technical activities, such as model building or investment appraisal, they often work alongside statisticians, mathematicians, operations researchers, accountants, or engineers. Chance, convention, and the influence of personalities necessarily affect the type of working relationship, but when economists move in significant numbers into a field hitherto regarded as the prerogative of a particular category of staff, friction is likely, especially when the newcomers question the effectiveness of existing procedures or resource allocations in such a way as to imply that the incumbents had not really thought seriously about their activities. Hostile reactions are almost inevitable when the application of cost-benefit analysis, planned programme budgeting, or policy analysis and review threatens well-established official procedures, hierarchical responsibilities, and career prospects. In a number of countries the rise of the economists has caused serious resentment, partly because of their combination of expertise and adaptability. But it is the belief that they have occasionally arrogantly exceeded the limits of their competence that has led one critic to coin the term 'econocrats.'[19]

(d) *Professional ethics and standards*

One valuable social and intellectual by-product of the large-scale employment of economists in government has been the heightened sensitivity to problems of professional ethics and standards, issues which in earlier periods were considered, if at all, only indirectly in the course of methodological debates about the nature and scope of economic sci-

19. Peter Self, *The Econocrats and the Policy Process: The Politics and Philosophy of Cost-Benefit Analysis* (London, 1975). The author is especially concerned with the misuse of cost-benefit analysis.

ence or the relationship between the 'art' and the 'science' of political economy (latterly explained in terms of 'positive' and 'normative' economics).[20] Government service has not merely stimulated a collective self-consciousness, it has also provoked constructive discussion of the profession's social responsibilities, especially in the policymaking process.

Broadly speaking, during the 1950s and 1960s there was a marked surge of professional self-confidence among economists, especially in Western countries, but also more generally, where the successful avoidance of a postwar slump and large-scale unemployment was widely attributed, rightly or wrongly, to the effective application of Keynesian doctrines in the public policy arena. More recently much of that optimism has been dissipated with the reemergence of significant unemployment combined with slower economic growth and serious inflation, and there has consequently been a good deal of heart searching about the nature and limitations of the economist's knowledge and its applicability to practical problems.[21] Experience of government employment has led many economists to adopt a healthy scepticism about earlier simplistic textbook descriptions of economics as a 'positive' science, and the familiar dichotomy between 'ends' and 'means' now appears much less clear-cut than was once the case.

Given the generally accepted interpretation of the nature and objectives of science it might seem that all the professional economist need do in dealing with policy issues is to abide by the 'rules of the game'[22]—that is, to be honest about the limitations of his knowledge; to refrain from presenting his personal judgements or predilections as though they were scientific truths; and to recognise the dangers of subjectivity, even in empirical matters. But such worthy counsels may not be capable of implementation in practice if only because the economist is a human being, with imperfect knowledge, and insufficiently aware

20. The best general account of these issues is to be found in T. W. Hutchison, *'Positive' Economics and Policy Objectives* (London, 1964). See also his *Economists and Economic Policy in Britain 1946–1966* (London, 1968); and my two essays: "Value Judgements in Economics," *Yorkshire Bulletin of Economic and Social Research* 16 (Nov. 1964): 53–67; and "Methodology and Professionalism in Economics: A Subordinate Theme in Machlup's Writings," in Jacob S. Dreyer, ed., *Breadth and Depth in Economics: Fritz Machlup—The Man and His Ideas* (Lexington, Mass., 1978), pp. 23–35.

21. Cf. the sources referred to in note 13, supra. Also T. W. Hutchison, *Knowledge and Ignorance in Economics* (London, 1977), pp. 1–8.

22. However, as Michael Polanyi has wisely observed, "all formal rules of scientific procedure must prove ambiguous, for they will be interpreted quite differently according to the particular conceptions about the nature of things by which the scientist is guided." *Personal Knowledge* (Chicago, 1958), p. 167.

of his personal and professional prejudices, or at least incapable of deciding how far to discount them in making policy recommendations. Contrary to earlier teachings, more often than not policy objectives are controversial, conflicting or incompatible, or obscure, sometimes as a result of deliberate concealment by policymakers. Moreover, they invariably transcend the boundaries of economics, as traditionally defined. Economic theory is abstract, limited in scope, and capable of a remarkable variety of extensions, adaptations, and interpretations which constitute a source both of strength and of weakness in policy debates. Beyond this, the available data on relevant past and current conditions are usually incomplete and unreliable; the future is uncertain; forecasting methods are far from satisfactory; and it is usually difficult to know how far ahead to trace the implications of any policy proposal. In short, the list of difficulties is formidable.

In seeking a code of professional conduct for government economists it is helpful to distinguish between internal and external dimensions.[23] With respect to the former, the economist wastes his time if he proposes policies which cannot conceivably be adopted; but within the constraints of his job he must set out the various policy options fully and honestly and present his recommendations. If his advice is rejected, he should accept defeat, lick his wounds, and live to fight another day. But if he repeatedly accepts defeat passively, in the hope of future victories, he will run the risk of reducing his effectiveness to the point where he becomes not merely neutral, but neuter. On the other hand, if he fights too fiercely, he will quickly become *persona non grata* and be either by-passed or dismissed.

Considered from an external standpoint, an adviser also has responsibilities to the public, by explaining the government's philosophy and policy objectives, but in so doing it is obviously difficult to draw the line between partisan advocacy and merely instructing or informing the public and his fellow professionals.[24] At times the economist can preserve his integrity only by remaining silent when faced with official policies of which he strongly disapproves, and if his silence proves embarrassing or unacceptable to his employers, he should resign. Whether, and if so when, to resign, and whether to resign silently or

23. In the discussion of these matters I have drawn freely on Walter W. Heller, *New Dimensions of Political Economy* (Cambridge, Mass., 1966), ch. 1, and my unpublished "Report of Discussions" at the Royaumont Conference on The Role of the Economist in Government, April 1974, sponsored by the Ford Foundation.

24. The most valuable brief account, focusing on political as well as more narrowly ethical issues, is the American Economic Association symposium published in *Challenge*, March/April 1974, pp. 28–42, entitled "How Political Must the Council of Economic Advisers Be?" The participants included Herbert Stein, James Tobin, Henry Wallich, Arthur Okun, Eileen Shanahan (chairman), et al.

loudly in a blaze of publicity, are matters to be left to his professional conscience. But resignation, however conducted, is a once-for-all decision, a confession of failure, and a gesture unlikely to have any effect on policy. Some cynics maintain that government employees are merely or mainly involved in rationalising policies that make little or no economic sense, but which have been adopted solely for reasons of political expediency. This suspicion is reinforced by the contention that there is a self-selection process whereby radical, eccentric, or highly original individuals are discouraged from entering or, if they enter, from staying in government employment. Government employees serve the ruling sociopolitical establishment and doubtless reflect the views of the dominant professional group in the discipline. However, if there are regular changes of government regime, changes of economic advisers may merely suggest that each administration is getting the advice it wants, rather than detached or independent professional opinion. And the wider and more contentious the divisions within a disciplinary profession, the more plausible this suggestion appears.

The preceding paragraphs of course apply with special force to the most senior economic advisers, those who are closest to the centres of power and political decision, and the issues involved have been richly demonstrated in a series of publications by former members of the President's Council of Economic Advisers in the U.S.A., a body which has displayed a unique combination of professional and political participation in economic policymaking. Economists serving in the middle and lower ranks of the hierarchy seldom face such acute problems of professional integrity; but they, too, can become frustrated and embittered if their contributions are repeatedly ignored or misused and their recommendations rejected. If they remain in public service indefinitely under such circumstances their sense of professional commitment will be impaired and they will become indifferent, lacking in drive and imagination. The higher civil servant economist may experience similar reactions, especially if he knows that his political master regards him as incompetent or his proposals as objectionable. He may for a time console himself with the thought that politicians come and go, and there is consequently a temptation to hold on for a while in the hope that matters will improve. Alternatively he may seek a transfer to another department, overseas mission, or international agency. But such an escape is simply cowardly in a situation where the minister wilfully and repeatedly ignores the evidence of forecasts, and deliberately deceives or withholds information from the public. In some governments secrecy is effectively maintained (though officials may be serving ministers who deliberately 'leak' information when it suits their purpose); and eventually, in extreme cases, the economist may have no option but to violate the official secrecy regulations if he deems it his duty to expose a dishonest or incompetent politician or senior official.

By comparison with non-economist bureaucrats the government economist may be subject to special temptations because he has access to confidential data (e.g. which may affect the course of share prices), and he may be more aware of the costs of bad policies. Moreover, he is often directly in the firing line because the economic policies are controversial and dependent on predictions known to be subject to significant but indeterminate margins of error. Given his dual loyalty to his employer and to the values and standards of his profession, the tension between them may at times become unbearable. In such circumstances his links with academic economists may not only be a source of comfort but also an ever-open escape route—especially in those cases noted earlier where exchanges between universities and government are frequent and well-established.

With respect to standards of professional performance it is clear that academic criteria are not necessarily relevant to public-service employment, where the emphasis is on 'useful' knowledge, in some sense of that vague expression. Nevertheless, in recent years it seems clear that the gap between academic and government economics has been narrowing significantly in many countries, and the proportion of genuine intellectual innovations originating within government agencies has been growing markedly—though of course it is difficult to confirm this impressionistic judgement. This is especially likely where an idea or technique is directly dependent on the author's knowledge of the practical functioning of the economic system and its institutions. Government experience, it is said, has greatly stimulated the translation of economic analysis and research into operating rules for public policy, and into quantifiable concepts. And if government employment has served to narrow the long-standing gap between theoretical and applied economics, this is a contribution of no small importance.

Government economists tend to believe, with some justification, that their contributions are undervalued by the economics profession, as contrasted with brilliant new theories or technical achievements which have little or no conceivable practical application.[25] Most of the

25. There are, of course, exceptions to this generalisation. Moreover, the situation depicted in the text may be changing. In Britain for example, a number of current and ex-government economists have been awarded life peerages, knighthoods, and other honours during the past two decades and have been honoured by their professorial colleagues. In India it is now customary to elect a government economist as President of the Indian Economic Association in alternate years. More generally, it is obvious that the prestige of the academic profession varies considerably from time to time, place to place, and discipline to discipline.

profession's accolades go to academic members, partly because government economists' work cannot be readily evaluated, since so little of it is published or even completed in publishable form, owing to the pressure of work. And in rare cases where a government economist becomes known to the public he may be found guilty by association with policies determined by others against which he has offered unsuccessful resistance. Strictly speaking, the work of academic economists and the work of government economists are not merely different, but incommensurable, and it may be proper to speak not of one profession but two—with business economics as a possible third category.

V. *The Polity*

(a) *The political system*

In considering the political context within which the government economist performs his duties the relevant considerations include such elements as the degree of stability, adaptability, and conflict or consensus; the stage of economic development; and the position on the spectrum of control extending from democracy to authoritarianism.[26] In the brief historical period covered in these studies, new states emerged in India and Israel, while Italy, Japan, and Norway underwent significant transitional changes during or after World War II, and Hungary and Brazil somewhat later. Moreover, in almost all the cases considered here the political system has been at times under such pressure for economic and social change—usually as the result of a combination of overeager political leadership and rising public expectations—as to warrant serious consideration of the dangers of political overload. And the economists, as a professional group, have usually been directly involved in efforts to reconcile and achieve a complex interrelated set of economic and social objectives.

Professional economists constitute a subgroup within the political culture—whether as political leaders, members of legislatures, government employees (our primary concern in these essays), journalists, or scholars—and like other subgroups they have their own attitudes and conventions, which both reflect and react on the wider community. Where political socialisation is advanced there are unlikely to be marked disparities between the economists' norms and values and those of the political leadership and the bureaucracy, although there may be transitory periods of discord when circumstances are changing

26. This and the next paragraph are based on Gabriel A. Almond and G. Bingham Powell, Jr., *Comparative Politics: A Development Approach* (Boston, 1966), esp. chs. 1, 2, 11; and the essays in Joseph La Palombara, ed., *Bureaucracy and Political Development* (Princeton, 1963; 1967).

rapidly—when, indeed, the economists may either be leading innovators or resistant to developments which they regard as disruptive to previously established economic and social goals. They are, on the whole, more likely to be in harmony with the polity where secularisation is well advanced—that is, where rationality, analysis, and empirical relevance are evident in political action. (These conditions were lacking in Hungary during the early postwar years, in Brazil prior to the mid-1960s, and in Italy throughout most of the post-1945 period.) Where traditional orientations and attitudes have been displaced by more dynamic decisionmaking processes (for example in less developed countries undergoing rapid modernisation), the economist is likely to be able to make significant contributions to the gathering and evaluation of information, the setting out of alternative courses of action, the selection of one or more of the most feasible options, and the effort to assess the outcomes.[27] In such situations, however, the economic adviser is liable to work under severe constraints owing to the mismatch between political objectives, administrative conditions, and available resources.

(b) *The structure of government*

The government economists' functions and effectiveness obviously depend directly on the positions they occupy in the official structure. The number of conceivable variants is so great that the studies presented here have concentrated on the principal economic policymaking units or agencies—e.g. key departments such as the Treasury, and the Ministry of Finance and/or Economic Affairs; the planning bureau (if there is one); the central bank; specialist economic advisory agencies; or such 'para-statal' bodies as play an important role in economic decisions. Even this brief list suggests the impossibility of dealing in detail with more than a few major components of the machinery of government, and the scope for more extensive studies is obvious. Of particular interest is the comparatively recent utilisation of economists in 'social' departments (e.g. education, health, and social security), not to mention much more obviously economic ministries as defence, transportation, agriculture, labour, and overseas trade. Beyond this, in recent years there has been a substantial growth of employment opportunities for economists and other professionals in state, provincial, and municipal governments. Hence it is hardly necessary to emphasise that we are only beginning to scratch the surface.

Among the organisational factors affecting the economist's work are these:

27. Cf. the article by Giles, cited n.7 supra, which contains references to Zambia, Lesotho, and Swaziland, as well as Malawi.

(a) his level in the system—technical tasks usually being performed in the lower and middle reaches, whereas at the 'top of the office' functions and responsibilities more closely resemble those of generalist administrators, and even of political appointees;

(b) whether he is an isolated adviser or specialist, a member of a team, or merely one of many suppliers of economic expertise from within or outside the organisation;

(c) the size and influence of the department or agency employing him; of course similar specialist functions occur in several different branches of government, and nominal similarities may conceal practical differences—e.g. owing to variations in departmental policies;

(d) the degree of politicisation of the bureaucracy and the economic service;

(e) the extent of the government's interventionist policies—e.g. whether primarily macroeconomic or microeconomic.

Economic forecasting may serve as an example of the range of possibilities, for this may or may not be centralised and will have varying relationships with the central statistical service and the key policy-making committees or councils. The nature and extent of contact between forecasting and model-building units and other parts of the bureaucracy which supplies them with data is another variable; so is the extent to which forecasts are published—a matter which directly affects the relationships between forecasters, politicians, and the public.[28]

Enough has been said to reveal that the economist's activities and influence are necessarily determined to a large extent by the context in which he works, and there is no ideal organisational structure that will maximise his effectiveness. Most government economists prefer to occupy a position in or close to the centre of decisionmaking, but an effective contribution is dependent on an appropriate relationship between the level of activity, the flow of information, and the area of responsibility.

VI. *Conclusion: The Role of Economists in Policymaking*

For many readers the main interest in this collection will be the assessments in the following studies of the nature and effectiveness of the

28. For example in Sweden there is virtually complete publicity of forecasts by the governmental, but independent, Swedish Business Cycles Institute. Its forecasts are based on the assumption that government policy will remain unchanged, and they appear together with the Finance Bill published by the Ministry of Finance, in which the Minister gives his opinion of prospective developments. In Britain the long-standing refusal to publish official forecasts has recently been abandoned, and outside users now have access to the official Treasury model.

professional economists' contributions to policymaking. Such an interest is understandable enough, given the importance of the economic problems governments have encountered during the period in which significant numbers of professional economists have been employed as civil servants and policy advisers.

Without seeking to anticipate the conclusions to be drawn at the end of the collection it is appropriate at this stage to discount exaggerated expectations by noting some of the serious difficulties facing those seeking to assess the 'influence' of professional economists in government.

The main point, perhaps, is to emphasise that in a strict sense there is no such thing as 'economic policy,' for policy is always affected in some degree by non-economic as well as economic factors, and it always has implications and effects which transcend the narrow and somewhat artificial boundaries of the economist's field. Why, then, should we expect to get precise answers to questions about the influence of economists on policy?

Effective policymaking involves at least three distinct phases: a correct diagnosis of the problem, which depends on accurate information and comprehension of the economic processes at work; the formulation of appropriate and feasible policy recommendations; successful implementation of those recommendations. Needless to say, the process may break down in any one or all of these phases, owing to lack of information, imperfect knowledge of economic processes, inability to predict the future, adoption of 'wrong' policy recommendations (which, for various reasons, may be second or third best from the economist's standpoint), time lags, and inefficiency in implementation— which may be thwarted or distorted by any one or a combination of political, administrative, or legal obstacles.

On the other hand, successful policy (however defined) may be due to a favourable conjuncture of economic, political, bureaucratic, and professional elements—including no small measure of good luck, especially with respect to timing.[29]

29. As Walter Heller conceded, in recounting the story of a famous U.S. policy decision, "it was the Council's good luck . . . to have the 1964 tax cut come when the economy was still moving forward." Had it occurred as an offset to an incipient downturn "we would have lost the force of the *post hoc ergo propter hoc* reasoning that has undoubtedly been gaining popular acceptance for positive fiscal policy." Cf. his essay "Economic Policy Advisers," in Thomas E. Cronin and Sanford D. Greenberg, eds., *The Presidental Advisory System* (New York, 1969), p. 36. The complexities of the American political and legislative system had in fact significantly delayed the implementation of the tax cut. For a somewhat less sanguine interpretation of the episode see Harry G. Johnson, "The Keynesian Revolution and the Monetarist Counter-Revolution," in Elizabeth S. Johnson and Harry G. Johnson, *The Shadow of*

Broadly speaking, given the political setting and the bureaucratic system, the effectiveness of any group of professionals involved in the policy process depends on a number of readily specifiable conditions,[30] including:

(a) the nature of their expertise;
(b) the extent to which their expertise is recognised (i.e. the 'authority of knowledge' accorded to them);
(c) their access to centres of power and information (especially that which they exclusively control or generate);
(d) their skill in communicating with their clients, and in coalition forming;
(e) the degree to which their recommendations accord with the prevailing political and bureaucratic climate of opinion;
(f) their effectiveness in 'working the machine,' i.e. comprehending and manipulating the norms, procedures, constraints, and culture of the administration;
(g) the extent of their ability to avoid involvement in areas where they cannot help, or where no clear solutions are available.

The case studies that follow cannot, of course, be expected to cover all these aspects systematically. The nature of the problem is indicated by the lighthearted proposal by one penetrating observer of the Whitehall scene who suggested that the Royal Economic Society should compile a record of official lifetime averages by which to gauge individual economists' success in making predictions. He concluded, after a thorough survey of the record, that the average performance is roughly correlated: negatively with ideological dogmatism, party-political fervour, and subservience to fashion; neither clearly positively or negatively with mathematical and geometrical facility; and positively with institutional experience and with knowledge of historical cases and institutional, administrative, and political processes.[31]

These remarks, it should be noted, were based on the published record of economists many of whom had, admittedly, spent periods in government employment. How much more difficult it would be to compile a score sheet for those involved within the bureaucracy whose performance is not or cannot be recorded![32] How can one assess the im-

---

Keynes: Understanding Keynes, Cambridge and Keynesian Economics (Chicago, 1978), p. 193.

30. This approach will doubtless strike some readers as excessively taxonomic. For a recent attempt to introduce a more theoretical approach see Alan Peacock, *The Economic Analysis of Government and Related Themes* (Oxford, 1979), esp. pp. 213–42.

31. Hutchison, *Economists and Economic Policy*, p. 262.

32. This is especially true of those contributions which entail the prevention or mod-

pact of an economic adviser whose recommendations are fed into and become lost in the policymaking process? Is he to be held responsible for sound policies badly executed, or recommendations overruled, reversed, or ignored by politicians more concerned with catching votes than promoting economic welfare? Over what time span should the effects of his recommendations be considered if they are detectable, and how far can he legitimately be blamed for failures due to unforeseeable developments beyond his control?

Needless to say, not all these questions will be answered, or indeed even asked, in the essays presented here. But they will help to suggest why the study of economists in government is both fascinating and important.

---

ification of foolish or harmful actions, a process which Alan Peacock has expressively termed "damage minimisation." As William R. Allen has stated, American economists in government have reported that "incredibly important decisions were being made with incredibly insufficient information by incredibly unanalytical people." In such situations the economist's function is to "keep them from doing something dumb, just completely dumb." Op. cit., pp. 79–81. This recalls the impressions of British economists in the generalist environment of Whitehall in the early postwar years.

Britain: the rise of the specialists

A. W. Coats

I. *Introduction and Historical Background*

One of the most striking features of Britain's history has been the continuity of her ideas and institutions. Political, economic, and social change has usually been slow and gradual, and even world wars seem more often to have accelerated existing trends than to have brought about fundamental changes of mood or direction. This makes it peculiarly difficult to decide where to begin an account of the post-1945 expansion of the role of the economist in government. One obvious starting point is the publication of J. M. (later Lord) Keynes' *General Theory of Employment, Interest and Money* (1936), which is generally acknowledged to be the most important book written by an economist in this century. But there is an obvious danger of exaggerating the influence of any single individual thinker on the subsequent course of events, more especially as there is still vigorous and seemingly endless controversy about the precise antecedents, character, and significance of the *General Theory*, the relationships between Keynes' own ideas and those of his disciples the Keynesians, and the validity and influence of Keynesian economics.[1]

Fortunately, the details of this controversy need not concern us here. Even his most ardent critics acknowledge that Keynes' ideas exerted a powerful and direct impact on both the scientific community and the prevailing conception of the ends and means of economic and social policy. Moreover, as Keynes himself was continuously engaged throughout the 1930s in public debates about current economic and social problems and in government advisory work, some account of the context and nature of his influence on prewar, wartime, and immediate postwar affairs up to his untimely death in 1946 is unavoidable.

From the present standpoint the most relevant phase of Keynes' prewar career was his work through the Economic Advisory Council established by the second Labour government in January 1930, as part of the official machinery for handling the acute unemployment prob-

---

1. For example, the essays in Don Patinkin and J. Clark Leith, eds., *Keynes, Cambridge and the General Theory: The Process of Criticism and Discussion Connected with the Development of the General Theory* (Toronto, 1978); also, T. W. Hutchison, *Keynes Versus the 'Keynesians'?* (London, 1977); and Elizabeth and Harry G. Johnson, *The Shadow of Keynes* (Oxford, 1979).

lem.[2] The council itself did not survive the 1931 crisis, for it uneasily combined a 'representative' group of businessmen and trade unionists with a 'technocratic' group of experts who, as Winston Churchill observed in 1930, could examine complex matters "requiring high, cold, technical, and dispassionate or disinterested decision."[3] However, that same year the Prime Minister, Ramsay MacDonald, accepted Keynes' proposal to create a Committee of Economists to diagnose current problems and propose possible remedies.[4] Other committees followed, especially the Committee on Economic Information which functioned from 1932–39, and together they constituted the major channels through which economic expertise reached high Treasury officials, some of whom eventually proved responsive.[5] The results were by no means dramatic or immediate in policy terms. The process was one of permeation rather than conversion, and it was somewhat impaired by disagreements among the experts.[6] Nevertheless, it was through these committees that academic economists, especially Keynes himself, effectively undermined the notorious 'Treasury view' well before the *General Theory* had made its full impact.[7] It was a valuable learning experience for both sides, one that paid rich dividends in wartime, for example, in accelerating the acceptance of Keynes' policy proposals.

In organisational terms the council and the committees were precursors of such wartime organs as Stamp's Survey of War Plans, the Central Economic Information Service, and, far more important, its two offspring: the Economic Section of the War Cabinet Offices and the Central Statistical Office, both of which will be more fully considered below. The beginnings were necessarily modest, for there is clear evidence of powerful civil service opposition during the 1930s to any

2. Howson and D. Winch. I have drawn heavily on this source in this and the following paragraph.

3. In his Romanes Lecture, *Parliamentary Government and the Economic Problem*, quoted by Howson and Winch, p. 155.

4. Howson and Winch remark that "this must have been the first occasion that an official body consisting entirely of economists was entrusted with such a far ranging brief" (op. cit., p. 47). It should be noted that the work involved investigatory as well as merely advisory functions.

5. This was especially true of Sir Richard Hopkins and Sir Frederick Phillips. Hopkins, who became Permanent Secretary of the Treasury from 1942 to 1945, was a defender of the 'Treasury view' in 1930, but became a wholehearted supporter of Keynes from the autumn of 1940. Ibid., pp. 151–52.

6. The economists who served on one or another of the committees included A. L. Bowley, G. D. H. Cole, H. Dalton, D. H. MacGregor, A. C. Pigou, L. Robbins, D. H. Robertson, J. Stamp.

7. The 'Treasury view' was an expression coined by Keynes to describe the official opposition to expansionist anti-depression measures. Cf. Howson and Winch, pp. 18, 27.

proposals to expand the technocratic element significantly or to create any substantial number of specialist posts for economists. The economist members of the Council were, of course, part-time advisers or consultants who retained their academic posts; and their full-time economist staff was confined to one senior member, H. D. (later Sir Hubert) Henderson, plus two juniors on the payroll and a third unpaid assistant.[8] Outside this tiny band there were also a small number of other civil servants who could legitimately be regarded as competent economists, most notably R. G. (later Sir Ralph) Hawtrey, whose official title was Director of Financial Plans, at the Treasury, from 1919. Also, following a short-lived post-1918 experiment with a General Economic Department at the Board of Trade, the post of Chief Economic Adviser to the Government was created;[9] but as it transpired, this official played little if any part in domestic economic policy for most of the period, being primarily occupied with quasi-diplomatic functions associated with imperial and international economic relations.

Before turning to the war and postwar periods one further notable prewar development must be recorded, namely, the creation of a professional economist unit in the Ministry of Agriculture, in 1934, and in the Department of Agriculture for Scotland.[10] This innovation was completely ignored in the recent scholarly study of the Economic Advisory Council, an omission reflecting the authors' acceptance of the conventional preoccupation with high-level Keynesian macroeconomic policymaking. There are, of course, other important functions for economists in government, and the Ministry of Agriculture experiment constitutes further evidence that professionals were beginning to gain a foothold in official circles. In organisational terms, the agricultural economists were the first group of recognised economists employed within a government department, as contrasted with Henderson's unit in the Cabinet Office, which was designed to service a group of advisory bodies composed of outsiders. The location of the experiment in agriculture is also historically significant, for during the interwar years the government developed a more actively interventionist policy for agriculture than for any other sector of the economy, and this formed the basis of an expanded wartime and postwar agricultural

8. The three junior members were H. V. Hodson, Colin Clark, and Piers Debenham. For a short time R. F. (later Lord) Kahn was Assistant Secretary to the Committee of Economists.
9. Between 1919 and 1946 this post was held, successively, by Sir Hubert Llewellyn Smith, Sir Sydney Chapman (sometime Professor of Political Economy at Manchester), and Sir Frederick Leith-Ross.
10. See A. W. Coats, "The Development of the Agricultural Economics Profession in England," esp. pp. 382–85. The first "economic student and investigator" post was created in 1924, and three qualified assistants were appointed in 1934.

policy which generated an unbroken tradition of agricultural economics and statistics up to the present. The personnel employed in the prewar period were engaged on modest, indeed sometimes literally down-
to-earth, tasks which have typically been ignored or looked down on
by other economists. Yet it was in the Ministry of Agriculture, rather
than in the Cabinet Office, that the predecessors of today's vastly expanded army of departmentally based government economists are to
be found.

In World War II, as in 1914–18, the exigencies of the situation generated an urgent demand for relevant economic ideas, techniques, and
data, and this time the economics profession was much better equipped
to make a constructive contribution. The broad intellectual foundations of macroeconomic policy had been laid and with respect to economic expertise there was direct continuity of personnel and approach
in the transition from peace to wartime. The initial buildup of the
administrative apparatus was slow and hesitant, even for a time after
Churchill succeeded Neville Chamberlain in May 1940, but there gradually evolved an expanding and flexible organisation for coordinating
production, allocating scarce labour, materials, and shipping space,
and controlling prices and production. However, even at the peak of
the process the machinery of government fell some way short of full-
scale centralised economic planning.[11]

Between 1939 and 1945 qualified economists and statisticians enjoyed unprecedented opportunities for government employment.[12]
Oddly enough, although Keynes was drafted into the Treasury as an
economic adviser early in the war, he never became a salaried civil servant. Yet from his informal position he came to exert a major impact on
official thinking and on the aims and direction of policy until his death.
His collection of articles *How to Pay for the War* (1940), which incorporated such seminal concepts as "the inflationary gap" and "output
potential," constituted the intellectual basis of Kingsley Wood's innovative Budget of 1941. An associated development from the same general source was the first official wartime effort to construct estimates of
national income and expenditure by Richard Stone and James Meade,
also in 1941.[13] From that time onwards the expanded conception of the

11. Cf. Hancock and Gowing. This is, of course, but one of a series of official histories of wartime economic and social affairs.
12. For a useful general account of this period see Winch, *Economics and Policy*,
ch. 12. "Keynesian War Economics and Post-War Plans." Also the general survey by
Leruez, *Economic Planning and Politics in Britain*, chs. 1 and 2; and the essays by
wartime government economists in Chester, *Lessons of the War Economy*.
13. At that time an earlier pioneering effort was unknown. Cf. *Inland Revenue Report on National Income; with an Introduction by Richard Stone* (Cambridge, 1977).
See also Stone's essay, "The Use and Development of National Income and Expenditure Estimates," pp. 83-101.

role of the budget as a central tool of economic policy and the data provided in the national accounts became integral components of wartime and postwar economic management. The relegation of monetary policy to a subordinate role was also largely due to Keynes, who argued persistently and effectively in favour of so-called cheap money.

The explicit wartime commitment to Keynesian peacetime goals was made in the path-breaking 1944 White Paper on *Employment Policy*, which announced the government's acceptance "as one of their primary aims and responsibilities the maintenance of a high and stable level of employment after the war." While conceding that in proposing this extension of state control over the volume of employment the government was "entering a field where theory can be applied to practical issues with confidence and certainty only as experience accumulates and experiment extends over untried ground," the document went on to disclose the intention to "establish on a permanent basis a small central staff qualified to measure and analyse economic trends and to submit appreciations of them to Ministers."[14]

In the present context this declaration is of symbolic as well as practical significance, since it both acknowledged the success of the technocratic component in wartime economic policymaking and also guaranteed its survival into the postwar era. The general character of the economists' wartime contribution can be described briefly, since it can be explored in the available secondary sources.[15] Shortly before the outbreak of hostilities three members of the aforementioned Committee on Economic Information were brought together to form the so-called Stamp Survey of Financial and Economic Plans, which helped to provide some guidance in the initial transition from peace to war.[16] Several months later the Survey was expanded, by the inclusion of additional economists and statisticians, to form the Central Economic Information Service, which was located in the Cabinet Offices rather than the Treasury because of the broad range of its responsibilities. This body in turn was divided early in 1941, on Churchill's orders,[17] to form the Economic Section, which continued in existence

14. Cmd. 6527, London, H.M.S.O. (1944), p. 26. In fact the permanence of the central staff, in the Economic Section, was not assured until the early 1950s.

15. In addition to the works by Winch, Leruez, and Chester, already referred to, the account in Lord Robbins, *Autobiography*, ch. 8, is especially valuable. Research into this period is already well under way. Important new material has recently become available in Donald Moggridge, ed., *The Collected Writings of John Maynard Keynes*, vols. 22–24 (London, 1978, 1979).

16. The members were Lord Stamp, H. D. (later Sir Hubert) Henderson, and H. (later Sir Henry) Clay.

17. The instruction is reprinted in Winston Churchill, *The Second World War* (London, 1949) vol. 2, app. A, p. 608. Robbins gives a vivid impression of the economists' dissatisfaction with the situation before they came under Anderson's wing. The

(after its transfer to the Treasury in 1953) until 1969, and the Central Statistical Office, which still survives in a greatly expanded form. The immediate motive for the division was Churchill's determination to establish a single authoritative supply of statistics, for he had been exasperated by the provision of conflicting departmental estimates. But the organisational details are less important than the fact that once the Economic Section came directly under the aegis of Sir John Anderson, as Lord President of the Council, its prestige, effectiveness, and influence soared. Anderson was not merely a great administrator; he also commanded Churchill's confidence, and under his leadership the Lord President's Committee became, in Churchill's words, "a parallel cabinet concerned with Home Affairs."[18] Anderson took his economic experts seriously, although he did not, of course, always follow their advice; and as the members of the Economic Section and the Central Statistical Office were increasingly enlisted to provide expert advice on a wide variety of departmental and other committees, their influence spread. As Lionel (later Lord) Robbins, the Director of the Economic Section for most of the war period, has revealed in his autobiography,[19] the dons rapidly gained practical experience, working alongside other temporary and permanent officials. Instead of intermittent contributions in the form of briefs and reports which might be ignored or dismissed by ministers and senior officials, they became active participants in the discussion and formulation of policy. In the special circumstances of the wartime emergency, and with the additional weight provided by their association with Anderson, they played a far greater role than they could have done in more leisurely peacetime conditions, when the goals of policy are less simple and direct. Nevertheless, the wartime practice set a precedent which decisively affected postwar developments.

One of the most unexpected features of the British case is the fact that the economists' acknowledged success in wartime and the conscious adoption of full employment as a major postwar policy objective did not automatically generate a substantial demand for professional economists in the peacetime civil service. During the first two postwar decades macroeconomic management was undertaken with the aid of only a handful (i.e. less than 20) professional economists. Perhaps even

personnel had been largely recruited by A. F. Hemming, who had been on the secretarial staff of the prewar Economic Advisory Council committees.

18. Cf. his statement in the House of Commons, 24 Feb. 1942, quoted by Chester, p. 9. For comments on Anderson's role and influence see, also, Robbins, p. 175, and the biography by Sir John Wheeler-Bennett, *John Anderson, Viscount Waverley* (London, 1962).

19. Robbins, loc.cit.

more surprising, however, was the dramatic transformation of that situation after the Labour government's election in October 1964, during which time the number of professional economist posts in Whitehall grew approximately twentyfold to a peak of 390 in 1979 (cf. Table 1).[20]

This transformation cannot be explained simply in political terms, even though the change of administration was followed by a major effort to redirect economic and social policy and a determination to 're-form' the civil service, a long-cherished objective of the British left. It is, of course, broadly true that the Labour Party has been more favorably disposed towards economic planning and technocratic interventionism in economic and social affairs than the Conservatives; but if politics had been the sole determinant, there should have been a substantial number of economists employed under the postwar Labour regime, from 1945 to 1951, and a diminution rather than a continuing upward trend during the Conservative government of 1970-74.

Politics aside, there are various other reasons for the peculiarities of the British postwar experience to be considered in the following paragraphs. Briefly, they include: overconfidence in the efficacy of high-level peacetime macroeconomic management, stemming largely, no doubt, from the acknowledged success of the wartime Economic Section and the almost unquestioned dominance of Keynesian views of economic policymaking up to the 1970s; the absence of any clear conception of peacetime economic planning on the part of the postwar La-

Table 1. Economists and statisticians in the British Civil Service

	Economists[a]		Statisticians[b]	
	Numbers	% change since 1950	Numbers	% change since 1950
1950	17 (37)		104	
1964	21.5 (46.5)	26 (26)	128	23
1970	208.5 (242.5)	1226 (661)	266	293
1975	365	2150	477	459
1980	379	2229	538 (1979)	517

[a] Compiled from information supplied by the Treasury and the Ministry of Agriculture and Fisheries. The figures in brackets include agricultural economists who were not part of the Government Economic Service until 1974. The basis of calculation differs from that in Table 2, below.

[b] Compiled from information supplied by the Central Statistical Office.

20. The reasons for this remarkable expansion are considered briefly below. For relevant background material see Booth and Coats. "The Market for Economists in Britain, 1945–75," pp. 436–54.

bour government;[21] rapidly waning official, public, and even socialist enthusiasm for direct economic controls; the long period of Conservative rule from 1951 to 1964, and especially the 1950s, when conscious efforts were made to reduce the extent of government intervention and the size of the civil service;[22] difficulties on the supply side, owing to the reluctance of many of the temporary wartime civil servants to remain in government employment after the end of hostilities; a continuing shortage of trained economists in the 1950s and early 1960s relative to the rising demand in the universities and in business;[23] the unfavourable public image of the civil service, compounded by official reluctance to offer specialists preferential pay and conditions; the heavy reliance on temporary or short-service professional economists, which tended, at least for a time, to obscure the long-term problems on the supply side; and the prevailing generalist, so-called 'intelligent layman' or amateur tradition in government employment, which restricted the opportunities for specialists to rise through the hierarchy and participate in top-level decisionmaking.

This is a formidable catalogue; not all of the items it contains can be fully considered here. The post-1964 transformation reveals that at least some of the earlier obstacles could have been overcome, given sufficient determination and foresight on the part of ministers and senior civil servants. But to leave the explanation at that point would be to overlook the fact that already from the early 1960's there had been perceptible changes both in the government's view of economic planning and in the official attitude towards the employment of specialists, especially economists, within the government. On a political level, the manifest failure of the economy to grow at a satisfactory rate led to a shift from the loosely managed 'welfare capitalism' of the 1950s to a revival of interest in economic planning, largely modeled on French experience. This change, described by a perceptive French observer as "the conversion of the conservatives,"[24] led to the establishment of the National Economic Development Council, with consequences for the economics profession which will be considered later. Almost simultane-

21. For a useful review of the literature on this subject see Leruez, ch. 2; also, for valuable details on the immediate postwar situation, Bernard Donoughue and G. W. Jones, *Herbert Morrison: Portrait of a Politician* (London, 1973).

22. The numbers in the Administrative Class, which included the highest-level officials as well as economists and statisticians, fell from 4,600 in 1950 to 3,400 in 1964, and rose again to 4,000 by 1970. *Annual Abstract of Statistics*.

23. Cf. Booth and Coats (1978).

24. Leruez, ch. 3. The subsequent developments are well treated in chs. 4 and 5. See also the valuable recent study by P. Meadows, "Planning," in F. T. Blackby, pp. 402–17. This volume is the work of a team of economists under the auspices of the National Institute of Economic and Social Research.

ously, within the Civil Service, there was a conscious drive for improved efficiency in management under the direct influence of the Plowden Committee on the Control of Public Expenditure, which reported in 1961, but also, more fundamentally, as a by-product of widespread dissatisfaction in Parliament and in Whitehall with the existing administrative organisation and utilisation of resources. While the immediate effects on the government economists' position were limited, even after the reorganisation of the Treasury in 1961–62, the longer-run implications were much more significant. However, instead of pursuing such matters now, thereby extending this chronological introduction, it is appropriate to consider these items later under the appropriate topical subheadings.

II.   *The Supply of Economists: Definition;*
Qualifications; Numbers; Market Conditions

In the absence of a generally accepted definition, the term 'economist' is used here to describe a person with a recognised academic qualification in the subject and a job title which acknowledges the specialisation. This is the most appropriate criterion from the standpoint of professionalisation, since the assignment of a suitable designation is ipso facto recognition of the need for trained expertise in the performance of the functions involved. However, as applied in British central government the term may be considered unduly restrictive, since for most of the postwar period the bulk of official economic work, from low-level routine functions to high-level economic decisionmaking, has been undertaken by non-economists. It is true, of course, that some members of the elite generalist Administrative Class had taken undergraduate courses or even degrees in economics, but in many cases they soon lost touch with their academic background while occupying a sequence of administrative posts. Promotion within the hierarchy was determined more by on-the-job performance than by educational qualifications. Given the anti-specialist ethos of the central bureaucracy, which reflected traditional educational prejudices, it is clear that the majority of key decisionmakers in postwar Britain, including ministers, Governors of the Bank of England, and heads of the nationalised industries, have had no formal training in economics. It should, however, be conceded that there is no conclusive evidence that trained economists necessarily make the best economic decisionmakers!

Unlike the situation on the European continent, there has been no direct link between the training of economists and lawyers in Britain. But given the comparatively low cultural status generally accorded to technical and scientific education both in the academic world and the civil service, it is easy to understand why the number of government economists and statisticians was so low at the end of the war and grew so slowly during the first two postwar decades.[25] Although some British universities have awarded specialist degrees in economics since the early years of this century, the practice is not yet universal. Indeed Oxford, one of the most prestigious institutions with a strong tradition of supplying graduates for the public service, has no 'single honours' degree in economics, the Modern Greats (or P.P.E.) course comprising a variable mixture of studies in Philosophy, Politics, and Economics. While this may well be an admirable preparation for entrants into the generalist Administrative Class, it is by no means adequate as a training for economic specialists. Moreover, it is impossible to determine, without specific information, how much economics training any given Oxford P.P.E. graduate has received; and the same is broadly true of the holders of early postwar London University B.Sc. (Econ.) degrees and the innumerable 'joint' degrees still awarded by many universities. For civil service recruits in the first two postwar decades the quality of the degree (and, some would add, the institution by which it was awarded) was usually far more important than its subject matter. This was not true of statisticians or agricultural economists; but the majority of early postwar recruits to the Economic Section were employed as high-level economic administrators and advisers, rather than technicians. By today's standards many were deficient in mathematical and quantitative techniques, and it was not until the mid-1960s that any significant number of civil servants had obtained the master's or doctor's degree in economics—a by-product of the slow development of postgraduate research and instruction in Britain.

However, in this as in other respects conditions were changing rapidly during the 1960s. Early in that decade there was a growing demand for experienced academic economists in their thirties or older who could occupy middle-rank posts and command the respect and attention of senior officials. Unfortunately, such individuals were not only few in number but also, in some cases, reluctant to enter the public service at a time when the universities, the main focus of their career aspirations, were entering a rapid expansionist phase. By going to Whitehall they would not only be out of sight, out of mind, but their publication opportunities would be restricted and, consequently, also their academic promotion prospects. Younger economists were, admittedly, somewhat less scarce. But there were few opportunities for ap-

25. For a more detailed account of the matters discussed in this and the next paragraphs, see Booth and Coats (1978).

prentices in the only specialist unit, the Economic Section, which was deliberately kept small, whereas if they entered a large government department they could hardly expect to make a significant impact at a junior level, especially as they were liable to become immersed in routine administrative duties.

Several ways of relieving the shortage were considered as part of the growing effort to improve the quality and efficiency of management. One novel suggestion was the provision of preferential postgraduate awards for economics graduates, the argument being that this was the stage at which professional career decisions were made. However, this scheme was rejected both as a potential interference with university autonomy and as an invitation to other specialist groups to claim comparable treatment. For young entrants with few or no qualifications in economics or statistics, a small number of cadetships or bursaries were provided, and attempts were made to place Executive and Research Officers with economics training in appropriate posts. Most significant, however, was the establishment of the Centre for Administrative Studies in 1963, designed to provide short courses in economics for generalists to enable them to perform economic functions more effectively and to enhance their ability to communicate with the few recognised government economists. In addition, refresher courses were provided for administrators who had previously studied economics.[26]

These developments constitute significant evidence of a growing awareness of the need for more specialists, not merely economists, in the public service, a change of outlook which was followed by a variety of efforts to improve the in-service training facilities for civil servants. Hence, when the reforming zeal of the new Labour administration was added late in 1964, it gave a strong impulse to a movement which was already under way. Several years earlier the Conservatives' 'conversion' to economic planning had given birth to the National Economic Development Council, a public agency outside the main departmental structure, but drawing in part on data and expertise supplied by the regular civil servants. The Council's office, Nedo as it soon became known, quickly built up an economic staff almost as large as that in the Treasury, and when the Department of Economic Affairs was created in 1964, after the change of government, most of the Nedo economists moved into the new ministry. There was also a rapid buildup of economists in the newly established Ministry for Overseas Development, and an even more dramatic development was the appointment of three

---

26. Cf. Desmond Keeling, "The Development of Central Training in the Civil Service 1963–70," *Public Administration* 49 (Spring 1971): 51–71.

prominent academic economists, Thomas (later Lord) Balogh, Robert Neild, and Nicholas (later Lord) Kaldor, as special advisers to the Prime Minister, Chancellor of the Exchequer, and Inland Revenue Department, respectively. This innovation caused a mild sensation at the time, and its implications for the professionalisation of government economics will be considered below. At this stage, however, its significance for the supply of economists must be emphasised, for it revealed the government's determination to give them a more prominent and influential role in the formulation and implementation of policy. Some of those who had hitherto dimissed the civil service as an unsuitable arena for the exercise of their talents responded readily to the determined efforts now being made to seduce them from their ivory towers. Most of the new recruits were temporary, which was already the established practice for members of the Economic Section; but because many were not enlisted through the normal recruitment procedures, they soon became known as 'irregulars.'[27] One important lesson was that if the conventional personnel practices could be overcome, stretched, or circumvented and if the prospect of government employment could be made to appear stimulating enough,[28] then obstacles to growth in the supply of economists which had hitherto been deemed insurmountable could in fact be overcome.

Although the invasion of the irregulars was essentially a short-term response to an immediate demand, it proved to be the onset of a remarkably rapid and sustained upsurge in the number of economists in Whitehall.[29] Those officials responsible for personnel matters were, it is true, anticipating a long-run increase in the numbers of economists and statisticians; but no one seems to have foreseen how fast or how far it would go—partly, no doubt, because the new government's political position was decidedly shaky at first, and it was thought that if the Conservatives were returned, the process might be halted or reversed. With the benefit of hindsight, however, it is clear that the process was affected not only by changes in political attitudes and the official view of the role of specialists in government but also by more general trends in the market for economists.

To sum up a complex story the full details of which are still unclear,[30] it appears that a marked expansion in the output of econom-

27. Brittan, "The Irregulars," pp. 329-39. See also Shanks, "The Irregular in Whitehall," in Streeten, pp. 244–62.
28. It is worth noting that a substantial group of economists was recruited for Nedo at a time when government departments were finding it very difficult to recruit economists. When the Department of Economic Affairs was established, late in 1964, the Nedo economists were transferred to it virtually en bloc, as mentioned above.
29. Cf. Table 1.
30. Cf. Booth and Coats, "The Market for Economists."

ics graduates from the early 1960s through to the early 1970s was accompanied by a sustained growth of their job opportunities, whereas more recently the slackening of demand both from business and the universities, coupled with increases in civil service salaries and favourable pension provisions, has greatly enhanced the relative attractiveness of government employment. As will be indicated later below, there has been a growth of career-mindedness on the part of Whitehall economists during the present decade, whereas up to the early 1960s the professionals in the Economic Section had usually regarded their government experience as a temporary intermission in a permanent academic career. In this respect, as in others to be noted below, the differences between British government economists and statisticians have narrowed, for the latter have almost invariably regarded the civil service as a lifetime career.

III.   *General Social and Cultural Attitudes Towards Intellectuals, Professionals, and Experts*

The dramatic increase in the numbers of civil service economists, statisticians, and other professionals during the past decade or so may suggest that there has been an underlying transformation in traditional anti-specialist social and cultural attitudes. However, it is far from easy to assess the precise extent and significance of this movement, especially as the civil service is one of the more entrenched and prestigious of British institutions, and its reform has been a hotly debated matter, especially since the early 1960s.

No doubt the roots of recent changes in social and cultural attitudes must be sought in the wartime emergency when the general desire for postwar reforms which would ensure that wartime sacrifices were not in vain contributed to a markedly leftward shift in public opinion.[31] The enthusiastic reception of Sir William (later Lord) Beveridge's welfare state proposals, and the general acceptance of full employment as a major policy objective, entailed a commitment to more active interventionist policies for the sake of greater economic and social equality, as well as prosperity. In the educational field the postwar expansion and democratisation of the universities, and the shift towards the social and natural sciences and technology, constituted manifestations of a modernisation process which might have been more rapid but for the slow rate of economic growth (by European standards), for this severely limited the resources available for educational experiments. And in these circumstances the delayed impact of modernisation on the civil service itself seems somewhat less surprising.

31. For an excellent general account of the process, see Addison, *The Road to 1945*.

From the standpoint of civil service reform, by far the most important single postwar landmark is the Fulton Committee's report of 1968, although enough has already been said to indicate that significant internal developments were already under way some years before that date. Unfortunately the question of the extent to which pre- and post-Fulton changes have effectively modernised and professionalised the civil service, which was one of the Committee's principal avowed aims, is still highly contentious; so too is the related question of the extent to which the highest ranks of the service have been opened to able candidates from broader social backgrounds. A massive recent House of Commons review of the post-Fulton decade concluded that the pace and extent of change had been disappointingly slow, and even some of the senior officials who gave evidence expressed regret and even bewilderment at the apparent failure of their efforts to correct the heavy statistical bias among new entrants in favour of independent (i.e. fee-paying) schools, Oxford and Cambridge universities, and arts graduates, as contrasted with social and natural sciences graduates.[32]

Various explanations of this state of affairs have, of course, been offered. Civil servants, on the defensive, have naturally stressed the difficulties of transforming a vast bureaucratic organisation within a short period, whereas overeager reformers have blamed bureaucratic inertia or deliberate resistance to change. Some of those specialists whose salaries, conditions of service, and promotion opportunities have, at least until very recently, improved out of all recognition, have been inclined to express dissatisfaction because their gains have fallen short of their rising expectations. Casual empiricism suggests that while conditions are now in many respects (and especially for specialists) remarkably different from those obtaining in the 1950s, Britain still lags well behind the U.S.A. and most northern and western European countries in respect of the role accorded to professional economists in government. It seems that the persistence of traditional cultural and social attitudes, as reflected in bureaucratic styles and procedures, has significantly delayed the impact of modernisation, even though there has lately been a rapid closing of the gap.

IV. *Professionalisation*

(a) *Economists, statisticians, and agricultural economists*

Operational definitions of professionalisation are difficult to formulate and apply, but there seems little reason to doubt that the

---

32. *House of Commons, Expenditure Committee, Eleventh Report, 1976–77, Civil Service* (London, H.M.S.O.).

Keynesian revolution and the subsequent wartime and postwar activities of economists in government have done more than anything else to enhance the public reputation and influence of the economics profession in Britain. Although there is evidence that professional self-consciousness was growing among the economists around the turn of the century, their principal organisation, the Royal Economic Society (RES) adopted a distinctly limited and cautious policy until the later 1960s.[33] This is true whether it is compared with the American Economic Association or its closest British counterparts, the Royal Statistical Society (RSS) and the Agricultural Economics Society (AES). The statisticians' organisation is stronger and more venerable and has been more active, for example, in petitioning the government on behalf of its members, usually with the object of obtaining additional resources for the improvement of official statistics; and shortly after the war the RSS shocked a number of leading economists, who were members of both organisations, by proposing to establish qualifying examinations for statisticians.[34] A comparable proposal for economists would probably have been unthinkable, and in the event the economists succeeded in thwarting the scheme. The agricultural economists, despite their limited numbers and lower prestige, also developed a more active organisation in the 1930s than the RES, largely owing to their collective association with and dependence on the Ministry of Agriculture, a link which stimulated their sense of professional solidarity and *esprit de corps*.[35] At least as far as the pre-1965 period is concerned, a broad comparison of the three groups reveals that in each case the degree of professional coherence, organisation and self-consciousness within the civil service has roughly paralleled the situation outside.

There are obvious reasons why British government statisticians were organised and professionalised in advance of the economists. Their numbers were greater; they had a recognisable shared technical expertise; and they were, as a group, more civil service career oriented than the economists, most of whom were, until very recently, on temporary or short-service appointments. A coordinated and systematised body of official statistics is obviously indispensable, and since World

33. Cf. A. W. Coats, "The Origins and Early Development of the Royal Economic Society," *Economic Journal* 78 (June 1968): 349–71; A. W. Coats and S. E. Coats, "The Changing Composition of the Royal Economic Society and the Professionalisation of British Economics," *British Journal of Sociology* 24 (June 1973): 165–87.

34. The evidence was published in *Journal of the Royal Statistical Society* 109A (1946), esp. pp. 490–502. The growth of the Statistician Class is discussed in Sir Roy Allen, "On Official Statistics and Statisticians," pp. 509–26.

35. Coats, "Development of the Agricultural Economics Profession."

War II the evolution of centralised Keynesian-type national income accounting has reinforced the need for a unified statistical apparatus and centralised management of statistical staff throughout the public service. The Central Statistical Office was the natural focus for co-ordination and management, but owing to the established tradition of departmental autonomy in staffing matters, those organisational functions were necessarily performed by persuasion and convention rather than by formal authority. From the later 1960s, however, the effective influence of the CSO increased through the Head of the newly formed Government Statistical Service.

The need for formal organisation of agricultural economists was much less pressing than for statisticians because their numbers were smaller and they were mainly concentrated in two departments.[36] As long as the economists were, to all intents and purposes, confined to the Economic Section and severely limited in numbers, informal management was sufficient. It is true that after the Treasury reorganisation of 1962 they were increasingly 'bedded out' within Treasury divisions and were working alongside non-specialist administrators. Management panels for economists and statisticians were in fact established before the hectic influx of irregulars in the early months of the new Labour government, but that development made it necessary to provide a more effective administration of the expanding but still scarce supply of economic expertise. In an effort to introduce a measure of order and system A. K. (later Sir Alec) Cairncross, the Director of the Economic Section and Economic Adviser to H.M. Government, was made Head of the newly formed Government Economic Service early in 1965, in addition to his economic advisory duties. But although the Treasury ultimately controlled the funds available for staff appointments, in practice Cairncross possessed limited powers to control or direct the new wave of temporary officials, though he endeavoured to check the proliferation of specialist economist units, which were rapidly becoming fashionable. More important than the details of these developments is the fact that the new arrangements, though initially designed to meet immediate needs, accelerated the progress of professional autonomy and self-control within the government machine. The need for specialised knowledge in managing the appointment, placement, and promotion of specialist personnel was reinforced by a trend away from the macroeconomic generalists who had predominated in the Economic Section towards microeconomists, a movement encouraged by the increasing attention already being paid to economic planning and

36. That is, the Ministry of Agriculture and Fisheries and the Department of Agriculture for Scotland.

regional development from the early 1960s. Cairncross found it virtually impossible to act as central recruiting agent and manager of a proliferating corps of specialists in economic forecasting, transport, industrial, and development economics while simultaneously performing his duties as Economic Adviser to the government. The employment of professional economists spread from the Treasury through the obvious economic departments to education, health and social security, foreign affairs, and defence—branches of government which hitherto had employed no professional economists whatsoever. The creation of the Civil Service Department (CSD) in 1968 to take charge of establishment (i.e. personnel) matters formerly undertaken by the Treasury, also contributed to the extension of professional autonomy. The economists and statisticians came to be regarded as 'well-managed classes' who did not require detailed supervision or control at a time when CSD officials were preoccupied with other more pressing matters.

Oddly enough, when the Government Economic Service was established, the agricultural economists were excluded, initially on the grounds that they were a specialist cadre who could not, like other economists and general administrators, move from one department to another if required to do so. This was an increasingly unrealistic contention at a time when, as already noted, the development of specialisation among other government economists was proceeding apace.

(b) *Professional self-consciousness, organisation, ethics, neutrality*

It is difficult to generalise about the effects of these processes on the development of the economists' professional self-consciousness. Despite the limited numbers employed in the Economic Section up to the mid-1960s, it would be erroneous to suggest that they were not professionally self-aware, even though most of them regarded the academic rather than the civil service community as their sociological reference group. They fully appreciated that they occupied a privileged position close to the centre of the policymaking process, and probably also realised that they were regarded by some officials, including statisticians and agricultural economists, as semi-academic theorists or backroom boys rather than operational civil servants.

With the growth of scale there inevitably developed a measure of specialisation, division of labour, and hierarchy which had been largely absent in the Economic Section. From the later 1960s the Economist members of the First Division Association of civil servants became more concerned about such matters as pay, career management, and promotion, and in recent years the practice of annual semi-formal negotiations with the head of the Government Economic Service has become customary.

Prior to the mid 1960s the professional economists in Whitehall were too few to exert any effective group pressure, had they sought to do so. In fact, they seem to have had a modest conception of their individual and collective role. In his *Autobiograpy* Robbins recalled that the Economic Section's wartime success had been due in considerable measure to its members' willingness to make themselves useful to ministers and senior officials, and to their acceptance of established civil service values and traditions.[37] Had they differentiated themselves too sharply from their non-economist colleagues, claiming special attention or consideration because of their knowledge or insight, they would presumably have encountered greater resistance and correspondingly diminished their impact. Robbins' successors, James Meade and Robert Hall (later Lord Roberthall), seem to have adopted the same general approach, and the latter seems even to have gone out of his way to minimise the need for any substantial number of professional economists in government.[38]

In retrospect, while this professional modesty may have enhanced the economists' initial acceptance and ensured them a place near the heart of the economic policymaking process, it may have inhibited the long-run perception of the need for their services within departments. Their general situation certainly changed little during the 1950s, but after that time a more favourable climate prevailed both within and outside the main departmental structure. In this respect a notable development was the appointment of an experienced economist, Sir Robert Shone, as the first Director-General of the National Economic Development Office. Through his Economic Director, Sir Donald MacDougall, who was already well known as an academic and ex-government economist, a substantial staff of general and industrial economists was assembled with unprecedented speed, and although the organisation was outside the established departments, it was close enough to exert a significant indirect demand for economists in Whitehall itself. There was both cooperation and some rivalry with existing

37. Robbins, *Autobiography*, p. 184, where he stressed the need "to become part of the machine and accept its logic rather than pretend to some special status. . . . If we had not been prepared to conform to the normal rules and normal routine, or if those who ran the machine had been hostile, the experiment would have failed."

38. Cf. Sir Robert Hall, "The Place of the Economist in Government," p. 122, where he remarked that "there is no obvious reason why most of those who are engaged in activities within the province of the economist should themselves be professional economists." For a valuable insight into Hall's position within the government machine, see the article by one of his junior colleagues, Robin Marris, "The Position of Economics and Economists in the Government Machine," pp. 759–83.

departments, which were put under added pressure to adopt a more thorough and professional approach to the preparation and presentation of economic policy proposals. Nedo was prominent in the campaign for increased economic growth during the years 1962–64, and on Labour's accession to power in October 1964, MacDougall moved to the Department of Economic Affairs to take charge of economic planning and public affairs under a new Permanent Secretary, Sir Eric (now Lord) Roll, another internationally known economist with both academic and governmental experience. MacDougall took with him most of his Nedo economists, and both in the DEA, and from 1969 as Head of the Government Service, his economic staff expanded rapidly. Unlike Cairncross, his immediate predecessor in the Treasury, MacDougall had no misgivings about working in charge of a large body of professionals.[39]

While the DEA was designed as a major economic department to challenge the Treasury's supremacy, other substantial groups of professional economists were assembled, most notably in the Ministry of Overseas Development, from 1964, and at the Ministry of Transport, from 1966. In both instances an enthusiastic minister, Barbara Castle, provided the initial stimulus; but in both cases the process became cumulative, largely because of the professionals' desire to work with their own kind. These examples were subsequently followed in other departments, though in a less spectacular manner.

By comparison with their American peers British economists have expressed remarkably little concern about questions of professional ethics or integrity arising from government employment. Doubtless the well-established respect for civil service neutrality has shielded them from most of the dangers that are only too familiar to their counterparts in some other countries; and some weight must be accorded to the practice of 'inning' and 'outing' which enhanced the short-service academic economists' feelings of independence and reduced the risks of professional obsolescence to which the permanent civil service economist is subject. There was, however, one period when the threat of political interference loomed large in Whitehall, namely when Balogh, Neild, and Kaldor were appointed to top-level advisory posts and were followed by an influx of irregulars, many of whom also appeared sympathetic to the new Labour government. For a time Cairncross's posi-

---

39. For Cairncross's views on this point, see his "On Being an Economic Adviser," p. 290. In fairness to MacDougall's predecessors it should be noted that whereas recruitment was a *sine qua non* of success with new ventures such as Nedo or DEA, it was always subordinate to the main economic advisory responsibilities of the Director of the Economic Section. It was not until 1969 that any formal provision was made for the recruitment and personnel management functions of the G.E.S.

tion as the chief government economist seemed to be undermined, if not actually jeopardised, while those of his colleagues who did not fear the taint of politicisation nevertheless resented the intrusion of inexperienced newcomers, however academically distinguished, who were appointed above their heads. In practice, however, the initial over-anxiety soon died away. Almost all the government economists benefited in some degree from the boom in the demand for their services, and it was not always possible to distinguish politically motivated irregulars from economists who could have (or indeed had) been appointed to the pre-1964 Economic Section. After a phase of uneasiness and dislocation, compounded by the hectic pace at which the new administration set about its ambitious programme, conditions soon settled down with regulars and irregulars working smoothly alongside each other. Professional solidarity and *esprit de corps* may have prevailed over short-term disturbances. Within two or three years many of the more prominent 'political' economists (as they were known in official circles) left the civil service, often somewhat disillusioned by their failure to transform Whitehall as completely as they had overoptimistically expected,[40] while others, who acquired a taste for government work and became fully assimilated into the Whitehall community, stayed on and became permanent civil servants.

Apart from the increase of scale, one other permanent legacy remains from this period—the practice of appointing Special Advisers to ministers whose function is to provide technical as well as political advice, somewhat on the lines of continental ministerial 'cabinets.' Their numbers have been small, and they have usually been selected by and attached to specific ministers on a temporary basis, but their influence may well have been considerable, for they can interpret official recommendations and, when disagreements arise, take a much stronger line than regular civil servants if they choose to do so. By no means all the Special Advisers have been economists. But it was probably the economists who led the way, and it is noteworthy that despite severe Conservative criticism of Labour's irregulars, the practice of appointing Special Advisers was continued after the Conservatives regained office in 1970.[41]

(c) *Relations with other professionals*

The rapid expansion of the professional economist cadre in Whitehall was accompanied by broadly similar trends among other profes-

40. This overoptimism was not merely a manifestation of political bias or reforming zeal; it also reflected the contemporary wave of enthusiasm for new models, concepts, and techniques in economics in the heyday of what is usually termed 'positive' economics. This tide of professional self-confidence receded rapidly in the early 1970s.

41. For instructive insights into the role of Special Advisers, see Mitchell, "Special Advisers," pp. 87–98.

sional groups, but as yet there is little detailed comparative analysis or commentary on the process. Given the growth of professional autonomy and self-control it would be surprising if tension and friction had been entirely absent. For example, during the Fulton Committee's investigation a merger of the economist and statistician classes was seriously contemplated but was eventually abandoned, largely because the statisticians feared it would work to their detriment.[42] In other instances the introduction of economists into departments aroused opposition or misgivings among entrenched professional groups such as the road engineers in Transport, where the process was sudden and dramatic in the later 1960s, tax inspectors in Inland Revenue, or prison officers in the Home Office. In some respects the response was not essentially different from that of generalist administrators, who, it has been said, "have tended to resist any development of specialisation, save in limited and pragmatic ways which can be combined with the maintenance of their generalised career opportunities."[43] Additional problems may arise when the newcomer claims or is supposed to possess superior powers of formal analysis, since his advent implies that the incumbents "have been sitting around for years mindlessly carrying on their activities without ever asking whether what they were doing was worthwhile or whether there might not be better ways to do the same thing."[44]

During the past decade and a half there have been two parallel, and at first sight contradictory, trends in Whitehall professionalisation. As noted earlier, the extent of professional recognition, autonomy, and self-control has grown substantially, but at the same time there has also been an increasing number of 'mixed divisions' in which a variety of professionals work side by side either under a professional head or generalist administrator. Such a development is doubtless inevitable, given the increasing complexity of modern society and governmental processes. Yet this intermingling and collaboration has not been accompanied by a blurring or obliteration of professional distinctions. In other words, with varying degrees of success methods have been devised to reconcile organisational flexibility and efficiency with the needs and interests of the participating professional groups.

---

42. Other reasons included the recognition that the respective functions and spheres of the two groups were distinct, even though on some matters they worked closely together. The economists were by no means unanimously in favour of a merger. From the standpoint of professionalisation the issue is of interest, since the two groups resisted the bureaucratic urge for order and administrative simplicity for the sake of preserving their respective professional interest and identities.

43. Self, *Administrative Theories and Politics*, p. 182.

44. Heclo and Wildavsky, p. 283.

V. *The Location, Functions, and Spread of Government Economists*

As so few professional economists were employed in Whitehall during the first two postwar decades, it is hardly surprising to find that apart from occasional outside consultants, the nationalised industries, local government, and even the Bank of England were virtually without economists at the time. There were, admittedly, one or two exceptions to this generalisation which can be ignored for the present purpose;[45] and it is worth noting in passing that local government employment in Britain, unlike central government, has not been dominated by the amateur or 'intelligent layman' tradition. Engineers and lawyers have often held key positions in county and municipal bureaucracies.

Something must, however, be said of the Bank of England both because of its potentially strategic importance and because in some respects it epitomises the British situation. As is well known, the Bank has had a long and proud history, and even after its nationalisation in 1946 it retained for a time much of its former independence. During the war period, when concern with materials and manpower shortages took precedence over purely financial considerations, the Bank was responsible for exchange controls and the sterling area, and its officials played a significant role in the vital discussions of postwar international trade and payments proposals. Their misgivings about the outcome appeared to be confirmed by the 1947 convertibility crisis, and thereafter the Bank acquired a virtually autonomous position on certain policy matters. For much of the early postwar period it remained almost aloof from Whitehall. Despite the secrecy surrounding its activities, it is known that the Governor occasionally gave advice (e.g. on Bank rate changes after the initial 'cheap money' period) directly to the Chancellor of the Exchequer without the intermediation, sometimes even without the knowledge, of the Economic Adviser to the Government.[46] During the 1950s there seems to have been a kind of tacit division of labour between the Economic Section and the Bank—partly, no doubt, because of Keynesian ideas, which were interpreted as assigning monetary policy a role subordinate to fiscal policy in the economic management process, but also because the Section's primary

45. For example, Sir Ronald Edwards, formerly a Professor of Industrial Economics at the London School of Economics, was head of the Central Electricity Board. Another LSE economist and former Economic Section member, Ralph Turvey, served as a consultant and economist in the same organisation. The National Coal Board has also occasionally had an economist on its staff.

46. There was a famous, though still officially secret, conflict between the Bank and the Treasury economists in the mid-1950s over the proposal to introduce convertibility of sterling. The Bank was eventually defeated after a protracted struggle.

functions and reputation had evolved in wartime, when monetary and financial matters had been relegated to a secondary place. Yet another reason is the fact that up to 1960 the Bank seems to have been "positively averse to economics."[47] Although in 1933 it had appointed an Economic Adviser (Professor Sir Henry Clay, who retained that office until 1944) and one other economist, it actually reduced its economic and statistical staff in wartime and was devoting fewer staff resources to domestic matters in the 1950s than in the 1930s. Its personnel were often recruited from the City of London or directly from independent schools rather than the universities, and though many probably took elementary economics as part of the Institute of Bankers' qualifications, the level of their formal knowledge was usually distinctly limited.

The publication of the Redcliffe Committee's Report on the Working of the Monetary System in 1950 "marked the beginning of a change, which gathered momentum in the succeeding years."[48] There was a virtually complete rethinking of the Bank's role. The provision of monetary and financial statistics was transformed; the Bank began to employ economists and other specialists in its general office and to publish data and commentaries on economic affairs. In the past two decades cooperation with the Treasury has greatly improved, especially since the Bank recruited a number of distinguished economists into its higher policymaking positions, some of them former members of the Economic Section.[49] Here too the professionals' encroachment on the intelligent laymen's domain has been inexorable, if inordinately belated. And in the process the Bank has lost some of its traditional independence.

One of the by-products of this history is that even during the 1960s and to a somewhat lesser extent in the 1970s, the Treasury was seri-

47. "The Work of the Economic Intelligence Department," *Bank of England Quarterly* (Dec. 1976), p. 436. This is by far the best published account of the Bank's economic and statistical work. It gives vivid hints of the interwar resistance to infection "with the ideas or the language of an economist." A 1925 memorandum proposing the appointment of an economist stated: "He should be fully qualified, as far as degrees etc., indicate; must not be a crank, and must have the gift of applying economics to practical affairs. A man chosen from the Cambridge School, if under the influence of Mr. Keynes, might perhaps have acquired this desirable aptitude; but if he had also followed this Economist in his progressive decline and fall, dating from the "Tract on Monetary Reform," he would be worse than useless" (ibid.). On the matters in this and the next paragraph I am indebted to Professors Leslie Pressnell and Richard Sayers.

48. Ibid., pp. 436, 440–46.

49. They included C. MacMahon and J. C. R. Dow, both of whom had served in the Economic Section. Dow is now a Director. It should be noted that the comments in the text refer to top-level policymaking staff. According to figures published in *The Economist*, 15 June 1974, the Bank's staff of economists had grown from 12 to 45 in the preceding dozen years. However, the precise status and functions of this staff are not known to this writer.

ously undersupplied with monetary expertise, a state of affairs doubtless reflecting both the customary division of labour with the Bank and the persistence of the Keynesian focus on fiscal rather than monetary matters. Until quite recently the Treasury's econometric forecasting models apparently contained no monetary equations whatever. Thus there has been no parallel between Britain and those countries where the central bank has been both an integral component in the policymaking process and a major supplier of economic expertise to the government.[50]

As already indicated, prior to the mid-1960s British government economists were concentrated mainly in the Economic Section and actively engaged in the policymaking process at a variety of levels. Unfortunately, owing to the restrictions imposed by the Official Secrets Act, it is impossible to provide a detailed description and evaluation of their roles and influence. Nevertheless, a reliable general impression can be derived by extrapolating from accounts of the wartime experience, by piecing together published reports, and by interviews.

The Economic Section's postwar position was determined largely by wartime precedents and by decisions taken before the end of hostilities. Before agreeing to succeed Robbins as Director, Meade obtained an assurance that the Treasury's wartime economic advisers—Keynes, Lord Catto, D. H. (later Sir Dennis) Robertson, and Henderson —would not remain indefinitely, and that he would, ex officio, have a place on the crucial Budget Committee. This was probably the Section's most important single means to exert an influence on policy throughout the 1950s. While the Section was still in the Cabinet Office Meade was invited by the Chancellor, Hugh Dalton, to approach him directly whenever he wished; and Hall retained that right after the Section moved into the Treasury in 1953. Yet neither seems to have availed himself of this privileged access in practice, believing that it would be more likely to arouse official suspicion and hostility than if he worked in the customary way through the senior Treasury staff, who were in almost daily contact with the Chancellor.

Other members of the Section also worked mainly by assimilating themselves into the established administrative processes rather than by direct assertion or by seeking special facilities. They played a major role in the preparation and production of the postwar Economic Surveys and became deeply involved (together with some of the C.S.O. statisticians) in the slowly developing economic forecasting machin-

50. As for example, in Mexico. See Roger Ai Camp, *The Role of Economists in Policy-Making: A Comparative Case Study of Mexico and the United States* (Tucson, Ariz., 1977), esp. p. 55.

ery. In addition they attended a variety of official policy committees and their subordinate, usually interdepartmental, working parties; wrote briefs and memoranda on current issues, sometimes directly for ministers; made independent studies of topical and prospective problems; prepared materials for ministerial speeches and replies to parliamentary questions; and made themselves generally useful to administrators. Theirs was a very flexible organisation—a kind of high-level fire brigade, ready to be deployed against almost any economic emergency, equipped with little or no supporting technical or clerical staff, but able to draw on a kind of accumulated goodwill and cooperation from a variety of government departments and agencies. In the early postwar period when the Section's future was still in doubt, they were, in a sense, on trial. While often seeming academic in tone and inclination, they knew that their effectiveness and impact depended on their ability to be relevant and constructive—for example, by becoming involved in issues at an early stage, before official attitudes had hardened. Their success, which seems to have been considerable, probably depended less on their specialised academic knowledge and professional skills than on their individual qualities and abilities—e.g. tact; patience; adaptability; the capacity to work quickly under pressure; the ability to communicate with non-specialists; skill in the arts of persuasion; a sense of timing; grasp of bureaucratic procedures and conventions, or more colloquially, the capacity to 'play the machine'; appreciation of the problems of administrative feasibility and political practicality; recognition of the limits of one's professional expertise; and sheer stamina. In general, the Section's members seem not only to have avoided arousing the traditionalists' hostility; they also won the confidence, respect, and occasionally even the admiration of their official colleagues, some of whom have paid generous tribute to the lessons they learned from collaborating with economists. This undoubtedly helps to explain part of the rising demand for economists (and to a lesser extent, statisticians) in the 1960s as their supporters moved up the civil service hierarchy and used their influence to create new technical or economic advisory posts.

By present-day standards most of the economists employed in Whitehall in the first two postwar decades were, by virtue of their academic training and mental outlook, closer to the generalist than the specialist end of the spectrum. Unlike the agricultural economists and statisticians, they were generally regarded as economic administrators rather than mere technicians. In some degree this reflects the fact that economics is a more value-oriented subject, more sensitive to political considerations than more narrowly technical disciplines; and as is well known, at the higher official levels administrative appraisal contains a relatively large economic component and a smaller technical component, whereas the nature of technical appraisal varies less with changes of administrative level. As Hall remarked, reflecting on the predominantly macro preoccupations of the 1950s, "the special province of the economist is the economic system as a whole, and the relations between the workings of its different parts."[51] In a similar vein one of the most outstanding early postwar generalists, Lord Bridges, acknowledged the economist's potential contribution to the coordination of policy by remarking that "it is economic factors more than anything else which have compelled departments to work together."[52]

At present there is insufficient evidence on which to base a judgement of the economists' effectiveness. But in the early postwar years it seems clear that one of their most important functions was "damage minimisation," as one leading economist recently put it, by correcting the fallacious economic reasoning employed by non-economist officials.[53] An indication of the need for economic education in the Treasury at that time is provided by the official who subsequently admitted:

> I was flung in at the deep end. I learnt about exchange rates through the process of reading briefs on devaluation. I learnt about budgets by making and preparing one as Secretary to the Chancellor. I did it knowing I had not the faintest idea of the basis on which the Budget was put together. I did not even know what a deficit was. It came as a great flash of light when someone told me that what you did when you had a deficit was borrow.[54]

That confession may not reveal a typical situation. But there are certainly retired Permanent Secretaries of economic departments who generously acknowledge how much they learnt 'sitting by Nellie,' i.e. alongside articulate trained economists. And the changing climate of

51. Hall, "The Place of the Economist," p. 125.

52. Sir Edward (later Lord) Bridges, *Portrait of a Profession* (Cambridge, 1950), p. 23. As Martin Albrow has remarked, "It is only a slight exaggeration to argue that a professional will come closer to the centres of power and influence the more he relinquishes his specific professional function . . . such a process is built into the professional career as the professional role widens to include administrative and other duties . . . professionalism may enhance the listening ability of the official, but it increases his distance from the noise" (*Bureaucracy*, London, 1970, pp. 149, 177). In this sense the early postwar economists were probably less 'professional' than their more technically sophisticated successors of the 1970s. But economics has at least, until recently, usually been a vocationally non-specific discipline; hence its suitability as a component in the administrative decisionmaking process.

53. See, for example I. M. D. Little, esp. pp. 35–36. This seems to have been a common experience at that time.

54. Anon., quoted in Heclo and Wildavsky, p. 41.

opinion in the Treasury over the whole period is suggested by a leading government economist, who remarked in the mid 1970s:

> Nowadays economic language is talked throughout the Treasury. And instead of the economists feeling strange, it is the administrators, who do not know any economics, who feel embarrassed. . . . And the fact that the top people are economically trained means that you have to put up a decent economic argument . . . and this is the way it should be.[55]

The spread of economic literacy has certainly gone much further in the Treasury than in most departments, but there were evidently still some embarrassed administrators recently even in that enlightened citadel. As with the growth of numeracy and familiarity with the handling and interpretation of statistics, there has been a veritable revolution in Whitehall during the postwar period, and its effects will continue to be felt long after the mere expansion of numbers has ceased.[56]

The progress of economic literacy and numeracy has undoubtedly been very uneven, and dependent on a chance combination of personalities and circumstances. At times, as with the creation of new departments like the DEA or the Ministry of Overseas Development or divisions within established departments such as the Ministry of Transport or the Board of Trade, the dissemination of economic ideas and data has increased suddenly. In other cases, however, a lone economist has been imported into a department because a minister or senior official had the vague notion that it might be helpful "to have a tame pundit around the place."[57] Such an individual has had to find his own way around, learn the ropes, and spend considerable time explaining in elementary terms the kind of analysis and advice he can provide. Needless to say, the results have often been meagre, especially until the newcomer has won the confidence of significant colleagues and discovered how to keep his ear close to the ground without losing his dignity. Sometimes the initiative for such an appointment comes from outside the department, e.g. from the need to deal with an international agency, or closer to home, from the need to defend expenditure proposals under Treasury fire. Indeed, it is not unlikely that in some instances the initiative has come from the Treasury itself in the form of a

55. The author of this remark wishes to remain anonymous.
56. As noted by Lord Armstrong, who has since retired as Head of the Civil Service, "over the time that I have been in the Civil Service, I have seen a really quite remarkable revolution in the attitude of the decision-takers to the kind of information they require, and this has been followed by a very large increase in the number of statisticians in the Government service" ("Management Training," p. 96).
57. This is an actual quotation from an interview.

gentle hint that unless the department's expenditure proposals are more skillfully presented and more cogently argued in future they are unlikely to be approved.[58] There have even been unfortunate instances when the new appointee has come directly from the Treasury, arousing suspicions that he has been planted as a spy.

During the past decade or so the economists' functions in Whitehall have changed markedly for a variety of reasons: the increase of specialisation, division of labour, and other organisational developments consequent upon the growth of numbers; the introduction of new and more complex techniques—most notably in the vastly expanded forecasting process, but also in the widespread use of such tools and approaches as cost-benefit analysis, output (or planned programme) budgeting, investment appraisal, and econometric model building; the growth of specialist operational and research units in the larger departments; and the increasing range, variety, and detail of government's intervention in economic and social affairs. Of course there are still economic administrative tasks of the kind undertaken in the heroic days of the Economic Section, especially by the increasing number of economists in senior posts where the distinction between purely economic functions, administration, and policymaking becomes unavoidably blurred.[59] But given the scale and complexity of the current bureaucracy, such economic administrators nowadays often have substantial managerial as well as advisory responsibilites. In this respect the functions of senior economists are becoming more like those of senior statisticians, many of whom have normally had charge of considerable numbers of subordinate technical and supporting staffs. By contrast, the Economic Section's personnel often worked in isolation or in pairs.

The development of more interventionist policies, especially since the revival of enthusiasm for economic planning in the early 1960s, has contributed to a major shift of emphasis in the utilisation of professional economists from broad macroeconomic management towards more specific and detailed microeconomic work. Admittedly the dis-

58. There is a penetrating discussion of this and related matters in Heclo and Wildavsky, passim.

59. As Sir Alec Cairncross has noted, any economist who believes that he and his professional peers can successfully take over the management of economic policy, "has never been present at the kind of discussion between economists, administrators, and ministers, at which it is by no means uncommon for the economist to talk politics, the administrators to talk economics, and the ministers to discuss administrative problems." See his "Economists in Government," p. 203. In 1969 there was only one economist post at Under Secretary level and above, apart from the Head of the Government Economic Service. By 1977 there were four such posts in the Treasury alone, and fifteen throughout the civil service.

tinction between macro and microeconomic issues is difficult to sustain in practice; the two are in many cases interdependent, and there has been no simple abandonment of the earlier type of Keynesian macroeconomics despite mounting reservations about its theoretical foundations and practical effectiveness. But in recent years the main growth in demand for economists, both as technicians and as economic administrators, has been in the formulation, implementation, and evaluation of specific policies focused on some one aspect or segment of the economy. A case in point is the development of regional policy, where the success of any given measures will depend crucially upon their applicability to the special conditions and problems of the area concerned, as well as their general analytical soundness and compatibility with other current policies.[60] Hence in many macroeconomic policy issues there is a need for detailed factual knowledge of the subject matter, whether it be an area, an industry, a mode of transport, or an aspect of economic and social life such as housing, education, or health. To say that most departmental economists are engaged on micro rather than macroeconomic activities may be an oversimplification, especially as some are technicians whose contributions consist of the application of their specific skills to any of a wide variety of problems. Nevertheless it is clear that the changing character of government economic work, as well as the growth of numbers, specialisation, division of labour, and professionalisation, have combined to reduce the gap which at one time differentiated the general economists (or economic administrators) from the departmentalised specialists in agricultural economics. And indeed, curiously enough, it is arguable that since the initial British approach to the EEC, a major new departure in economics and political affairs with especially important implications for the agricultural sector, the trend in agricultural economics has been in the opposite direction to the trend in government economics generally—namely, away from their established preoccupation with the microeconomic details of domestic agricultural production and pricing towards a broader concern with the role of agriculture in the national and international setting. Here too there has been a shift of emphasis rather than a sharp break with the past. But as in other branches of government economic work, it has been accompanied by considerable advances in analytical sophistication and technical complexity.

In addition to changes in their functions, there has been a remarkable 'spread' of economists beyond the Treasury, in which they were for so long concentrated. The extent of this movement is indicated in Ta-

60. For an account of the employment of economists in one major region, see A. W. Coats, "The Changing Role of Economists in Scottish Government," pp. 399–424.

ble 2, which lists the main concentrations[61] of economists and statisticians in the mid 1970s. Some of the implications of this movement for the economist's working conditions (e.g. whether he is a loner or a member of a substantial unit or team) have already been mentioned.

VI. *The Nature of the Political System and Bureaucracy; the Role of Economists in Policymaking*

At the beginning of this study the continuity of British history was stressed, and this theme is also relevant when considering the general characteristics of the political and bureaucratic environment in which the professionalisation of government economics has evolved during the past four decades. Throughout that period the political system has been democratic (doubtless somewhat less so in wartime and in the immediate postwar transition); government has been dominated in succession by two major parties which, for all their superficial differences and mutual antagonisms, differ much less in their practice than in their ideology or rhetoric; the balance of political support has shifted remarkably little, with the consequence that Parliamentary majorities have at times, at least until the present (1980) government, been disturbingly small and uncertain, and it is not too much to say that there has been a fundamental consensus—admittedly with some significant changes of emphasis and differences in detail—on the basic objectives of economic and social policy. Indeed, for these and related reasons, many observers maintain that the continuity—in other words, the inability to shake off the shackles of the past—has been the major reason for Britain's inability to escape from her depressingly persistent economic problems, such as a slow rate of economic growth; a low level of manufacturing productivity; inadequate investment and technological innovation; outdated managerial and labour attitudes and practices; balance of payments weakness: excessive overseas financial and political commitments (until recently); and a general lack of economic and social capacity to adapt to the demands of twentieth-century modernisation.[62]

This is obviously not the place to embark on a general survey of

61. Government Economic Service staff were also employed at that time in the Cabinet Office (Central Policy Review Staff), Civil Service Department, Customs and Excise, Ministry of Defence, Office of Fair Trading, Home Office, Board of Inland Revenue, Royal Commission on the Distribution of Income and Wealth, Welsh Office, Civil Aviation Authority, Commission for Industrial Relations, Office of Manpower Economics, Monopolies Commission, National Economic Development Office, Post Office, and Price Commission.

62. It should perhaps be added, given the experience of the later 1970s, that some other leading countries appear to be encountering somewhat similar problems, albeit in a less acute form.

Table 2. Major concentrations of economists and statisticians in the British Civil Service, 1974 and 1980

Government Economic Service	1974[a]	1980[b]
Department of the Environment (D.O.E.)	73	(60)
Department of Trade and Industry (D.T.I.)	43	(44½)
Treasury	58	(65½)
Ministry of Overseas Development (O.D.M.)	29	38
Department of Employment (E)	20	21
Department of Health and Social Security (D.H.S.S.)	14	20
Department of Energy	10	20
Foreign and Commonwealth Office	10	9
Scottish Office	9	24[(c)]
Education	7	7
Others	17	81
TOTAL	290	

Government Statistical Service[d]	1974	1980[e]
D.O.E.	45	68
D.T.I.	78	57
Treasury	7	12
O.D.M.	14	15
E.	20	42
D.H.S.S.	30	42
Ministry of Agriculture, Fisheries, and Food	12	18
Ministry of Defence	37	32
Central Statistical Office	56	55
Office of Population Censuses	32	29
Civil Service Dept.	28	8
Home Office	17	25
Inland Revenue	14	21
Others	52	96
TOTAL	442	520

[a] Compiled from Government Economic Service Directory, 1974. There were also 23 economists in the Ministry of Agriculture, Fisheries and Food and 11 in the Department of Agriculture and Fisheries, Scotland, who were then excluded from the G.E.S.

[b] Data applying to October 1, 1980, supplied by Government Economic Service. These figures do not include economists on loan outside the G.E.S.; on study leave; in Nedo or Administrative posts; and those recruited by the Price Commission and other non-departmental bodies.

[c] The Scottish Office figure includes agricultural economists in the Department of Agriculture and Fisheries, Scotland. The agricultural economists in the Ministry of Agriculture, Fisheries and Food are included in the table among "other" economists.

[d] Compiled from Government Statistical Service Directory. It should be noted that the Statistician Class in the British Civil Service is broadly parallel in salary and status to the Economist and Administrative Classes.

[e] Data supplied by the Central Statistical Office.

postwar British economic and social history, especially one coloured unduly by the justifiable disappointments of the past decade or so. From the standpoint of the 1930s there have been substantial achievements, notably a steadily rising standard of living, and the avoidance of serious depressions and widespread unemployment. With respect to the present subject, changes in the size, composition, and structure of the civil service and the educational system have been significant, even though too slow and gradual in the early postwar decades. Within the government machine there has been a significant breakdown of anti-specialist prejudices and a corresponding readiness, on the part of senior civil servants and ministers of both parties, to place more reliance on qualified social scientists, technologists, and other experts in making policy decisions.

The temptation to draw significant parallels between the rapid expansion of the Government Economic Service in the past decade or so and the concurrent rise in the trends of inflation and unemployment has, of course, proved irresistible to some commentators. On occasions it has provided harmless amusement in the form of references to the "plague of economists" in Whitehall[63] which unduly flatter the economics profession by exaggerating its influence (much as socialist and sentimentalist historians overstated the pernicious influence of the classical economists in the early nineteenth century). From another standpoint, however, the matter cannot be dismissed so lightly, for serious scholars have attributed at least part of Britain's ills to the failures of Keynesian economics and the bad advice given by government economists, and even to a species of *trahison des clercs* on the part of the professional establishment, especially Cambridge and Oxford members.[64]

Needless to say, these important but highly controversial contentions cannot be adequately explored here. Despite a veritable flood of analysis, interpretations, reminiscences, journalistic disclosures, and scholarly studies of Britain's postwar economic ideas and policies, we still lack detailed knowledge of when, how, and to whom economic ad-

63. Cf. M. M. Postan's well-known article of that title originally published in *Encounter*, 1968, and reprinted in his *Fact and Relevance: Essays on Historical Method* (Cambridge, 1971). An amusing editorial in the *Guardian* (25 July 1974) discussed the correlation between the number of economists in government and the growth of such undesirable phenomena as inflation, airline hijackings, and terrorist outrages, suggesting that "if it can be shown that the value of money varies inversely in proportion to the quantity of advice received, an important watershed in the field of economic theory will have been passed."

64. See, for example, Harry G. Johnson, "Keynes and British Economics," in Milo Keynes, ed., *Essays on John Maynard Keynes* (Cambridge, 1975), pp. 108–22; T. W. Hutchison, *'Positive' Economics and Policy Objectives* (London, 1964), esp. the concluding chapter; also his *Economics and Economic Policy in Britain, 1946–1966*.

vice was offered, and precisely how far, if at all, it entered into the decisions actually taken.[65] The combination of an (at least partially) effective Official Secrets Act, a strong and sustained tradition of civil service anonymity, and a predominantly consensual style of administration[66] constitutes a significant obstacle to scholarship. In some instances—such as the economists' unsuccessful efforts to persuade the Wilson government to devalue the pound between 1964 and 1967—the general content and thrust of economic advice and its reception are well known. But this was an unusual episode and on the whole—for example, by comparison with the USA[67]—British students of economic thought and policy labour under serious handicaps.

However, despite these difficulties, some broad concluding observations can be made about the changing postwar role of British government economists. As professionals, they now play an enormously increased role in policymaking in the broadest sense of the term—which includes the choice of policy objectives and assignment of weights to them; the selection of means to attain those ends; and the implementation and adaptation of existing policies in response to changing circumstances. Underlying the decisions there is now infinitely more relevant economic and statistical data, which are nowadays prepared and presented in a much more sophisticated form and analysed in more subtle and varied ways. Doubtless not all of this represents a net gain, for the proliferation of analyses and data may generate confusion and indecisiveness on the part of policymakers, especially when there is a babel of conflicting voices. Indeed, it is appropriate at this point to note the tendency, especially among scholars, to exaggerate the deliberateness and rationality of the policymaking process, which can be countered by reference to Cairncross's timely warning that "The atmosphere of a large government department is frequently almost indistinguishable from that of the loony bin. I use the term in no pejorative sense; it is simply one of the facts of official life."[68]

65. Of course in many cases it is impossible to know exactly what occurred and why. As Cairncross has remarked, "it is often very hard even for those at close quarters with policy-making to know what does in the end shape the decisions that ministers take—or, still more, do not take. . . . Where the issue is in dispute, who except the minister (or even including the minister) knows what clinched the matter? It is very rarely that one can say with confidence that the decision would have been different if *x* had not been there. The people who think they know and say so may, in fact, be ill-qualified to judge." *Essays on Economic Management*, p. 210.

66. For a good recent example from a large literature see Christoph, in Dogan, ed., pp. 25–26. There is an excellent account of the upper-level civil service working atmosphere and relationships in Heclo and Wildavsky, passim.

67. See, for example, the very detailed documentation used by the contributors to Craufurd D. Goodwin, ed., *Exhortation and Controls: The Search for a Wage-Price Policy, 1945–1971* (Washington, 1975).

68. From an unpublished paper, "Writing the History of Economic Policy," (1970),

On the same occasion Cairncross referred to the temptation to exaggerate the influence of policy and the danger of neglecting the noneconomic factors involved, considerations that have been especially important in recent British history. The predominantly 'consensual' relations between British ministers and top-level civil servants encourage 'mutual political protection,' a practice based squarely on the traditions of collective ministerial responsibility and bureaucratic anonymity. Changes of government, however sudden or unexpected, have only temporarily affected this state of affairs,[69] even in the most dramatic postwar instances when the Labour Party came to power in 1945, and again in October 1964, supposedly with deep-rooted suspicions of the bureaucratic machine and a fierce determination to change the course of postwar history. In the latter episode, as always, the civil servants prepared themselves for the new regime by studying the campaign programmes and endeavouring to predict and clear the ground for new policies, some of which were discussed in private with leading members of the opposition before the election. As with so many potential British revolutions, the accompanying efforts to politicise the government economic service and reform the bureaucracy proved to be disappointing to their most ardent proponents.

The manifest failure of Labour's attempt to shift the balance of power within the bureaucracy by creating the D.E.A. as a counterweight and policymaking rival to the Treasury is yet another example of the underlying continuity of the British system of government.[70] Curiously enough, some of those who are most critical of civil service traditionalism and most anxious to accelerate its reform also recognise that "The greater the professionalism and expertise of our bureaucracy the greater its power. So we need to match any increase in civil service professionalism by at least a corresponding increase in the capacity of our Ministers and Parliament to control our bureaucratic machine."[71] Yet while there has been a widespread tendency to overrate the importance of bureaucrats and experts—a view that the economists them-

---

quoted by permission. For a useful discussion of the role of rationality (which economists tend to overrate) and other elements in policymaking processes see Geoffrey Hawker, R. F. I. Smith, and Patrick Weller, *Politics and Policy in Australia* (University of Queensland Press, 1979), ch. 1, and sources cited therein.

69. This is in marked contrast to the situation in Belgium. Cf. Drs. G. Stienlet, *Economists and the Civil Service System: The Belgium Case* (Centrum voor Economische Studien, Katolieke Universteit te Leuven, 1978).

70. Some of the postwar structural changes in Whitehall have been changes of nomenclature and form rather than substance, and it is noteworthy that the post-Fulton removal of establishments (i.e., staffing) matters from the Treasury to the CSD has not been an unqualified success. A return to the status quo ante-1968 is by no means unlikely.

71. Lord Crowther Hunt, Evidence to the *House of Commons Expenditure Committee*, op. cit. n.32 supra, 3:1108.

selves have too seldom discouraged[72]—there is no doubt that in a democracy the ultimate responsibility must be with their masters, the politicians, and through them the electorate. In the British case it appears that in addition to the inertia of the past we have suffered unduly in recent years from short-term administrative and political disruptions consequent upon changes of government. As Michael Stewart has noted in a cogent analysis of the structural, technical, management, and political influences on the course of events,

> Incoming government have spent their first year or two abolishing or drastically modifying the measures—often quite sensible—of their predecessors, and pressing ahead with the measures—often unrealistic or irrelevant—which they have formulated in opposition. After a year or two they have come to closer terms with reality, and changed course, but by that time much harm has been done, and the benefits that would have accrued from continuing the policies they inherited have been lost.[73]

To the extent that this diagnosis is correct the remedy lies not in the sphere of economics, but in the need for more responsible opposition and the development of a degree of bipartisanship with respect to the primary ends and means of economic policy. British postwar experience suggests that this desirable objective is unlikely to be attained either easily or rapidly. While economists have undoubtedly learned much in that time about the complexities of policymaking processes and the intractability of economic and social problems, in dealing with such matters they necessarily tend "to direct their attention to facets that can be illuminated by the methods of inquiry they find congenial. Their instruments are efficient within a range; but they often choose to ignore what lies outside it. . . . So it happens that, on occasions, their inquiries do not penetrate beyond the periphery of fundamental problems."[74] Nevertheless, despite the undeniable limitations of economics as science—limitations that become the more obvious as economists participate more actively and continuously in government—it is clear that they can make a constructive, if usually modest, contribution to public affairs.

72. During the 1960s some economists encouraged false public expectations by exaggerating their ability to influence the course of policy. A few years later when the now familiar combination of inflation and unemployment became obvious, they were given a disproportionate share of the blame for policy failures.

73. Michael Stewart, *The Jekyll and Hyde Years: Politics and Economics Since 1964* (London, 1977), p. 241. There is support for this emphasis on the disturbing effects of repeated policy changes in the editor's concluding "General Appraisal" in Blackaby, esp. pp. 652–53.

74. G. C. Allen, *The British Disease* (London, 1976), p. 19.

VII. *Concluding Reflections*

This study began by emphasising the continuity of British ideas and institutions. In the light of events since the general election in May 1979 it may be appropriate to conclude by asking whether this generalisation still holds good, for there have recently been significant, even seemingly dramatic, changes in government attitudes and practices. The first government in our history to be led by a woman Prime Minister has so far displayed an unusual determination to reverse the decline of the British economy (in itself no novel objective) by adopting strong policies that represent a conscious and deliberate break with the past. The fact that these policies are widely believed to be wholly or largely inspired by an economist—an American, Professor Milton Friedman—is of added interest from the standpoint of these studies. And as Mrs. Thatcher's administration has the largest Parliamentary majority for some years, and therefore (at least on paper) the political means to implement her party's campaign promises, the current experiment is likely to be of great interest to future students of economic thought and policy.

It is, of course, much too early to judge how far this apparent discontinuity is either real or lasting. The current severe economic recession, though obviously not confined to Britain, has been accompanied here by unprecedentedly high interest rates, a sharp increase in the value of sterling, a high level of bankruptcies, and the worst unemployment since the early 1930s. How far the government is directly responsible for these conditions—some of which are novel, while others simply represent an accentuation of existing trends—is a matter of intense controversy. But whatever the verdict, the shift towards monetarism, loosely defined, raises important theoretical and practical questions about the government's ability to measure and control key monetary variables. Moreover, it entails a significant change from the earlier approach, according to which monetary factors were not ignored but were regarded as "peripheral to the forecast mainly because examination of past relationships suggested that their influence was not strong."[75]

Post mortems on this period may eventually shed new light on the role of economists in British government, but these investigations, like the present study, will doubtless continue to be severely inhibited by the Official Secrets Act.[76]

75. Blackaby, p. 628.
76. Despite considerable public pressure during the past decade or so this measure remains virtually intact. With respect to the machinery of government there are other significant signs of continuity. As in the mid-1960s the opposition, through the Fabian Society, is once again examining proposals for the reform of the civil service, including

There have, however, been several recent developments relevant to our subject which are worth noting by way of conclusion. Firstly, it is clear that the peak in the numbers of professional economists and statisticians in Whitehall has been passed, partly as a result of the government's determination to reduce public expenditure and the size of the civil service. Secondly, unlike the first two postwar decades, the days of 'inning and outing' are virtually over: almost the entire corps of professional economists in Whitehall now consists of career civil servants. Thirdly, while the present government has continued the practice of appointing special advisers—not all of whom, of course, are economists[77]—the latest appointee as Head of the Government Economic Service, Professor Terry Burns (formerly of the London Business School) has had no previous experience of working in the Civil Service. Unlike his predecessors, most of whom had earned reputations both as academics and as experienced economist-administrators, Burns is a leading econometrician and forecaster. As an isolated case, his appointment can hardly be regarded as a portent of politicisation, even though many of the career professionals would probably have preferred to see the promotion of an insider. But whatever his impact on policy may be, Burns' arrival in Whitehall is further evidence that highly technical economic expertise is now securely placed at the top of the generalist bureaucracy.

suggestions concerning the role of special advisers and the powers of the Prime Minister. At the same time the government is reported to be reviewing the Fulton Committee's reforms with a view to abolishing, or reducing the role of, the Civil Service Department, by restoring to the Treasury control over personnel management. Plus ça change, plus c'est la même chose.

77. The latest (i.e. November 1980) appointment of an economist Special Adviser, in this case to the Prime Minister, is Professor Alan A. Walters of the Johns Hopkins University (formerly of the LSE).

Bibliography

Addison, Paul. *The Road to 1945*. London, 1975.

Allen, C. G. "Advice from Economists—Forty-Five Years Ago." *Three Banks Review* (June 1975). Reprinted in his *British Industry and Economic Policy* (London, 1979).

Allen, Sir Roy. "On Official Statistics and Statisticians." *Journal of the Royal Statistical Society* 133A (part 4, 1970): 509–26.

Allen, W. R. "Economics, Economists, and Economic Policy: Modern American Experiences." *History of Political Economy* 9 (1977): 48–88.

Anderson, Sir John. *The Organization of Economic Studies in Relation to the Problems of Government*, Stamp Memorial Lecture. London, 1947.

Armstrong, Sir William. "Management Training for Statisticians and Opportunities to Enter Top Management." *Journal of the Royal Statistical Society* 136 (part 1, 1973): 95–99.

────. *Professionals and Professionalism in the Civil Service*. Welwyn Garden City, 1970.

──── William (Lord). *Personnel Management in the Civil Service*. London: H.M.S.O., 1971.

Blackaby, F. T., ed. *British Economic Policy 1960–74*. Cambridge, 1978.

Booth, A. E., and A. W. Coats. "The Market for Economists in Britain, 1945–1975: A Preliminary Survey." *Economic Journal* 88 (1978): 436–54.

────. "Some Wartime Observations on the Role of the Economist in Government." *Oxford Economic Papers* 32 (July 1980): 177–99.

Brittan, Samuel. *Steering the Economy: The Role of the Treasury*. London, 1971.

────. "The Irregulars." In Richard Rose, ed., *Policy-Making in Britain: A Reader in Government* (New York, 1969), pp. 329–99.

Brown, R. G. S. *The Administrative Process in Britain*. London, 1970.

Cairncross, Sir Alec. "On Being an Economic Adviser." Reprinted in *Factors in Economic Development* (London, 1962), pp. 272–91.

────. "The Work of an Economic Adviser" (1967) and "Economists in Government" (1970). Reprinted in *Essays in Economic Management* (London, 1971), pp. 184–96, 197–216.

Chester, D. N., ed. *Lessons of the War Economy*. Cambridge, 1951.

────, and F. M. G. Willson. *The Organisation of British Central Government 1914–1956*. London, 1957.

Christoph, James P. "Higher Civil Servants and the Politics of Consensualism in Great Britain." In Mattei Dogan, *The Mandarins of Western Europe: The Political Role of Top Civil Servants* (New York, 1975), pp. 25–62.

Coats, A. W. "The Development of the Agricultural Economics Profession in England." *Journal of Agricultural Economics* 27 (Sept. 1976): 381–92.

────. "The Development of the Economics Profession in England: A Preliminary Review." In L. Houmanidis, ed., *International Congress of Economic History and History of Economic Theories* (Piraeus: Piraeus Graduate School of Industrial Studies, 1975), pp. 277–90.

────. "The Changing Role of Economists in Scottish Government, Mainly Since 1960." *Public Administration* 57 (Spring 1979): 399–424.

Coddington, Alan. "Economists and Policy." *National Westminster Bank Quarterly Review*, Feb. 1973, pp. 171–88.

Devons, Ely. *Papers on Planning and Economic Management*. Edited by Sir Alec Cairncross. Manchester, 1970.

Dow, J. C. R. *The Management of the British Economy 1945–60*. Cambridge, 1964.

Hall, R. L. "Reflections on the Practical Application of Economics." *Economic Journal* 69 (Dec. 1959).

Hall, Sir Robert. "The Place of the Economist in Government." *Oxford Economic Papers*, n.s. 7 (June 1955): 119–35.

Hallett, G. "The Role of Economists as Government Advisers." *Westminster Bank Review*, May 1967, pp. 2–20.

Hancock, W. K., and M. M. Gowing. *British War Economy, History of the Second World War*, United Kingdom Civil Series. H.M.S.O., 1949.

Hargrove, Erwin C. *Professional Roles in Society and Government: The English Case*. Beverly Hills, 1972.

Heclo, Hugh, and Aaron Wildavsky. *The Private Government of Public Money*. London, 1974.

Henderson, P. D. "The Use of Economists in British Administration." *Oxford Economic Papers*, n.s. 13 (Feb. 1961): 5–26.

Howson, Susan, and Donald Winch. *The Economic Advisory Council 1930–1939: A Study in Economic Advice During Depression and Recovery*. Cambridge, 1977.

Hutchison, T. W. *Economics and Economic Policy in Britain, 1946–1966*. London, 1968.

Jewkes, J. "Second Thoughts on the British White Paper on Employment Policy." In *Economic Research and the Development of Science and Public Policy* (New York, 1946).

Keeling, C. D. *Management in Government* London, 1972.

Leith-Ross, Sir Frederick W. *Money Talks: Fifty Years of International Finance*. London, 1968.

Leruez, Jacques. *Economic Planning and Politics in Britain*. London, 1975.

Little, I. M. D. "The Economist in Whitehall." *Lloyds Bank Review* 44 (April 1957): 29–40.

Marris, Robin. "The Position of Economics and Economists in the Government Machine: A Comparative Critique of the United Kingdom and the Netherlands." *Economic Journal* 64 (Dec. 1954): 759–83.

Mitchell, Joan. "Special Advisers: A Personal View." *Public Administration* 56 (Spring 1978): 87–98.

Moser, C. A. (Sir Claus). "The Statistician in Government: A Challenge for the 1970's." *Transactions of the Manchester Statistical Society*, Session 1970–71, pp. 1–39.

———. "Staffing in the Government Statistical Services." *Journal of the Royal Statistical Society* 136A (part 1, 1973): 75–88.

Peacock, Alan. *The Economic Analysis of Government, and Related Themes*. Oxford, 1979.

Postan, M. M. "A Plague of Economists." Reprinted in *Fact and Relevance: Essays on Historical Method* (Cambridge, 1971).

Robbins, Lord. *The Autobiography of an Economist*. London 1971.

Roll, E. "The Uses and Abuses of Economics." *Oxford Economic Papers*, n.s. 20 (Nov. 1968): 295–300. Reprinted in his *The Uses and Abuses of Economics, and Other Essays* (London, 1978).

Salter, Sir Arthur J. *Slave of the Lamp: A Public Servant's Notebook*. London, 1967.

Seers, Dudley. "Why Visiting Economists Fail." *Journal of Political Economy* 70 (Aug. 1962): 325–28.

Self, Peter. *Econocrats and the Policy Process: The Politics and Philosophy of Cost-Benefit Analysis*. London, 1975.

———. *Administrative Theories and Politics*. Toronto, 1972.

Shanks, Michael. "The Irregular in Whitehall." In Paul Streeten, ed., *Unfashionable Economics: Essays in Honour of Lord Balogh* (London, 1970), pp. 244–62.

Stone, Richard. "The Use and Development of National Income and Expenditure Estimates." In D. N. Chester, ed., *Lessons of the War Economy* (Cambridge, 1951), pp. 83–101.

Thomas, Hugh, ed. *Crisis in the Civil Service*. London, 1968. Essays by

Roger Opie, "The Making of Economic Policy," pp. 53–82; and Dudley Seers, "The Structure of Power," pp. 83–109.

Williams, Alan. *Output Budgeting and the Contributions of Micro Economics to Efficiency in Government*, C.A.S. Occasional Paper No. 4. London, 1967.

Wilson, Harold. "Statistics and Decision-Making in Government: Bradshaw Revisited." *Journal of the Royal Statistical Society* 136 (part 1, 1973): 1–16.

Winch, Donald. *Economics and Policy: A Historical Study*. London, 1969.

Australia: economists in a federal system

A. Petridis

I. *Historical Background*

Prior to 1940 there were very few economists in the Australian government but a small group of academic economists were very active 'outsiders.'[1] This study necessarily begins with a brief examination of interwar and Second World War developments, and especially the role of the 'outsiders,' before examining the expansion of economists in government after 1945.

Prior to the Second World War the Australian Public Service (A.P.S.) employed only a small number of graduates of any sort and these consisted entirely of graduates in fields such as engineering, medicine, law, and science who were regarded as professional appointees. Economists were certainly not regarded as falling into the professional category, and non-professional entry was, until 1933, restricted to persons under twenty years of age.[2] The predominant method of recruitment by examination at the upper secondary education level was consistent with the 'egalitarian' view[3] that all entrants to the service should be at the same level, and that access to the highest positions should be open to everyone.[4]

After the expansion of 1919–24 the Australian economy had begun to stagnate, and by 1929 had "drifted into depression."[5] Recruitment policies for the A.P.S. meant that it was ill equipped to interpret Australia's economic problems and to provide economic advice and guidance to the government. Successive Australian governments therefore turned to the small group of economists (there were only five full professors of economics in 1930) for advice on especially pressing economic problems.[6] Two economists stand out as having had the

1. See Corden, pp. 57–59.
2. See Schaffer, "Australia," in Ridley, pp. 57–91.
3. See C. J. Hayes, "The Commonwealth Public service," *Public Administration* (Sydney) 15 (March 1956): 1–24.
4. For a review of recruitment policies up to 1940 see R. S. Parker; S. Encel, "The Recruitment of University Graduates," pp. 222–31; idem, "The Commonwealth Public Service"; idem, "Graduate Recruitment—A Rejoinder," pp. 28–34 and 49–50; and H. A. Scarrow, "Graduate Recruitment—A Reply," *Public Administration* (Sydney) 14 (March 1955): 51–55.
5. L. B. Schedvin, *Australia and the Great Depression*.
6. See C. D. Goodwin, *The Image of Australia* (Durham, N. C., 1974), esp. ch. 9.

greatest impact on government policy in this time—L. F. Giblin and D. B. Copland. They are best known internationally for their review of the Australian tariff (along with Bridgen, Dyason, and Wickens) which led to the development of Australia's elaborate tariff system.[7] The role of this group of economists, who at times publicly promoted their views on policy, has not always been judged a success,[8] but its significance lies more in the close contacts and influence they had with the governments of the day. The groundwork was laid for gradual changes in the recruitment policies of the public service, for the full-time participation of many academic economists in Australian wartime governments, and the subsequent take-off in the number of permanently employed graduates, especially graduates in economics.

In response to the rising numbers of university graduates, and to lobbying from universities and the Public Service Board (P.S.B.),[9] the government amended the Public Service Act in 1933 to permit the appointment of 'generalist' graduates to the service. Government attitudes were gradually changing, reflecting the changing supply and demand conditions for graduates in the social sciences. However, from 1934 to 1941 (when the scheme was suspended because of the war) only 82 graduates were appointed—so few largely because of the low salary levels at which appointments had to be made. Of these, 42 had some training in economics, although only 6 had bachelor of economics degrees. The significance of these appointments lay in the unusually rapid promotion of the appointees, which very quickly placed them in positions where they were able to influence the future direction of the public service in war and peace.[10]

There were two other noteworthy developments in the 1930s which were apparently initiated by Copland and Giblin. The first was the appointment of an economist with a D.Phil. from Oxford and a Ph.D. from the University of Chicago to the post of Assistant Statistician and Economist. He had been Lecturer in Economics in Tasmania before coming to Canberra in 1932. This appointee rose to the position of Secretary to the Treasury after the Second World War. The second was

7. See J. B. Bridgen et al., *The Australian Tariff: An Economic Inquiry* (Melbourne, 1929); N. Cain, pp. 1–20; D. B. Copland, "A Neglected Phase of Tariff Controversy," *Quarterly Journal of Economics*, Feb. 1931, pp. 289–308; and L. F. Giblin, "Some Economic Effects of the Australian Tariff," *Joseph Fisher Lecture in Commerce* (Adelaide, June 1936). Space considerations preclude an examination of the many other significant policy initiatives in which these economists participated.

8. See Schedvin, ch. 10, for more detail on the policy prescriptions of these economists.

9. *Report of the Conference of Universities of Australia* (Melbourne, 1929), and Public Service Board Report 1929–1930 (Melbourne), p. 21.

10. Information supplied by the P.S.B. See also Encel, "Recruitment of University Graduates to the Commonwealth Public Service," p. 226.

the creation in 1938 of the position of research officer. The first such officer was appointed to the Research Section of the Bureau of Census and Statistics, and the appointee was an economics graduate who eventually became secretary of a major economic policy department. Several similar research officer appointments were made to the same Research Section of the Bureau of Census and Statistics, and to other branches of the Treasury Department. The Research Officer, Grade 1 level, became the usual appointment level for all graduates appointed to the Third Division[11] after 1945.

Adjustment to war

The A.P.S. was technically ill-equipped to meet the demands of a total war economy.[12] The need for reliable data on the human and other resources of the wartime economy was satisfied by the Bureau of Census and Statistics, the only branch of the A.P.S. which had built a small nucleus of economists in the 1930s. For some years prior to the war the Commonwealth Statistician had also been the Economic Adviser to the Treasurer.[13] But the Bureau of Census and Statistics apart, it was the outsiders who played a major part in the planning, coordination, and effective operation of Australian economic and social policies.[14] It is well documented in the literature of public administration that an 'official family' emerged, consisting of cabinet ministers, certain senior officials such as permanent heads of departments, academic economists on temporary appointments to the A.P.S., and the new group of research officers, plus a few other economists and businessmen from private banks and industry.[15] In 1939 the Financial and Economic Advisory Committee, consisting of economists attached to and sometimes directing various departments, had been formed to advise on individual policy issues.[16] The A.P.S. grew from 13 depart-

11. The A.P.S. consists of four divisions. The First Division contains all Permanent Heads of Departments. The Second Division is made up of those public servants exercising senior executive or professional functions under the permanent heads. The Third Division consists of officers engaged in a wide range of administrative, clerical, and professional work. Most graduate appointments are made to this division. The Fourth Division contains technical and clerical workers.

12. See D. B. Copland, *Giblin*, p. 8; and idem, "The Recruitment, Training and Organisation of the Public Service," *Public Administration* (Sydney) 4 (March 1944): 137.

13. See Lyall, "Graduate Preference," pp. 294–320.

14. See Walker, *The Australian Economy in War and Reconstruction*.

15. See "Commonwealth Policy Co-ordination," based on a Report of A.C.T. Regional Group of Royal Institute of Public Administration, *Public Administration* (Sydney) 14 (Dec. 1954): 193–213. See also E. J. B. Foxcroft, "The Changing Balance of Government in Australia," *Public Administration* 6 (Dec. 1946): 184–92.

16. "Commonwealth Policy Co-ordination," pp. 196ff. See also S. Encel, "Cabinet Machinery in Australia," *Public Administration* (Sydney) 15 (June 1956): 106–11.

ments in 1939 to 25 at the peak of wartime activities, and economic advice was being provided to the government on a very wide range of macroeconomic and microeconomic problems.[17] In the Australian case the economists' impact was probably greatest on manpower, employment, and wages policy, and on price control, rationing, and resources management.[18]

It is easy and may be misleading for an economist to look at the wartime Australian economy and see the hand of the new breed of economists in every government move. Nevertheless, the following highly significant conjuncture of events and relationships should be described. The young graduates employed under Section 36A of the Public Service Act entered the A.P.S. when a favourable climate of opinion had been created at the political level by the role of the academic economists in the 1930s. On technical matters the established public servants were at a disadvantage vis-à-vis this group of relatively freshly trained graduates.[19] Partly because of the lopsided age structure of the A.P.S. and the unimaginative interwar recruitment policies and partly because they appear to have been accorded special treatment in the promotion stakes, the progress of this group to positions of power and influence was exceedingly rapid. Finally, although the A.P.S. grew rapidly during the war, it was still sufficiently small for constant, close contact between the members of the group, which encouraged the development of an *esprit de corps* and a sense of common purpose which exercised a profound influence on postwar developments in Australia.[20]

The World War experience dramatically changed the prevailing views on the kinds of targets that governments could hope to achieve. The Labor Party leadership and the Labor Treasurer, J. B. Chifley, were ready to maintain the greatly increased level of government intervention in the economy in peacetime, so that 'full employment' could

17. See E. J. B. Foxcroft, "The Changing Balance of Government in Australia," and W. E. Dunk, "New Problems of Management in the Public Service," *Public Administration* (Sydney) 6 (Dec. 1947): 433–41.

18. For examples see Copland, *Giblin*, esp. part III; Walker, *The Australian Economy in War and Reconstruction*; D. B. Copland, *Price Stabilization* (Melbourne, 1943); and "Essays in Honour of Sir Douglas Copland," *Economic Record* 36 (March 1960).

19. See Encel, "Recruitment of University Graduates," p. 226. Of course, some of these new entrants to the A.P.S. were equally disadvantaged initially by their comparative lack of knowledge of administrative and bureaucratic practice. However, Walker has argued that they were less handicapped in this respect than many of the temporary appointees from business and industry. See Walker, esp. ch. 5.

20. Some of the points in this paragraph have been made in interviews by members of this group who are now retired. See also "Commonwealth Policy Co-ordination," supra n.15, in which the reasons for the great influence of this group are examined.

be achieved. Thus the Australian preparations for the peace were planned to maintain the government's growing interventionist role. Chifley fully comprehended and supported Keynesian policies of government intervention, and there now existed a bureaucracy in which a number of young economists, led by Dr. H. C. Coombs, enthusiastically pushed the Keynesian line. The culmination was the presentation on 30 May 1945 to the Australian Parliament of a *White Paper on Full Employment*.[21] A month earlier the Australian Government had presented another White Paper on *Some Problems of Economic Policy* by D. B. Copland which was also interventionist in nature, drawing on and emphasising the Keynesian theoretical framework. The strength of the Australian commitment to Keynesian policies to achieve full employment is exemplified by the approach adopted by Australian delegations to various international economic conferences in the 1940s. At an International Conference in San Francisco in 1945 the Australian delegation was instructed by the Treasurer to press for the inclusion of a full-employment pledge in the charter of the organisation which was being created to replace the League of Nations.[22] The intellectual ferment generated by the 'new economics' had found a fertile environment in the A.P.S. in the 1940s.

Developments since 1945

The direction in which the A.P.S. was to develop and the role played by economists in that development had been presaged by the events up to and including the war. Two main effects are discernible. First, the placing of a much greater emphasis on economics-type degrees as the principal form of graduate qualification, to such an extent that it could reasonably be regarded as the 'generalist' qualification; and the second, the permanent appointment of a group of economists (many of whom had temporary appointments in wartime) to form the nucleus of an influential group of top-level administrators, who also provided policy advice to governments as economist-specialists. Three phases are clearly identifiable in the postwar development of the A.P.S. leading up to the current period.

21. See Copland and Barback, *The Conflict*, pp. 1–80. See also J. S. G. Wilson, "Post-War Employment Policy," *Australian Quarterly* 16 (Sept. 1944): 30–40; idem, "Rehabilitation and Full Employment: Problems and Policies," *Australian Quarterly* 17 (June 1945): 12–22; D. H. Merry and G. R. Bruns, "Full Employment: The British, Canadian and Australian White Papers," *Economic Record* 21 (Dec. 1945): 223–35; J. S. G. Wilson, "Prospects of Full Employment in Australia," *Economic Record* 22 (June 1946): 99–116; L. G. Melville, "Some Post-War Problems," *Economic Record* 22 (June 1946): 4–23; D. B. Copland, "Professor Jewkes and the Alternative to Planning," *Economic Record* 47 (Dec. 1948): 191–203; and K. Laffer, "Economic Controls Under Full Employment," *Australian Quarterly* 23 (Dec. 1951); 21–30.
22. L. F. Crisp, "The Australian Full Employment Pledge," p. 18.

The first phase from the end of the war to the middle of 1952 was, not surprisingly, associated with a rapid growth in the recruitment of graduates, including those with economics-type degrees. But in this early phase, recruitment of economics graduates was not with a view to providing specialists. This is true even of appointments to newly created branches in the Treasury, the new department of Post War Reconstruction, and the Prime Minister's Department. Some of these graduate recruits occupied Research Officer positions requiring a university degree, which in over half the cases was specified as an economics degree.

The A.P.S. grew rapidly as the Labor government moved to implement a variety of interventionist economic policies. Between 1945–46 and 1951–52, of 1479 graduates appointed, 610 (41 percent) entered administrative positions, and it has been estimated that half of these (i.e. 20 percent of all graduate appointees) held economics degrees, while half of the remainder may have had arts degrees with a major in economics.[23] This compares with the mere trickle of 194 graduates in the dozen years up to 1945–46. Thus the growth in graduate recruitment reflected the growth in the A.P.S. as a whole, but the increased emphasis on graduates in economics was a direct result of the special factors which had placed men with a 'bias' towards economics in positions of power to influence the nature of recruitment. Perhaps it was inevitable that they should favour the recruitment of persons in their own image.[24]

Although economics graduates may have been sought for their 'generalist' qualities, information supplied by the Public Service Board points to the location of a significant proportion in the central policymaking departments of the public service. The Treasury's simple function as keeper of the books was superseded by the requirement that fiscal policy—and to a much lesser extent at this stage, monetary policy—as reflected through the annual budget should be used as instruments of economic policy to achieve at least full employment with stable price levels, equilibrium in the balance of payments, a satisfactory (greater) rate of economic growth, and "desirable" changes in the distribution of income.[25]

It was a logical development for the Treasury to become the government's chief source of advice on economic policy and for it to serve

23. See Public Service Board, *Annual Report* (Canberra, 1970).
24. See J. G. Crawford, "The Role of the Economist in the Public Service," pp. 1–16; and Encel, "The Commonwealth Public Service and Outside Recruitment," esp. pp. 40–43.
25. See E. Russell, *A Historical Survey of Fiscal Policy, 1945–1966* (Adelaide, 1967).

as the centre for coordination of government economic policies. These functions were reinforced by the strength of character, great competence and economic comprehension of J. B. Chifley, who was by then in the dual role of Treasurer and Prime Minister. The primacy of the Treasury's role had been established by 1949 even as plans were being made for the abolition of various temporary wartime departments, including Post War Reconstruction, which had loomed as one of the Treasury's few rivals. Thereafter the Treasury's expansion was steady rather than spectacular through the 1950s and 1960s, but with increasing professionalisation so that it is now the repository for some of the ablest graduates in economics in the country.[26]

In the 1950–52 period the Australian economy was confronted by a series of crises associated with inflation, balance-of-payments deficits, and the first substantial increase in unemployment since the war. Expenditure restraint was one of the key components of the fiscal policy which the Treasury devised to deal with the 1950–52 situation, and in July 1951 the Liberal Country Party government, which had presented itself as less interventionist than the Labor Party in the election campaign, ordered a cut of 10,000 in the staffs of Commonwealth departments and authorities, 8,500 of which were to be in the public service. The implementation of this decision ushered in the second phase of postwar development of the public service.

During the next decade the A.P.S. encountered difficulties because of the relative decline in its graduate intake. In 1951–52 the graduate intake into the administrative areas had declined to 113 from 160 in the previous year, partly reflecting the effects of the decision to reduce the size of the public service. But supply considerations also began to loom large. The surge in graduate appointments in the period 1948–49 to 1950–51 was derived from the large number of ex-service graduates who had been provided by the postwar Commonwealth Reconstruction Training Scheme. By 1951 this source of graduates was beginning to dwindle. Furthermore, the lower birth rate during the depression resulted in the Australian population being depleted at the age groups most likely to attend a university, so that despite an increase in university participation rates the output of graduates barely matched the demand in an Australian economy that was growing steadily but unspectacularly. Between 1952 and 1961 only 664 graduates were appointed to administrative occupations, amounting to 32 percent of total graduate appointments for the period (compared with 41 percent for the period 1945–51). The Public Service was clearly feeling the pres-

26. See L. F. Crisp, "The Commonwealth Treasury's Changed Role," pp. 315–30; and idem, *Ben Chifley* (London, 1960).

sure of competition from private employers for graduates in economics and related disciplines.[27] Despite a slight improvement in the recruitment of social science graduates in the mid-fifties the P.S.B. commented in its Annual Report that it had "recommended to the Government the establishment of a Committee to review the recruitment processes and standards of the Commonwealth Service."[28]

The government responded to the PSB's recommendations and to backbench and party pressures, by instituting an inquiry into public service recruitment under the chairmanship of R. J. F. Boyer. The Boyer Committee first met in October 1957 and presented its report to the Prime Minister in November 1958.[29] In its chapter on "Recruitment for Higher Administration" it declared, "if the Commonwealth Public Service is to give adequate help to present and future Governments in discharging their responsibilities for guiding the economy of Australia . . . no effort must be spared to ensure that the Service shall obtain its proper share of the highest ability in the country, and that the best use shall be made of the talents obtained."[30] The Boyer Report had a much greater effect on the P.S.B.'s policies and organisation than the consequent legislation revealed.[31] Coincidentally, in 1960 a new chairman had been appointed to the Public Service Board. He had been one of the first research officer economists in the late 1930s and had wide experience of policy matters in war and postwar periods, having been extremely close to the Treasurer and Prime Minister, J. B. Chifley. In the 1950s he had gained further experience at the International Labour Office, and now proceeded to zealously apply this experience to the A.P.S.'s recruitment problems.

Some of the amendments to the Public Service Act (1960) recommended by the Boyer Committee made it easier for the P.S.B. to recruit graduates. In the period 1960 to 1972 the composition of the A.P.S. was radically transformed. There was an even greater emphasis than before on the hiring of graduates with economics-type degrees. The subsequent deployment of these recruits determined whether they could be regarded as working as economists or generalist-administrators, but the distinction was not usually made in the recruitment and advertising literature. The purpose seemed to be to obtain as many graduates as possible, regardless of the functions they were to

27. Public Service Board, *Annual Report*, 1952, p. 12.
28. Public Service Board, *Annual Report*, 1956–57, p. 5
29. *Report of the Committee of Inquiry into Public Service Recruitment* (Canberra, 1958). For a summary of the Boyer recommendations see Caiden, *The Commonwealth Bureaucracy*, pp. 306–8.
30. Boyer Report, para. 108.
31. Caiden, *The Commonwealth Bureaucracy*, p. 195.

perform. At the same time public servants were encouraged to obtain degrees through a refurbished 'free place' scheme and the introduction of a fees-reimbursement scheme. Once again economics was the dominant choice as a major subject. Major new cadetship schemes begun in the early sixties provided full salaries and benefits while cadets studied for their degrees, most commonly in economics and statistics, although there were also cadetships offered in other subjects. Of the total number of university economics graduates, some 5 percent per annum entered the A.P.S. during the 1950s, rising to 8.6 percent in 1961, peaking at 16.5 percent in 1968, and stabilising at about 15.0 percent thereafter.

In 1961 a very important judgement by the Commonwealth Arbitration Court,[32] in the Professional Engineer's case, had finally convinced the P.S.B. that it was operating in a larger labour market consisting of both a private and a public sector. This was reflected consistently in the Board's more aggressive graduate recruitment policies throughout the sixties. The implementation of a Graduate Allowance Scheme in 1965 was a response to the competitive recruitment pressures emanating from the private sector of the economy. These allowances were paid to university graduates employed on clerical/administrative duties "in order to bring their total remuneration up to minimum prescribed levels related to the nature of the qualifications held."[33] But the A.P.S. was still experiencing difficulties in recruiting 'good' graduates, especially in economics, which led the P.S.B. in 1968 to investigate the possibility of offering a 'marked' differential in premium pay rates for 'good' graduates in economics. This scheme did not come to fruition, but it is one more indicator of the determination with which the recruitment of graduates, and especially graduates in economics, was pursued.

Inevitably, the transformation of the A.P.S. produced a reaction within the service itself. For one thing the departments needing specialist economists found themselves competing with departments which hired graduates as generalist-administrators. Considerable interdepartmental competition, and some friction, were generated between departments. From time to time departments seeking well-qualified graduates as economists-specialists had organised separate recruitment campaigns. In the later 1960s some of these departments were given special permission to mount expensive recruiting campaigns outside Australia, which were not very successful. In keeping with international trends there was a greater emphasis on econometric applications, including models of the Australian economy, and the overseas

---

32. See the text following Table 3 below.
33. Public Service Board, *Annual Report, 1967–68* (Canberra, 1968), p. 21.

advertisements especially sought competent econometricians. But in the relatively tight labour market of the time, very few overseas graduates were recruited.

By 1970 the number of graduates in the A.P.S. had apparently expanded much more rapidly than the availability of jobs requiring graduate qualification. In many departments graduates with job or career expectations became dissatisfied at the menial and undemanding duties assigned to them.[34] The P.S.B. began to adopt a more questioning attitude to graduate recruitment, drawing to a close in 1972 as the P.S.B. moved to wind down or eliminate a number of recruitment and incentive schemes instituted in the 1960s, and as the Australian Labor Party came to power in December 1972.

The Labor Party was elected on a wide-ranging platform of change and reform and in the first few months acted with a sense of urgency and haste which placed enormous pressure on the A.P.S. The normal recruitment procedures were stepped up, but like the British situation in 1964, "A large number of academic and other 'outside' economists became interested in using their skills for the solution of practical problems and were commissioned by the Labor government to reexamine the various economic and social issues confronting the country."[35] Inevitably there were some problems of communication and conflicts of policies as the 'outsiders' endeavoured to establish their authority. Cabinet ministers began to express considerable dissatisfaction with policy advice through the established channels, especially as economic conditions began to deteriorate after July 1974.[36] Soon after, the Labor government decided to initiate the first full-scale review of the Australian Public Service in over fifty years.[37] This Royal Commission, headed by Dr. H. C. Coombs comprehensively examined many areas of the A.P.S. and recommended a long list of changes, many of them intended to improve the processes of economic policymaking. But by the time of the Royal Commission's final report the Labor government had been swept from power.[38]

The newly elected Liberal-Country Party government had promised to reduce the role of government in the economy and had made no

34. See Lyall, "Graduate Preference."

35. F. H. Gruen, "Australian Economics 1967–1977," *Joseph Fisher Lecture in Commerce* (Oct. 1978).

36. G. Hawker, R. F. I. Smith, and P. Weller, *Politics and Policy in Australia* (St. Lucia: University of Queensland Press, 1979), esp. ch. 9.

37. *Royal Commission on Australian Government Administration, Report and Appendix*, vols. 1–4 (Canberra, 1976). Here cited below as either Coombs Commission or R.C.A.G.A.

38. See Hazlehurst and Nethercote, *Reforming Australian Government*, and Smith and Weller, *Public Service Inquiries*.

commitment to implement the Coombs Commission recommendations.[39] The current situation in the A.P.S. is one of zero growth, apparently across all categories of employment. The present government is relying to a much greater extent on the traditional sources of public service expertise and advice. In these circumstances, bureaucratic politics and the relative distribution of 'power' will determine which departments and which categories of employment will be affected most by the no-growth policies of the government.

II. *The Supply of Economists*

The definition of an economist in the Australian Public Service

There is no separate designation of 'economist' in the A.P.S., although from time to time a few 'economist' positions have existed, which have not necessarily been filled by people with training in economics. Thus, it is not possible to define an economist purely in terms of the position occupied, as may be the case in some other countries. The Research Officer category which was created in 1938 has usually been filled by graduates, although an economics degree has not always been a prerequisite.

An economist in the A.P.S. can therefore be defined only in terms of an amalgam of functions and characteristics. Someone has to choose 'appropriate' subjective weights for these factors—the qualifications held, the techniques and the type of analysis used, the nature of the material analysed, the subject matter, and less clearly, the uses which may be made of such analyses. It would seem a simple matter to define as economists those individuals having an economics degree working in the major economic-policy making departments of the A.P.S. In fact it is difficult to determine whether the techniques and the type of analysis used are those of the economist, and further, whether they are in some sense the predominant methods of work.[40] Thus, a large proportion of

39. See Gruen, "What Went Wrong?" pp. 15–32; G. Hawker, "The Use of Social Scientists"; and R. Forward, "Ministerial Staff under Whitlam and Fraser," *Public Adminstration* (Sydney) 36 (June 1977): 159–67.

40. In April–June 1978, 75 senior public servants in the three major economic policy departments of the A.P.S. were interviewed. The interviewees were all in the Second Division, branch heads or division heads, who would have been directing, supervising, or actively participating in economic analysis. Three of the 75 questions which they were asked concerned their perceptions of an economist in the A.P.S. Seventy percent thought a pass or honours degree in economics was the minimum qualification for a 'professional economist' and 13 percent thought a degree in any discipline, not necessarily economics was required. In another question, 21 percent indicated that to qualify as a 'professional economist' an individual would have to spend 100 percent of his time on economic analysis, 15 percent thought 80 percent of his time on economic analysis, 29 percent thought 60 percent of his time on economic analysis, and 27 percent thought

those employed in the Treasury, Finance, Prime Minister and Cabinet, and Business and Consumer Affairs departments, and in the Bureaux of Agricultural Economics, Industry Economics, Transport Economics, and the Reserve Bank of Australia are probably engaged in work which qualifies them to be classified as economists. But there is also a significant proportion who, because of the great emphasis on economics degrees as a generalist qualification, are engaged in non-economic work that may be routine administrative or purely clerical in nature. In addition, there are a small but significant number of individuals holding the B.A. degree, usually with a major in economics, who are performing work which would qualify them to be regarded as economists. Non-graduates performing economic work are now a negligible category.[41] It follows that in the A.P.S. the application of a rigorous definition of an economist would be inappropriate, and would leave very few individuals in such a classification.

The nature of academic qualifications in economics

The evaluation of academic qualifications in Australia is relatively uncomplicated because until recently the number of degree granting institutions was small and standards were relatively homogeneous.[42] In 1950 there were just six fully accredited universities, by 1960 there were nine, and in 1978 there were eighteen. There are three main degrees awarded by Australian universities, all of which were once regarded as preparation for practicing as an economist. These are the Bachelor of Economics, Bachelor of Commerce, and Bachelor of Arts degrees, each of which may be awarded as a three-year pass degree or, with a fourth year of study, as an honours degree. The Bachelor of Economics degree now seems to be the minimum qualification that an economist would be expected to possess in the A.P.S. The typical economics degree has been modelled on comparable degrees in British universities.

The fourth honours year is an extremely intensive, highly de-

---

40 percent of time on economic analysis. Of the 75 interviewees, just one third classified themselves as 'professional economists' working in the public sector. Of course, the interviewees often responded to the above three questions, and to others in the questionnaire, with qualification to their answers. Space does not permit a more detailed examination of responses here. See also n.60 below.

41. It is notable that time and again interviewees in the A.P.S. survey stressed that even in cases where individuals were not working as economists they believed that the quality of their work was improved by their economics training. This is also a recurrent view in some earlier published work. See for example, Sir John Crawford, "The Role of the Economist in the Public Service," and the references quoted therein.

42. See Auchmuty, Harman, and Selby-Smith, "The Universities of Australia," and L. H. Short "Universities and Colleges of Advanced Education: Defining the Difference," *The Australian University* 11 (May 1977): 3–25.

manding course in which students are expected to work at the frontiers of knowledge in at least some areas of economics. The honours degree is a very sound and quite specialised preparation for potential public service economists.

The Bachelor of Commerce and Bachelor of Arts degrees differ from the economics degree in the extent of their emphasis on other specialisations, rather than economics. Because of this element of choice, Arts and Commerce degrees from Australian universities cannot be regarded as a sufficient preparation for economists in the A.P.S., with two exceptions. At one Australian university the B.Com. degree has a structure comparable to the B.Ec. degree and at another university all students majoring in economics were until recently granted a B.A. degree. Thus, about a third of Commerce graduates, and a half of Arts graduates with majors in economics can be regarded as part of the potential pool of economists.

In the decade after 1967 Australian universities were able to shake off the problems of rapid postwar change and rapid growth in student numbers. The quality of the staff, as measured by the proportion holding higher degrees, rose very substantially, and inroads were made into the high student/staff ratios. The output of writing and research is now very much greater than a decade ago, and as Gruen has observed, Australian academic economists are now frequent contributors to the international literature.[43] At the same time, there has been some change in emphasis in the teaching of economics. There are two strands to this change, both parallelling international experience. One has been an even greater tendency to emphasise specialisation in economics, and to require a high degree of technical competence. This trend has been accompanied by a marked increase in the number of courses offered in economic statistics and in econometrics. However, there are signs that this phase is now ending, partly affected by the growth of a political economy movement on the Joan Robinson model. The second trend has been for the teaching of economics to be less 'old fashioned' Keynesian in its bias, and more pro-Friedmanite and/or libertarian in its approach, a trend undoubtedly reinforced both by economic events and by the new generation of younger academics, many of whom have been trained in the United States.

The number of economists

Statistics of employment and qualifications in the A.P.S. must be examined with a great deal of caution. The major problem is the changes in coverage of those classified in various categories of govern-

43. F. H. Gruen, "Australian Economics 1967–1977," p. 3.

ment employment. In the following brief statistical examination data will be presented excluding the now dismantled Postmaster-General's department.

Table 1 indicates that approximately one quarter of all graduates in the A.P.S. have degrees in economics, while the growth rate in the employment of graduates in economics and in all graduates was approximately the same, at 12 percent, in the period 1968–1976. However, the growth rate for graduates in economics was faster than that for the Third Division (the major entry point for graduates) during the same period, and it was even faster in the period 1960–1967, when a number of major recruitment campaigns were mounted by the P.S.B. That the A.P.S. is a major employer of graduates in economics can be crudely gauged from the fact that between 1950 and 1977 economics graduates have accounted for between 10 and 15 percent (12 percent in 1977) of all graduates from universities, and yet the proportion of graduates in economics in the A.P.S. is considerably higher at 25 percent. A significant phenomenon has been the extent to which economics degrees have been obtained after appointment to the A.P.S. In 1977, for example, 47.6 percent of graduates in economics had qualified after appointment to the A.P.S., reflecting the Public Service Board's (and perhaps the government's) provision of various incentives to study economics. Appointments after graduation in the period 1967–1977 have never fallen below 10.9 percent of all graduates appointed, and in the boom years of 1973 and 1974, when the Labor government was attempting a large number of new initiatives, graduates in economics accounted for 20.1 and 17.1 percent of all graduates appointed, respectively. In 1976 and 1977, affected by the new governments' policies, graduates in economics have still accounted for approximately 11 percent of a reduced graduate intake. Furthermore, the data in Table 2 indicate the much

Table 1.   Graduates in the A. P. S., 1968–1976

Year	1968	1972	1976
Economics graduates[a] number:	1860	2497	3647
Total graduates:	7280	10375	14150
Economic graduates as percent of total grads.:	25.6	24.1	25.8
Economics graduates as percent of Third Division Staff:	4.88	5.08	6.11

[a] Includes degrees in Economics, Commerce, Arts (Economics) and Science (Economics).

Source: Data provided by Public Service Board, Canberra, and *Statistical Yearbook*, Public Service Board, Canberra, 1977, pp. 106–7.

lower rate of separations for graduates in economics,[44] while those in Table 3 indicate that graduates in economics accounted for over 32 percent of promotions of graduates in 1967, 1972, and 1977.

These data need to be treated with caution, but they imply that in the period considered economics graduates were more likely to be promoted than other graduates. Overall the data are consistent with the historical review which has indicated the great significance of economics graduates in the A.P.S. However, as will be seen, only an estimated 15 percent of economics graduates in the A.P.S. are likely to be working in positions requiring the application of the expertise of a professional economist.

The market for economists

There are several reasons why it is not a straightforward matter to examine the 'market for economists.' First, their output is obviously not homogeneous as between those employed in government and those employed in the private sector. Further, the nature of their output clearly changes with on-the-job training and with promotion. On the salary side, direct dollar comparisons are invalid unless they have been adjusted for the various fringe benefits available in both sectors. Finally, since there is no separate category of economist in the A.P.S., and since positions in the private sector are not always or even usually advertised as requiring economists, it is simply not possible without the undertaking of a separate major research project to delineate a market for economists. Of course, it should be possible to make some deductions from observations about equilibrium imbalances of supply

Table 2. Separation rates (%) for permanent Second and Third Division staff: qualification level for 1967, 1972, 1977

Year	1967	1972	1977
Qualification level:			
Graduate, Economics	1.6	4.9	6.6
Graduate, other	4.1	7.5	9.6
Diplomates	1.4	8.9	21.2
Other 2d and 3d Div. staff	10.7	7.6	9.8
All 2d and 3d Div. staff	8.0	7.1	9.2

Source: Public Service Board, Canberra.

44. This does not appear to be due to inferior opportunities elsewhere, as unemployment rates for graduates in economics and commerce are lower than those of graduates in most other areas except medicine, dentistry and law. See for example, *First Destinations of 1977 University and College Graduates* (Graduate Careers Council of Australia, 1978).

Table 3.   Promotions to Second and Third Division positions: type and level
of qualification, 1967, 1972, 1977

Year	1967	1972	1977
Graduates, Economics	412	618	894
Graduates, other	781	1320	1887
Other	5783	6621	8443
Total	7621	9349	12082

Source: Public Service Board, Canberra.

and demand, and there is also some information available from surveys
of relative pay rates carried out from time to time by the Public Service
Board.

The Engineer's judgement of June 1961 was a watershed in pay fix-
ation for the A.P.S. because the arbitral authorities determined new
salaries for engineers within a community (or market) framework, and
not as part of any notional A.P.S. structure. The Public Service Board
determined to press for the implementation of the principles of the Engineer's judgement to all positions in the A.P.S. At the same time the
Board increased its own collection of data on relative public and private rates of pay. But in 1966, when the Professional Officers Association followed the example of the engineers and initiated a work value
case for a proposed new category of economist, the Public Service
Board opposed the application principally on the grounds that the
economist's functions could not be separated from the clerical and
administrative functions performed by graduates. Ultimately none of
the unions involved in the economists' case pressed the matter
strongly, and the case was allowed to lapse.

What evidence is there on relative rates of pay in the public and private sectors for the categories of interest? At the graduate recruitment
level the Public Service Board frequently reported difficulty in obtaining a sufficient number of graduates qualified in economics in the
period 1960–1972.[45] Presumably shortages at the port of entry would be
reflected, with a lag, in shortages at other levels in the internal labour
market. The implication is that salary rates lagged behind those in the
private sector. The implementation of special recruitment drives for
economics and commerce graduates in the sixties, the competition between the Treasury and other departments for honours graduates in
economics, and the special permission granted for some departments
to advertise internationally for specialists in economics and econometrics, all point to a lagging public salary structure. A late 1974 sur-

45. See the *Annual Reports* of the Public Service Board.

vey of generalist (non-professional) graduate recruit commencing rates indicated that for a three-year degree these rates were up to 10 percent higher in the private sector, with the differentials tapering off to a low of 3 percent for four-year degrees and for honours degrees. Also, on the basis of a private survey and information supplied by the P.S.B., crude comparisons of changes in gross salary rates between March 1975 and March 1978 show that the A.P.S. rates are lagging, by up to 5 percent, behind increases in average weekly earnings in the economy as a whole for positions at around the graduate recruitment level, and by up to 14 percent for positions at the senior management level. None of this is surprising, given the system of plateau wage indexation since 1975, the greater competitive flexibility of the private sector, and the avowed policy objective of the government since December 1975 to reduce the size of the public sector. It can however be safely predicted that if this trend continues, and if the Australian economy emerges from the present long drawnout recession, the A.P.S. will be hard pressed to service the increasing level of activity, and well qualified economists will be one of its scarce resources.

III. *Professionalisation*

It has been noted above that the economics profession was well established in the universities by 1945, and that many academic economists were also 'professional' advisers, commissioners, board members, etc., in a variety of government activities impinging on economic issues. But the smallness of the numbers of economists involved undoubtedly hindered the process of professionalisation. Through the initiative and foresight of D. B. Copland, however, the Economic Society of Australia and New Zealand had been founded in 1925, and the society's journal, *The Economic Record*, began biannual publication in November 1925, with the number of issues per annum being increased in the fifties and again in the sixties.[46] The impetus to further professionalisation after 1950 came from three main sources. Between 1950 and 1965 it came from the rapid growth of numbers studying and teaching economics at universities, and the concomitant increase in employment opportunities for graduates in economics. After 1965 it came also from a rapid rise in the proportion of academic economists who had higher degrees and who regularly contributed to the economics literature. The annual meetings of the Economics Section of the Australian and New Zealand Association for the Advancement of Science (ANZAAS) provide the main forum for personal contact between professional economists and for a mutual exchange of ideas.

46. See "Essays in Honour of Sir Douglas Copland," *Economic Record* 36 (March 1960), esp. pp. 143–46.

With increasing numbers of professional economists, the professionalisation process inevitably produced some complementary and some competitive developments. Membership of economic societies grew in each of the six states and the Australian Capital Territory, and proceedings of annual and biannual or special conferences are now regularly published. In 1962 a second journal, *Australian Economic Papers*, began biannual publication. In the 1950s professional economists were engaged in full-time research only at the Australian National University in the Research Schools of Social Science and Pacific Studies. A second full-fledged research institution in the form of the Institute of Applied Economic and Social Research at Melbourne University was established in the early sixties. In 1968 it commenced publication of the quarterly *Australian Economic Review* which concentrated almost entirely on aspects of the Australian economy and carried regular reviews and forecasts of the economy. The *Australian Economic Review* has a much broader readership than the other journals, being widely read in the business community and frequently quoted by the financial press in Australia. By 1970 professional economists had decided that they needed another specialised forum since the Economics and Statistics section of ANZAAS was attacting a very wide range of papers on diverse subject matter sometimes only peripheral to economics. Thus the Conference of Economists was established on an approximately annual basis (there have been seven conferences between 1970 and 1978). This conference very quickly grew in size, and it has been characterised by more complex and specialised contributions to economic theory and applied econometrics. Specialisation has therefore been the third major force in the professionalisation of economics, and the force which will be most significant in the next decade. The process of professionalisation has been hindered, however, by the lack of recognition of economics as a profession in the A.P.S., even though, as we have pointed out, economics graduates, in terms of recruitment, promotion, and influence, have played a significant role in this organisation.

Economists in Australia have usually been awarded a status somewhere between the professional in medicine, law, science, and engineering[47] and the generalist graduate in, for instance, history, politics, and classics. It is probable that the status of economists in the

47. This group has occupied an exalted position in Australian society, being perceived as practical men of action rather than as intellectuals who argue about philosophical fine points. There is a thread of anti-intellectualism running through Australian society which has rarely been directed against these professionals. Usually this group has received remuneration and recognition in public and private employment exceeding that of other university graduates. See C. J. Hayes, "The Commonwealth Public Service," *Public Administration* (Sydney) 11 (March 1956): 15. See also B. B. Schaffer, "Australia," in Ridley, *Specialists and Generalists*.

A.P.S. has never been higher in the public mind than it was during the Second World War. At the time they were seen to be providing data, analysing problems, and suggesting solutions which were tied up with the very survival of the Australian economy and society in its existing form. But in the postwar period, although many of these economists moved to positions of power, and although the number of graduates in economics recruited to the A.P.S. rose steeply, the trend to greater professional recognition of economists was halted. The abortive attempt by the unions in the mid-1960s to establish a separate professional category of economist in the A.P.S. undoubtedly marked the end of this trend.

As the A.P.S. had recruited such a large proportion of its graduates from those with majors in economics, the all-embracing nature of the relevant union's claim for an economist category, with separate and higher salaries, would have created a very difficult and complex situation. But in addition to the P.S.B's reluctance to recognise the economist as a separate profession, it seems likely that the Liberal-Country Party government would also have opposed such recognition. The leader of the government in the mid-1960s, R. G. Menzies, had expressed views, as long ago as 1942, which indicated that he did not categorise the economist as a professional.[48] The government and the public view probably did not differ greatly from this even in the sixties. When the Committee of Economic Enquiry (the Vernon Report) commissioned after the major recession of 1960–1962 presented its report in 1965, the government had no difficulty in rejecting all of its recommendations and in identifying the report as the work of economists hellbent on planning.[49] In the decade since this view was expressed, attitudes have changed but slowly, and despite the increasing technical competence of economists, they are still not regarded in the same light as professionals in science, engineering, and the like.

While the external view has failed to ratify the increasing professionalisation of economists, internally the situation is different. In the key macroeconomic policy advising departments of the Treasury, Finance (which was hived off from the Treasury in 1977), and Prime Minister and Cabinet there are cells of professional economists.[50] Those cells located in the Treasury are the largest, and in

48. R. G. Menzies, "The Australian Economy During War," *Joseph Fisher Lecture in Commerce*, 1942.

49. See P. Samuel, "Policies for Economic Growth: The Vernon Report," *Australian Quarterly* 37 (Dec. 1965): 11–25, and also *Economic Record* 42 (March 1966): 1–180. The Report recommended the establishment of a high-level advisory body of professional economists somewhat akin to the U.S. Council of Economic Advisers.

50. Other important groups of professional economists have been located in the Bureau of Agricultural Economics, the Industries Assistance Commission, the Trade Prac-

terms of academic qualifications, undoubtedly the most technically competent of the three departments. The Treasury has more honours graduates in economics than any other department and has usually succeeded in employing, at least temporarily, the major share of graduating first-class honours people available for employment in the A.P.S. each year.[51] There is another highly professional group of economists at the Reserve Bank, which is the other major employer of graduates in economics. It does not come under the Public Service Act, and it operates a policy of more rapid promotion for graduates with first-class and upper second-class honours degrees, than other graduates in economics recruited by the Bank.[52]

In the absence of formal professional recognition the professionalisation of these groups has mainly been reflected in their participation in the professional activities described earlier in this section. Economists from these groups have been very active in the various conferences and have contributed regularly to the Australian journal literature in economics, especially in the 1970s. The Reserve Bank has organised seminars since the sixties at which academic staff from universities have presented papers and been able to exchange ideas with Reserve Bank staff. The scope of these seminars has been widened to conference status and the proceedings published by the Bank.[53] One of the major forces tending to unify the academic and government economists has been the upsurge in model building of the Australian economy, by the Treasury, the Reserve Bank, and the Industries Assistance Commission. In Australia, government departments are better equipped than economists elsewhere to develop the teams required for such projects, and they have readier access to data. This has been a desirable development, helping to reinforce a sense of professional identity amongst a select group of economists.

The relatively small number of professional economists in the A.P.S. only partially explains the congenial relations between them

---

tices Commission, and the Bureaux of Transport Economics and Industry Economics. The sense of professional identity of these groups has grown along with an increasing demand for more sophisticated policy advice.

51. In 1977, according to figures supplied by the Treasury, 76 percent of staff had economics qualifications, and 9 percent other qualifications; 52 percent of those with economic qualifications had honours degrees, 12 percent had masters degrees, 2 percent had Ph.D.s, and the remaining 34 percent had pass degrees.

52. According to figures provided by the Reserve Bank, 11 percent of all staff held economics-type degrees, just under 1 percent had other degrees, and 50 percent of those with economics qualifications had honours or higher degrees.

53. See *Conference in Applied Economic Research* (Reserve Bank of Australia, Dec. 1977). The only other government publication in the economics field is the *Quarterly Review of Agricultural Economics*, published by the Bureau of Agricultural Economics.

and other specialists in the A.P.S. Probably more significant is the domination of particular departments by economists and the very low interaction between economists and other specialists that occurs. Another reason why relations between economists (and other specialists) and generalists have been relatively congenial is the apparent access of all these categories to top positions in the A.P.S.[54] One of the interesting phenomena here is the large number of professionals in law, science, medicine, etc., who have seen fit to take second degrees in economics. This factor highlights the great extent to which economics training has been regarded as both a generalist and a specialist qualification. Its effect may be observed in the Second Division of the A.P.S., where the proportion of staff with qualifications in economics is significantly greater than the proportion with such qualifications in the Third Division.

IV. *Functions of Economists in Government and Their Role in Policymaking*

The multitude of tasks which may sometimes be performed by British economists have been described elsewhere by A. W. Coats.[55] A similar list could be prepared for economists in Australian government. In relation to their training in economics, the tasks performed by economists may occasionally require a high degree of economic competence, economic research, and advice, but in the Australian context as elsewhere these tasks nearly always shade by imperceptible degrees into tasks which are indistinguishable from other research type tasks performed by non-economist graduates or occasionally by non-graduates. As the economist progresses up the hierarchy it is likely that at the middle levels a greater proportion of tasks performed will be of a more analytical and economic nature, but at or near the top of the hierarchy they are more likely to be purely administrative, and less often, a mixture of both.

Is it possible, then to classify meaningfully those groups of economists in the A.P.S. who were categorised as professionals in Section III above? Broadly speaking they can be subdivided into two categories according to the dominant form of activity. In the first category are those economists whose essentially administrative tasks require them to utilise advanced economic knowledge in order to (a) organize and supervise research work by subordinates, (b) provide specific advice on economic problems, and (c) represent their department in interde-

54. Crisp, "Specialists and Generalists."
55. A. W. Coats, "Economists in Government: A Research Field for the Historian of Economics," *History of Political Economy* 10 (1978): 312–13.

partmental discussions and discussions with outside agencies, private groups, and bodies at the state, national and, occasionally, international level. In the second category can be placed those economists who are engaged almost solely in economic research and/or policy advice which requires a high level of technical economic expertise in either (a) a very narrow speciality, most often associated with microeconomic analysis and techniques, or (b) technical economic knowledge on a broad front with associated research and policy advice, most often associated with macroeconomic analysis and techniques. Those in the second category probably approach most closely to the academic economist in terms of qualifications, breadth of knowledge of economic principles and techniques, and 'impartiality' of advice. They are concerned primarily with analysing economic trends and the like, and advising on the economic consequences of policy largely in isolation from the administrative and political environment. But even in these instances their purity is 'sullied' by some minimal amount of administrative and policy-implementing activity. The basic conclusion is that only a few (between one hundred and two hundred) economists in the A.P.S. perform tasks which conform to the 'pure' model of what an economist does. The remainder perform a wide range of heterogeneous tasks requiring varying degrees of economic expertise.

The nature of the bureaucracy and the influence of economists on policymaking

A catalogue of the tasks performed by economists, however, does not inform us about their relative impact on policy. The categorisation of economists according to the extent that their tasks were administrative rather than policy-advising has merely served to underline the difficulty of examining such a complex process. One writer has suggested eight different meanings of the word 'policy,' and these meanings could be multiplied, with elements of each meaning appropriate in different circumstances.[56] The dividing line with administration is thin, tenuous, and perhaps meaningless.

There is no doubt that the single most important factor influencing the impact of economists on policy in Australia is the bureaucratic and political context. In fact the conservative 'incremental' model probably fits the Australian case best. Thus, there is a very great stress on hierarchy in the A.P.S., leading to a preoccupation with questions of

56. Parker, "Policy and Administration," pp. 113–14, and G. D. Greenberg et al., "Developing Public Policy Theory: Perspectives from Empirical Research," *American Political Science Review* 71 (Dec. 1977): 1541.

rank and status. In such a hierarchy advice is passed up the line to the minister, and there tends to be "over emphasis on the official and impersonal role of the individual public servant" resulting "in an unduly rigid conception of who was allowed to do what and with whom."[57]

There is obviously a subtle, delicate, and complicated interrelationship between senior public servants and ministers. There is no doubt that, to varying degrees, officials may exercise considerable influence on the minister's policies. In Australia some permanent heads have placed on record their attitudes to policy advising, and in each case they have stressed their belief that they have an influence on policy.[58] The retired permanent heads (all involved with economic policy) who were interviewed for this project were in general agreement with this view. One former permanent head said that "the economist/adviser should have a view on policy based on what he thinks the future of the economy should be." Another permanent head said that the role of the public servant was "persuasive only. He either persuades or fails to persuade the minister." A common view amongst all those interviewed was that the economic adviser must tell the minister when he is heading for trouble. The extent to which senior public servants have an impact on the minister's policies, however, also depends upon the minister's knowledge and expertise, his personality and relationship with the permanent head, his standing with the cabinet and the electorate, and the political and economic circumstances in which policy is being made. No doubt the strength of character of particular senior public servants is also of importance.

Does it make a difference if the permanent heads (and for that matter, the deputy secretaries) of departments have been trained in economics in a disproportionate number of cases? In 1978, out of 54 permanent heads (or persons of equivalent status in the First Division) 22 (40 percent) had Bachelor of Economics or Commerce or higher degrees. A further 16 had Bachelor of Arts degrees, more than half of which were with majors in economics. The remaining 16 had law, engineering, science, and medical degrees. Amongst deputy secretaries, 16 out of 34 had Economics or Commerce degrees, a further 8 had Arts degrees, and the remainder, other degrees or no degrees. The interval between acquiring their qualifications and the time at which they filled their current positions would certainly cast doubt on the direct applica-

---

57. Emy, *The Politics of Australian Democracy*, p. 541.
58. J. G. Crawford, "The Role of the Permanent Head," *Public Administration* (Sydney) 13 (Sept. 1954): 153–65; and idem, "Relations Between Civil Servants and . . . Policymaking"; Dunk, "The Role of the Public Servant," p. 113; and Wiltshire, *Australian Public Administration*, ch. 2.

bility of their qualifications, although those in major economic-policy departments could certainly keep in touch with the main developments in economics through the well-established public service procedure of circulation of selected material.[59] What is significant, however, is that the mode of thought, the technique of analysis of the economist, and the manner of presenting information would be familiar to these senior public servants. It is the method of approach which they would often prefer, and which they would therefore expect other public servants to also use. Thus it provides a channel through which other public servants trained in economics are also able to exert a significant qualitative influence on policy.

In order to throw further light on this and other aspects of policymaking in the A.P.S. it was decided to interview selected Second Division officers. A questionnaire was devised and administered by this writer and an experienced research assistant.[60] Only the section of the questionnaire concerned with aspects of policy is reported here.

Interviewees were asked in separate questions to indicate how often they saw the permanent head and the ministers on policy matters. Contact with the permanent head was fairly frequent, but with the minister it was much less frequent. It could be said that for most of those interviewed ministerial contact on policy matters was rare. This seems consistent with the hierarchical view of the operation of departments mentioned earlier. It means that the impact of these public servants, 68 percent of whom had degrees in economics or commerce, would be limited to the indirect contribution they made to minutes briefing, minutes passing through the permanent head/deputy secretary channel.

When the interviewees were asked, How much input do you make to the policy recommendations of your superior officer? over 80 percent indicated "large" input or "considerable" input. This represented their individual judgement of the extent to which the policy recommendations they produced were incorporated into the permanent head's recommendations. Even discounting for normal human reaction to such a question, it implies a considerable impact on policy. In one de-

59. It should also be noted that many officers of these departments participate in the various conferences where the most recent developments in economics are being presented and discussed. See Section III above.

60. Initially 100 Second Division officers were selected, not randomly, from the three major macroeconomic policy departments, including about 20 selected from a fourth department concerned mainly with microeconomic policy. The selection was based on information kindly supplied by the Public Service Board on qualifications of officers, and on a judgement that the public servants selected were likely to be involved in the policy process. Ninety-nine agreed to be interviewed, but for organisational, leave, and other reasons, only 75 useable interviews were made. The average duration of interviews was 75 minutes, and although a questionnaire was used, interviewees were encouraged to qualify their answers or add to them in any way they thought fit.

partment a few officers at first-assistant-secretary level had direct access to the Prime Minister and in addition to briefing him on submissions from their own department were apparently also briefing him on submissions from other departments.

Another question was aimed at finding out whether in writing their recommendations, public servants usually presented a range of options. Just over 40 percent of interviewees said they presented options in policy submissions to the permanent head in over half the cases, but the remainder indicated that their input to the permanent head was less often presented in the form of options. A range of options was even less common in material passing from the permanent head to the minister, in the opinion of those interviewees (a much smaller proportion) who chose to answer this question. This is an area in which there is obvious scope for personal preferences and prejudices to intrude. It should be noted that this was one question to which interviewees made numerous qualifications. Some made the point that ministers differed greatly in their attitudes and abilities, some being passive and preferring definitive guidance rather than options.[61]

Finally, on the question of the extent to which the interviewees confined their recommendations to what was understood to be government policy, a wide range of qualitative answers were obtained. But the general tenor of the responses seemed to differ as between those in the major macroeconomic policy departments, and those in the other department. In the former case they generally seemed to confine themselves to government policy as they understood it, while in the microeconomic policy department the economists unambiguously regarded themselves as in the business of generating new options, even if they were outside existing government policy. Most of the economists interviewed from this department would have fallen into the 'pure' economist category suggested above.[62] On the other hand, this group were less certain that they had a significant impact on policy. The explanation for these differences may be that in the macroeconomic policy departments the economists were engaged mainly in short-run policy making, while in the other department they were engaged in policy work of a more long-term nature.

In general a case has been established for the proposition that economists in the Australian government may have a significant impact on policy. Beyond that it is not possible to go at present because the last two links in the chain, involving politicians as ministers and the role of the Cabinet, have not been thoroughly investigated. Nor has the role of pressure groups outside the government been examined. These consid-

61. See R. F. I. Smith, "Ministerial Advisers: The Experience of the Whitlam Government," *Australian Journal of Public Administration* 36 (June 1977): 133–158.
62. See Section IV above.

erations have not prevented other observers from reaching firm conclusions on the impact of economists on policymaking. Most observers have written about the impact of the Treasury on economic policy rather than the impact of economists. The Coombs Commission noted that "the Treasury has command of the information on which financial and economic policy is based, that it is equipped to interpret the relevance and significance of that information, and that it approaches its task of informing and advising the Treasurer with a coherent and some would say almost doctrinal force and persuasiveness."[63] The Commission accepted the repeated charges from other public service departments, former Treasurers and other politicians, from academic economists and other academics, and from other private individuals, that the role of the Treasury in policy advice was too dominant. According to the Commission, criticisms made in submissions "express the belief that Treasury is too privileged, too powerful, and too prone to substitute its own judgements, its own values and its own priorities for those of other departments, ministers and the government itself."[64] To the large extent that Treasury is staffed by economists, it is economists who play the major role in creating this impression.[65] The Treasury has a highly trained group of economists who have helped to develop a sophisticated economic philosophy which may be reflected in policy submissions and in policies adopted.[66] The mark of the economist is clearly visible on the free market philosophy which underlies much of Treasury thinking.

It is precisely in the area of economic policy that politicians have been least satisfied with the bureaucracy. This dissatisfaction emerged most strongly in the 1970s, and found its most vehement expression in Labor government circles, although the Liberal-Country Party government also had its share of troubles.[67] In the difficult economic circumstances of the seventies, the professional consensus of the previous two decades on economic policy virtually evaporated, but most observers believe that the Treasury department provided one of the few constant views on economic policy. There is no doubt that the Treasury preference was both for a continuity in economic policy and

63. *R.C.A.G.A. Report*, para. 11.3.5, p. 366. The Labor Government, it seems, eventually accepted the view being pushed most forcefully by the Treasury. The 1975 Labor Budget was described as "moderate and responsible" and was widely believed to have been a Treasury document—which the previous Labor budgets certainly were not.

64. Ibid., para. 11.3.13, p. 319.

65. See Weller and Cutt, *Treasury Control in Australia*, esp. ch. 3.

66. See John Edwards, "The Economy Game."

67. *R.C.A.G.A. Report*, para. 11.3.13, pp. 369–70. Also para. 10.1.1, p. 299. See also Weller and Cutt, pp. 22–27.

the closest possible adherence to its recommendations. Well-established and 'well-tried' policies as recommended by the Treasury have always appeared cautious and conservative and certainly not innovative. Treasury policy appears to have largely prevailed with the present government, with only minor modifications, concerning the degree of protection and the freedom of the exchange rate to fluctuate.

Policy advisers in Australia have never been constrained by a set of economic targets clearly articulated by politicians and the public. Until the mid-seventies there has been little or no informed public discussion on targets and instruments of economic policy. The policy advisers have simply had vague general targets to aim for embracing moderate growth in all real incomes, and 'low' rates of inflation and unemployment. As a result of the economic events of the seventies there is probably a better public understanding of economic issues now than ever before. This has made the task of explaining and selling Treasury policies to the public relatively easier.[68] The primacy of Treasury in the economic-policy arena has been restored, although governments in the seventies have nurtured alternative sources of advice—in the case of Labor by bringing in outside advisers and strengthening the economic secretariat of the Prime Minister's department and several other departments, and in the case of the Liberal-Country Party government by concentrating on strengthening the Prime Minister's department and by splitting the Treasury into the departments of Treasury and Finance.[69]

The Australian press, and the public whose views it helps to formulate, seem in no doubt about the large influence of economists on economic policy, especially those in the Treasury.[70] However, in the final analysis, regardless of the inputs made by economists, strong politicians and political views have prevailed. Thus the Treasury's opposition to the Whitlam government's 25 percent unilateral tariff cut is well known; its opposition to the Fraser government's implementation of tax indexation and the major devaluation of the Australian dollar in November 1976 are similarly well known.[71] And dissatisfied governments have available to them sanctions such as shifting permanent heads, reorganising or, as in the case of the Treasury, splitting departments and depriving them of some of their functions.[72]

68. See W. Kasper, *Formation and Co-ordination of Economic Policy* (Canberra, 1975), and *The Processes of Economic Policy Making In Australia*, pp. 22–27.

69. See Weller, "Splitting the Treasury," pp. 29–30.

70. See Paul Kelly, "Our Leading Public Servant," *National Times*, 28 Oct. 1978, pp. 8–11.

71. See F. Gruen, "What Went Wrong?" and idem, "The Twenty Five Per Cent Tariff Cut."

72. P. Weller, "Splitting the Treasury," p. 29.

When asked for their impression of the impact of the high proportion of economics graduates on the development of the A.P.S., most of the senior public servants interviewed responded with a positive view of the contribution of economics graduates. This is not surprising, given the fact that most of those interviewed were themselves graduates in economics or commerce. There were, however, some more critical responses. Several of the interviewees felt that the large number of economists in the A.P.S. led to a great deal of conflicting policy advice being generated, which was seen to cause some indecision and confusion in the formulation of policy proposals. A number of others felt that there was an overemphasis in the A.P.S. on the use of economic factors in the analysis of what were essentially social problems. They believed that a multidisciplinary approach should be cultivated which would help to counter the tendency to perceive particular problems through the narrow lens of a single specialism. In addition, a few respondents felt that economics graduates were insufficiently pragmatic in orientation, with reference to such areas as report writing and managerial decisionmaking. These general criticisms are not necessarily consistent with each other, nor do they alter the basically positive view of the contribution of economics graduates which emerges from this research.

Why, then, have Australian governments employed such a large number of graduates in economics? In our estimate less than 15 percent of graduates in economics are employed in roles where they advise on policy or act as policy innovators. The historical survey in Section I above pointed to a number of significant events linked to an almost inexorable bureaucratic process in which the emphasis was placed on graduate recruitment, especially in economics and commerce. It was to a great extent the judgement of the bureaucracy, reflecting underlying cultural attitudes towards 'practical' training, which led to the emphasis on the recruitment of specific types of graduates. Within the bureaucracy the economics graduate was seen as an organiser of economic intelligence and, more importantly, as potentially the most able of administrators, with the ability to bring an economic dimension to the diverse and growing range of tasks to be performed in an expanding economy. For better or for worse, it is this attitude which has so profoundly influenced the nature of the Australian Public Service.

I am grateful to my research assistant Mr. R. W. McKenzie, who participated in the design of the questionnaire and carried out much of the interviewing for this project. I am also grateful to the Public Service Board, Canberra, for supplying me with data and other information, and I am especially grateful to Mr. B. G. McCallum of the Board's Office. This research was partly supported by a grant from the Australian Research Grants Council.

Bibliography

A.C.T. Regional Group. "Commonwealth Policy Coordination." *Public Administration* (Sydney) 14, no. 5 (Dec. 1955).

Auchmuty, J. J., G. S. Harman, and C. Selby Smith. "The Universities of Australia." *Commonwealth Universities Year Book* (London: 1978) pp. 2–8.

Butlin, S. J. "Of course I know no Economics, But. . . ." Some Comments on Provision for Economic Teaching and Research in Australia." *Australian Quarterly* 20, no. 3 (Sept. 1948).

Caiden, G. *The Commonwealth Bureaucracy*. Melbourne, 1967.

———. "Tackling Bureaucratic Inertia: Some Personal Reflections on the Royal Commission on Australian Government Administration." *Australian Quarterly* 49, no. 1 (March 1977).

Cain, N. "Political Economy and the Tariff: Australia in the 1920's." *Australian Economic Papers* 12 (June 1973).

Cochrane, D. "University Education for Administration and Management." *Public Administration* (Sydney) 19, no. 3 (Sept. 1960).

Copland, D. B., ed. *Giblin—The Scholar and the Man*. Melbourne, 1960.

———, and R. H. Barback, eds. *The Conflict of Expansion and Stability: Documents Relating to Australian Economic Policy, 1945–52*. Melbourne, 1957.

Corden, W. M. *Australian Economic Policy Discussion: A Survey*. Melbourne, 1968.

Coster, P. R. *Graduate Recruitment Review*. Canberra, 1974.

Crawford, Sir John G. "Relations Between Civil Servants and Ministers in Policy Making." *Public Administration* (Sydney) 19, no. 2 (June 1960): 99–112.

———. "The Role of the Economist in the Public Service." *Public Administration* (Sydney) 22 no. 1 (March 1963): 1–16.

Crisp, L. F. "The Commonwealth Treasury's Changed Role and Its Organizational Consequences." *Public Administration* (Sydney) 20 (Dec. 1961).

———. "The Australian Full Employment Pledge at San Francisco." *Australian Outlook* 19 (1965).

———. "Specialists and Generalists: Further Australian Reflections on Fulton." *Public Administration* (Sydney) 29 (1970): 197–217.

———. *Australian National Government*, 4th ed. London, 1978.

Cutt, J. *Economists, Policy Analysis and Government*. St. Lucia: University of Queensland Press, 1976.

Dunk, W. E. "The Role of the Public Servant in Policy Formation." *Public Administration* (Sydney) 20 (June 1961).

Dye, T. R. *Understanding Public Policy*, 2d ed. Englewood Cliffs, N.J., 1975.

Edwards, J. "The Economy Game: Treasury and Its Rivals." *Current Affairs Bulletin* 51, no. 12 (May 1975): 4–11.

Emy, H. V. *Public Policy: Problems and Paradoxes*. Melbourne 1976.

———. *The Politics of Australian Democracy*, 2d ed. Melbourne, 1978.

Encel, S. "The Recruitment of University Graduates to the Commonwealth Public Service." *Public Administration* (Sydney) 12, no. 5 (Dec. 1953).

———. "The Commonwealth Public Service and Outside Recruitment." *Public Administration* (Sydney) 14, no. 2 (March 1955).

———. "Graduate Recruitment—A Rejoinder." *Public Administration* (Sydney) 14, no. 2 (March 1955).

"Essays in Honour of Sir Douglas Copland." *Economic Record* 56 (March 1960).

Farran, A. "Reflections on Policy Making and the Public Service." *Public Administration* (Sydney) 34, no. 2 (June 1975).

Gruen, F. H. "The Twenty Five Per Cent Tariff Cut: Was It a Mistake?" *Australian Quarterly* 47 (June 1975): 7–20.

———. "What Went Wrong? Some Personal Reflections on Economic Policies Under Labor." *Australian Quarterly* 48, no. 3 (Dec. 1976).

———, ed. *Surveys of Australian Economics*. Sydney, 1978.

———. "Australian Economics 1967–1977." *Joseph Fisher Lecture in Commerce*, Oct. 1978.

Hawker, G. "The Implementation of the R.C.A.G.A: What Happened to the Coombs Report." *Australian Quarterly* 49, no. 1 (March 1977).

———. "The Use of Social Scientists and Social Science in the Inquiries of the Labor Government." Sociology Section, *Australian and New Zealand Association for the Advancement of Science*, 1977.

———. R. F. I. Smith, and P. Weller, *Politics and Policy in Australia*. St. Lucia: University of Queensland Press, 1979.

Hazlehurst, C., and J. R. Nethercote, eds. *Reforming Australian Government*. Canberra, 1977.

Higley, J., and D. Smart. "Why Not Ask Them? Interviewing Australian Elites About National Power Structure." *Australian and New Zealand Journal of Sociology* 13, no. 3 (Oct. 1977).

Kasper, W. *The Processes of Economic Policy Making in Australia: Report to the R.C.A.G.A.* Canberra, 1976.

Lyall, E. A. "Graduate Preference: A Case Study in Administrative Dogmatism." *Public Administration* (Sydney) 28 (1969): 294–320.

"Lyndhurst Giblin." *Australian Quarterly* 23, no. 1 (June 1951).

Parker, R. S. *Public Service Recruitment in Australia*. Melbourne, 1942.

———. "Policy and Administration." *Public Administration* (Sydney) 19, no. 2 (June, 1960).

Reid, G. S. "The Changing Political Framework." Address to the Australian Institute of Political Science, Summer School. Canberra, 1978.

Report of the Committee of Inquiry into Public Service Recruitment. Canberra, 1958. Also known as the Boyer Report.

Ridley, F. F., ed. *Specialists and Generalists: A Comparative Study of the Professional Civil Servant at Home and Abroad*. London, 1968.

Royal Commission on Australian Government Administration. *Report and Appendix*. Vols. 1 to 40. Canberra, 1976. Also known as the Coombs Commission, or *R.C.A.G.A.*

Schedvin, L. B. *Australia and the Great Depression*. Sydney, 1970.

Smith, R. F. I., and P. Weller. *Public Servants, Interest Groups and Policy Making: Two Case Studies*. Occasional Paper no. 12, Department of Political Science. Canberra, 1976.

———, and ———. *Public Service Inquiries in Australia*. St. Lucia: University of Queensland Press, 1978.

Spann, R. N., et al. *Public Administration in Australia*. New South Wales Government Printer, 1975.

Walker, E. R. *The Australian Economy in War and Reconstruction*. Oxford, 1947.

Weller, P. "Splitting the Treasury: Old Habits in New Structures." *Australian Quarterly* 49 (March 1977).

————, and J. Cutt. *Treasury Control in Australia*. Sydney, 1976.

Wheeler, F. H. "The Administrator in the Public Service—Responsibilities." Address to the South Australian Regional Group of the Royal Institute of Public Administration, May 1965.

Wiltshire, K. *Australian Public Administration*. Melbourne, 1974.

India: the aftermath of empire

S. Ambirajan

I. *The Establishment of the System*

In the last thirty years there has occurred a large infusion of trained economists into the decisionmaking and operational organs of the government of India in the belief that this would make a significant contribution to the stimulation of economic development of the country. The changed emphasis on the usefulness of economics and economists can be seen in the fact that from being on the bureaucratic periphery until not so long ago, economists have come to occupy some of the most sensitive and influential positions of power in India's administration. All this has taken place in the absence of any clear idea about either the nature of the expertise they possess or how they could be used in the government. This means that to comprehend this novel phenomenon of the existence of numerous economists within the government it becomes necessary to examine what the economists actually do in and for the government. This essay will be concerned with the following questions: What factors have caused the large employment of economists? Where do these economists come from? How are they recruited and trained? What is the process of decisionmaking, and where do the economists fit in? Is there any connection between the utilisation of economists and the 'economic' policies pursued?

Reasons for employing economists

There are two primary reasons for the increasing induction of economists into the Indian Government, the first of which is the spectacular growth of the Indian bureaucracy since 1945. Among this increased number of higher civil servants are many Economics graduates. For example, out of a total intake of 392 in the elite Indian Administrative Service from 1947 to 1963, no fewer than 134 had majored in Economics or Commerce.[1] Economics occupies a prominent and favoured position in the Arts Faculties of most universities and colleges in India. So when Economics graduates enter open competitive examinations, they are able to succeed in great numbers.

The second reason for the induction of economists into government

1. See V. Subramanian, p. 155.

was the need to change the bureaucracy India had inherited from its British rulers in accordance with the new political leadership's philosophy of state action.

Although the British government in India had not entirely refrained from intervening to regulate the workings of the economic system, it had been essentially a 'law and order' system of government in which 'administrators' enforced regulations based either upon existing laws or accumulated precedents. The government was then run by so-called 'generalists,' competent men who acquired considerable expertise in all branches of administration through field experience, but lacked deep specialist knowledge in any one branch.

Once India became independent, the government headed by Jawaharlal Nehru and the Indian National Congress adopted a pronounced interventionist policy, particularly in the economic sphere. Positive action could not take place merely on the basis of legal codes and past practices, but needed specialised knowledge about the structure and operation of the economy. Even members of the 'generalist' cadre of the elite Indian Civil Service had realised the utility of economics for practical administration. As a distinguished Indian civil servant noted, the layman's approach to economic problems could be simplistic: it was necessary to have an expert professional interested in "the deeper analysis" of economic problems.[2] Another senior civil servant who had been a magistrate, tax collector, judge, president of a cooperative bank, president of a municipality, and a central banker in the 1930s and the 1940s wrote: "I learnt the elements of Economics —which have stood me in good stead; it was inexact but it nevertheless was a science."[3]

In fact, the increasing utilisation of economic expertise had its immediate origins in the decade or so preceding India's attainment of freedom. This came about in two ways: namely, the changing attitudes of the Indian National Congress and other Indian groups, and the need for wartime economic administration in India.

Soon after the introduction of Provincial Autonomy in 1937, the Indian National Congress itself took the initiative, and its President, Subhas Chandra Bose, convened a conference of ministers of industries in Delhi in October 1938. The Congress agreed that only large-scale industrialisation could solve India's economic backwardness, and it was therefore necessary to prepare a comprehensive scheme of economic progress. Presently a national planning organisation, the National Planning Committee, was established, with Jawaharlal Nehru as

2. L. K. Jha, p. 589.
3. B. K. Nehru, in Joan Abse, ed., *My LSE* (London, 1977), pp. 26–27.

its chairman and the economist, K. T. Shah, as secretary. Defining planning, the Committee stated that under a democratic system planning meant "the technical coordination by disinterested experts of consumption, production, investment, trade and income distribution in accordance with social objectives set by organs representative of the nation." The National Planning Committee was an expert body,[4] and a number of its subcommittees did valuable fact-finding work and issued several useful reports on various aspects of planning such as trade, public finance, labour, industry, and agriculture. There were also other intellectual efforts by non-official agencies to think rationally about the Indian economy, all of which accepted the role of economists either explicitly or implicitly. Economists contributed to the three exercises in preparing national economic plans—the Bombay Plan, the People's Plan and the Gandhian Plan. Professor John Mathai, formerly of the Economics Department of Madras University, was one of the authors of the Bombay Plan. G. D. Parekh, who co-authored the People's Plan, was a student of economics and later became the rector of Bombay University, S. N. Agarwal, who single-handedly prepared the Gandhian Plan, taught economics and commerce at Nagpur University, and after India's independence became a member of the Indian Planning Commission.

However, the most interesting and novel suggestion for the utilisation of economists came from Mokshagundam Visveswarayya, the Diwan of the Mysore State. He proposed the establishment of Economic Councils composed mainly of expert economists and businessmen at the central, provincial, and local levels to provide advice and supervision. Thus the cabinet minister, on whom would devolve the duty of executing the programmes, would have at his side the "brainstrusting services of a General Economic Staff."[5]

Thus among the non-official and the nationalistic circles, a climate of opinion had been generated that favoured the utilisation of economists as experts, as innovational enclaves in the administrative structure. In addition, influenced by British wartime experience, the Indian government began to consider that economists could play a part in the formation and administration of policies. In 1938 the government had appointed its first economic adviser, Sir Theodore Gregory, who had both academic (he had been Sir Ernest Cassel Professor of Economics at London University) and advisory experience (he had been Economic Adviser to the Niemeyer Mission to Australia and New Zealand

4. For example, in the subcommittee on Trade, among others there were three economists associated with the preparation of the Report. They were Professors J. J. Anjaria, C. N. Vakil, and B. N. Ganguli.

5. For a short description of the proposal, see A. H. Hanson, p. 31.

in 1930). Gregory occupied that position until 1946. In the 1940s the British government in India decided to undertake a policy of rational utilisation of resources for economic development. Sir Ardeshir Dalal became Planning Member of the Viceroy's Executive Council. When Gregory responded adversely to his economic development plan proposal Dalal appointed an Indian economist, Professor C. N. Vakil, as his economic adviser.[6]

Therefore it is not surprising that many economists have joined the Indian bureaucracy since 1947. The Indian government had had great faith in economics as a technical tool since the days of Jawaharlal Nehru, and this certainly furthered its acceptance within the government.[7]

The supply of economists

The supply of economists in India to cope with this demand has never presented a problem since 1945. The first three Indian universities were founded in 1857, but subsequent additions were made, so that by the time India became independent, in 1947, there were nearly twenty universities with numerous colleges affiliated to them giving post-secondary school education. Now, after thirty years, there are more than a hundred universities, most of them granting degrees in Economics and Commerce. The number of graduates in Economics and Commerce runs into tens of thousands (Table 1). In 1973, for example, 57 universities (not including some of the large ones like Osmania, Calcutta, Aligarh Muslim, the 11 Agricultural universities and the 6 Institutes of Technology) granted 7,896 M.A. (Economics) degrees by course work. Of these, 261 candidates secured First Class marks. In the same period, 4,738 M.Com. degrees were awarded, with 348 Firsts. In addition, more than a hundred Ph.D.s in Economics are awarded by Indian universities every year.

Together with this increased university education in social sciences, ample resources are being channelled to both universities and

6. See C. N. Vakil, *Poverty, Planning and Inflation* (Bombay, 1978), p. xvii.

7. The following table shows the growth of employment in the occupational group comprising economists and statisticians in the central government service.

Class	1959	1971
I	226	1,271[a]
II	429	1,187
III	892	9,780

a including members of the IES and ISS cadres

Source: *Report of the Third Central Pay Commission* (New Delhi, 1973), 1:200.

Table 1. Higher education graduates: number and percent change since 1960.

Year	B.A. B.A. (Hon.) Economics	B. Comm. B. Comm. (Hons.)	M.A. Economics	M. Comm.	Doctorates
1960					
N	n/a	n/a	n/a	n/a	n/a
%	n/a	n/a	n/a	n/a	n/a
1964					
N	12522	17624	4106	2652	48
%	—	—	—	—	—
1970					
N	26963	39189	7720	5170	72
%	+115.3	+122.4	+88.0	+94.9	+50.0
1976					
N	40700	83214	12355	10101	91
%	+225.0	+372.2	+200.9	+280.9	+89.6

Source: University Development in India, Basic Facts and Figures 1971–72 (University Grants Commission, New Delhi, 1976).

semi-university institutes through the Indian Council of Social Science Research and the University Grants Commission for research related to the Indian economy. In the pre-independence period, apart from the Gokhale School of Economics and Politics, there were hardly any specialised institutes studying the Indian economic conditions. But in the last three decades many institutes have been established for this purpose—both at national and regional levels. Many of these institutes impart postgraduate training both by course work and research projects.

The extent of oversupply of economists can be gauged by the number of economists the government can employ in a given year. In 1975, there were 1,864 applicants, most with postgraduate experience, who sought 40 posts available in the Indian economic and statistical services. In the same year 173 persons applied for the Union Public Service Commission's fifteen vacancies for senior posts in the Economics/Commerce category, and all the positions were filled with suitable candidates except one reserved for candidates belonging to the Scheduled Tribes category.[8] The 1971 Census revealed that the total stock of B.A. (Arts)—of which Economics is a significant component—degree hold-

8. Certain posts are reserved in every category of employment for those belonging to underprivileged sections of the society such as those belonging to the 'Untouchable' castes and tribes.

ers in the country was 11,387,000, and 390,700 M.A.s and Ph.D.s. Similarly, the stock of B.Com.s was 267,800 and M.Com.s, 43,800. Among all these, 15.10 percent of the B.A.s, 16.3 percent of B.Com.s, 10.3 percent of M.A.s, and 7.07 percent of M.Com.s were seeking employment.[9]

While the availability of economists is impressive quantitatively, there is a large variation in the quality available. Whereas universities in general have continued to teach economics in the way it had been taught in the 1920s and 1930s, some universities have made important changes in their teaching programmes. In some of the leading universities economics has managed to cut itself away from the history-politics-sociology nexus and has attached itself to the mathematics-statistics yoke. The quantitative bias introduced into the economics curricula, and the imaginative innovations pursued by some universities in the 1960s, have accentuated the qualitative differences among Indian universities' economics graduates. In interviews, senior members of the profession both in academia and government lamented this state of affairs. Whereas government economists blamed the universities for bad curriculum planning and teaching, university professors suggested that deeper structural factors had caused the deterioration in the quality of graduates.

But despite the poor quality of a significant proportion of the economics graduates, the total pool is sufficiently large for the government to be able to recruit the professionally competent personnel it requires. (The available data are presented in Tables 2 and 3.) This was evident in conversation with senior economic advisers, who felt that the younger Indian Economic Service recruits selected by competitive examinations were much more competent professionally than the older members of the service who had been promoted from within.

The bureaucratic structure

During the British rule of India, ultimate authority was vested in the British Parliament, which meant the British Cabinet. The Secretary of State for India ruled the country from Britain. However, within India, the Viceroy and his Executive Council had the final say in all matters. The bureaucracy was hierarchically organised and, true to its British tradition, was very generalist in its approach. Usually the Executive Councillor was the supreme decisionmaker, but he was confidentially advised by his departmental secretary, who collected needed information from specialists. But economics was not considered a specialist

9. Government of India, Committee on Unemployment, *Report of the Panel on the Assessment of Unemployment and Underemployment*, pp. 40–41.

Table 2. Central government employment: number and percent change since 1960

Year	Administrative officials	Economists and economic investigators	Statisticians and statistical assts.
1960			
N	n/a	1040[a]	472[b]
%	—	—	—
1964			
N	n/a	96[a]	318[b]
%	—	−90.8	−32.6
1970			
N	3457	1569	801
%	—	+50.9	+69.7
1976			
N	n/a	n/a	n/a
%	—	n/a	n/a

[a] Economists only, as economic investigators' figure is not known.
[b] Statisticians only, as statistical assistants' figure is not known.
Source: Data collected by the Director General of Employment and Training, Ministry of Labour, Government of India. (These data are collected from Government agencies on a voluntary basis and are therefore not reliable.)

subject, and every secretary was in effect his own economist.[10] As the functions of government were relatively few, the secretaries were able to manage things. Indeed the functions were so limited that the executive councillors themselves could take all vital decisions. For special issues, it was always possible to leave the matter in the hands of a Royal Commission.

Conditions changed—particularly in the 1930s—and the Indian decisionmaking system responded to the increased pressures by augmenting the secretaries' discretionary authority. Experts slowly trickled into the system and, as we have seen, 'Economics' became a specialist subject, and an economic advisor was appointed. In the thirties, with the increased need for some economic expertise, it was decided to

10. The idea that university trained economists were prejudiced and not useful for practical decisionmaking persisted for a long time. L. K. Jha who was selected to serve in the Finance and Commerce Pool of the Indian Civil Service in the late 1930s gives his experience: "In fact I have on good authority that Sir Eric Coats, who as Finance Secretary, along with the Auditor General, and Commerce Secretary and the Chairman, Central Board of Revenue had the responsibility of selecting officers for the pool, had reservations about taking me into the Pool on the ground that I had studied Economics in Cambridge and might have imbibed dangerous theoretical ideas which may prevent me from learning from experience." Jha, p. 587.

Table 3.   Public sector employment: number and percent change since 1960

Year	Professionals	Social scientists	Economists	Statisticians	Social science workers
1960					
N	432406	60511	1695	2997	3834
%	—	—	—	—	—
1964					
N	719230	49993	367	1703	7442
%	+66.3	−17.4	−78.3	−43.2	+94.1
1970					
N	884588	67820	559	1981	9870
%	+104.6	+12.1	−67.0	−33.9	+157.4
1976					
N	n/a	n/a	n/a	n/a	n/a
%	n/a	n/a	n/a	n/a	n/a

Source: As for Table 2.

allocate some members of the Indian Civil Service with appropriate qualifications to the so-called Finance and Commerce Pool.[11] Approximately four officers with six to eight years' service were selected every year to administer monetary policy and international trade arrangements.

Since 1947, although many changes have occurred, the decision-making apparatus has not been fundamentally changed. The new Constitution adopted in 1950 adapted the inherited British system to the federal framework. At the topmost level the policymaking body became the Parliament (Lok Sabha) and the Cabinet. Instead of advising and working under the Executive Councillors and the Viceroy, the civil service now had to work with and advise the Cabinet and the Prime Minister.[12]

As governments[13] were of the 'law and order' variety until the 1940s, problems came up through the hierarchy (instead of new projects or programmes being initiated from the top) and were decided upon by officers at successively higher levels. The basic bureaucratic structure consisted of the Minister, Secretary (Department), Joint-

11. Resolution No. F. 28(6) Ex 11/36 of the Government of India Finance Department. See R. N. Thakur, p. 273.

12. The relationship between the minister and his secretary was reported upon and procedures laid out by the 1937 Report of the Government of India Secretariat (Maxwell) Committee. These are followed to this day. See Misra, pp. 158 ff.

13. We are at present concerned only with the central government. The state governments are more or less similar, and in any case very subordinate to the centre.

Secretary (Wing), Deputy-Secretary (Division), Under-Secretary (Branch), Principal Section Officer (Section), Section Officer Class II, Assistants. In this hierarchical structure, decisions on cases actually start at the under-secretary level. All the cadres below that position have only the function of receiving references, preparing papers, searching for precedents, and in general submitting all the necessary information to help the officers to reach decisions.

Since the mid-1940s interventionism has entailed policies generating at the top and traversing downwards for implementation. Under these circumstances the role of the secretary to the ministry is to assist and advise the minister in policymaking and subsequently to implement the policies formulated.[14]

Two questions now arise: Does the minister have recourse to other advice? And how does the secretary arrive at the policies? The first question is easily answered: the minister gets considerable advice from the party secretariat and any economists or others he consults unofficially. It is certainly up to him to get whatever advice he wants and from wherever he wants it. He can also appoint special officers to investigate specific problems. The second question is harder to answer, for when problems were simple and relatively straightforward the generalist secretary could decide policies without much difficulty. In the present changed circumstances all ministries have many advisers of various kinds. The secretary will certainly need such advice because he is at the apex of a huge organisation, and he cannot be expected to master the details of all the departments and satellite organisations.

The process of decisionmaking

Karl Marx once said, with considerable accuracy, that the British government in India was one immense writing machine. This was so because of the need to inform Britain of the reasons for taking particular actions, but also because of the peculiar nature of the higher civil servants' tenure in India. As early as 1899 Viceroy Lord Curzon pointed out how significant differences between the higher civil service of India and Britain were responsible for the enormous quantity of the written material in India. In Britain all departments at Whitehall were manned from top to bottom with clerks and officers with long experience. The department as a whole accumulated ample knowledge of the rules, precedents, and procedures. But in India the situation was such

14. Government of India, Administrative Reforms Commission, *Report of the Study Team on the Machinery of the Government of India and Its Procedures of Work*, part II, vol. 1 (New Delhi, 1968), pp. 6–7.

that the British officers at the Central Secretariat had a limited tenure as they made their way up, often serving the districts and states. They did not progress solely in the service of the Government of India's Central Secretariat office. Hence they were dependent on the clerks lower down the scale for briefings for decisionmaking.[15] This system suited even post-1947 India because the files were always fully informative, and it facilitated the secretaries' task of giving evidence to the many parliamentary watch-dog committees. The presence of written material relating to particular decisions in the form of 'noting' discouraged arbitrariness, thus protecting both the minister and the civil servant.[16]

Any proposal or item for which a decision is required must go through this process of 'noting.' In fact, once a letter, memorandum, or proposal enters the system from any source whatever, it becomes either a 'Paper under Consideration' or a 'Fresh Report.' It can travel vertically downwards or upwards, or horizontally from one department to another at specified levels for noting. Specialist-experts are either located within the department's hierarchies in an advisory capacity or are situated in parallel structures outside the department. These specialists perform two functions. They either originate a note by identifying a problem and then let the note meander around the various levels of the bureaucracy; or, what is more normal, they give their comments as experts on a note that originated elsewhere in the system. In some departments (e.g. Commerce, Economic Affairs) the noting system has given way to 'Papers of Problems,' and there are also 'Position Papers' which can be sent for comments outside the bureaucratic framework.

Location of economists

As we have seen, Indian government economists are of two types. The first is the economist whose training bears no relevance to the position he holds in government. He may or may not perform 'economic' functions, but if he does, that is quite incidental. There are individuals

---

15. See Curzon's Minute dated 24 May 1899: "Reforms in the System of Filing, Noting and Interdepartmental References," p. 658.

16. Op. cit. supra, n.14, p. 62. The system of 'noting' is described by the Administrative Reforms Commission thus: "It is through the process of noting that the bulk of decision-making takes place, and it is the notes of a particular case that relate the decision taken on that case to past practice and precedents. The central place occupied by noting as a phenomenon is complementary to the position of the structural pattern of officers and office. The office note became necessary to the process of administration because the time of the officers, who were few and hard pressed with responsibilities, had to be served. The office was thus trained to produce notes which would be so self-contained in the matter of facts and precedents as to enable the officers to take decisions easily and quickly.

with economic training in Parliament as well as in the various cadres of government service performing generalist services. Indeed, individual economists have captured some of the vital areas of administrative power. The second type of government economists is those who have entered on the basis of their professional expertise. They hold a variety of positions, e.g. as research assistants, research officers, consultants, members of permanent and semi-permanent commissions, analysts, counsellors (in the case of embassies abroad), and advisers.

In addition, a considerable amount of government economic work is carried on in numerous organisations indirectly connected with the government under contract from different governmental organs. For example, the National Council of Applied Economic Research founded in the 1950s with large government patronage was actively encouraged by Mr. V.T. Krishnamachari, then vice-chairman of the Planning Commission.

Recruitment

Whatever the methodological controversies that rage in the academic arena, the official perception of the duties of an economist *qua* economist seems clear enough. According to the National Classification of Occupations, the economist is one who

> makes studies, conducts research, prepares reports and formulates plans designed to aid in solution of economic problems arising from production and distribution of goods and services. Studies whole process through which man makes a living and satisfies his wants for products, shelter, service or amusement and conditions favouring or hampering economic development. Devises methods for collection and analysis of economic and statistical data and compiles and interprets such data. Prepares reports and formulates plans based on studies in economic field and interpreted and analysed data. Advises and consults private industrial concerns or government agencies on matters such as operating efficiency, marketing methods and fiscal problems. May specialise in any branch of economics, such as agricultural, financial or industrial, international trade, labour or prices, or in taxation or market research and be designated accordingly.[17]

Specifically, in the case of the Ministry of Industry, the economic adviser's office was expected

17. *National Classification of Occupation*, prepared by the Directorate General of Employment and Training of Occupational Information Unit: Ministry of Labour, Employment and Rehabilitation, Government of India, March 1969, no. 110.10.

to render technical advice on matters of economic nature. The office compiles and publishes the official index number of wholesale prices in India and reviews trends in wholesale prices periodically. The office examines trends in industrial production and assists in formulation of industrial policies and import policies. It also renders advice and assistance on the allocation of foreign exchange for the import of raw materials and other maintenance inputs.[18]

The functions are sufficiently broad-based to include a variety of work some of which—like the collection of statistics—needs no particular expertise in economic theory. On the other hand, some tasks require considerable specialised knowledge and experience. While the government of India has accepted that individuals with proper background can equip themselves with the necessary economic expertise to perform the economists' tasks,[19] it has generally been considered appropriate to recruit economists for certain jobs; and the government has also recognised the need to provide a modicum of economic expertise for non-economists who might have to take charge of economic work.

Economists enter the administration in two ways. Firstly, through individual appointments by the ministries on an *ad hoc* basis, which are subsequently regularised. Membership of commissions and economists' panels are also directly controlled by the administration. Similarly 'consultants' are appointed on a limited-term basis directly by the Planning Commission. All such appointments involve considerations such as the 'Old School tie,' political affiliations,[20] personal/family relationships,[21] and so on. It is only fair to say that until now, appointments to senior positions have seldom been made unless the appointee has appropriate qualifications and solid achievement. However, it is to be expected that the ideological position of the economist selected will not vary markedly from that of the minister, for as Paul Samuelson has said: "he who picks the doctor from an array of competing doctors is in

18. Government of India, Ministry of Industry, *Report 1976–77* (New Delhi, 1977), pp. 3-4.

19. Pitambar Pant, who was one of the most influential individuals in the government of India in the area of economic policymaking, was originally trained as a physicist.

20. An economist—distinguished in his own right—told me that he was appointed to head an enquiry in a state because he and one of the party bosses of that state had been colleagues some years previously, and also because they had moved in the same political circles.

21. To give an important example: the late Mr. V. K. Ramaswami, who was Deputy Economic Adviser and Chief Economic Adviser respectively from 1955 to 1969, was the son of Mr. V. T. Krishnamachari, who was the Vice-Chairman of the Planning Commission at the time of his appointment.

a real sense his own doctor. The Prince often gets to hear what he wants to hear.''[22] In the Indian situation the array of competing doctors has been so small, and the range of ideological differences among economists so insignificant, that the politicians have usually been able to appoint economists as members of commissions or special economic advisers without the stigma of ideological bias.

Secondly, many more economists join the government as a career, and are selected by the Union Public Service Commission (U.P.S.C.),[23] which selects members of the Indian Economic Service through competitive examinations as it does for other services. The Indian Economic Service and the Indian Statistical Service had their origins in the early 1950s when the need for collecting and processing statistical material relating to economic affairs for developmental policy began to be recognised. Until then different ministries had recruited economic personnel through the U.P.S.C. to suit their individual requirements. Mr. V. T. Krishnamachari, vice-chairman of the Planning Commission, felt that it was necessary to have a pool of economists for routine economic work in order to avoid the inevitable delays in getting special *ad hoc* appointments made by the U.P.S.C. Professor P. C. Mahalanobis, the honorary statistical adviser to the Cabinet Secretariat, apparently suggested that there should be a central economic statistical pool, but the various ministries favoured a regular service from which they could readily draw the personnel required. The idea was that whereas economic advice on important policy matters could be secured on a part-time temporary basis from leading economists attached to universities and research institutes, day-to-day problems were to be tackled by the permanent officers belonging to the Indian Economic Service. According to Mr. L. K. Jha, it was also considered a good policy to have available ''a regular breed of economists who would have grown with the headaches of the government.''

The Indian Economic Service was constituted in 1961 as a Class I central service on a par with the Indian Administrative Service, Indian Foreign Service, and Indian Police Service, but with special Indian Economic Service rules. Guidance for running the cadre is provided by the Indian Economic Service Board, consisting of the Chief Economic Adviser and representatives from the various 'economic' ministries. When the Service was established, all the previous irregular appointments as economists were absorbed into it.[24]

22. "Economists and the History of Ideas," *American Economic Review* 52, no. 1 (March 1962): 17.

23. U.P.S.C. is one of the four institutions (the others are the Supreme Court, the Comptroller and Auditor-General and the Election Commission) embodied in the Indian Constitution as a safeguard for the Indian system of democratic government.

24. In the 1950s when the number of economists increased, there was considerable

The Indian Economic Service has four grades, depending upon the basic salary. On 1 January 1976 the total number employed was 440 (as against the authorised strength of 556), with 51 in Grade I, 67 in Grade II, 177 in Grade III, and 145 in Grade IV. All are graduates with a fair sprinkling of postgraduate degrees, including doctorates.

Appointment to the Indian Economic Service is either by competitive examination or promotion or direct recruitment. Every year approximately 75 percent of the vacancies at Grade IV level are filled by direct recruitment through a competitive examination conducted by the Union Public Service Commission for candidates from all over India. Candidates are usually fresh from the universities or recent graduates. Out of a total of 1,350 marks, 250 marks are awarded for *viva voce* tests. Examination papers include General English, General Knowledge, Essay, Statistics, and Economics. In recent years about a dozen recruits are absorbed into the Service annually at this level, selected from a few hundreds who appear for the examination, and the total entry by this method to date is about 160. The Indian Economic Service is a Class I service, and up to 25 percent of the vacancies in the lowest grade (Grade IV) are reserved for the promotion of persons with appropriate qualifications in economics and experience in economic work from Class II, which is a lower service. Thirdly, a certain number of senior posts at levels above Grade IV are recruited from outside by the U.P.S.C. Originally it was 25 percent at Grade I, 50 percent at Grade II, and 25 percent at Grade III. However, at present direct recruitment by advertisement for specific posts and interview is reserved for only 25 percent of the vacancies in Grades I and II.

Training

It has been repeatedly asserted that for India to move from a negative to a positive approach to government, administrators must possess extra skills, especially a knowledge of economics.[25] Thus economics is regarded as one of the useful qualifications for the generalist cadre, the Indian Administrative Service (I.A.S.); and some training in econom-

---

frustration among them because they did not belong to any Service. The Indian Economic Service was instituted partly to rectify this situation. A cynical view often expressed by informants belonging to Grade IV of Indian Economic Service was that it was erected to provide a 'Service Haven' for one or two top influential government economists so that they could be given 'line' positions!

25. It has been pointed out that even the collector and senior engineer of the district will have to take crucial and and far-reaching decisions concerning a variety of subjects for which they need a certain amount of expertise in economics. As Robert Wade points out in a paper on the efficient use of irrigation water, they "should have sufficient understanding of economics to grasp why certain changes in cropping pattern are desirable in the wider social interest." "Water Supply as an Instrument of Agricultural Policy: A Case Study," *Economic and Political Weekly* 13, no. 12 (March 1978): 13.

ics is provided, initially for a year at the L.B.S. National Academy of Administration,[26] to make the recruits to the Indian Administrative Service fully professional. During this period they take courses in economics, the administrative history of India, general administration, criminal law and procedure, district administration, and regional languages. The coverage being wide, the content obviously cannot be anything but superficial.[27]

The generalist Indian Administrative Service, and other selected cadres, subsequently get additional training for periods of up to two months. Similar short courses are given by many other institutions, such as the Indian Institute of Public Administration, Administrative Staff College, Indian Institute of Foreign Trade, Institute of Applied Manpower Research, Indian Institutes of Management, Jawaharlal Nehru University, and so on. Most of these are courses sponsored by the Ministry of Home Affairs Department of Personnel Training Division. In addition a few one-year scholarships are provided for the study of economics at such places as the London School of Economics, Maxwell School, Oxford University, Williams College, and Harvard University.[28] However, there is no systematic approach to training in any subject, let alone economics, and only a minority of personnel gets into any of these schemes.[29]

26. This was set up in Mussoorie in 1959, incorporating the I.A.S. training school at Delhi and the I.A.S. Staff College at Simla. In 1966 it was renamed Lal Bahadur Shastri National Academy of Administration in honour of the late Prime Minister of India.

27. For example, in 1977 the Economics lectures covered the following topics. The candidates could not have absorbed much, given the work load and the limited time available: "Basic Economic Concepts, National Income, Economic Development, Balanced versus unbalanced growth, Economic Planning in underdeveloped and developing countries, Planning under Socialism, The Indian Plans, Monetary Policy, Fiscal Policy, Price Policy, Industrial Policy, Agricultural, Food, Labour and Population Policies, Economic Overheads, Social Services, Foreign exchange, Foreign trade, Deficit financing, Employment problem, Statistics as an aid to administration, Some selected topics of contemporary importance." Source: *Probationers' Handbook 1977*. See also Prasad, p. 230.

28. Only a handful can go abroad in any year, and I am informed by many civil servants that there is very keen competition for these scholarships. Selection is influenced by the candidate's academic record, the level at which he passed his competitive examination, his performance and, more importantly, his 'connections.' Opinions differ about the value of these trips. One (his basic degree in Chemistry) who had been to Oxford for a year said that although he had not learnt much economics, he enjoyed the welcome break from his bureaucratic chores. Another (degree in English Literature) told me that he had learnt a lot of useful things at Harvard, and it had spurred him to learn further tools and techniques of economic analysis for management. Yet another who spent a year at L.S.E. said he did not learn anything new that he could not have learnt at home provided he had had the year free.

29. For a critique of the various training programmes see Maheshwari, "Training in Public Administration in India."

Economists recruited as professionals should not require any additional training. However, this applies only to those appointed at the middle and high levels, and not to the young recruits fresh from the universities. By the time they are appointed and are ready for service, they will have spent 24 months in training in five stages of varying lengths.

The Government of India has an arrangement with the Institute of Economic Growth attached to the Delhi University School of Economics to provide each year ten months' training for the newly recruited members (Probationers) of the Indian Economic Service. The topics covered include the tools of modern economic analysis in planning, and the formulation and evaluation of economic policies.

After this stage, the probationers are sent to the L.B.S. National Academy of Administration at Mussoorie for four months' training similar to that given to the generalist service. The third stage is a month either at the Reserve Bank's Bankers Training College at Bombay or at any of the allied financial institutions. The fourth stage is important because during this period of about eight months they work in the various ministries or public sector undertakings, almost as apprentices. The concluding stage—introduced in 1977—is a month spent in a district observing, and participating in the economic administration at the village level.

Policy process

In a policy process we can identify conceptually the following six self-explanatory stages: invention/initiation/anticipation; estimation; selection; implementation; evaluation; termination.[30] However, few economists have experienced the whole life cycle of economic policies.

During the policy process files travel in many directions, both vertically and horizontally. Government economists rarely have the opportunity to think out the overall policy framework. They invariably react to something specific, using their knowledge of economics while doing so.[31] Even at the very top level—i.e. when they have the opportunity to think out the broad issues—they react to established political param-

30. See Garry D. Brewer, "The Policy Sciences Emerge: To Nurture and Structure a Discipline," *Policy Sciences* 5, no. 3 (Sept. 1974): 240–41.

31. Cf. the following comment by Robert K. Merton: ". . . the problem may be presented to the intellectual at progressively advanced points in the *continuum of decision*: at the point where alternative policies are being considered or when a specific policy has been adopted and there is need for information on means of implementing this policy through a definite program of action or finally, after a given program has been put into practice and there is a demand for assessing the effectiveness of the program." *Social Theory and Social Structure* (New York, 1968), p. 269.

eters. In other words, policy formation and economic advising are on-going processes. The system never has a completely clean start. Even such a fundamental decision as the creation of a Planning Commission is really the 'termination' stage of an earlier policy of leaving economic management free. Policies generally do not emerge from a clear pattern of problem–alternatives–chosen policy at any one time.

It is possible to indicate the broad nature of problems faced by different government organs. Some will be concerned with purely day-to-day matters. The very administration of the affairs will involve taking decisions that will have an impact on the total policy. At the other end, there are those concerned with very long-term projections. Some organs are more concerned with policy and less with administration, and others *vice versa*. Table 4 indicates this broadly.

Policy formation is continuous and periodically under review. Just as the financial budget is prepared annually by the Treasury with a general review of policies, so other organisations and policies operate with different time patterns. Some ministries review their policies every three or six months, whereas other organisations—such as the Planning Commission—may reconsider their policies every five years. Of course in the event of a sudden upheaval (e.g., famine, foreign invasion) the executive and bureaucracy may have to rethink the whole gamut of policies. But otherwise the process of policy formation is continuous at all levels, and representatives of different organs of the government invariably meet in working groups to hammer out policies. For example, a typical industry working group will

a. estimate the domestic demand both on a regional and national basis;
b. suggest a policy framework covering pricing, freight, etc.;
c. recommend capacities and production targets for the next three to five years;
d. suggest the most advantageous way of securing the targets.

Table 4.

Organ	Function	Time Horizon
Planning Commission	Policy	Long/Medium term
Finance Ministry	Policy/Administration	Day-to-day/Short/Medium
Operating Ministries	Policy/Administration	Day-to-day/Short/Medium
Reserve Bank of India	Policy/Administration	Day-to-day/Short term
Public Enterprises	Administration	Day-to-day
Committees and Commissions	Policy	Depends upon the frame of reference

The working group will include senior members of the relevant ministry (in this case, the Department of Industrial Development), representatives of the Director General of Technical Development, Department of Science and Technology, C.S.I.R., industrial commissions, and the Planning Commission who would invariably be economists from the different divisions. In this process of continuous revision and rethinking of policies, the economist as expert brings to bear the fruits of the latest research in order to improve the overall performance.

The economist as expert can play three roles. Firstly, as an adviser he responds to any request for his comments on economic issues and may work with other bureaucrats and technical experts in decisionmaking groups.[32] Secondly, the economist can serve as a "technical auxiliary to policy-makers—to provide the quantification which can make their decisions more precise."[33] And thirdly, he may construct economic models which go to other operational divisions to be translated into specific policies or policy packages in combination with materials provided by other economists. In the ongoing policy process the economist may at some stages be a technical auxiliary and at others an adviser. There are relatively few model builders in the system.

II. *The System in Operation*

An understanding of what economists can in principle contribute to the policy process leads to the broader and more speculative subject of the economists' experience in the Indian government. In general Indian administrators, politicians, and economists suggest that economists can play a large part and in fact do play some part at all the stages of policy formation. However, there are some differences of opinion as to what part economists have been playing, how they have played it, and how effective their presence has been.

The economist in bureaucracy

Economists who have worked at all levels (i.e. as model builders, economic advisers, and technical auxiliaries) explained that there was a great demand for their type of work, the nature of which necessarily depends on their location. At the broadest policy level—e.g. in the Perspective Planning Division of the Planning Commission, or the chief

---

32. The economist functions here "as a policy adviser who makes (explicitly or not) certain value assumptions." As the economist gathers administrative experience, he is able to provide correct advice. In view of his working in close proximity to political activity the economist, according to Peter Self, is able to "marry his techniques with practical judgements, and to gain utility at the expense of purity." *Administrative Theories and Politics: An Inquiry into the Structure and Processes of Modern Government* (London, 1972), p. 213.

33. Ibid., p. 212.

economic adviser's office—there is considerable emphasis on model building, because an abstract picture of the likely outcome of different sets of assumptions is required.

In such places, lower-level personnel perform the technical auxiliary functions of gathering and interpreting data for the model builders. But in the narrow policy *cum* implementation locations the economist functions more in an advisory role—sometimes reacting and at other times making specific policy proposals. When his advice is sought, it is designed to reveal the extent to which a particular short- or medium-term measure will fit into the overall long-term pattern and how it relates to changing long-run economic situations. For instance, one economist in the Finance Ministry said that the economists' function was like that of a 'brains trust,'[34] from which administrators could solicit a *technically* informed opinion even on routine administrative matters. A secretary of an economic ministry[35] noted that he regarded his economic adviser as "a repository of all information on economic matters" and that he "very often picked his brain for ideas."

With few exceptions, economists in the Indian government seem to have fitted extremely well into the niches carved for them by the bureaucracy, for two reasons. The first is the Indian government economists' consensual character. Economists and bureaucrats repeatedly stressed the limited extent of conflict among economists on theoretical or ideological issues. Their capacity to discuss and arrive at mutually agreeable conclusions was repeatedly highlighted. An economist member of the Planning Commission said that once the 'facts' are known, "on all basic issues all competent professional economists generally agree." Another economist maintained that there were differences of opinion on matters of detail, but nothing on broad policy issues. One senior administrator claimed that conflicting views, if encountered, were more apparent than real. "If the right questions are asked," he said, there can be "no problem with conflicting views." Another economist echoed this view, saying that "if the basic issues are clear, economists need not differ considerably." Given the economic magnitudes and compulsions of economic reality this is understandable, and in any case those few who feel strongly about their own positions soon leave the government service.

This consensual attitude is attributable to the widely accepted so-

34. The Chief Economic Adviser of the Department of Economic Affairs of the Finance Ministry is responsible for preparing the annual Economic Survey tabled in the Parliament along with the Year's Budget.
35. A catch-all term to indicate ministers who deal with economic aspects—commerce, industry, steel, finance, etc.

cial democratic ideology[36] and the neoclassical training received by all the economists, whether at home or overseas. More than one economist attributed this similarity of attitudes and outlook to the fact that virtually all the top advisory positions in the 1950s and early 1960s were filled by former students of Cambridge and the London School of Economics. One added that this 'commonality' of outlook would always exist because the new recruits, though coming from different universities, could develop an *esprit de corps* by going to the L.B.S. Academy together at the beginning of their career, and by frequently meeting as professionals.

Broadly speaking the economists, bureaucrats, and politicians spoke a similar language. Consider for example, a major aspect of Indian economic policy, viz. Detailed Planning. The politicians think of it as a symbol, a panacea, a concrete manifestation of the avowedly socialistic aims. The bureaucrats—most of whom come from a higher social stratum[37]—distrust businessmen, consider them socially inferior, and think they ought to be controlled. What is better than planning for the purpose? The economists—while nurtured on the milk of neoclassical microeconomics—nevertheless have doubts about the working of the free-enterprise system because until recently most of the top economic policy advisers had their higher education in Britain, where "the emphasis was typically on the inadequacy of the Invisible Hand."[38] Thus there is a broad general agreement about the nature of economic policy, and given their common orientation, the economists can work in harmony with the rest of the policymaking framework.

The second reason why the economists have fitted in well is their realisation that their survival in the bureaucratic system depends on their willingness to transcend the limits of their expertise. Virtually every government economist ensures that he is above all a bureaucrat[39] or, as one economist put it, "an informed generalist." Indeed, economists seem to have been anxious to become bureaucrats, as exemplified by their fight for the establishment of a special service, the desire to belong to a cadre, their persistent clamour for promotion

36. According to Bhagwati and Srinivasan (p. 155), in India "an official's efficacy and possibly even his ability to get ahead in life depend significantly on whether he can operate within the broad framework of mild-to-strong left wing politics." By and large they are able to work within this environment because they often accept this ideology unconsciously. After all, economists, like all human beings, are creatures of the environment!

37. See Rosen, pp. 232-33.

38. Padma Desai and Jagdish Bhagwati, "Socialism and Indian Economic Policy," *World Development* 3, no. 4 (April 1975): 219.

39. Economists in the Indian government, as elsewhere, believe that they are not oracles to be consulted rarely (to use Sir Alec Cairncross's felicitous expression), but

through the hierarchical set-up, and their resistance to lateral entrants into the system.

It is a testimony to the neutrality of the Indian bureaucracy (including the economic component) that though the government recently changed after three decades of monolithic rule, it made no drastic changes in the advisory bodies. Some shuffling in the advisory personnel undoubtedly took place, but nothing revolutionary occurred. Professor Sukhamoy Chakravarty left the Planning Commission, and Professors Raj Krishna and D. T. Lakdawala joined. Dr. I. G. Patel, who was reputedly close to the new Prime Minister, was appointed head of the Reserve Bank of India. But given the size of the bureaucracy these changes seemed insignificant, and there was hardly any trauma in the minds or attitudes of the government economists.[40] One economist candidly admitted that it was difficult at first, but once the broad thrust of the party in power was known, "we are able to work smoothly."[41]

This continuity can be attributed to two factors. Firstly, economists claimed that they were simply bureaucrats and, as permanent civil servants, they had no option but to carry out the wishes of their political masters. As one economist put it, the political masters provide the value judgement, and the economists' duty is simply "to apply . . . economic logic to that."

Secondly, government economists claimed that there were no significant differences between the economic policy of the defeated Congress Party and that of the victorious Janata Party. In other words, the 'objective function,' that is, the total bundle of policies and overall priorities, has been stable over long periods irrespective of changes in government.

---

part of the bureaucratic structure in which they also participate in the implementation of policy. Thus they have to take everyday decisions in the process of actually implementing policy. While economists at the upper levels (e.g. Economic Advisers) are not encumbered with many administrative chores, those at the middle levels (e.g. Deputy and Assistant Economic Advisers) are also often given administrative responsibility, such as the allocation of foreign-exchange quotas, or deciding which imports should be liberalised. Another routine chore involves preparing answers to be given by the minister.

40. According to the Vice-Chairman of the Planning Commission, Indian government economists are "quite flexible in their views," and they are quite prepared to "rethink." The situation was no different when Mrs. Indira Gandhi came back to power once again in January 1980. Apart from the Planning Commission membership, very little change occured.

41. It is believed that the Annual Economic Survey which was to be presented to the Parliament soon after the Janata government came to power had to be rewritten three times to make it acceptable to the new finance minister.

The influence of economists

Many distinguished economists have served in the Indian government, and others continue to do so,[42] but their influence on policymaking is difficult to estimate precisely.[43] Some economists' influence is at least partly attributable to their association with the leaders of the Indian National Congress from the pre-independence period. For example, Professor J. J. Anjaria was involved in the deliberations of the National Planning Committee, of which Jawaharlal Nehru was chairman. Similarly Nehru knew Professor P. C. Mahalanobis long before India achieved freedom. Others can exert influence because of their formidable academic record, and when this is combined with the dazzling sophistications of modern theoretical analysis which these economists of the post-mid-1950s period display, they appear irresistible to the political and bureaucratic bosses, who, for the most part, possess only a general education.[44] Compared to these new-style econ-

42. I have excluded overseas economists who have visited India to advise on various aspects. The Planning Commission and the Indian Statistical Institute were the main organisations which absorbed these economists. Their influence, while not easy to quantify, was nevertheless not without significance. We can give a few examples here. Ragnar Frisch's work in 1955 in the Indian Statistical Institute on multi-sectoral models and Jan Sandee's work, again at the Indian Statistical Institute, in 1957/58 on linear-programming models influenced the Planning Commission economists' theoretical approach. Similarly the work of Alan Manne, Richard Eckaus and Louis Lefeber (along with similar work done by Indian theorists like Ashok Rudra, Sukhamoy Chakravarty, and Kirit Parikh) done at the Indian Planning Commission and the Indian Statistical Institute influenced the Fourth Five Year Plan's authors. W. B. Reddaway's assistance to the Perspective Planning Division is also noteworthy. See Bhagwati and Chakravarty, pp. 3–11. Again, Nicholas Kaldor's advice on the Wealth Tax and Expenditure Tax was favourably received, and implemented at least partially. Many economists from Western countries came to India in the fifties and sixties to advise. The Ford Foundation brought a number of advisers such as Sir John Crawford from Australia and David Hopper from the United States. The M.I.T. Center for International Studies Program sent people from many countries, including I. M. D. Little, J. Mirrlees, and Donald McDougall from Britain, Richard Eckaus and Arnold Harberger from the U.S.A., Trevor Swan from Australia. Occasionally economists from other governments' agencies have had a significant impact on the Indian government's economic policy. For example the joint work of D. G. Pfoutz (Supply Adviser to the U.S. Agency for International Aid in New Delhi in the 1960s) with Indian and American co-workers had, in the words of K. N. Raj (p. 233), "considerable influence on the policies urged upon the Government of India by international agencies like the World Bank and which were ultimately adopted by it."

43. According to Bhagwati and Desai (*India, Planning*, p. xiv), the four most influential economists in the Government in the fifties and sixties were K. N. Raj, I. G. Patel, V. K. Ramaswami, and Pitambar Pant.

44. Given this, it is possible for the finance minister to be completely lost, and leave everything to the bureaucrat–economic adviser axis. Writing about Y. B. Chavan, who had just been given the Finance portfolio, the *Economic and Political Weekly* commented: ". . . he is likely to be as much a prisoner of bureaucrat's hands as his predecessor . . ." 5, no. 27 (4 July 1970): 1030.

omists, with their array of mathematical, econometric, and programming techniques, the old-style literary economists must have looked drab.

The economist's impact on policy decisions depends upon his location and the nature of the policy. His influence is greater in ministries which deal with particular problems within a narrow range of options—Commerce, Industry, Transport, Railways, etc. But in the Ministry of Finance, the economists' influence is different because the 'basic notes' emanate from the various operational ministries. One senior economist claimed that the Finance Ministry was merely 'residual,' in the sense that problems come to it only if they happen to be outside the narrow range of ministerial responsibilities. The Finance Ministry's task is to see that the various individual items fit into a coherent total framework.

The Ministry of Finance is responsible for annual budgeting, expenditure control, and the important aspects of policy which have the broadest impact on the entire Indian economy, such as money, banking, taxation, and international economic relations. The Reserve Bank of India plays altogether a subordinate role, and is very much under the control of the Finance Ministry. The economists have ample opportunities to shape the overall policy framework, notwithstanding the influence of political and administrative considerations. Most members of Parliament and ministers have virtually no detailed understanding of economic affairs; hence the finance minister and his bureaucrats, including the economists, can exert a large influence on the formation of the government's macroeconomic policy. Almost all the contents of the finance minister's important annual budget speech emanate from the researches conducted in the Department of Economic Affairs.

The nature of the question at issue largely determines whether the economist will be listened to. The more specific and technical the problem, the greater the chance that his solution will be accepted. One senior economist in the Department of Economic Affairs has found that whilst his advice on the level of a government-controlled price of a minor commodity will be accepted largely without question, this will not be true of a major issue, such as the extent of deficit financing. Obviously, the greater the repercussions of a given policy, the wider the groups affected; and consequently political considerations become very relevant.

Ultimately what economists are able to accomplish depends upon their intimacy with the ministers and bureaucrats with whom they work. As one leading practitioner of the art of economic advising has said, it is a "difficult and long task to build up confidence" on the part of ministers and administrators. The senior economic advisers appreciate that this is the crucial element in determining the adviser's effectiveness. Administratively inexperienced politicians usually seem to depend much more heavily on advisers who have a greater knowledge of how the system works. In the opinion of Dr. M. Mukherjee, a close associate of Professor P. C. Mahalanobis both at the Indian Statistical Institute and at the Cabinet Secretariat, it was not Mahalanobis's expertise but his friendship with the Prime Minister and his power of persuasion that were responsible for his immense influence. Even on specific issues, such as the decision to devalue the rupee in 1966, the impact of government economists is often explained in terms of personality factors.

The 'good' economic adviser

What makes a good economic adviser? The uniform and predictable opinion is that he should possess 'technical expertise.' Although a significant proportion of those questioned did not define this attribute, they probably had in mind someone with a broad understanding of micro and macro economics, economic history, institutional structure, and economic development, and a solid grounding in statistical methods. Most urged that they used fairly elementary economic analysis and made it clear that the more involved sophisticated economic theory was not of much use. One of the top economists even declared: "I don't believe we have really any useful theory. Much of what we have is of no relevance to us." In many areas it was said that because economic theory is in a constant flux there is no "given stock of knowledge." Thus while economic theorists' views should be known, they need not be given undue importance, because "most economic advice stems from commonsense, not from what we learnt." Policy advice was given on the basis of some raw data, off-the-cuff reasoning, unstated but ever-present ideological preferences,[45] and "legal-administrative commonsense" (to use a phrase of Professor Raj Krishna), rather than on the basis of professionally rigorous economic analysis.

But if received economic theory is not all that useful, what should economists possess? Most held the view that economists should be able to understand and talk the 'language of economics' without speci-

---

45. A leading Indian government economist, Bimal Jalan, who is very much respected by other government economists, has remarked: "much of the economic advice which is offered as being technical and objective is in reality often based on personal and political value judgements about means and objectives of development and social change" (*Essays*, p. 1).

fying particular areas. While received economic theory might not offer much, the 'technique of analysing' was valuable.

Techniques of analysis acquired after a thorough study of economics, though essential, are not sufficient by themselves. It is of equal importance that the economist should be able to communicate with the generalist administrator and the professional politician.[46] The academic economist addresses himself mainly to fellow professionals whose social background, ideology, and training broadly resemble his own. But the government economist has to deal with people from all walks of life and all strata of society. If he wants to be an efficient economic adviser he should be able to put across his ideas and to persuade diverse kinds of people. The economist will obviously use his tools and knowledge of economics in arriving at a particular decision,[47] but that is only for his personal satisfaction. The politician/administrator is interested in the advice and not overmuch concerned with how it was derived. Thus a good economic adviser reaches a decision and communicates it in non-technical language. One very eminently successful economic adviser summed it up thus: 5 percent technique, 20 percent capacity for leadership, 40 percent persuasive ability, and the rest luck.

Politics and the government economist

Even these two qualities, viz. knowledge and persuasive power, are insufficient, and as one senior economist with the Ministry of Food and Agriculture said, "sturdy commonsense" and "proper judgement"[48] are essential to the good economic adviser. This means that he has to understand the political parameters of the subject on which he is asked to give advice, although the informant quickly added that economic advisers "don't actually trim their views to suit their political masters." That economic advisers have to be conscious of the views of the ministers is acknowledged universally; they cannot be oblivious to the political situation in which farmers, industrial labour, and organised business wield considerable power. Realities of life, e.g. social phenomena,

46. The government economist must also be able to work extremely quickly, sometimes producing instantaneous decisions. One economist said the civil servants must think "we are magicians" to be able to produce memoranda on quite complicated and technical subjects, at short notice.

47. Nevertheless this is very important. Some significant changes in economic policy have been preceded by rigorous theoretical work: for example, the decision to give agricultural price support; the decision to promote capital-intensive techniques; and even the policy of reducing farm size through land reforms. See Raj Krishna, p. 31.

48. 'Intuition,' 'insight,' 'hunch,' are some of the words used in this context by numerous economic advisers. This particular capacity seems to be of more importance than anything else. Indeed, ex-government economists with widely different ideas and attitudes agree on the need for these qualities.

political circumstances, and international conditions, have to be taken into account in tendering advice. As one bureaucrat put it, "we don't want textbook positions" where the economists can surround themselves with a wall of *ceteris paribus*.

Another bureaucrat-economist pointed out that as in any selling system, the economic adviser must know the client's requirements. Having this knowledge he must match his supply without "of course compromising his first principles."

The economic adviser is interested in introducing some rationality into the decisions arrived at, but in taking a particular line he has to take something that is "feasible even if it is not the ideal" if he is to be effective. In his desire to be practical he will very often have to consider the drastic political and administrative compulsions. Hence it is quite possible for the same economic adviser to give "different advice to different political masters." This does not mean dishonesty, said another economist.

Drastic and bold shifts from established policy cannot be successfully initiated by economists without the full cooperation of their political masters and the generalist administrators. If a government economist—however senior and eminent—tries to do that, he will fail; as an economist told me, "even a hundred Ashok Mitras" (referring to the former chief economic adviser, who left the government) "cannot change the society functioning within the government." Yet time and again, both politicians and administrators have suggested that the economic adviser should not be passive and wait to be asked for advice, but be an 'ideas-man,' taking the initiative in suggesting policy lines while also taking account of the realities of life.

So far the 'political masters' have apparently been fairly careful in selecting economic advisers.[49] Mr. C. Subramanyam—the former finance minister who was reputed not only to listen to experts in general and economists in particular, but also to act boldly upon their advice—said that a good economic adviser, besides having sound technical competence, must have an open mind and not ride his own particular hobby horse. He himself believed "in hearing alternative views of a wide spectrum of economists." But if an economist simply promotes his own viewpoint "we listen to him but will not act upon it." This accorded fully with the experience of Dr. Ashok Mitra, who had resigned as chief economic adviser. He claimed that his views were such that

49. It is very rare indeed for economic advisers to be mavericks. Those few who enter, leave the service as soon as they find they can achieve very little. A secretary of an economic ministry, referring to the question of selecting the right economic adviser, said: "We have been in this business for a long time. We can pick the good from bad."

the ministers either did not refer to him matters for advice or, after doing so, never acted upon it.

Because of the nature of the ideological overlay, different economists can give different prescriptions for the same malady. Hence the minister always has the possibility of finding someone to agree with his point of view. When conflicting economic advice is tendered, a minister claimed, "we use our political judgement."

On the whole, economists in the Indian government claim that politicians are not irrational. As Dr. Manmohan Singh at present member-secretary of the Planning Commission and formerly finance secretary, and himself an economist, remarked: "Economic rationality is not the only one. There are other rationalities also." In brief, then, the economist should analyse the arguments and wishes of the politicians before dismissing them as irrational. One bureaucrat felt that politicians listened to "reason and rationality" except when their particular interests were at stake, so that a specialist adviser could have a meaningful relationship with the politician.

Conclusions

One unmistakable conclusion is that economists have, on the whole, had a distinctive part to play in the government's policymaking organs. They have not only increased in numbers but have also been accepted as part of the system. Within limits, they have had considerable influence in shaping policy. Certainly the macro allocations of large investments have been the work of economists since the early fifties.

Even if economists become mere technical accessories to the politician's actions, the fact that they bring to government a knowledge of the economic world, and a systematic way of examining it in terms of costs and benefits, is of great value to the country's administration.

On the other hand, they are not entirely without thwarted hopes. While many of these frustrations are inherent in the situation of specialists in administrative structures dominated by generalists, some are also due to certain peculiarities in the Indian administrative system. As an Indian government economist with more than twenty-five years' experience has said: "The established system does not accept the economic adviser easily."

Firstly, the most important frustrations stem from the subject matter of economics, for although many accept the ideal of 'positive economics,' there nevertheless exists the hidden doubt as to exactly what economists are 'specialists' in. For example, what can the economist say that is purely 'economic' when he is asked to suggest a policy to 'ban poverty'? His advice naturally turns out to be what Peter Self characterised as the "broad but shallow"[50] kind.

The main problem is knowing what precisely the economist can do and when he should be consulted, for it is virtually impossible to find a basis on which a file should be sent laterally to the economist for his views instead of going to the next step upwards or downwards in the generalist hierachy.[51]

No civil servant could give an answer to the question, What sorts of material go to the economist? The uniform answer was, "Material pertaining to economic aspects." Nobody could clearly specify what these "economic aspects" comprised. One administrator (recalling the view of the United States Supreme Court judge on pornography: "I can't define it, but know it when I see it!") suggested that while they couldn't be precisely defined, they could still be identified for administrative purposes.

The economic adviser's role is nowhere precisely charted. In some cases there is hardly any practical distinction between an economic adviser and a joint-secretary. The adviser is simply in charge of a 'wing' and does all that a generalist administrator does. When this is not the case, there exists a considerable element of discretion in the sort of material that goes to the economist for advice. This is unavoidable, because the policies to be decided range from such major decisions as the nationalisation of the banking sector to almost insignificant matters, such as the increase of the maximum foreign exchange allowed for a student who proceeds overseas for higher studies. Because of the diversity of the policies, each is unique, and the economist operates under different sets of circumstances such as the political climate, constraints of time, the authority to whom the economist is responsible, and the data available.

Certain obvious subjects—prices, investment, costs, balance of payments, monetary policy, etc.—are automatically referred to the economist for his comments. But there are numerous less obvious subjects at the disaggregated level of analysis where the generalist administrator feels he can do without the specialist's assistance. Thus the extent to which the economist is imaginatively used depends upon the personality of the administrator. If he is very zealous of his own functions and powers, he will obviously not be interested in seeking the

50. Self, p. 211.
51. What is and what is not 'routine' is determined at the Senior Research Officer level.

economist's comments.[52] If, on the contrary, the bureaucrat possesses what an economist called the "Vision of the Administrator," then he will refer matters to the economist in order to gain fresh insights into the problem.[53]

Secondly, the economist usually has to play second fiddle in the concert. If he is involved in data gathering and analysis of information, he merely provides assistance to those responsible for decisionmaking. If, in contrast, he is an adviser, his advice will be sought only at the discretion of the politician or bureaucrat. Policy matters, for instance, cannot go to the Cabinet without the financial adviser's comments, but there is no such compulsion to present the economic adviser's views. Similarly, the field of the generalist (say the joint-secretary) is precisely defined, whereas that of the equivalent-ranking economic adviser is not; the consequence is that the economic adviser is either underutilised or overwhelmed with a multitude of routine issues which can be dealt with at a fairly low level.

Power resides with the generalists and, as elsewhere, they usually attach importance to administrative considerations, such as ease of decisionmaking, economy, short-term solutions, and a desire to avoid upsetting the political bosses.[54]

Specialists and technical personnel in general are usually smothered by the generalists at the top who preside over a bureaucratic ma-

52. There are a few of this type. As one joint-secretary in the Ministry of Industrial Development bluntly put it: "Mostly we don't need economists' advice and I don't take them."

53. When pressed for an example, the economist told how the secretary of the Department of Civil Aviation initially asked the government economists to consider the long-term implications of purchasing new aircraft for the Indian Airlines Corporation. Now such consultation is treated as a routine matter.

54. Obviously it has not been difficult for the Indian bureaucracy to come to terms with changing political conditions, or for the individual bureaucrat "to have a common mind with his minister" (to use a phrase from Lord Redcliffe-Maude; cited in Self, p. 165). In this connection it is worth mentioning the recent controversy about 'commitment' in bureaucracy. A large section of the Indian bureaucracy seems to feel that as the 'directive prinicples' are enshrined in the Constitution, it is impossible for civil servants "to take a philosophic position that they may be neutral in any of the programmes which are in furtherance of these objectives." Chaturvedi, p. 44. However, such an easy solution is not available to the economist who also has a loyalty to his discipline, which need not always point the same way as the politician-bureaucrat faces. It was said of even an "intensely loyal" economic adviser such as the late Mr. V. K. Ramaswami that "in his role as a policy maker he was sometimes a troubled man. When it came to policies he questioned, he felt an obligation to reach a calm and balanced attitude, but his friends knew what an effort this required." Obituary notice in the *Indian Economic Review*, n.s. 4, no.2 (Oct. 1969): 96. 'Commitment' often meant subservience on the bureaucrat's part, and one who resigned the Economic Advisership rather than acquiesce told me bluntly that he was at that time "serving a bunch of crooks."

chine that concerns itself with procedures and precedents.[55] But in the case of economists as specialists, the problem is accentuated because many generalist-administrators in India seem to believe that economics is not all that difficult and that they can easily perform the economist's function and even improve upon the advice tendered. Worse still, when the bureaucrat happens to know some economics, as one experienced generalist said, the "economist-administrator is a poor user of the economic adviser."

Thirdly, civil service rules for a regulatory state manned by generalists tend to be structured in a self-contained manner. India is no exception. In the words of Ramaswami R. Iyer:

> The Brahminical penchant for metaphysics and subtle argument is clearly evident in the gusto with with we pursue the elaborations and complexities of civil service rules and regulations . . . . A consequence of this tradition is perfectionism of a kind . . . to devise systems which are completely self-contained and can provide answers to all questions, leaving no need or room for a reference to anything outside them. . . .[56]

If this is the case, then why approach the economic adviser at all if the answers are contained in the rules and regulations? Thus the generalist often tends to ignore the economist.

Fourthly, as noted earlier, policymaking is an ongoing process. Moreover, policy formation rests primarily with the ministry concerned, and neither the Planning Commission nor the Finance Ministry is integrally involved.[57] One civil servant who has held very senior positions in the Ministry of Finance and Economic Affairs reported that economic advisers of different ministries ultimately had only to provide a rationalisation of their "Ministry's point of view" and defend it (sometimes against their judgement) especially against the criticisms of the Finance Ministry and the Planning Commission. Thus the economists' function was to put policies in "appropriate and appealing packages." Even the Planning Commission's economists are not entirely free agents. One informant, very much involved in the Commission's operations for a long period, said that the first four chapters of the First Five Year Plan document, which provide the plan's rationalisation, were written jointly by Professor K. N. Raj and Dr. K. S. Krishnaswamy under the supervision of Professor J. J. Anjaria. Apparently Mr. Gulzarilal Nanda, the then Planning Minister, personally asked

55. See De, pp. 712–13.
56. Iyer, p. 706.
57. See Dayal, "The Crisis," p. 13.

this team to expand the chapter on employment from its original six pages to the fifty pages it eventually became so that it would look impressive. As is well-known, the First Five Year Plan came out years after the Plan was supposed to have been conceived and launched. This illustrates how the economist can be trapped within the bureaucratic structure and frustrated, not only when the politicians' pragmatic interest overrides their considered judgements, but also by the system itself.[58]

It may be added that the economist is often personally and professionally unsuited to working within a system which robs him of his intellectual autonomy. But this has not, as yet, led in India to the sort of wholesale flight from the bureaucracy that Merton reported in the United States.[59]

Economists and other specialists in India rarely resign, because the public service has unequalled social and financial advantages. Indeed, as many generalist-administrators reported, even those economists who come into government service for short-term assignments endeavour to get themselves appointed to permanent positions.[60]

One high-ranking government economist confessed: "I offered to resign on the issue of . . . . But on how many things that you disagree with can you do so?" Hence instead of opting out of the system, the economist adjusts himself to its demands. Sometimes, as Professor

58. A typical example of disregarded advice which an economic adviser must tolerate is given by Dr. Mitra, p. 38: "One day I find a note from the Department of Food that food prices are rising in Bihar and U.P. (Uttar Pradesh) and we must do something about it. People are in distress. And what can we do about it? One major feature then is that the State Governments in both States are rather inefficient. They are not able to maintain the public distribution system. The off take from the ration and fair price shops is very poor. But something has to be done. The Government cannot make any impact. This is what the note suggested: In both U.P. and Bihar, there is an extensive network of private trading agencies and private traders are experienced in dealing with foodgrains. Therefore, the Government should really sell a part of its public stock of grains to private traders in Bihar and U.P. and the private traders in their turn will distribute the foodgrains. The conclusion was that 3 million tonnes of foodgrains should be straightaway released to the private traders. Then I exploded. I issued a stiff note. But the policy was implemented. From March '72 to September '72 our entire foodgrain stock in the public sector came down from 9 million tonnes to something like 2 million tonnes. Some 3 million tonnes was handed over to the private traders at around Rs. 1.15 a kilo which these people held back and sold later in the season for Rs. 3.50 a kilo."

59. R. K. Merton, supra n.31, p. 276.

60. According to Balraj Mehta (p. 36) many economists in government "are not willing to quit yet but are openly expressing their doubts about the worth of their contribution to the nation's welfare and development. There are of course many others who will remain in the positions they occupy for purely career considerations. But even they are found to be pathetically apologetic about their role." This point has been echoed by university economists as well. See Dr. B. Datta, "Role of the Economist," his presidential address to the Indian Economic Association, p. 214.

Bardhan has charged (Bardhan, p. 372), the economist in government takes the "easy way out of essentially playing the game as the politicians want him to and or providing them the opportunity to wrap their designs with the respectability of his technical expertise."[61] But perhaps more often he tries to use—through formal or informal channels—whatever influence he has to make policy decisions as informed and rational as possible.

Success in this depends upon random factors, such as his personality and the relationships he manages to establish with the bureaucrats, politicians, and his own subordinate economists. On the whole it would appear that economists have been grafted on to the system as an afterthought. In other words, economic analysis is not yet systematically built into the administrative structure as an integral part of the decisionmaking processes. The result of this informality and lack of institutionalisation is that while there are a number of brilliant individual performers, there is neither a tradition nor a framework which can utilise their full potential. Instead, the individual economists are embedded in the administration at various points as if haphazardly. Inasmuch as they form part of the bureaucracy, they either adopt bureaucratic mores and avoid the uncertainties involved in departures from established procedures or they remain frustrated, having entered the system and finding nowhere else to go.

My sincere thanks are due to the many government and academic economists, politicians including ministers, and permanent civil servants who discussed with me various aspects of the subject of the study. As the informants wished to remain anonymous, I have refrained from identifying them in the text.

61. See also Shourie, "Economics, Economists and Policy-Makers," pp. 147–56. Shourie refers to a striking feature of the economists in Indian government, namely "the enthusiasm with which some of them take on the role of legitimisers" (p. 153).

Bibliography

Appleby, Paul A. *Public Administration in India: Report of a Survey*, New Delhi, 1953.
———. *Re-examination of India's Administrative System with Special Reference to Administration of Government's Industrial and Commercial Enterprises*. New Delhi, 1956.
Association of Indian Universities. *Universities Handbook, India*. New Delhi, 1975.
Bardhan, Pranab. "On Welfarism versus Radicalism in Planning." *Economic and Political Weekly* 9, no. 9 (2 March 1974).
Bhagwati, Jagdish, and Sukhamoy Chakravarty. "Contributions to Indian Economic Analysis: A Survey." *American Economic Review* 59, no. 4, part 2, suppl. (Sept. 1969).

————, and Padma Desai. *India, Planning for Industrialisation: Industrialisation and Trade Policies Since 1951*. London, 1970.

————, and Padma Desai. "Socialism and Indian Economic Policy." *World Development* 3, no. 4 (April 1975).

————, and T. N. Srinivasan. *Foreign Trade Regimes and Economic Development: India*. New York, 1975.

Bhalerao, C. N. *Public Service Commissions in India: A Study*. Delhi, 1966.

Brecher, Michael. *Nehru: A Political Biography*. London, 1959.

Chaturvedi, Mrigendra. "Commitment in Civil Service." *Indian Journal of Public Administration (I.J.P.A.)* 17, no. 1 (Jan.–March 1971).

Chaturvedi, T. N. *Quest for Commitment in Public Services*. Cabinet Secretariat, Government of India. New Delhi, May 1975.

Curzon, G. N., Lord. "Reforms in the System of Filing, Noting and Interdepartmental References." *I.J.P.A.* 12, no. 3 (July–Sept. 1966).

Dasgupta, A. K. *Planning and Economic Growth*. London, 1965.

Datta, B. "The Role of the Economist." *Indian Economic Journal* 22, no. 3 (Jan.–March 1976).

Dayal, Ishwar. "The Crisis in Administration." *Quest*, no. 97 (Sept.–Oct. 1975).

————, K. Mathur, A. Datta, and U. K. Banerjee. *Dynamics of Formulating Policy in Government of India: Machinery for Policy Development*. Delhi, 1976.

De, Nitish R. "Public Administration and Plan Implementation." *I.J.P.A.* 20, no. 4 (Oct.–Dec. 1974).

Deshmukh, C. D. "The Role of the Central Services in Economic Development." *I.J.P.A.* 7, no. 2 (April–June 1972).

Faber, Mike, and Dudley Seers, eds. *The Crisis in Planning*, vol. 1. London, 1972.

Gadgil, D.R. *Indian Planning and the Planning Commission*. Laski Memorial Lectures. Ahmedabad, 1958.

Goldhamer, Herbert. *The Adviser*. New York, 1978.

Gorwala, A. D. *Report on Public Administration*. Delhi, 1951.

Government of India. *Occupational and Educational Pattern in India: Public Sector*. Issued by the Directorate of Employment and Training.

————. *National Classification of Occupations*. New Delhi, 1968.

————. *Report on Indian and State Administrative Services and Problems of District Administration*. By V. T. Krishnamachari. New Delhi, Aug. 1962.

————. Committee on Unemployment. *Report of the Panel on the Assessment of Unemployment and Underemployment*. New Delhi, 1972.

————. *Notes on Office Procedure*. New Delhi, 1975.

————.Organisational Set-Up and Functions of the Ministries/Departments of the Government of India. 5th ed. New Delhi, 1974.

————. *Report of the Third Central Pay Commission*. Delhi, 1973.

Government of India. Administrative Reforms Commission. Reports of Study Teams. 1. *Machinery of the Government of India and Its Procedures of Work*. Part 1 (Delhi, 1967). Part 2 (Delhi, 1968).

————. 2. *Machinery for Planning* (1967).

————. 3. *Financial Administration* (1967).

————. 4. *Public Sector Undertakings* (1967).

————. 5. *On Recruitment, Selection, U.P.S.C. State P.S.C.s and Training* (1967).

Haggerty, William J. *Higher and Professional Education in India*. Washington, 1969.

Hanson, A. H. *The Process of Planning: A Study of India's Five Year Plans 1950–1964*. London, 1966.

Iengar, H. V. R. *Planning in India*. Delhi, 1974.

Indian Council of Social Science Research. *A Survey of Research in Economics*: vol. 1, *Methods and Techniques*. Bombay, 1977.

Indian Economic Association. *The Diamond Jubilee Commemoration Volume*. Madras, 1977.

Iyer, Ramaswami R. "Understanding Our Bureaucracy." *I.J.P.A.* 12, no. 4 (Oct.–Dec. 1966).

Jalan, Bimal. *Essays in Development Policy*. Delhi, 1975.

Jha, L. K. "Economic Administration: A Personal View." *The Administrator* (Journal of Lal Bahadur Shastri National Academy of Administration) 21, no. 2 (Summer 1976).

Khosla, R. P. "Future of Generalist." *I.J.P.A.* 14, no. 1 (Jan.–March 1968).

Krishna, Raj. "Economic Research in India: A Brief Survey of Trends, Gaps and Possible Priorities." Mimeographed, Jan. 1974.

Krishnamachari, V. T. *Planning in India: Theory and Practice*. 2d edition. Bombay, 1977.

Kumar, Virendra. *Committees and Commissions in India 1947–1973*. 7 vols. Delhi, 1975–77.

Lal Bahadur Shastri National Academy of Administration. *Probationer's Handbook*. Mussoorie, 1977.

Maheshwari, Shriram. "Training in Public Administration in India." *I.J.P.A.* 17, no. 4 (Oct.–Dec. 1971).

Malenbaum, W. *Prospects for Indian Development*. London, 1962.

Mars, Theo. "The National Academy of Administration: Normative Vocabularies and Organisational Reality." In Bernard Schaffer, ed., *Administrative Training and Development: A Comparative Study of East Africa, Zambia, Pakistan and India*. New York, 1974.

Mehta, Balraj. *Failures of Indian Planning*. New Delhi, 1974.

———. "Rise and Fall of Planning." *Indian Express*, 27 May 1977.

Misra, B. B. *The Administrative History of India 1834–1947*. London, 1970.

Mitra, Ashok. Interview, *Sunday* 5, no. 13 (12 June 1977).

Muttalib, M. A. *The Union Public Service Commission*. New Delhi, 1967.

Pai Panandikar, V. A. "Study of Public Administration in India." In *A Survey of Research in Public Administration*, vol. 1. Bombay, 1975.

———. *Government Systems and Development*. Bombay, 1975.

Paranjape, H. K. *The Reorganised Planning Commission: A Study in the Implementation of Administrative Reforms*. Delhi, 1970.

———. *Poverty of Policy and Other Essays in Economic Policy and Administration*. Bombay, 1976.

Potter, David C. "The Shaping of Young Recruits in the Indian Civil Service." *I.J.P.A.* 23, no. 4 (Oct.–Dec. 1977).

Prasad, B. *The Indian Administrative Service*. New Delhi, 1960.

Raj. K. N. "Growth and Stagnation in Indian Industrial Development." *Economic and Political Weekly* 11, nos. 5, 6, 7 (Feb. 1976).

Rosen, George. *Democracy and Economic Change in India*. Berkeley, 1967.

Self, Peter. *Administrative Theories and Politics: An Inquiry into the Structure and Processes of Modern Government*. London, 1972.

Shourie, Arun. "Controls and the Current Situation: Why Not Let the Hounds Run?" *Economic and Political Weekly* 8, nos. 31, 32, 33 (Aug. 1933).

————. "Economics, Economists and Policy-Makers." *Economic and Political Weekly*, Annual Number 1975, vol. 10, nos. 5, 6, 7.

Simha, S. L. N. *Essays on Finance*. Bombay, 1967.

————. *All the Bank's Men*. Madras, 1976.

————. "Economists' Role in Policy Making." *The Hindu*, 29 Dec. 1975.

Singh, Batuk. *The Union Public Service Commission*. New Delhi, 1974.

Singhvi, L. M. "Parliament in the Indian Political System." In A. M. Kornberg and L. D. Musolf, eds., *Legislatures in Developmental Perspective*. (Durham, N.C., 1970).

Sivaraman, B. *The Role of Civil Services in Administration of India*. Department of Personnel, Cabinet Secretariat. New Delhi, Sept. 1970.

Srinivasavaradan, T. C. A. "Some Aspects of the I.A.S." *I.J.P.A.* 7, no. 1 (Jan.–March 1961).

Subramanian, V. *Social Background of India's Administrators*. New Delhi, 1971.

Swaroop, S. N. *Background of the I.A.S. Officers: A Comparative Study*. Cabinet Secretariat. New Delhi, Aug. 1971.

Taub, R. P. *Bureaucrats Under Stress*. Berkeley, 1969.

Thakur, R. N. *The All India Services: A Study of Their Origin and Growth*. Patna, 1969.

Union Public Service Commission. *Annual Reports*.

Vakil, C. N. "Ministers and Economists." *Indian Express*, 1 May 1978.

Weiner, Myron. "Political Interviewing." In Robert E. Ward et al., *Studying Politics Abroad: Field Research in the Developing Areas* (Boston, 1964).

Norway: the powerful servants

Trond Bergh

Introduction

Norway's Minister of Finance from 1973 to 1979, Mr. Per Kleppe, Labor politician and economist, expressed some years ago the opinion that his country, particularly in contrast with Great Britain, had lately succeeded in developing a new economic policy free of "conventional thinking on economic interrelations." He explained Norway's eminence by pointing out that while there were almost "watertight bulkheads between the government and the country's excellent economists in Great Britain," the Norwegian situation was characterized by intimate cooperation between politicians and economic experts. The new economic policy was first and foremost a result of practical application of "the work of a generation with economic models in the spirit of Ragnar Frisch."[1]

Although Kleppe's conception of the British situation may be contested, this is a far from unusual description of the role of economists in Norwegian economic policymaking. In public debates throughout the whole postwar period economists have been given a considerable share of the honor and the blame for the development of the economy because of their alleged influence on governmental economic policy. The journalistic search for powerful civil servants has usually concentrated on economists.[2] The economists themselves have tried to modify this impression by pointing out their servant relationship to the government. On the other hand they have done little to correct the impression that they are entitled to a considerable share of the honor for the postwar economic success. As a whole, their influence has been most consistently stressed, and warned against, by their main opponents in the political arena, i.e. leading business organizations and, until they came into office themselves, also the non-socialist parties. Within the professional community they have been particularly strongly attacked for undue exercise of power by the emerging social sciences.

1. *Dagbladet*, 23 Oct. 1976.
2. Mr. Eivind Erichsen, the top economic adviser in the Ministry of Finance, has, for example, been described as "the most influential civil servant in Norway" (*Aftenposten*, 11 Oct. 1973).

However, whether the commonly accepted picture of the powerful economics profession is in accordance with reality has never been systematically studied. The methodological problems are, of course, formidable, but a combination of different approaches, including historical background studies and detailed case studies, no doubt will enhance our insight into the role and importance of economists in government. Besides, the more troubled economic waters of the 1970s and the new wave of criticism against Keynesian macroeconomics obviously provide new and stimulating starting points for a reconsideration of the role of government and of government economists. Is, for example, the picture of the powerful economics profession in Norway rather a myth nourished by a general overestimation of the role of government and by the economic stability of the 1950s and 1960s?

In this essay attention will primarily be concentrated on the postwar period. However, we will also point out certain earlier developments. These will help to explain why economists have been increasingly employed in the government machinery and will provide some background insights into their role and functions after 1945.

In the Norwegian case there are two main reasons for concentrating on the postwar period. The first is that it was not until after the war that the new generation of 'Frischian' economists had 'grown up' and, as a critic put it, were "ready to be let loose on a defenceless society."[3] The other reason is the radical change in the economists' status and positions in government after the war. Generally speaking, in the interwar years economists had had to content themselves with outside influence on economic policy, e.g. through professional journals and newspapers and only sporadically as members of public commissions, whereas since 1945 a considerable number of economists have been part of the political and administrative apparatus responsible for the formulation and implementation of economic policy. In 1938 there were only some 20 economists in the ministries, of whom almost all were in lower level jobs. By 1950, however, the number had increased to about 100, of whom a considerable number occupied leading administrative posts.[4]

The contrast between the interwar and the postwar period can eas-

3. The Conservative leader Mr. C. J. Hambro in a parliamentary debate on economic policy and planning in 1947 (*Stortingstidende 1947*, p. 392).
4. About 40 of these 100 economists were 'social economists' graduated from the University of Oslo from 1939 onwards, i.e. after the introduction of a new 'social economics' degree whose chief architect was Professor Frisch. This degree succeeded the 'state economics' degree, which had been introduced in 1905. In 1950 there were about 40 'state economists' in the ministries as well. The remaining 20 were business economists graduated from the Norwegian School of Economics and Business Administration in Bergen, which was founded in 1937. Most of them were employed on a temporary basis.

ily be exaggerated, for there are instances in which economists played extremely important parts in economic policymaking between the wars, the most powerful of all being Mr. Nicolai Rygg, Governor of the Bank of Norway and architect of a heatedly disputed monetary policy.[5] Nevertheless, the conventional view is that the theoretical and technical revolution initiated in the 1930s, and the massive employment of economists on almost all levels of the civil service after the war, have, on the whole, made the economics profession more influential and instrumental in the economic policymaking process and have thereby given economic 'rationality' a more decisive role in the shaping of economic policy.

In a study of a profession, which this primarily is, the obvious criterion for the definition of an 'economist' will be formal, university-level education. In Norway there are two different types of education in economics aspiring to professional status. The University of Oslo offers a degree in "social economics," and the Norwegian School of Economics and Business Administration in Bergen a degree in business economics. Only graduates from these two institutions are generally accepted as 'economists.'[6] Thus, the number of Norwegian economists is fairly small. In 1977 there were some 6,500 economists, of whom a little more than 5,000 were business economists. In contrast with most of the countries represented in this collection, economics in Norway is an elitist education.

The standard definition of a 'professional' underlines the combination of education and occupation. Consequently we should not necessarily include all persons in government with an educational background in economics, but only those who do 'economic' work. However, the difficulties involved in deciding exactly what 'economic' work is and for what kinds of functions economics actually qualifies limit the usefulness of this definition in our case. One way out of this definitional problem is to regard as economists only those in posts which are explicitly defined as economist posts by the employer. But in Norway this type of job description system has only relatively recently been established and will not give any guidance to the early postwar years. On the other hand, unlike the situation in Britain, there is little reason to assume that there has been any significant number of economists in government doing primarily 'non-economic' work, if we apply a fairly wide definition of 'economic' functions. Therefore, we may generally

5. Traditionally the director of the Central Bureau of Statistics was an economist as well.

6. There is also a private institute in Oslo (Bedriftsøkonomisk Institutt) which educates business economists. However, graduates from this institute are usually not regarded as having the same status as the business economists graduated in Bergen.

include all economists who have obtained one of the two economics degrees.

In addition to the two economics degrees, some elements of economics are integrated into a few other academic disciplines. During the nineteenth century the economics course for law students was the only university education in the discipline, and law students still read some economics. Agriculturalists and engineers are also being offered courses in economics. For our purpose, jurists' knowledge of economics and its importance for the relationship between economists and jurists in government will be of particular interest.

The two economics degrees are in several respects very different. The social economics education was primarily intended to fill the need for civil service economists, while the business economics education was established to produce economists for the private sector. Thus, in reality there are not one, but two economics professions, and there are two different professional organizations. Here we shall focus on the social economics profession. However, since the late 1950s the demarcation line between the labor markets of social economists and business economists has become less sharp, and there is now a considerable number of business economists in the civil service who must be included in this study.

In addition to an examination of professional economists and related professions, we must also turn our attention to the level and nature of economic literacy among politicians and the general public. This is a difficult but highly relevant theme. We may, for example, assume that the extent of amateur knowledge influences the position of professional economists in government in a variety of ways.

This essay is primarily designed to contribute to introducing a new field of research; therefore more questions will be asked than answered. The investigation is meant to include most of the civil service.[7] However, after presenting our findings on the concentration of government economists we shall focus on the ministries responsible for macroeconomic planning and management, where the most influential economists are supposed to be found.

Historical and contemporary background

Today most governments in industrialized countries, whatever their political and ideological flavor, employ a considerable number of

7. Our definition of the civil service will include the following three categories as defined by the Central Bureau of Statistics: (1) the ministries and the Audit Department, (2) other Central Administration departments, and (3) other civil services. Excluded are schools, universities, and equivalent institutions, government enterprises, defense, and medical and health services.

economists. This general long-term trend has inspired some general explanations which emphasize the trend towards increasing state intervention and the links between industrialization and professionalization. Nevertheless the wide divergencies of individual nations within this common framework are perhaps more interesting than the general trend, for the timing and scale of the introduction of economists in government vary considerably from country to country, and these variations have a direct bearing on the actual functioning of government economists.

The ideal of the rule of law was the fundamental ideological element governing the functions of the state in Norway in the nineteenth century. The philosophy was that the state, which Norwegian historians have called the civil servant state, should be 'tied' by general rules and laws in order to obtain maximum predictability in its performance. In such a system the making and interpretation of law became the state's main function, and thus the state was in a sense a non-political body. The state functions were in the hands of the civil servants, recruited almost exclusively from the law profession, which could supply the state with the skills and knowledge it needed. In 1889, 98 percent of all the civil servants with university education in the ministries were jurists.[8] Thus, historically Norway has been part of the continental *Rechtsstaat* tradition and its *Juristenmonopol*.[9]

As in the case of Germany, this system was the object of continuous criticism even during its golden age in the nineteenth century. But it was only towards the end of the century that essential changes took place. In 1884 parliamentary rule was introduced in Norway, and this change in constitutional practice strongly accelerated the development away from the dominance of the rule of law and towards discretionary politics based on electoral strength. At about the same time Norway entered a relatively late but rapid process of industrialization which also contributed to the extension of state responsibilities within industrial as well as social policy.

This type of development, described by Habermas as a transition from *Ordnungspolitik* to *Prozesspolitik*, led the state to undertake com-

8. Wilhelm Aubert, "Norske jurister: En yrkesgruppe gjennom 150 år," *Tidsskrift for rettsvitenskap* 77 (1964): 311.

9. The Norwegian 'rule of law' state is analyzed by Francis Sejersted in "Rettsstaten og den selvdestruerende makt—Noen refleksjoner over det 19 århundres embedsmannsstat," in Rune Slagstad, ed., *Om staten* (Oslo, 1978), pp. 46–85.

Although the *Juristenmonopol* is the most characteristic feature of the nineteenth-century civil service, too little attention has been paid to the growth of technical expertise (for example, engineers) which took place from the 1840s on onwards. This new technical staff were probably more instrumental in the economic modernization of Norway in this century than the jurists.

mitments that presupposed skills and knowledge different from those provided by jurists. Initially the jurists were challenged by such new specialist professions as engineers and agriculturists. These new professions were integrated into the civil service by the establishment of new specialist institutions, under administrative and juridical surveillance of a permanent secretary, either outside or within the ministries. Thus, this first wave of professionalism did not essentially weaken the *Juristenmonopol* on generalist functions, and as late as 1940, 79 percent of the civil servants in the ministries were still jurists.[10] Consequently, the economics profession was the first to threaten seriously the status quo.

Although the economists started to aspire to generalist jobs as late as after the Second World War, the *idea* of an alternative generalist education was old. As early as by the turn of the century the need for an economics and social science education for civil servants as a supplement to and partly as a substitute for law was strongly advocated both outside and inside the civil service. It was argued that law had become too limited and no longer met the demand for knowledge in a state whose functions were no longer mainly juridical, but economic.[11] However, as long as such an alternative knowledge and profession was lacking, the jurists' position remained unchanged. It was only towards the end of the 1930s, when Professor Ragnar Frisch (1895–1973) drastically reformed Norwegian economics, that the discipline could aspire to full academic and professional status. Thus, the new role of economists after the war can be regarded as a natural consequence of professional developments.

We know from countries like Great Britain and Germany that a strong established civil service tradition can effectively prevent changes in state functions as well as in recruitment policy. In Germany the jurists have succeeded in protecting their monopoly even since 1945.[12] A somewhat similar, but weaker, element of tradition can also be found in the Norwegian case and can, to some extent, explain why some 45 percent of the professionals in the ministries are still jurists.[13] We may, probably, assume that jurists have tended to recruit jurists, even in cases where they were not the obvious choices, although some leading civil service jurists from the turn of the century have been ad-

10. Aubert, p. 312.
11. See for example, Dr. Sigurd Ibsen in *Samtiden*, 1896, p. 205, and Professor Lie Henriksen in *Statsøkonomisk Tidsskrift* 14 (1900): 134.
12. John A. Armstrong, *The European Administrative Elite* (Princeton, 1973), p. 173.
13. Per Lægreid and Johan P. Olsen, *Byråkrati og beslutninger* (Bergen, 1978), p. 100.

vocates of a new generalist education based on social sciences and in particular on economics. Nevertheless, their dominant position at the University of Oslo (until 1948 the only Norwegian university) was the jurists' most effective means of protecting their generalist monopoly.

The jurists were largely responsible for the late development of economics as an academic discipline. Although from the beginning of the century onwards they had acknowledged the need for economics in the civil service, until the 1930s they argued that the economics element in the law degree was sufficient to meet this need. When the first degree in economics was introduced in 1905, many leading jurists considered that it ought mainly to function as an additional education for jurists. However in the long run, given the progress in economics, this strategy could not work. Yet even in 1934, when the government proposed to establish a degree examination in economics which would, in practice, open up generalist jobs for economists, the jurists argued—in vain—against it. They were willing to accept economists as specialists, but not as generalists.[14]

Having lost their monopoly of economic knowledge and the battle over educational reforms, the jurists' possibilities of retaining their *Juristenmonopol* had weakened considerably. They had less power than their German counterparts, for their civil service organization did not possess the same kind of authority, and they had never had the opportunity to exercise control through special entrance examinations or post-entrance education. Indeed, the civil service jurists offered surprisingly little resistance when, from 1945 onwards, the government decided to introduce the economists as a new and important civil service profession. One reason was that the newcomers did not invade the existing jurist precincts, but acquired administrative and professional leadership in quite new areas, such as macroeconomic planning, and in new agencies where juridical knowledge was definitely of minor importance. Perhaps even more important was the fact that the jurists no longer had any reason to regard the advent of a new civil service profession as a threat to their position in the labor market. By contrast with the interwar period, the first ten to fifteen postwar years were characterized by an enormous surplus demand for professionals, especially for jurists, even in the civil service.[15]

Among the political parties, the Liberals were the first to press for the modification of the *Juristenmonopol* as an element in the party's

14. For the jurists' strategy see the following government documents: Ot. prp. [Parliamentary Bill] 27 (1904–5) and Ot. prp. 15 (1934).

15. One consequence of the demand surplus was that the percentage of non-professionals in the ministries rose sharply after the war.

traditional opposition to centralized state authorities. Later the Labor Party reinforced the scepticism towards the civil service jurists, although historically this party had been an opponent rather than a spokesman for Norwegian economics, which was regarded as a typical 'bourgeois' discipline. However, this attitude changed during the 1930s because the Labor Party, more easily than any other party, could identify itself with the new tendencies in economics associated with Keynesianism and planning. These ideas revived the party's interest in educational reforms and new research in economics. The introduction of the new degree in economics at the University of Oslo in 1934 was more actively supported by the Labor Party than by any other party.

This new awareness of economics was a consequence of new tendencies in the party's ideological orientation. In the 1920s the Norwegian Labor Party was more radical and revolutionary than its Scandinavian counterparts. Its reformist ideology was established in the early 1930s, and in 1935 it formed a minority government. However, despite cooperation with Frisch on a program to overcome the economic crisis, its prewar economic policy had very few Keynesian elements.[16] But during the war, belief in the 'new' economics and the possibility of planning or managing the economy gained new ground. Together with the new challenge presented by the need for rapid and effective postwar reconstruction these developments finally persuaded the party to adopt a new economic policy in 1945 based on a combination of economic planning and Keynesian ideas on monetary and fiscal policy with the three main policy objectives of full employment, economic growth, and income redistribution. Thus, for the Labor Party the employment of economists in government was a means of materializing its reformist social-democratic ideology.

Labor's attempt to establish an alternative to market forces was not the only line of development leading to calls for more public employment of economic experts. During the 1930s leading industrialists were even more enthusiastic advocates of a more 'rational' economic policy (inspired, for example, by William Beveridge's idea of an economic general staff) based on economic research and expert advice as a reaction against the strong tendencies towards political opportunism and indecision that characterized the interwar years. In these circles, too, economic 'rationality' was seen as a means of stopping the expansion of the public sector and state interventionism.[17] However, by their

16. On the Labor Party and Keynesianism during the 1930s, see Helge W. Norvik, "Krisepolitikk og den teoretiske nyorientering av den økonomiske politikken i Norge i 1930-årene," *Historisk Tidsskrift* 56, no. 3 (1977).

17. The industrialist who most forcefully advocated public employment of economic experts was Mr. Johan Throne Holst.

political and financial support for developing Norwegian economics they actually made considerable contributions to the establishment of what many industrialists later labeled the socialist Oslo School in economics.

During the German occupation, by contrast with Great Britain and the U.S.A., economists were not systematically absorbed into government service. The government in exile established a small administration in London in which a few economists were given prominent positions. But the real breakthrough came after the war, when economists in some countries were leaving the government service. In Norway the position obtained during the early postwar years was never lost.

Although war damage was relatively small in Norway, the war was the immediate cause of the breakthrough. Wartime regulations were maintained longer in Norway than in most countries, thereby creating a greater demand for qualified civil servants than the academic professions could meet. But this wartime emergency was not unique in its impact on recruitment policy, and the decisive reason for change was the introduction of the 'new economic policy,' especially the ambitious macroeconomic planning. Indeed, the first important 'cell' of economic planners was a national budget office which was established in November 1945.

Thus the breakthrough for economists in government was the result of a combination of long-term developments and immediate postwar pressures. The situation in 1945 facilitated the realization of civil service changes advocated since the turn of the century and which even then would have been a natural response to changes in the state's functions. The delay was due to a combination of civil service tradition, political hesitation, and the backwardness of Norwegian economics. During the 1930s Norwegian economics emerged as an academic discipline and developed in a direction which made the Labor Party, the new leading party, its natural political ally. These developments were accelerated during the war and given their first practical application in 1945.

The continued political dominance of Labor largely explains why the first few postwar years were not an isolated episode for economists in government. From 1935 to 1965 the Labor Party was continuously in power, and with a majority between 1945 and 1961, hence the political conditions for a systematic and continuous development of an activist economic policy were more favorable than in most Western countries. The economic growth and stability further explains both Labor's dominance and the economists' civil service success, for they got their fair share of credit for the apparent success of economic policy and planning. Growth rates were especially high during the reconstruction period 1946–50, when the economists were establishing themselves in the government offices.[18] No doubt these years were unusually favorable for the exercise of their new role, and their prestige would surely have been more doubtful in a less favorable economic climate.

However, the growth in the number of government economists has not exactly paralleled the economy's growth rate. On the contrary, it has had very distinctive phases of expansion and stagnation. The first phase of expansion lasted until the mid-1950s, when the number of economists in the ministries increased from about 20 to 125.[19] Then followed a long period of stagnation lasting to the end of the 1960s, and the numbers did not increase substantially again until the 1970s. Thus the development of a more comprehensive system of economic planning and management has not been automatically followed up by the employment of more economists in government. By and large, during the first postwar years, planning policy was concentrated on the coordination of rationing and the special regulations necessitated by economic reconstruction. But ambitions were higher for example with national budgeting, the pride of Norwegian government economists and the most important tool of short-term (one year) planning, which was regarded as being adaptable to all kinds of economic situations and compatible with a variety of ends and means. Consequently, the planning apparatus was not merely maintained, but strengthened and expanded during the 1950s. New sectors of the economy were included in the national budget model. Regional and physical planning was introduced, and the national budgets were supplemented by long-term (four year) programs. While most countries had regarded the long-term plans for the OEEC as a once-for-all event, the Norwegian Labor government saw it as the starting point for permanent long-term planning.[20]

The early 1950s also saw a comprehensive change of economic policy instruments. The detailed microlevel regulations were abolished and general fiscal and monetary instruments took their place, and although this change may have diminished the capacity for effective economic management, it increased the need for economic analysis.

The 1960s were characterized by several innovations in economic policymaking and planning. Early in the decade Norway, like many other countries, witnessed a revival of interest in planning against the background of falling rates of growth. This resulted in a strengthening

18. On the political and economic development in Norway after 1945, see Trond Bergh and Helge Pharo, eds., *Vekst og velstand. Norsk politisk historie 1945–1965* (Oslo, 1977).
19. Of the 125 economists about 70 were social economists, 30 state economists, and 25 business economists.
20. The development of national budgeting in Norway after 1945 is described by Petter Jakob Bjerve in *Trends in Quantitative Economic Planning in Norway* (Oslo, 1968).

of medium- and long-term planning and the introduction of long-term state budgeting.[21] Another expanding sector was the so-called sector planning, leading to the establishment of planning divisions in most government ministries. Sector planning was designed as an extension of central macroeconomic planning, but in practice it increased the problems of central coordination.

Given this background, the stagnation in the number of government economists is somewhat surprising. By contrast with Britain, the Norwegian planning renaissance was not accompanied by any explosion in the employment of economists in government. The early developments in Norwegian planning during the 1940s and 1950s provide a partial explanation, but the main reason lies on the supply side. From the early 1950s onwards there was a decline of interest in the study of social economics and in the status of the Oslo School of economics.

Consequently, from the mid 1950s onwards the supply of social economists was insufficient to meet the government demand for economists, with the result that the Norwegian government lost its former prominent position among Western countries as a leading employer of economists. These professional obstacles were more important than the fact that the non-socialist parties formed a coalition government in 1965. Indeed the government maintained and strengthened the planning apparatus, and the tendency to identify the Oslo School with socialism was diminishing.

Up to this point the development of macroeconomic planning and management had been the principal dynamic element in the employment of economists in government. During the second wave of expansion, starting in the early 1970s, the situation changed somewhat. Given the economic problems of the 1970s, general macroeconomic planning has been on the defensive. Instead, new importance was first attached to selective instruments and microeconomic planning. Lately, however, there has been a tendency towards a renaissance for a more comprehensive use of the market forces, particularly within monetary policy.

The idea of comprehensive economic planning having been questioned, the status of government economists has definitely been declining. Even when the apparatus for long-term planning was considerably strengthened in January 1980 by the establishment of a ministry of long-term planning, the new scepticism towards economists was illustrated by the fact that most of the new jobs were filled not by economists but by sociologists and other social scientists.

21. On long-term and short-term plans, see Trond Bergh, "Ideal and Reality in Norwegian Macroeconomic Planning 1945–1965," *Scandinavian Journal of History* 3 (1978): 75 ff.

Thus the main expanding sectors for economists have not been the central-planning institutions but agencies dealing with industrial developments and employment problems and other sectors which have been hit by the economic 'crisis.' In addition, the very extensive state participation in North Sea oil exploitation has created a new and important market for economists in the civil service. In contrast with earlier decades, the 1970s have been characterized by both increase and spread of the employment of economists in government.

The strong political will behind the introduction of economists in the Norwegian civil service must have enhanced the economists' potential influence as a civil service profession. In the end, even the civil service jurists regarded the newcomers without distrust. The political aim of using the economists as instruments in a new departure in economic planning and policymaking may account for the integration of the planning economists into the centers of the political and bureaucratic decisionmaking processes. The planning agencies have never had such semi-independent, semi-official status as, for example, in Holland, Sweden, and to some extent Great Britain. (Whether this 'Norwegian' solution in the long run and under all circumstances is favorable from the point of view of the economists may, of course, be questioned.)

The civil service and the market for economists

The traditional and still fashionable way of locating power is by identifying persons in top jobs. However, concentration is no longer so much upon individuals as upon the *network* of top positions in formal organizations. One obvious deficiency is the disregard of informal or 'hidden' centers of power, but in the Norwegian case this is probably no fundamental criticism, given the smallness and openness of the political and bureaucratic systems and the strong tradition of highly formalized civil service procedures.[22]

Among the approximately 7,000 professional economists (social and business economists) in Norway, probably two thirds today work in the private sector. However, among the social economists, which form the smaller group, there is a clear majority of public (state, regional, and local) employees. In 1977 there were a little more than 1,000 social economists in public jobs; and of these, some 600 were working in the state (central government). About one third of these 600 were employed in the ministries. But while about 11 percent of the total

22. One of the most serious criticisms against studies of power and influence is that the conclusions and the identifications of holders of power to a certain extent are a result of the choice of explanatory model. This weakness may be reduced somewhat by combining a series of different models and approaches, some of which will be applied in this essay.

number of employees in the ministries were social economists they constituted only 1.4 percent of the total number of civil servants in the state apparatus. In the ministries they still lag far behind the jurists, who constituted 44 percent of the total ministry employees in 1976 (cf. Table 1).[23]

Primarily because of the low status of university studies of social economics during the 1950s and 1960s[24] the relative share of social economists in the ministries has increased only insignificantly since the middle of the 1950s. One consequence of this decline of social economics was a change in the role of business economists, whose subject has generally been more popular than social economics and not subject to the same serious cyclical fluctuations. The 1950s was a period of stagnation but not of decline, and the 1970s growth has been much more conspicuous. Thus, while business economists were not originally intended for government service, from the late 1950s they began to fill some of the gaps created by the shortage of social economists, and they have definitely proved to be successful in government. In 1976, 8 percent of the professionals in the ministries were business economists, and today there are more business economists than social economists in the central government as a whole.[25]

23. The main sources for statistics on economists in government are: *Norges Statskalender* (The Norwegian State Calendar)—Annual issues, *Lønns- og sysselsettingsstatistikk for statens embets- og tjenestemenn* (Wages and Employment Statistics for Central Government Employees).—Central Bureau of Statistics, 1959, 1963, 1969, and annually from 1973 onwards, *Statens sentrale tjenestemannsregister* (The Central Register of State Employees). Some statistics, particularly on incomes, also produced by the professional organizations.

24. In 1960 an all-time low was reached with only two graduates. See *Historisk Statistikk 1978* (Oslo, 1978), p. 631.

25. The following table shows the number of economists in the ministries for years since 1959:

Year	State and social economists	Business economists
1959	112	23
1969	102	43
1972	162	95
1977	190	136

Source: Wages and Employment Statistics for Central Government Employees

The reduction of the number of state and social economists between 1959 and 1969 is due to the fact that the decrease in the number of state economists was higher than the increase in the number of social economists.

In the state as a whole there were 591 social economists and 571 business economists, and if the trend of the 1970s has continued the business economists are today far the biggest economics profession in the state. Between 1969 and 1977 the number of business economists increased by 175 percent against 57 percent for the social economists.

Table 1.   Total number of central government economists

Year	Number[a]		Percent change since 1950[a]	
1950	281	(236)	—	—
1955	329	(264)	17.1	(11.9)
1959	486	(343)	73.0	(45.3)
1969	585	(377)	108.2	(59.7)
1973	942	(516)	235.2	(118.6)
1977	1162	(591)	313.5	(150.4)

[a]The figures in parentheses include state and social economists.
Source: Wage and Employment Statistics for Central Government Employees.
Only permanent employees are included.

Even though the situation was particularly difficult during the 1950s and 1960s, there has been a continuous postwar surplus demand for economists and intensive competition for candidates between the public and the private sectors. Throughout the whole postwar period the salary level for social economists has probably been higher in the private than in the public sector. The earliest existing figures, for 1957, showed an average difference of 26 percent and in 1977 it exceeded 30 percent. The differences are narrower for the lower age groups, but increase with the number of years from graduation.[26] But generally speaking social economists' average income level is equal to that of the jurists. Among social economists in government, incomes are highest in the ministries, owing to their particularly favorable positions in the hierarchy.[27]

Theoretically one might assume that income differences of this order would influence the quantitative and qualitative distribution of social economists in favor of the private sector. However, in the Norwegian case this seems unlikely, for the civil service still has a surprisingly powerful capacity to attract the majority of social economists, especially the most talented. A higher percentage of the best candidates goes to the civil service rather than to industry, and although there has recently been a tendency for talent to go into the private sector, it is weaker than might have been expected, given the income differences.[28]

Another reason for discounting the importance of income differ-

26. *Sosialøkonomen*, 1, no. 1–2 (1958) and 21, no. 3 (1978).

27. In 1977 (Oct. 1) the average monthly income in the ministries were: for jurists kr. 9,130, for social economists kr. 9,376 and for business economists kr. 8,704. *Wages and Employment Statistics for Central Government Employees* (Oslo, 1978), p. 51.

28. *Yrkesundersøkelse for siviløkonomer, sosialøkonomer og stats-økonomer i 1970* (NAVF's Utredningsinstitutt 1972:6), pp. 43–44.

ences is the very limited mobility of social economists between the public and the private sectors. A study of the 1970–1974 period showed that the majority of recruits came from the universities and left with a pension. There was also a higher degree of mobility within the civil service, and most of those who left prior to retirement were in lower-level jobs and had relatively short service. The higher up the hierarchy, the greater the stability, despite the especially high income differentials between top-level economists in the two sectors.[29] Consequently the investigation casts doubt on the supposed existence of a powerful and self-recruiting elite moving extensively and without friction between the top levels of the private and public sectors. Nor does it support the conception of the civil service as a sort of waiting room or springboard for business careers.[30]

One essential reason for the low mobility from private to public sector is the strength of the traditional civil service career pattern. Most top jobs can be reached only by long and continuous service. The system encourages loyalty among those already in the service and discourages entry from high-level private employment. The civil service protects its members and erects barriers against potential intruders. In addition, the strong attraction of the civil service for social economists is a by-product of educational and professional socialization. We have seen that social economics was initially mainly seen as a training for public service, and government service still has retained much of its status and prestige within the profession.

Demand surplus is often supposed to increase the possibilities for influence by 'oppositional' elements in the professions and to change the balance struck by civil servants between political and professional loyalty in favor of the latter. There may be an element of truth in this contention, but in general conditions for 'oppositional' economists have been unfavorable in the Norwegian civil service. Socialization to civil service values is strong, and economists unwilling to adjust themselves usually leave the service quite early. The relatively high mobility among young economists is probably the result of a kind of 'cleaning process' in the civil service.[31]

Income statistics show that business economists' average incomes

29. Lægreid and Olsen, p. 130.

30. In quantitative analyses there is, of course, a danger of overestimating the bearing of aggregate numbers. No doubt there have been some few and important examples of mobility, particularly from the public to the private sector. Recent cases are Mr. Egil Bakke, the present top economist in the Federation of Norwegian Industries, and Mr. Sverre W. Rostoft Jr., director of the Federation of Norwegian Private Banks. Both Bakke and Rostoft are former ministerial employees.

31. Lægreid and Olsen, p. 130.

exceeded those of social economists owing to their strong foothold in the private sector. In the state sector the business economists' average income was 4.7 percent lower partly owing to their lower status and position in the official hierarchy.[32] Higher incomes constitute one of the main reasons for the growing popularity of business economics, and for the relative decline in recruitment to social economics. This may indeed be the most serious threat to qualitative decline among government economists, for government service has hitherto had less attraction for business economists, especially the most talented ones.

With more than 20 percent of the professionals in the ministries, the two economics professions have become a very 'visible' and essential part of the Norwegian civil service. However, the power-elite model concentrates on top-level positions, and we shall therefore proceed to look more closely at the actual location of the civil service economists.

The location of economists in government

The most striking characteristics of the location of economists in the Norwegian civil service is that the majority are spread over a very large number of institutions and agencies. Nonetheless, we will focus our attention on the economists in the relatively small, policy-oriented ministries (somewhat like the structure of the Swedish ministries) because of their important position in the policy process and the numerical strength of their economic staff.

There is, of course, a concentration of economists in the economic policy ministries (cf. Table 2). In 1977, 45 percent of the social economists were employed in the ministries of Finance, Trade, and Industry. Historically the hegemony has shifted somewhat between the Ministry of Finance and the Ministry of Trade. In 1945, the former was supposed to become the planning ministry, but in 1947, during a serious currency crisis, almost all the newly employed economists and the planning functions were transferred to a new Ministry of Trade, together with Mr. Erik Brofoss, the former Minister of Finance. Mr. Brofoss was the brain and driving force behind the new planning policy, and the planning apparatus was therefore placed under his leadership. In this respect, Mr. Brofoss was the Norwegian equivalent of Britain's Sir Stafford Cripps. However in 1952 another strong personality, Mr. Trygve Bratteli, later Prime Minister, took over the Ministry of Finance and the planning functions were divided between the two ministries. National budgeting and short-term management were taken over by Mr. Bratteli, while Mr. Brofoss was to be responsible for long-

32. *Wages and Employment Statistics for Central Government Employees* (Oslo 1978) p. 47.

Table 2.   State and social economists in the ministries

Ministry	1946	1960	1970	1977
Prime Minister's office	—	1	2	1
Foreign affairs	3	2	2	4
Education	3	3	4	7
Justice	1	—	—	1
Labor and local government	—	5	12	20
Trade and shipping	5	28	21	29
Industry	—	9	14	25
Fishery	3	3	4	7
Agriculture	—	3	3	5
Communication	11	6	7	17
Environment[a]	—	—	—	5
Wages and prices[b]	—	2	4	12
Finance	5	20	22	33
Defense	2	5	5	8
Reconstruction[c]	8	—	—	—
Family and consumption[d]	—	2	2	—
Social affairs	3	2	—	15
Total	44	91	102	189

[a] Established 1972.
[b] Established 1955.
[c] Abolished 1950.
[d] Established 1956, abolished 1972.
Source: Norges Statskalender and Statens sentrale tjenestemanns-register (1977).

term planning. In the 1960s the renaissance of the primacy of the Ministry of Finance was complete when it also took over long-term planning.[33] However, the establishment of the Ministry of Long-Term Planning in 1980 has once more modified its dominance somewhat.

Historically the Ministry of Trade is of particular interest because it represented the first attempt to construct a new ministry mainly on economic expertise, and it still is the only ministry where economists have been in a majority among the professionals. On the other hand, the most typical and hard-core 'cells' of social economists are to be found in the Finance Division (state budgeting) and the Economy Division (short-term planning) in the Ministry of Finance.[34] Also contributing to the ministry's position as an economic 'superministry' is the low profile of the Prime Minister and his office in economic policymaking. There has usually only been one economist attached to the Prime Minister's office.

33. Trond Bergh, "Ideal and Reality," pp. 77 ff.
34. In 1977 a third of the social economists in the ministries were employed in the Ministries of Finance and Trade.

Outside the ministries, the Central Bureau of Statistics is by far the most important employer of economists. In the Bureau, which cooperates closely with the Ministry of Finance and is the center of a highly centralized statistical service, economists have nearly a monopoly of professional jobs.[35] Special mention must also be made of the Bank of Norway, where economists traditionally dominate. By contrast with the Bank's interwar position, and in the interests of coordination and planning, the government has since the war been stressing its subordination. However, some of its independence remains and, as shown later below, this has some effect on the functions of the Bank's economists.

There has been a small, but not unimportant number of part-time consultants and advisers in the ministries. Professor Trygve Haavelmo was particularly influential as an adviser to the Minister of Finance, Mr. Bratteli, during the 1950s. Indeed, Haavelmo has been the most influential university economist as far as policymaking is concerned, for Frisch's contribution seldom went beyond the technical aspects of model building.[36] There have generally been extensive contacts between government economists and university economists, a great number of whom regularly do contract research for the government.

Originally social economists were afraid of becoming a 'proletarian' profession, whereas in fact they soon established themselves as an elite profession in government. Throughout the whole postwar period they have had a relatively high percentage of the top jobs, especially in the ministries. In 1976, when 13 percent of the professionals were social economists, they occupied no less than 21 percent of the top jobs. In contrast, the representation of business economists in the administrative elite has so far been considerably smaller.[37]

The need for interdepartmental coordination has increased enormously since the war as part of the planning process. Economists have performed these coordinating functions effectively more than any other profession. They are generally in majority in the expanding system of interdepartmental councils and committees.[38]

Another factor which has enhanced the Norwegian economists' role in the planning processes is the absence, by contrast with most countries in western Europe, of a top representative council. The idea of a process of decisionmaking in which employers, employees, and

35. In 1975 there were about 70 full-time social economists in the Central Bureau of Statistics.
36. Besides, politically Frisch disagreed more and more with the Labor Party, particularly on free trade and international economic integration.
37. Lægreid and Olsen, p. 61
38. Jorolv Moren, ed., *Den kollegiale forvaltning* (Oslo, 1974).

the big industrial and agricultural organizations cooperated directly and formally with the government was one of the cornerstones of the original strategy for the new postwar planning organization. But although an Economic Coordination Council was established, it soon lost its importance and was abolished in 1954. Some ten years later an unsuccessful attempt was made to reestablish such a council during the planning renaissance. Thus, macroeconomic planning has very much been in the hands of the planning economists, even more so than originally intended.[39]

So far we have distinguished between economists as civil servants and economists in political positions. However, there is no better reason for retaining this distinction than there is for differentiating clearly between politics and administration. Rather, the intimate interrelations and overlapping between the two levels have been important conditions for the strategic positions of government economists and their relatively harmonious cooperation with the political leaders. Traditionally, law has been the dominant professional background for members of government, and it still is; but social economists have considerably modified their dominance. Between 1965 and 1976, 23 percent of the ministers were jurists and 13 percent were social economists. Indeed, a majority of the postwar ministers of Finance and Trade have been social economists, and the latter's position has been particularly strong among deputy ministers (*statssekretærer*). In Parliament both jurists and economists have had a much weaker position. Between 1973 and 1976 only 5 percent of the 155 representatives had a professional background as social economists.[40]

One of the characteristics of government economists in Norway is that a number have been shuttling between the civil servant and the political cadres. Several ministers and deputy ministers, among them Mr. Brofoss, the most important link and 'bridge builder' between the profession and the Labor Party, started their careers as civil servants, served as minister for some years and then returned to civil servant status (usually, but not always outside the ministries). This kind of shuttling, which reflects the technocratic and 'non-ideological' attitude towards economic policy which was particularly strong during the early postwar years, has usually, but not always, been successful. Mr. Brofoss was a success both as a civil servant and as a politician, whereas the qualified success of Mr. Petter Jakob Bjerve, the first head of the National Budget Office (1945–1947) and Director of the Central Bureau of Statistics (1949–1980) as Minister of Finance (1960–1963) is

39. Cf. Bergh, "Ideal and Reality," p. 98–99.
40. Lægreid and Olsen, p. 100.

usually explained by his unwillingness to make sufficient allowances for the political aspects of the minister's role.[41]

In view of the blurred distinction between government economists and politicians it comes as no surprise to find that economists are the politically most active professionals in government. In 1976, 60 percent of the social economists in the ministries were or had been members of a political party, compared with 34 percent of the jurists and 31 percent of the business economists.[42]

This, together with the shuttling between the civil service and politics, especially under Labor governments, has lent support to the contention that most government economists are Labor sympathizers. There have been no systematic studies of political allegiances, but student gallup polls and trade union affiliations give no support to the theory of massive Labor membership.[43] Nevertheless, it is well known that a considerable number of top government economists have been members of the Labor Party. Therefore, party sympathies may have played some part in government economists' career patterns, but only in cases where their professional qualifications were beyond doubt.

Social economists have, in varying degrees, been dependent upon or in competition with other professions. In addition to the historical relationship between law and economics referred to earlier, and the continued, although modified, numerical dominance of jurists, political scientists and sociologists have recently been introduced as supplementary experts to economists. In 1976, 5 percent of the professionals in the ministries belonged to the social science group.[44] The most successful attempt at cooperation between economists and social scientists has been in long-term planning. However, even this has been a qualified success, partly because economists have tended not to regard interdisciplinary cooperation as the best way of establishing a broader overall perspective in planning. This attitude is probably one expression of the unwillingness, especially among social economists, to accept the scientific status of the social science disciplines. Besides, the high degree of specialization within social economics has caused problems of interdisciplinary communication. Oslo School economics has created a gap between social economics and the social sciences, and communication is scarce even at university level.

The long-lasting dominance of jurists in the civil service is partly

41. Bjerve himself has said that he resigned in 1963 because he felt too uneasy being responsible for government decisions with which he as an economist disagreed. *Dagbladet*, 26 Sept. 1973.
42. Lægreid and Olsen, pp. 74 ff.
43. Ibid., p. 75.
44. Ibid., p. 100.

due to their control of recruitment processes. Similarly, we can assume that economists have obtained a certain control in their own strongholds. The main reason for this assumption is the fact that neither before nor after 1945 has there existed any centrally coordinated and consistent policy of recruitment. Consequently, individual ministries and professions have had extensive autonomy, in this area. Thus, economists have had a decisive say in recruitment to divisions for economic policy and planning. Given economists' attitudes towards neighboring professions and towards their own mission, we may assume that this control has encouraged self-recruitment. On the other hand, the recent increase in the number of social scientists in long-term planning has been encouraged by leading government economists and most emphatically by Mr. Kleppe, former Finance Minister and from 1980 head of the new Ministry of Long-Term Planning. Thus there seems to be a similarity between the historical development of jurists' attitudes towards economists and that of economists to social scientists.

The Labor governments have tried to develop a more 'representative' civil service, i.e. one that reflects the social and economic composition of society as a whole. The Labor Party has traditionally had an anti-intellectual bias, and the number of academics in the party leadership has always been small, for example by contrast with the Swedish Labor Party. However, the party has been careful not to go too far in introducing laymen into the civil service. Its main instrument has been a long-term strategy of democratizing education and modifying the upper-class bias associated particularly with jurists.

In this strategy social economists have played an important part, although this was not the main reason why the civil service was opened to the economics profession. Background data on social economists show that they are far more 'representative' socially than government jurists : indeed, they have a more typically blue-collar background than any other profession in the ministries.[45] However, the importance of this feature has been exaggerated somewhat. In the relatively equalitarian Norwegian society early socialization has probably been of less importance for civil service values and attitudes than later educational and institutional socialization.

As we have seen, economists, have obtained a relatively favorable position in the formal bureaucratic structure, especially in the economic policy ministries. They occupy a network of top positions and dominate the principal economic policy divisions and the interdepartmental coordinating functions. Hence they are close to, and to some extent a part of, the political leadership. But their spread seems to have

45. Ibid., p. 83.

encouraged conflicts within their ranks, for there is a strong tendency to identify themselves with their institutions.

What do economists in government do?

A complete survey of the activities of government economists would comprise a very long list, including most of the typical civil service functions, both on the technical and administrative level. Hence we shall concentrate on the main characteristics and peculiarities of the economists' functions.

As a consequence of their concentration on macroeconomic policy and planning, the economists' activities differ in one essential respect from those of other government professionals. While jurists are still mainly involved in decisions in individual cases in accordance with law and established usage, the functions of the planning economists are innovative and creative—and some would add, more political. They cannot rely on precedent, but are supposed to anticipate and prepare for future problems and developments. Hence they must identify new problems, take new initiatives, and propose new solutions and policies. They are occupied with problems of a general nature rather than individual cases, although there has recently been a certain shift of emphasis from macroeconomic to microeconomic problems.

These special functions of economists may seem incompatible with traditional conceptions of the proper role of civil servants. Nonetheless, one of the most serious problems in the planning process is the economists' inability to fulfill their roles as innovators. Civil service tradition has taught them to try to anticipate and to interpret loyally the government's policies and priorities. This kind of extreme loyalty is perhaps one of the disadvantages of the close cooperation and political consensus between the bureaucratic and political facets of economic policymaking. Another problem is the formalized and hierarchical structure of civil service decisionmaking. To remedy this, economists have, with some success, tried to develop looser, more informal and egalitarian structures based on staff- and team-work and extensive oral communication.[46]

A questionnaire addressed to social economists in the ministries in 1976 showed that the three crucial functions were, in order, planning and reporting, budgeting, and coordination.[47] Among the typically technical functions within these categories economists have been particularly actively engaged in economic forecasting, by means of extremely complicated numerical models, which constitute one of the

46. Alf Inge Jansen, *Planlegging og organisasjon* (Dissertation, Oslo, 1967), p. 195.
47. Lægreid and Olsen, pp. 116–17.

main pillars of economic planning and management in Norway. This includes the development of models both for the whole economy and for particular macro sectors.

This extreme 'technification' of planning represents the activities that most directly relate to the economists' professional knowledge and skills. However, their success in the civil service has involved them in administrative functions for which an education in social economics seemingly provides little or no training. However, according to Norwegian civil service and Oslo School philosophy this is no serious handicap, since it is claimed that administrative capacity is being developed partly by practice and partly by postentry training (which started in the 1950s), and the important thing is that the administrative leaders are professionally qualified within the areas for which they are responsible. Besides, economists usually claim that economics, and especially macroeconomics, is superior to other kinds of specialist educations as a preparation for coordinating and administrative functions.

The two obvious objections against this system are the dangers that it may produce amateur administrators and outdated economists. The current emphasis on postentry administrative training constitutes an implicit acknowledgment of the dangers of administrative amateurism. And in addition to professional qualifications there is now a tendency to stress the importance of personality and ability to communicate and cooperate. At least until recently the government economists' professional qualifications seem to have presented no significant problems. Most top generalist economists continue to participate in professional debates, and some continue to teach at the university. The frequent use of university economists in contract research has also helped to strengthen professional identity. In addition, government economists have had some limited success in obtaining sabbatical years to enable them to keep up to date professionally. Their relationship with the university economists is usually the best test of the professional standards of government economists. Generally speaking, relations have been harmonious, although it seems as if the cordiality has cooled somewhat lately, especially between university economists and economists on the political level.[48]

Apart from coordination and control, one of the generalist economist's most important functions is economic (and political) advising of ministers and deputy ministers. This advising function is performed ei-

48. This somewhat cooler relationship may mean either that the government economists are less professionally up-to-date than before or, as is perhaps more probable, that the university economists have lost some of their sensitivity towards the political variable of economic-policy advising.

ther individually by specially appointed economic advisers (who are exempted from the regular administrative functions),[49] or the regular general directors or by committees or councils of economists. This kind of collective advising is institutionalized in general economic management and planning, but the committee reports are strictly confidential, in contrast with the practice in some other countries where the planning agencies and councils of economic advisers have a semi-independent position.

Advisory strategies differ somewhat. One of the two most popular forms is the 'menu strategy,' in which economists present a certain limited number of alternatives based either on different policy targets or on different instruments, leaving the final choice to the politicians. According to the second strategy, which seems to be increasingly popular, the economists present politicians with a single recommendation as a starting point of a dialogue between politicians and economists from which the final decision will emerge.

Even though there are still more jurists than economists in generalist positions, the economists have, in one sense of the word, succeeded them as *the* generalist profession. Earlier law provided the general insights and guidelines for the performance of the state's functions. However, in the modern interventionist state general insight into the economic mechanisms of society is more important and relevant than juridical knowledge. Hence economics has taken the place of law, and economists have displaced jurists.

This survey reveals that economists' functions in government go far beyond the more technical activities usually associated with their subject. It also shows that the 'non-economic' functions (narrowly defined) have become more rather than less important over the years. Moreover, it is now widely accepted that economics may be a valuable qualification for economic and political advising as well as for administrative functions.

Norwegian economics: characteristics and development

As educational socialization is important, and education in economics differs considerably from country to country, it is appropriate to provide some indication of the educational and professional background of Norwegian government economists.

The economic problems of the 1970s have generated a renaissance of amateur economists or economic 'quacks,' as one government econ-

49. This is a quite new practice. The first permanent, full-time economic adviser without ordinary administrative duties was appointed in the Ministry of Finance in 1979.

omist has labeled them.[50] In this sense the present situation is reminiscent of the 1930s. This tendency towards 'deprofessionalization' is the very opposite to the ideals of Norwegian economists, for their ambition has been to reach a level of professionalization comparable to that of doctors, architects, and engineers. They have not been content, as Keynes recommended, with the more humble aim of comparability with the dentists' profession. Nonetheless, Norwegian economics still has many of the characteristics of a proto- or semi-profession. For example, economists are still far from having a defined and undisputed job monopoly both outside and within the civil service. On the other hand, it is here that the most conspicuous changes have occurred since 1945. During the interwar years even the economists themselves found it difficult to pinpoint the offices that should be reserved exclusively for them. Today—after the establishment of a job description system in the civil service, partly as a result of claims from the economics profession—more than 200 jobs in the ministries alone are defined specifically as economists' jobs.

Professional organizations figure prominently in most theories of professionalization, and in the Norwegian case the role of the organization clearly illustrates both the would-be character of the profession and the use of organization as a means of accelerating the professionalization process. However, this strategy has had only a limited success as far as the social economists and their predecessors, the 'state economists,' are concerned.

The first economics association was established in 1883, not primarily as a professional body, but rather as a debating club for politicians, bureaucrats, businessmen, and a handful of university economists. Only in 1908, in the wake of the educational reform of 1905, was the first, after several unsuccessful forerunners, Association of Norwegian Social Economists established. The first relatively successful period was the 1930s, when the association played a certain role by lobbying for the educational reform of 1934; but it was not until 1955 that the association tried to establish itself as the trade union for social economists. However, it has never succeeded in becoming their only trade union. Today only about 60 percent are members of the association, and even fewer belong to its trade union division. To a large extent, factors other than professional identity have been decisive in the choice of trade union membership.[51]

50. Per Schreiner, leader of the Planning Division in the Ministry of Finance, in *Sosialøkonomen*, 21, no. 8 (1978): 32.

51. On the process of professionalization of state economics and social economics, see Trond Bergh, "Profesjonalisering og foreningsdannelse," *Sosialøkonomen* 21, no. 8 (1978): 4–11.

This is somewhat surprising, considering the conventional image of Norwegian social economics as an extremely homogeneous and self-assertive profession. This image is more than anything else attached to the name of Ragnar Frisch, who through his research and profession-building activities established the so-called Oslo School in Norwegian economics. How could one person dominate a whole profession to the extent that Frisch did? In small countries the dominance of one person is not unusual in the early stages in the development of professions, and there are parallels in other disciplines (e.g. philosophy and psychology) in Norway, and economics was indeed a small discipline when Frisch entered the scene. The only two professors had died at the end of the 1920s, and almost by himself (together with Professor Ingvar Wedervang), Frisch *was* the new generation of university economists. He came not to fight old opponents, but to fill a void. The low status of economics at the time encouraged new initiatives, but Frisch's charismatic personality was also of great importance. His ability to create enthusiasm and professional self-confidence, to establish useful contacts, to obtain political as well as financial support (both in Norway and abroad) is well known and recognized. The fact that early in his career Frisch became the first Norwegian economist with an international reputation added tremendously to his status in Norway as the undisputable leader of the economics profession. His professional role and importance was very similar to that of Jan Tinbergen in the Netherlands, although Frisch was probably less directly influential politically than Tinbergen.

The academic study of economics in Norway dates back to 1814. But only when economics was integrated into the study of law in the 1840s did it attract some attention. In 1905 the 'state economics' degree was established as a first step towards the 'independence' of economics as a university subject, a status that was achieved in the 1930s. In its early stages Norwegian economics was more influenced by German and Austrian tradition than by British—for example, in the practice of dividing the training of state economists into the three subdisciplines: theoretical economics, practical economics, and public finance.[52] Among the methodological and technical subjects some importance was attached to statistics, but apart from some elements of insurance mathematics, mathematical economics was excluded. However, with the new social economics degree, this changed drastically. It differed

52. The Continental impact, particularly from the German historical school, was also reflected in the so-called organic conception of the state, which perceives the state not only as a laissez-faire state, but also as a culture state. (I am indebted to Tore J. Hanisch for supplying me with information on pre-Frischian economic theory in Norway.)

both in extent (five years to two) and in content—and it was very different from economics degrees in most other European countries.[53] It involves an extreme concentration on theoretical economics, econometrics, and mathematical economics, and this methodological uniformity more than its theoretical orientation has been the essence of the Oslo School.

Critics claim that this methodological bias explains why recruitment for the degree has sometimes been catastrophically low. Interest in mathematics has been one of the principal motives among students, and there has usually been a high correlation between success in high school mathematics and success in social economics degree examinations. No such relationship has been observed in other western European countries.[54]

Frisch's theoretical orientation had Keynesian elements, but without any direct or acknowledged influence from Keynes. He regarded himself as a representative of a broad new trend among monetary theorists which he termed "the activist ideology." He believed that the ultimate justification for economics was the urgent need for active management and planning of the economy, and was mainly interested in the methodological and technical reorientation of the discipline. He introduced mathematical economics in Norway and was one of the international pioneers of econometrics. Nowhere else has quantitative economics dominated economics education so early and so completely as in the Norwegian case.

Frisch considered this redirection a necessary precondition for the practical application of economics and economists.[55] Many of his critics, within but especially outside the profession, have regarded this educational strategy as a way of disqualifying economists for civil service jobs. No doubt Frisch was preoccupied with the idea of developing 'scientific' economics and in a way regretted that so many of his best pupils were absorbed by the civil service. Nevertheless, he was convinced that his was the only correct strategy for an economics profession with practical ambitions. Education in economics had to be something more than "an advanced version of the art of conversation." He likened the role of mathematics in economics to that of cortisone in medical science.[56]

53. See J. F. H. Roper, *The Teaching of Economics at University Level* (Council of Europe, 1970).

54. Ibid., p. 25.

55. See, for example, Frisch's inaugural lecture in 1932 titled "Nyorientering av den økonomiske teori. Økonomikken som eksperimentalvidenskap" (Redirecting Economic Theory: Economics as an Experimental Science).

56. Frisch drew this parallel in a speech on 24 Nov. 1955, on the question of re-

The decline of social economics during the 1950s brought about the most intensive debate on the discipline up to that time and resulted in some, although not fundamental, changes. There was an increase in the number of optional courses and a diminution of the emphasis on theoretical economics. Instead, more time was devoted to practical and empirical economics at an early stage of the study.[57]

There was also criticism of the absence of a lower social economics degree. During the 1950s no more than about 50 percent of the students completed the course; consequently social economics was regarded as being an exclusive and elitist education. Subsequently a new, less advanced degree was introduced, but very few students were satisfied with it, mainly because the profession still hesitated to recognize the 'half-learned' economists (cf. Tables 3 to 6 for statistics in economics and related subjects).

The exclusivity of social economics may have had positive as well as negative effects upon the process of professionalization. The image of a highly theoretical and inaccessible science may enhance professional status, increase professional self-control, and give protection against outside control and competition from neighboring professions. This may, as in the case of macroeconomic planning, provide a basis for monopoly, but it may also weaken the profession's general position

Table 3.   New social science degrees

Year	Number	Percent change since 1946
1946	23	—
1950	46	100
1955	63	174
1960	50	117
1965	50	117
1970	202[a]	778
1975	511[a]	2122

[a]Includes lower and higher degrees.
Source: Historisk Statistikk 1978, p. 631.

forming and revising the social economics degree. On his attitude to quantitative planning models, see R. Frisch, *Economic Planning Studies* (Dordrecht, 1976).

57. Today the social economics degree is made up of these disciplines in the following order: (1) mathematics, (2) elementary theoretical economics, (3) elementary industrial economics, (4) sociology, (5) theoretical statistics, (6) applied statistics, (7) advanced theoretical economics, (8) advanced industrial economics, (9) monetary economics and public finance, and (10) one of the following six optional subjects: international economics, economic systems, business economics, econometric methods, law, and macroeconomic planning.

Table 4. New economics degrees

Year	Social economics		Business economics[b]	
	Number	Percent change[a]	Number	Percent change[a]
1946	30	—	67	—
1950	52	73	48	−28
1955	42	40	52	−22
1960	2	−93	62	−7
1965	22	−27	90	34
1970	77	157	183	173
1975	80	167	258	285

[a]Since 1946.
[b]Business economists educated abroad are not included.
Source: As for Table 3.

in the labor market. There are obvious drawbacks arising from overqualification, for example when seeking lower-level government jobs.[58]

Another consequence of the exclusivity of social economics is the low level of general public education in economics. Historically, enlightenment of the people was one of the main justifications for economics as a university subject. At the turn of the century a better general knowledge of economics was regarded as a necessary presupposition for universal suffrage, parliamentarism, and *Prozesspolitik*, and this was one of the arguments for the first educational reform in

Table 5. New law degrees

Year	Number	Percent change since 1946
1946	168	—
1950	333	98
1955	147	−13
1960	83	−51
1965	87	−46
1970	223	33
1975	340	102

Source: As for Table 3.

58. Social economists have lately witnessed an increasing competition from a newly established and very popular two-year economic-administrative education at the district high schools.

Table 6.   Share of total number of new degrees (percent) in economics, law, and social sciences

Year	Economics	Law	Social sciences
1946	8.9	15.4	2.1
1950	7.2	24.0	3.3
1955	8.4	13.1	5.6
1960	5.9	7.2	4.3
1965	5.6	4.4	2.5
1970	7.4	6.4	5.8
1975	7.7	7.8	11.7

Source: As for Table 3.

1905. Frisch and his pupils supported this philosophy. However, there has been a considerable gap between ideal and reality. Economics has played a very minor role in the general educational system, and the social economists themselves have shown a lack of ability and little interest in the diffusion of knowledge by popular scientific writings. Debates among social economists are usually conducted in exclusive circles within the profession. The participation of social economists in the general public debates on economic questions is surprisingly low in view of their 'utilitarian' philosophy. The low public profile has possibly had the effect of maximizing the effects of their rare statements in the media. On the other hand, the positive effects of a more active education of the public have been missed. No doubt this is one of the reasons for the popularity of economic 'quacks.'

The most successful informal educational process has probably taken place as part of the interaction between government and university economists and political, bureaucratic, and industrial elites. During the first postwar years the economists' position in government was largely due to the confidence they enjoyed among a few influential politicians with a footing in the economics profession and the Prime Minister's (Einar Gerhardsen) good relationship with these politicians. Later the politicians' and bureaucrats' awareness of the economists' limitations has grown, but so also their understanding of their potential contribution.[59]

During the first postwar years government economists tended to be somewhat overoptimistic and unrealistic about their role in economic

59. On the education of the political and administrative elite, see Petter Jakob Bjerve, "Utviklingstendensar i norsk planlegging gjennom 30 år," *Samfunnsøkonomiske studier nr. 26, Nasjonalregnskap, modeller og analyse* (Oslo, 1975), p. 37.

policymaking. Frisch once said that the economists' job was to eliminate three-fourths of the political struggle on economic policy. Above
all, Oslo School economists have regarded their mission as that
of increasing 'rationality' in economic policymaking, as a reaction
against the dogmas and shibboleths of interwar economic debates. In
1945 leading government economists stressed that debates on economic policy should dispense with such terms as liberalism, socialism,
and planned economy. Instead, concrete questions and the problems of
the day ought to be "discussed and analyzed fully in an unprejudiced
way."[60]

Besides this tendency towards depoliticization of economic policy,
the other striking characteristic of the Oslo School philosophy was the
conviction that it was possible to distinguish clearly between the functions of the expert and of the politician. This belief was based on
Frisch's analysis of the relationship between economics and politics
and his emphasis on the distinction between facts and values in economics (following Max Weber) which he published in 1936. While
conceding that the fact-value distinction was particularly difficult to
draw in the social sciences, he believed it could be done through the
economists' awareness of the value elements in his research.[61] This
was by no means an unusual argument during the 1930s. The peculiar
thing, however, is that it still has a very strong position among Norwegian social economists, and Frisch's 1936 analysis is still compulsory
reading for social economics students.

Even if we regard the distinction between economics and politics as
simply an ideal rather than an attainable reality, it has had considerable
importance for government economists because it goes hand in glove
with the traditional civil service ethics stressing political loyalty and
neutrality and professional independence.[62] This compatibility between professional ethics and civil service ethics has been extremely
conducive to the integration of economists into the government machinery.

Since the turn of the century, when law ceased to be the 'midwife'
and economics began to stand on its own feet, it has continued to be
part of the standard law training. And although the jurists' knowledge
of economics has remained at a fairly low level, a number of jurists

60. Odd Aukrust and Petter Jakob Bjerve, *Hva krigen kostet Norge* (Oslo, 1945), p.
321.

61. R. Frisch, W. Keilhau, and I. Wedervang, *Plan til en strukturoversikt for Norge*
(Oslo, 1936), pp. 7–12.

62. On civil service ethics, see Knut Dahl Jacobsen, "Lojalitet, nøytralitet og faglig
uavhengighet i sentraladministrasjonen," *Tidsskrift for Samfunnsforskning* 1 (1960):
231–48.

have gone on to take an additional degree in economics, and some of these jurist-economists moved into important political and bureaucratic positions after 1945, playing a major role as architects of the new economic policy.[63] The existence of such a group of interdisciplinary civil servants is surely one reason why conflicts between jurists and economists in government have been relatively harmless.

The degree in business economics introduced in 1937 differs markedly from the social economics degree: it is more heterogeneous and interdisciplinary and puts less weight on theoretical economics, econometrics, and mathematical economics. It is important to note that business economists, unlike social economists, have some theoretical background in administrative subjects. Nonetheless, social economists still constitute a majority of generalist economists.

The absence of pre-entry training in administrative topics constitutes the most obvious lack of correspondence between social economics education and the actual functions of economists in government. Even Frisch conceded that this might be a weakness,[64] but little has been done to change the situation. In other respects the social economics education seems relatively well adapted to what civil service economists actually do, although there is actually a quite complicated interrelationship between functions and education. Undoubtedly the influence of Frisch and his pupils on the prevailing conceptions of the proper education for and functions of economists in government have been very strong indeed.

Economists and the bureaucratic ideals

Civil servants are expected to be loyal to the policy of the government and to observe their professional independence. More often than not these ideals may be incompatible and lead to conflicts between the government and its civil servants. However, Norwegian government economists seem not to have regarded political loyalty as a particularly burdensome obligation. This is especially so for the economists in the economic-policy ministries, who have usually considered their ministers as being on their side against the 'party politicians.' This is especially true of the Minister of Finance, who, according to economists in the ministry, functions as counterbalance against political and tactical considerations in government.[65] Generally the economists themselves experience more conflicts between ministries than within them, and

63. Among these were Mr. Erik Brofoss, whose importance has been repeatedly stressed in this essay.
64. Cf. his speech on 24 Nov. 1955 on reform of the social economics degree.
65. Jansen, p. 157.

between different sectors and professions than between the bureaucracy and the political leadership.[66]

In this respect the economists differ somewhat from other professions in government, for whom the conflicts with the government are more prominent. Thus a high degree of consensus in the political and administrative system is not, by itself, a sufficient explanation of the relatively harmonious relationship between economists and politicians. There is probably a particularly strong accord between the value systems of economists and government politicians. Another relevant factor is the generalist character of the government economists' functions, for they are less closely identified with sectoral or regional interests than the other professions. This is illustrated by the fact that the economists' outside contacts are somewhat different from those of other professionals. The frequency of their contacts with local and regional interest groups and with individual, private citizens is particularly low, whereas contacts with organized groups on national and cross-sectoral level matters are much greater.[67]

The political loyalty of civil servants has an internal as well as an external aspect. With respect to the latter, tradition and unwritten rules say that civil servants may be politically engaged and participate in public debates as private citizens, the only exception (besides not being eligible for Parliament) being where political activity and civil service functions overlap. According to custom, civil servants in such cases are expected to refrain from expressing personal opinions, especially when they disagree with the government. Only once, during the debate preceding the referendum in 1972 on Norwegian membership in the EEC, have the government economists massively violated this rule.

The majority of the civil servants were, as was the government itself, in favor of membership, while most of the social economists, particularly in the Ministry of Finance, were opposed. Initially most of these kept out of the public debate for reasons of loyalty, in contrast with the advocates of membership among the civil servants, who were encouraged by the government to argue in favor publicly. As a consequence of their political disagreement with the government the social economists lost some of their prominence as civil servants and planners. In presenting its analysis of the economic consequences of membership or non-membership the government chose to disregard the macroeconomic planning apparatus in the Ministry of Finance, and instead left the job to the ministries of Industry and Trade, where sup-

66. Lægreid and Olsen, p. 160.
67. Ibid., p. 197.

porters of membership were in the majority. Of course, the government was perfectly within its rights in doing so; nevertheless, it represented a break with a solidly established practice. In the present context, however, the most interesting point is that the social economists so strongly disagreed with the published figures that they published a dissenting statement in conjunction with economists in the Central Bureau of Statistics, accompanied with alternative figures. In other words, they chose to demonstrate their professional independence rather than political loyalty to the government.[68] However, it is generally recognized that the EEC case was an isolated exception to the customary harmonious relationship between the economists and the government.

Harmony and consensus do not, of course, mean a total absence of conflicts and differences of opinion, and although civil service ethics prevent government economists from publicly expressing professional protests and warnings, expectations of political loyalty are not equally strong throughout the whole civil service. Officials outside the ministries are usually somewhat freer to criticize than those working within them. As far as economists and economic policy are concerned, the Bank of Norway in particular has established a tradition of public and independent criticism of the government. Thus the governor and vice-governor of the Bank, both usually economists and often recruited from the ministries, quite regularly function as a professional corrective to official economic policy. This critical attitude cannot be explained by a different theoretical orientation on the part of the Bank's economists. Rather, the most likely explanations are their institutional distance from ministerial day-to-day policy decisions and their freedom to disregard political and tactical considerations, both of which make it easier for them to apply economic 'rationality.'[69] The present vice-governor of the Bank, Mr. Hermod Skånland, has recently argued publicly along these lines in order to reestablish some of its prewar eminence in economic policymaking. The leaders of the Central Bureau of Statistics have had a function somewhat similar to that of the leaders of the central bank.

The change of government in 1965, when the non-socialist parties took power after thirty years of Labor rule, was the first serious

68. Jon Elster, Nils Petter Gleditsch, and Øivind Østerud, *De utro tjenere* (Oslo, 1974), pp. 56–80.

69. See, for example, Per Bratland, *Hvem har makt i Norge* (Oslo, 1965), pp. 25–26, on the role of Mr. Brofoss as governor of the Bank of Norway during the early 1960s. One of the consequences of the freer position of the central bank no doubt has been a more extensive and public debate on economic policy questions. The role of the bank as a guarantee for the professional point of view may also to some extent have served to ease professional frustrations among the economists in the ministries.

post-1945 test of the political loyalty of the civil service, and it is generally agreed that it stood up well. But even if the new government had wanted to change the composition of the civil service, it could not have done so overnight. The Norwegian civil service is extremely non-political. Very few civil servants leave for political reasons, and very few are appointed for the political reasons when changes of government occur. Even so-called 'irregulars' are very sparingly employed. All permanent civil service jobs must be announced publicly, and professional qualifications are usually of fundamental importance. In addition, the civil service is protected against politicization by the irremovability of civil servants, while the hierarchical structure and detailed rules of procedure also serve as impediments to 'political' appointees.

In this sense the Norwegian civil service is a 'closed' system: recruitment is based on professional skills, and the civil service is a life-long career. Thus, it comes very close to Weber's model bureaucracy. Civil servants are recruited among young professionals with little or no practical experience of or identification with other sectors; they adjust to civil service ethics and are rewarded for their loyalty by promotion.

The bureaucrats' neutrality is the most utopian of the ideals of civil service ethics. Nonetheless, economists have taken particular care to stress their neutral and non-political role. They have done so, for example, by drawing a sharp distinction between ends and means in economic policymaking. However, nowadays this distinction between the functions of the politician and the expert has very few adherents, and it has also become more difficult to characterize policy instruments as politically neutral. Economists are strongly involved in the formulation of policy ends, especially in macroeconomic planning, and are often in a position to make final decisions which are political rather than technical. We have also seen that the government has, to a certain extent, encouraged this deviation from traditional civil service ethics. Thus, it may seem as if some of the traditional bureaucratic ideals today are meant more for public consumption than for internal use in the civil service.

Against this background it is tempting to conclude that the compatibility between bureaucratic ideals and professional ethics was favorable to the introduction of economists in government, but that the practical and deliberate neglect of the civil servants' neutrality greatly facilitated their rise as an influential civil service profession.

The role of economists in decisionmaking: the case study approach

Previous paragraphs have dealt mainly with broad and general approaches to the study of the role of economists in government, but in addition more special and detailed analyses of their contribution in particular areas of policymaking processes are needed. Of course this approach cannot reveal the more permanent structural elements of power, and there are great difficulties in selecting a representative sample of case studies. The cases that have attracted most public attention are not necessarily more important and interesting than the many lesser cases that have escaped notice. For the present purpose a case has been selected which, though not necessarily representative, provides an insight into the economists' role at the height of their influence, i.e. the process of national budgeting.

Formally the national budgets are political documents reflecting the general economic policy strategy both verbally and quantitatively for a one-year period. Nevertheless, the government has usually played a relatively passive role in the preparatory process. After drawing up some general political guidelines, it has left the process to the civil servants, i.e. to the economists in the Economy Division in the Ministry of Finance, the Committee on the National Budget, and the Long-Term Program, which includes some of the most prominent top generalist economists. Thus the economists control most of the stages in the planning process, largely deciding which questions are political and which are purely technical. Thereafter, the politicians' function is to come to a decision on the questions put before them. Members of the government usually have neither the time nor the inclination to examine aspects of the plans about which no questions have been asked by the civil servants. The government usually accepts and adopts the plans without essential changes. This has led some scholars to conclude that there is every reason to regard the planning process as "an example *par excellence* of technocratic influence in the making of public policy."[70]

The treatment of the National Budgets in Parliament is even more summary than in the government. Parliament only debates the final, official version of the plans and therefore has very little chance of influencing the contents. It has no expert staffs of its own to prepare alternative plans, and it has only very limited access to the government's experts and their background studies. Consequently Parliament's treatment of the National Budgets is usually brief and ritualistic. Its situation was particularly difficult during the first postwar years when very few representatives had any profound understanding of the new economic policy. Over time, however, members of the Finance

70. John Higley, Karl Erik Brofoss, and Knut Groholt, "Top Civil Servants and the National Budget in Norway," in M. Dogan, ed., *The Mandarins of Western Europe* (New York, 1975), p. 266.

Committee in Parliament, which prepares the parliamentary debates on economic policy and planning, have gradually acquired a fairly respectable level of amateur knowledge in economics.[71]

The economists' dominance in national budgeting does not necessarily mean that the planning process is an example of a civil service run rampant. Their relatively free hand is a result of a deliberate delegation of functions and not of a government without control over its own machinery. There is every indication that the government has the motivation as well as the power to intervene when necessary and to redirect the process in accordance with its own policies and priorities. This has happened a few times, and in every case the economists have adjusted to the new signals, even when they have regarded them as economically unfavorable or even irresponsible. The EEC case cited earlier reveals that the delegation of the planning process to the economists is a reality only as long as they are assumed to agree with the government on the most important economic-policy questions.

On the other hand, the government does not always have a policy, and this gives the planners the opportunity to introduce new ideas and policies. They also have a certain freedom to operationalize and decide upon the exact contents of imprecise policy signals. As they act as the government's economic conscience and are free to decide which questions and problems are politically relevant, no doubt they largely decide where to put the focus of attention in economic policymaking. Moreover, even among politicians there has been a tendency to regard national budgeting and short-term management as primarily a technical question, on which they feel quite incompetent.

Less undisturbed, probably, is the dominance of economists in long-term planning, where the political importance of the process and the documents is more obvious. Therefore, a very tentative conclusion, which cannot be fully justified here, is that economists have strongly influenced ends as well as means in short-term management, but have been less decisive in the design of the long-term direction of policy goals and instruments. However, this does not mean to say that short-term economic management has been an unqualified success. The most obvious exception is the 1958 recession, which was considerably exacerbated in Norway because the economists miscalculated the demand-reducing effect of a 1957 tax reform.[72]

71. On the role of Parliament in long-term planning, which is very similar to that in short-term management, see Trond Bergh, *Utviklingstendenser i norsk makroøkonomisk langtidsplanlegging* (Oslo, 1976), pp. 42 ff.

72. This has been admitted even by government economists. See Odd Aukrust, *Tjue års økonomisk politikk i Norge: Suksesser og mistak* (Oslo, 1965), p. 27.

*Some concluding remarks on the influence of economists
in government*

Despite all the problems involved in defining and analyzing 'influence' it seems clear that the economists in the Norwegian civil service, and particularly in the ministries, have played an important part in public policymaking. They do not dominate numerically, but have by their position in economic policymaking and planning occupied the strategically most important jobs in the civil service. More than any other profession they have changed and expanded the role of civil servants. They have radically changed the process of economic policymaking. Their ambition was to increase 'rationality' in economic-policy making, and they have been successful in developing a new mode of thinking among policymakers, whether in government, Parliament, or the civil service. Major decisions are no longer taken without preceding economic analyses which cannot easily be overlooked. They have made it considerably more difficult than earlier for politicians to have their cake and eat it too.

What then have been the most important preconditions for the success of economists in government? There are certain political, bureaucratic, and professional conditions which deserve to be pointed out. On the political level we have stressed the importance of the remarkably high degree of political consensus between economists and politicians, which only recently has been fading somewhat, and the postwar political stability. It is usually said that strong and stable governments weaken the position of civil servants, while weak governments and frequent changes of power are supposed to strengthen the influence of the civil service. In the Norwegian case the opposite seems to have applied. In periods of relative political instability conditions have generally been unfavorable to economic 'rationality' and long-term considerations and solutions, while political stability has not encouraged short-term opportunism and irresponsible political outbidding.

A comparison between the pre-1961 period of Labor majority and the situation between 1961 and 1965 and during most of the 1970s, when Labor has had a minority government, illustrates the advantages economists derived from stable and strong governments.[73] This is not to say that conflicts between political 'opportunism' and economic 'rationality' were absent before 1961; but they definitely became more frequent and serious thereafter.

73. Government economists were, for example, sceptical towards several new social-policy initiatives and the expansive fiscal policy of the government during the early 1960s when it used quite radical social reforms as a means of regaining electoral support which it had lost in the 1961 election.

On the bureaucratic level, the integration of the planning agencies into the government machinery has been especially significant. This administrative solution, which reflects the government's early intentions to draw the planning economists into the policymaking processes, has brought expert advice closer to policy decisions and eased the problem of striking a realistic balance between professional and political considerations. It has helped to formalize and institutionalize the economists' role in economic policymaking. Of course, from the professional standpoint there are certain dangers in being too much inside government and too much bound by political loyalty, particularly in periods of increasing professional discontent. However, the semi-independent economists in the Bank of Norway, by indirectly also functioning as spokesmen of economists in the ministries, seem to have reduced this danger to some extent.

Professional dissension and strife are among the most serious weaknesses of most professions and provide a justification for politicians to disregard professional advice. But the homogeneity of the Oslo School has largely deprived Norwegian politicians of this opportunity. The economists' quantitative orientation has also strengthened their position, giving them a monopoly of the complex numerical models which are regarded as essential to the planning process. As a result only a very small number of specialists comprehend its intricacies. Although Oslo School economists regard these models as indispensable, there are indications that their real importance is fairly modest. Even a leading government economist has said that an able and experienced economist can reach the same main conclusions as the numerical models by calculating a little on the back of an envelope.[74] This undoubtedly raises the question whether the technical level in macroeconomic planning is unnecessarily and artificially high.

Professional homogeneity has so far been to the advantage of the economists in government, but in the long run it may have a serious negative effect—for example, by producing a kind of theoretical conservatism which impedes the search, both by economists and politicians, for new types of solutions to economic problems.

Despite the economists' indisputable success in government, there still is some way to go before the profession is satisfied with the course of events. Government economists frequently complain of the government's inability to commit itself to specific policies and priorities, and a leading government economist has contended that this is the most serious obstacle to effective and rational planning. If politicians could agree on policy targets, it would be easy for government economists to

74. Mr. Arne Øien, permanent secretary, in *Dagbladet*, 11 Oct. 1976.

find instruments to achieve them.[75] This applies especially to long-term policy, where even majority Labor governments have been hesitant to commit themselves to specific objectives. In situations where long-term and short-term policies conflict, the latter usually prevail. In the opinion of most economists, particularly among the university economists, this kind of political opportunism explains the economic problems of stagflation during the 1970s. They deny that there is a theoretical crisis in economics. The crisis is political. Economists know how to solve the problem, but their solutions are being thwarted by political indecision.[76]

Government economists are frequently accused of departing from their politically neutral official roles. On the other hand, the economists complain that politicians exceed their proper roles, since they have not been content to consider what policy instruments are politically acceptable, but have also pretended to know better than the economic experts what the economic consequences of alternative instruments will be. Thus, economists have not been satisfied with the division of labor and authority between experts and politicians. There has been and still is a problem of confidence.[77]

Although the economists primarily emphasize the political shortcomings, they are not blind to imperfections in economics. The relatively primitive state of economics, Mr. Bjerve has maintained, helps to explain the lack of political confidence in economists. They still have a long way to go, he added, before they have analytic tools that may qualify them as 'economic engineers.' Nevertheless, even he has seen political opportunism and indecision as the main problem.[78]

Whether the economists' increasing influence in government has on balance been beneficial or harmful is, of course, a matter for personal judgment. On the one hand they have contributed to an undesirable increase in bureaucratic power at the expense of democratically elected bodies. From another, equally legitimate, point of view, they have positively influenced policymaking by displacing political demagogues and substituting a process of 'rational' economic policymaking. As to their actual influence on economic development, international comparisons of economic growth rates and our emphasis upon government economists' concentration on short-term problems both suggest that their in-

75. Per Schreiner, *Langtidsplanlegging*, Memorandum from the Department of Economics, University of Oslo, 12 June 1964, pp. 1–2.

76. One of those who stress this publicly is Mr. Hermod Skånland, the present vice-governor of the Bank of Norway. He is an economist and member of the Labor Party.

77. P. J. Bjerve in *Teknisk revolusjon i økonomisk analyse og politikk?* (Oslo, 1966), pp. 5–6.

78. Ibid., p. 20.

fluence on long-term developments has been relatively modest, but their impact on the stability of the economy has probably been considerable.[79] Therefore, Frisch no doubt was essentially right when he in the early 1950s described his profession as "servants—but powerful servants."

79. Postwar growth rates in Norway have been very close to the western European average, while the fluctuations have been smaller than in most other countries.

Bibliography

Aukrust, Odd. "Tjue års økonomisk politikk i Norge: Suksesser og mistak" (Twenty Years of Norwegian Economic Policy: An Appraisal). Article no. 15 in the series *Artikler fra Statistisk Sentralbyrå*. Oslo, 1965.

———, and Petter Jakob Bjerve. *Hva krigen kostet Norge* (What the War Cost for Norway). Oslo, 1945.

Barton, Allan H. "Decision-making in a Planning Agency," *Social Science Information* 3, no. 4 (1963): 57–76.

———. *Sociological and Psychological Problems of Economic Planning in Norway*. New York, 1954.

Bergh, Trond. "Ideal and Reality in Norwegian Macroeconomic Planning." *Scandinavian Journal of History* 3 (1978): 75–104.

———. "Norsk økonomisk politikk 1945–1965." In Bergh and Pharo, eds., *Vekst og velstand. Norsk politisk historie 1945–1965* (Growth and Welfare: Norwegian Political History 1945–1965). Oslo, 1977, pp. 11–97.

———. "Profesjonalisering og foreningsdannelse" (Professionalization and the Establishment of Professional Organizations). *Sosialøkonomen* (The Social Economist) 21 (1978): 4–11.

———. *Utviklingstendenser i norsk makroøkonomisk langtidsplanlegging* (Trends in Norwegian Macroeconomic Long-Term Planning). Oslo, 1976.

Bjerve, Petter Jakob. "Government Economic Planning and Control in Scandinavia." In Henning Friis, ed., *Scandinavia Between East and West* (Ithaca, N.Y., 1950).

———. Planning in Norway 1947–1956. Amsterdam, 1959.

———. "National Accounts and National Budgets in Norway." *Bulletin of the International Statistical Institute* 33, part III (1953): 93–114.

———. "Trends in Quantitative Economic Planning in Norway," Article no. 21 in the series *Artikler fra Statistisk Sentralbyrå*. Oslo, 1968.

Bourneuf, Alice. *Norway, the Planned Revival*. Cambridge, Mass., 1958.

Elster, Jon, Nils P. Gleditsch, and Øivind Østerud. *De utro tjenere* (The Unfaithful Servants). Oslo, 1974.

Galenson, Walter. *Labor in Norway*. Cambridge, Mass. 1949.

Grunwald, Joseph. *"National Economic Budgeting in Norway."* Unpublished dissertation, Columbia University, 1951.

——— "Planned Economy in Norway: A Reply." *American Economic Review* 7 (1950): 410–15.

Hernes, Gudmund, ed. *Forhandlingsøkonomi og blandingsadministrasjon* (Negotiating Economy and Mixed Administration). Bergen, 1978.

Higley, John, Karl Erik Brofoss, and Knut Groholt, "Top Civil Servants and the National Budget in Norway." Mattei Dogan, ed., *The Mandarins of Western Europe*. New York, 1975.

Holben, R. E., "Planned Economy in Norway: Comment," *American Economic Review* 6 (1949): 1283–87.

Jacobsen, Knut Dahl, and Torstein Eckhoff, *Rationality and Responsibility in Administrative and Juridical Decision-making*. Copenhagen, 1960.

Klein, Lawrence R. "Planned Economy in Norway." *American Economic Review* 5 (1948): 795–814.

Lægreid, Erling, and Johan P. Olsen. *Byråkrati og beslutninger* (Bureaucracy and Decisions). Bergen, 1978.

Leiserson, Mark W. *Wages and Economic Control in Norway 1945–1957*. Cambridge, Mass., 1959.

Østerud, Øivind. *Det planlagte samfunn* (The Planned Society). Oslo, 1979.

Torgersen, Ulf. "The Trend Towards Political Consensus: The Case of Norway." *Acta Sociologica* 6, nos. 1–2; 159–172.

The United States: economists in a pluralistic polity

William J. Barber

In the United States—as in other countries considered in these studies—the participation of professional economists in government has swollen with the extension of the state's jurisdiction in economic life. This phenomenon is one of the striking characteristics of most societies in the middle decades of the twentieth century. Meanwhile the discipline of economics has changed in ways which have altered perceptions of the proper public agenda and of the contributions economists can make in its execution.

While these developments have been international in scope, a number of features of the American scene have given a distinctive national cast to the types of relationships worked out there between officialdom and the community of professional economists. Part of this distinctiveness derives from the structure of the American central government, with its calculated diffusion of power between executive, legislative, and judicial branches. As a result, the contrast with those countries in which a central focal point for macroeconomic policymaking can be readily identified—e.g., the treasury, the ministry of finance, or a planning commission—could not be more marked. In matters of fiscal policy, for example, the American executive branch initiates recommendations, but the ultimate shape of federal tax and expenditure programs is controlled by a Congress which is notoriously unresponsive to appeals for party discipline. Nor is there any assurance that monetary policy and fiscal policy will be optimally coordinated, since the former is determined by a central bank which is answerable to the Congress, not to the President.

The American governmental structure also presents yet another challenge to consistency in the development of overall economic policies. Some jurisdictional overlap between various components of a bureaucracy is perhaps inevitable anywhere. In the American case, however, interdepartmental competition takes a special form. Most of the established departments and agencies administer programs serving constituencies with strong Congressional reinforcement. The ambitious department thus has an incentive to cultivate its own congressional lobby and to resist central executive management. The problem of developing coherence in policy is further confounded by the presence and proliferation of independent regulatory commissions which enjoy certain immunities from presidential direction of their judgments. In short, the system institutionalizes conflict and rewards effectiveness in advocacy. In this respect, it can be sharply differentiated from practice in countries such as Japan where a tradition for molding consensus is prized. (The reader unfamiliar with the structure of the U.S. federal government is invited to consult Appendix A.)

The potential role of economists in the American system is further influenced by an ambivalence in public attitudes toward experts. The views of specialists—whether they be scientists, military planners, or economists—have typically been received with a guarded suspicion. Those of economists are especially vulnerable. President Truman, for example, reflected a widely held opinion when he once observed that "if all the economists in the country were laid end-to-end, they would never reach a conclusion." At the same time, the public can agree that the complexity of modern government requires technical expertise. Indeed the American bureaucracy has been more receptive to the absorption of experts than has been the case in countries in which the civil service tradition has been dominated by an administrative class of 'mandarins.'

The purpose of this essay is to convey the essential flavor of the interaction between professional economists and officialdom at the federal level. Particular attention will be directed to those features of the American system which differentiate it most sharply from practice in other countries.

I. *Economists and the Public Service:*
Establishing the Beachheads

In the conventional wisdom, the story of systematic linkages between economists and government is held to have begun with the creation of the Council of Economic Advisers within the Executive Office of the President in 1946. This innovation, however, was but the culmination of a trend which had been under way for nearly three decades.

As far as the profession was concerned, one of the landmark formulations of its public responsibilities was contained in Irving Fisher's presidential address to the American Economic Association in December 1918. Fisher then appealed to his colleagues to move beyond their base in the ivory tower and to make their talents available to government on a regular basis.[1] His views coincided with those of many who

1. Irving Fisher, "Economists in Public Service," *American Economic Review* 9 (March 1919): 5–21.

had done a tour in Washington during the First World War and were impressed by both what the economy and what the economists could accomplish. The lessons for peacetime seemed to be clear: continued collaboration between economists and government promised to offer benefits to all parties. Government, aided by economists, could spur efficiency in the private sector through the timely collection, interpretation, and dissemination of economic data. A 'new era' for economics was also held to be at hand: there was now an opportunity to place the discipline on solid empirical foundations. Wesley Mitchell, director of the newly formed National Bureau of Economic Research, captured the mood when predicting that American economics was on the threshold of "rapid theoretical development and constructive application" at a pace unrivaled since the period following the Napoleonic Wars.[2]

In this context, the first regular posts earmarked specifically for 'economists' in the bureaucratic establishment were created with the formation of a Bureau of Agricultural Economics within the Department of Agriculture in 1922. Shortly thereafter the statistical services of other cabinet departments were enlarged: e.g., in the Department of Commerce (with responsibility for monitoring trends in income and output) and in the Department of Labor (with primary concern for measuring changes in employment and price levels). Though modest by comparison with what was to come later, some innovative thinking was also applied in the 1920s to the role the federal government could play in stabilizing economic activity—particularly through the central bank's conduct of open-market operations and through the guidance the federal government could offer to state and local governments (which then controlled the bulk of public-sector spending) on the countercyclical timing of public works. Officialdom increasingly recognized the competence of economists as processors and interpreters of data by enlarging the space assigned to them in tables of organization and by increasing the frequency with which they were appointed to official advisory commissions. These beachheads for economists and economic statisticians were, of course, considerably removed from the higher reaches of economic policymaking. It is worth recalling, however, that the orthodoxy of these years largely presupposed that government could act indirectly as a catalyst to the efficiency and stability of the system, but that it should not interfere directly with the private sector.

With the crisis of the Great Depression, the character of the contacts between professional economists and government took on a quite

2. Wesley C. Mitchell, in R. G. Tugwell, ed., *The Trend in Economics* (New York, 1924), p. 33.

different form. Events posed a formidable challenge to the alleged self-adjusting properties of the economy to high levels of employment and output. The Administration which came into power in March 1933 was favorably disposed toward experimentation with extraordinary techniques of economic control, and it initially enjoyed the support of leading members of the business community, who were then calling for a collaboration of business and government in national economic planning. Economists in the academic mainstream, however, were generally unsympathetic toward these innovations. The policy elite in Roosevelt's First New Deal was thus dominated by a mix of lawyers and businessmen. Though a number of card-carrying Ph.D.s in economics were among those from whom the President sought counsel, the advisers with this certification typically held views which were at odds with the profession's prevailing orthodoxy. To the bulk of the professional community, the brethren who preached institutionalist and monetarist heresies in Washington were misguided and mischievous mavericks.

By the mid-1930s, the disjunction between official doctrine and the orthodoxy of the academic establishment was to produce some unanticipated consequences. A number of the profession's more imaginative younger talents—particularly those sympathetic to an activist fiscal policy—were then to find officialdom more congenial than academia. The career of Lauchlin Currie is a case in point. Denied a permanent appointment at Harvard,[3] Currie migrated to Washington where he joined the staff of the Federal Reserve Board, which was then under the leadership of an untutored but intuitive advocate of fiscal heterodoxy. Within the bureaucracy, the studies of academic refugees such as Currie were merged with research efforts in the Department of Commerce, where fundamental work on the redesign of the national income accounts was under way.[4] What began to emerge was a fresh perspective toward macroeconomic analysis and toward the appropriate agenda for government in promoting recovery. Indeed this cadre of bureaucratic insiders arrived independently at the central message of Keynesian doctrine for economic policy. By the time *The General Theory* was published, its contents were much more readily appreci-

3. Currie's position on public spending as a stimulant to recovery had put him at odds with senior members of the Harvard economics faculty. As John Kenneth Galbraith has remarked about this episode, Currie was among those who paid the price for being prematurely right. See Galbraith, "How Keynes Came to America," in *Economics, Peace, and Laughter* (Boston, 1971), pp. 43–59.

4. For a valuable discussion of the pioneering studies of Simon Kuznets and the group with which he worked in the Commerce Department in this period, see Carol S. Carson, "The History of the United States National Income and Product Accounts," *Review of Income and Wealth*, June 1975, pp. 153–81.

ated by a group of economists within government than by those operating from an academic base.

In the late 1930s the acceptability of the new doctrine was enhanced by its capacity to explain an otherwise perplexing phenomenon: the recession of 1937–38. This sharp downturn in economic activity—which occurred when the economy was well short of full-capacity levels of activity—caught official Washington totally unprepared. The analyses offered by the younger breed of economists seemed to supply the answer through statistical demonstrations of the major reduction in the "net contribution of government to spending" between 1936 and 1937. This line of analysis conveyed in turn a new understanding of the potential contribution of economists to government and to the successful management of fiscal policy. More official posts for economists were authorized, and the new breed of 'Keynesians' recruited those of common persuasion to fill them.[5]

By 1940 the beachheads were secure. Currie's appointment to the White House staff as economic adviser to the President—the first member of the profession to enjoy such exalted rank—gave formal recognition to the triumph of the new macroeconomics within the Executive Branch. But this achievement cannot be attributed solely to the persuasive skills of the advocates of a Keynesian approach to policy. The appeal of the new doctrine to senior policymakers owed much of its apparent capacity to speak to the most urgent political problem of the day: the necessity to design measures which could assure the achievement of high levels of employment. Moreover, as Currie advised Roosevelt in March 1940, it was now possible to blend 'sound economics' with the humanitarian objectives of the New Deal. From a Keynesian perspective, such a merger could be accomplished in an American context by designing 'offsets to saving' through redistributive taxation and income transfers to society's most vulnerable members.[6] This breakthrough had far-reaching implications for the position economists might occupy in government. As interpreters of the way the Keynesian model could best be translated into effective policy, professional economists—at least those with a competence in the new macroeconomic analysis—came closer to a monopoly position in the market for economic advice than had ever been the case before.

5. In this connection, see Lauchlin Currie, "Comments and Observations," *History of Political Economy* 10 (1978): 541–48.
6. Currie reported to Roosevelt that "the basic analysis is that of J. M. Keynes." While he did not believe that the line of analysis itself could be sold politically, it was still valuable in providing a "proper orientation of our own thinking in developing a coordinated program." Currie to the President, "Memorandum on Full Employment," 18 March 1940, Franklin D. Roosevelt Library.

Operationally, the application of the new macroeconomics to policy was to have its first trial run in the management of a wartime economy. As had been the case in 1917–18, the months following Pearl Harbor witnessed a sharp increase in the population of economists in official Washington. While the problems of economic mobilization were necessarily a central preoccupation, the groundwork for a new role for government in the postwar economy was also being laid. Blueprints drafted during the war years (most notably in a strengthened Bureau of the Budget, which had loaded its staff with Keynesians) called for a reorganization of government which would delegate unprecedented powers to economists. The institutional reform recommended by this group called for the placement of a staff of economic experts in the Bureau of the Budget with discretionary authority to alter the government's spending programs and tax schedules: i.e., the creation of a body with independent jurisdiction over fiscal policy and with an autonomy analogous to the Federal Reserve's control of monetary policy. Should forecasts for the economy point, for example, toward a shortfall in aggregate demand, this group would be empowered to trigger increases in public expenditures and/or reductions in tax rates. Its charge would be to keep the economy on a full-employment track through fiscal fine tuning.[7] On these matters, the sympathies of the younger breed of Keynesians and those of an older generation of institutionalists with an appetite for planning could converge.

This ambitious scheme did not survive legislative review. The overtones of centralized planning in the first drafts of the proposed 'Full Employment Bill' were unacceptable to a substantial body of congressional opinion. Vigorous objection was also raised to the suggestion that a group of anonymous experts, shielded by executive privilege, should be accorded such unprecedented power. Majority support could be found, however, for two propositions: first, that a recurrence of depression of the scale of the 1930s would be politically intolerable; and, secondly, that the federal government should henceforth accept responsibility for the macroeconomic climate. The issues to be resolved concerned the manner in which that commitment was to be formulated and the part that economists would be invited to play in honoring it.

II. *Economists as Macroeconomic Strategists*

The Employment Act of 1946 created a new institution—the Council of Economic Advisers—within the Executive Office of President. In

7. For a discussion of the debates which led to the passage of the Employment Act of 1946, see Stephen K. Bailey, *Congress Makes a Law: The Story Behind The Employment Act of 1946* (New York, 1950).

the annals of American governmental organization, this was a signal event. For the first time, institutional standing was accorded to economists at the pinnacle of national decisionmaking. This innovation remains unique for another reason: none of the other academically based learned professions have been accorded similar status.[8] It matters little that the compliment paid to economists was more than a little backhanded. The very idea of a presidentially appointed council—which had not been a part of the original proposals on planning for the postwar economy—was a concession to that wing of congressional opinion which was suspicious of faceless experts, but was prepared to tolerate them if their appointments required senatorial confirmation and if their work was available for congressional review.

The 1946 legislation was pathbreaking in yet another respect—it put the federal government on record in support of "maximum employment, production, and purchasing power." In the legislative process, the adjective 'full' had been deleted from the statement of the employment objective: the explicitly Keynesian imagery of such terminology offended some important political sensibilities. The meaning of the compromise language was to be a matter of continuing debate—particularly over the status of 'price stability' in the Act's stipulation of goals. For some years, proponents of an amendment which would give price stability equal standing with 'maximum employment' were deflected with the argument that such a revision would be redundant. The mandate to promote 'maximum purchasing power,' it was maintained, implied a commitment to anti-inflationary policies.[9]

Of more immediate practical significance was the failure of the Act to speak in detail about how the Council of Economic Advisers was to function and about how it should be assimilated into the regular apparatus of government. Early in 1946, an adviser to the Secretary of the Treasury anticipated an uncomfortable predicament for the Executive Branch: either the newly authorized Council could act as a central research agency or it could be structured as the central economic-policy organ of the government. Neither alternative appeared to be entirely satisfactory. Were it to become a high-level research group, its opera-

8. Subsequently, proposals have been circulated unsuccessfully in support of a Presidential council of social advisers and of a council of scientific advisers.

9. Ambiguity on this point was removed with the passage of the Full Employment and Balanced Growth Act of 1978 (otherwise known as the Humphrey-Hawkins Act) which specified that the maximum rate of increase in the consumer price index should be 3 percent by 1983. Unemployment targets were also set out for that year: the rate should not exceed 4 percent for workers aged 16 and over, nor 3 percent for workers aged 20 and over. If these goals were not already sufficiently daunting, the Act of 1978 further stipulated that a balanced federal budget and steady reduction in the share of national output claimed by federal spending should also rank high in the nation's priorities.

tions were likely to be 'academic' and of limited relevance to practical decisionmaking. On the other hand, its capacity to function as a policy-coordinating body was also limited. An organization without operational responsibilities of its own was held to be ill-equipped to shape economic strategy "because it would be isolated from those day-to-day decisions which form the very warp and woof of policy." An independent body with such authority was likely to be "irresponsible. And to the degree that it was irresponsible, it would almost certainly prove disruptive. An agency reduced to the position of critic after the event could prove an embarrassment to the Administration, but seldom a support."[10] Indeed the uneasiness of some members of President Truman's senior staff about the administrative implications of the Council of Economic Advisers (in the form prescribed by Congress in the Employment Bill of 1946) was sufficient to incline them to recommend a presidential veto. The argument that the bill's official declaration of national economic goals had benefits which outweighed its administrative defects ultimately carried the day. But Truman was unsuccessful in persuading his first choice for the job of chairman of the new CEA to accept. Harold D. Smith, Director of the Bureau of the Budget, declined the invitation, arguing that the occupant of the post would be placed in an impossible situation. In his judgment, the public and the Congress were likely to hold the CEA accountable for the nation's economic health, whereas the CEA—denied the operational fiscal authority which he held to be essential—would be unable to direct a satisfactory macroeconomic policy.

Though many questions remained to be answered, three points were at least clear about what the Council would *not* be. In the first place, it was not to be an overall planning body with independent operational authority. With the limited resources available to it, this possibility was automatically foreclosed.[11] Secondly, though its members could be presumed to be professionals of high competence, they could not expect to operate in an atmosphere of 'scientific' detachment. After all, they were charged, in the first instance, to report to the President on a timetable synchronized with the preparation of his annual budget messages and legislative proposals. Further, CEA's reports would also be transmitted to a Joint Committee of the Congress and would thus provide a framework for public debate on economic

10. J. Donald Kingsley to John W. Snyder, Secretary of the Treasury, "The Economic Council and the Organization of the Presidential Office," 6 March 1946, Harry S. Truman Library.

11. Throughout its existence, the total professional staff assigned to the CEA has usually been less than two dozen. Its total budget has frequently been compared unfavorably to that of the Battle Monuments Commission.

policies and programs.[12] Finally, it was clear that economists appointed to the CEA would not automatically enjoy a position of primacy in the shaping of macroeconomic strategy, despite the advantage of immediate access to the President. Within the Executive Branch, their positions would compete for presidential favor with those submitted by the cabinet departments. Moreover, even when the CEA position prevailed within the Administration, it might still be neutralized by actions of a Federal Reserve Board which the President could not directly control.

Few administrations have given identical answers to the question of how the CEA should function. Nevertheless, three distinct operational styles may be identified: a 'scientific harmony' approach, an 'inside consultant coordinator' approach, and a 'policy advocacy' approach. They diverge both in their 'inside' relationships (i.e., with the President and with operational departments and agencies) and 'outside' relationships (i.e., with the Congress, with the public, and with the external community of economists). Though no Council has been a pure case of any single style, a few examples can usefully illuminate the central properties of different operational models.

The prime exhibit of the 'scientific harmony' approach is to be found in the position of Edwin G. Nourse, the Council's first chairman.[13] He set out his understanding of the office in his letter of acceptance to President Truman:

> the Council of Economic Advisers is conceived as a scientific agency of the Federal Government. Its prime function is to bring the best available methods of social science to the service of the Chief Executive and of the Congress in formulating national policy from year to year and from month to month. . . . It should give a clearer and more comprehensive picture than we have ever had as to the economic state of the nation, as to the factors which are

12. This structure, it should be noted, contrasts strikingly with West Germany's Sachverständigenrat which has functioned as an external evaluator of national economic policy. For a detailed institutional comparison, see Henry C. Wallich, "The American Council of Economic Advisers and the German Sachverstaendigenrat: A Study in the Economics of Advice," *Quarterly Journal of Economics* 82 (Aug. 1968): 349–79.

13. Nourse, it may be noted, was a respected elder statesman of the profession at the time of his appointment. Though much of his research and writing had been in the field of agricultural economics, he had served as President of the American Economic Association. To the scholars in the profession, the other two members of the original CEA were less well known. John D. Clark, Dean of the College of Business Administration at the University of Nebraska, was a latecomer to the profession, having left a highly successful business career to take up graduate studies in economics. Leon Keyserling brought experience in the ways of Washington to the assignment; his professional certification, however, was as a lawyer.

tending to retard prosperity, and as to the probable effect of various remedial measures which may be under consideration by the Executive or the Congress.[14]

Nourse was further persuaded that members of the CEA should regard themselves as representatives of the broader community of economists. He sought to enlist the best energies of the profession—whether or not in government employ—into his vision of "economics in the public service." As he told his professional colleagues in the American Economic Association in December 1946: "I conceive this agency as the doorway through which the best thinking of systematic economics (not forgetting the lay brothers) may be brought into clear and effective focus at the point of executive decision as to national policy and action." The Council itself "should always remain a small assembly plant, using subassemblies, parts, and materials drawn from all corners of the field." Nourse wanted the Council to be in a position to say that the conclusions, evaluations, and recommendations it presented to the President were not merely the judgment of its own members. In most cases, he hoped to be able to report that they reflected "widespread consensus," and that "the conceptual tools, the analytical methods, the statistical techniques, the cause-and-result logic we used have been duly examined and approved in the profession."[15] Whether or not the profession could converge on a common position was more problematic; the American Economic Association has encouraged diversity within its ranks and its membership has never been totally committed to any single school. Nourse's vision, however, did recognize an important reality of American professional life: namely, that permanent commitments to public employment are seldom compellingly attractive to the nation's actual and potential Nobel Prize winners (though they may welcome temporary and less formal contacts with government).

As far as working relationships within the government were concerned, Nourse took the position that there should be "no occasion for the Council to become involved in any way in the advocacy of particular measures or in the rival beliefs and struggles of different economic and political interest groups."[16] From the perspective of the White House, however, such neutrality was less than helpful.[17] Members of

14. Edwin G. Nourse to President Truman, 29 July 1946, as reprinted in Nourse, *Economics in the Public Service* (New York, 1953), p. 107.

15. Nourse, "Economics in the Public Service," *American Economic Review* 37 (May 1947): 21–30.

16. Nourse to Truman, 29 July 1946, loc. cit.

17. Following a White House briefing in which Nourse's discussion of the prospects for the economy was filled with "on the one hand, on the other hand" qualifications, President Truman reportedly remarked to an aide: "Can't someone find us a one-armed economist?"

the White House staff felt obliged to adopt some extraordinary tactics in order to bring the language of the annual Economic Report into line with the Administration's programmatic recommendations.[18]

When put to the test, Nourse's grand design fell short. The three members of the original Council were unable to achieve consensus among themselves in their recommendations to the President, let alone among economists at large. Internal dissension also flared up over the appropriateness of public presentations by Council members. Nourse opposed and Keyserling favored on-the-record testimony before Congressional committees. Moreover, the Council was systematically by-passed on important economic policy initiatives; for example, the most imaginative approach to the agricultural problem in more than a decade was transmitted from the Department of Agriculture to the Congress without the foreknowledge of the CEA.

With Nourse's resignation in 1949, the style of CEA activities shifted dramatically. Keyserling, who succeeded him in the chairmanship, made no claim to neutrality in his conduct of the office. In his view, the CEA should be in the forefront of intra-Administration infighting on the shaping of economic policy and in public advocacy of the Administration's programs. This quality of partisanship enhanced the Council's influence with the government of the day, though it was to raise questions about its professional integrity. Even so, the first phases of the experience of economists in government at this level stimulated some impressive analytical achievements. Insights into aspects of growth theory worked out in the analysis of practical problems facing government put the CEA and its staff in advance of the textbooks.[19]

The 'consultant-coordinator' approach to economic advising has received perhaps its highest expression in the work of the CEA under Arthur Burns during the Eisenhower Administration. Some redefinition in the activities of the CEA was unavoidable in 1953 if the institution was to survive at all. Appropriations for the CEA were scheduled to lapse on 31 March 1953, and powerful political figures in the Republican Party's ranks were unenthusiastic about refreshing them. The new President's Advisory Committee on Government Organization diagnosed matters as follows:

18. For example, Charles Murphy, Legal Counsel to President Truman, has reported that Nourse's resistance to suggestions from the White House could be broken by exploiting his sleeping habits. Murphy has observed that "we found out along about midnight that Dr. Nourse would begin to agree to anything. So we'd do most of the work after midnight." Oral History Interview with Charles S. Murphy, Harry S. Truman Library, p. 122.

19. Walter S. Salant, "Some Intellectual Contributions of the Truman Council of Economic Advisers to Policy-Making," *History of Political Economy* 5 (1973): 36–49, is instructive on these points.

Despite the high hopes held for it, and some substantial accomplishments, the Council has not in general met the principal needs originally foreseen. Divided authority and responsibility among the Council members, and public discussion of opinions and judgments seriously detracted from the Council's effectiveness and prestige; and a certain lack of professional objectivity was suspected. The Council did not draw sufficiently on the best economic brains in the universities or in private industry.

In short, there does not now exist a Presidential staff facility to plan against the threat of economic disruption, and at the same time integrate its findings and advice with the policy considerations and determinations of the Secretaries and Agency heads at the Departmental level. This cleavage has existed despite the most important advantage of direct access to the President for consultation.[20]

Though the decision was made to go forward with a plan to resuscitate the Council with increased authority lodged in its chairman, the task of reformulating the function of the CEA was a matter of some delicacy. In these circumstances, a substantial change in the form—if not in the content—of economic advising activities was indicated. The climate also called for changes in personnel. It was not remarkable, of course, for a new Administration to bring new blood to the Council membership. Less expected was the almost complete turnover of the CEA's professional staff: only one member of the Truman staff group survived. In Nourse's vision of an ideal world, the same cadre of experts should be capable of serving any political masters with equal effectiveness.[21]

As remolded, the CEA regarded its primary function as the provision of private consultative services to the President. The advice it offered was, in turn, treated as privileged. On this ground, Council members refused to make themselves available to congressional committees other than the Joint Economic Committee. Moreover, appearances before that group were to be governed by a prior understanding that responses to questions were to be off the record.

Under Burns's direction, the Council also took on an active role as an educator within the Administration. This undertaking, though executed tactfully and inconspicuously, was of major significance. Many

20. Memorandum to President Eisenhower from the President's Advisory Committee on Government Organization, "Council of Economic Advisers," 20 April 1953, Dwight D. Eisenhower Library.
21. For a discussion of the reorganization of the CEA in this period, see Edward S. Flash, Jr., *Economic Advice and Presidential Leadership* (New York, 1965), esp. pp. 102 ff.

of the ranking political figures in the Executive Branch were ideo-logically persuaded that their mission was to undo the works of the Keynesian revolution—or at least to re-affirm the sanctity of balanced budgets as the overriding priority of policy. A Council concerned with insuring that the needed fiscal weapons were available to combat a se-vere downturn in economic activity thus faced an unusual challenge. It chose to address it in two principal ways. In the first place, its mem-bers quietly reviewed the position papers of senior cabinet officers with an eye to demonstrating that the economic effects of deficits need not always be bad. Secondly, it began to chart demand-sustaining types of intervention which would be acceptable within existing politi-cal constraints. One type of program was ideally suited to these specifications—a national highway-building effort. It could be financed through the government's Trust Fund accounts (and thus would not be visible in the conventional budget); it would be complementary to—not competitive with—the private sector; its spending tap could easily be turned off and on, depending on the state of the economy; and it prom-ised to improve the efficiency of the private sector and to strengthen the nation's defensive capability. Putting this program in place was not the work of a day. But this approach did provide a countercyclical buffer suited to conservative tastes.

While most of the energies of the Burns Council were necessarily devoted to macroeconomic problems, the CEA in this period also took on some responsibilities as a coordinator of the overall economic poli-cies of the government. This exercise, which was mounted by Burns, involved the formation of an Advisory Board on Economic Growth and Stability which met weekly under his chairmanship. Representatives of the main departments with economic responsibilities—including Com-merce, Agriculture, Labor, Interior, Treasury, State, and Defense—were gathered weekly for these discussions. The CEA thus widened its influence within the Executive Branch.[22] Its jurisdiction, however, was not complete: for example, the interdepartmental committee which put a program of oil import controls in place in the mid-1950s did so without the participation of the CEA.

This mode of operation, however, was not without its costs. For the most part, the CEA's external relationships during this period were allowed to wither. The Joint Economic Committee of the Con-gress—which was under the control of the opposition party during six of the eight Eisenhower years—regarded the CEA as downright

22. Cf. Scott Gordon, "The Eisenhower Administration: The Doctrine of Shared Responsibility," in Craufurd D. Goodwin, ed., *Exhortation and Controls: The Search for a Wage-Price Policy, 1945–1971* (Washington, 1975), esp. pp. 95–134.

uncooperative. As required by statute, the CEA submitted its annual reports to the Joint Economic Committee but did not participate further in the Congressional deliberation on economic policies. Hearings to review the CEA's work were thus dominated by expert witnesses drawn from outside. By the late 1950s the Joint Economic Committee of the Congress approached the status of an official opposition Council of Economic Advisers, and it had enlarged its staff of professional economists accordingly.

An unambiguous example of a third operational model—the 'policy advocacy' approach—is to be found in the Kennedy Administration's CEA, headed by Walter Heller. Its members were advocates of a specific strategy—Keynesian fiscal stimulation in which a tax cut was to be the operative variable. At the same time, they were well aware that their recommendations were likely to encounter formidable resistance—e.g., from budget-balancing sentiments in the Congress, from Treasury officials who feared that fiscal expansionism would aggravate balance-of-payments difficulties, from the Federal Reserve, where measures to neutralize inflationary pressures were held to be the major imperative of policy.

To widen their scope for maneuver, members of the Heller Council—as a condition of accepting appointment—insisted that they be allowed to speak openly in public forums. Hence, the ground rules of the Eisenhower years were scrapped. The task of educating the Congress and the public, as well as the President and his official entourage, was now held to be one of the CEA's fundamental responsibilities. The CEA was also authorized to take positions on its own behalf which did not necessarily reflect Presidential commitments. The annual *Economic Reports* were thus subdivided: one component was "The Economic Report of the President," which was limited to a review of the economic situation and to a discussion of the policies the President had determined to pursue; a second was "The Report of the Council of Economic Advisers" in which the CEA could analyze longer-term trends and survey policy options, including some which had not been accorded official blessing.

Within the government, the CEA pressed its case for a tax cut in regular meetings with the Secretary of the Treasury and the Director of the Budget (the 'Troika') and of the 'Quadriad' (the Troika plus the chairman of the Federal Reserve Board). What emerged was a package of arguments which ultimately neutralized its opponents. To those who clung to faith in balanced budgets, the Heller Council argued that a balanced budget remained the goal—but that it was a 'full-employment' balanced budget that mattered, and the attempt to achieve fiscal balance prematurely would produce an unbalanced economy. To those who feared that the expansionary strategies would spark price increases and produce further deterioration in the balance of payments, it argued that price stability could be achieved by educating the public to observe 'wage-price guideposts' which constrained increases in factor incomes within the bounds of productivity gains. Domestic economic expansion, it was argued, could be made compatible with balance-of-payments improvement by inducing an 'interest-rate twist' designed to lower long-term rates (for the purpose of encouraging domestic investment) while sustaining short-term rates at levels attractive to capital inflow from abroad. To those who favored increased government expenditures (particularly to address the plight of the unemployed in depressed regions) over tax reductions as the route to fiscal stimulation, it argued that residual pockets of poverty could be best dealt with at a later stage. The 'fiscal dividends' flowing from the rising revenues generated by growth in national income would mop them up. These exercises in advocacy did indeed give 'new dimensions' to political economy.[23]

The economics profession in the United States has probably never enjoyed higher public esteem than it did in the afterglow of the 1964 tax cut. The recommended medicine seemed to work. GNP increased as predicted, and unemployment declined. Meanwhile, the budget deficit was narrowed and fiscal dividends to finance a 'war on poverty' were in sight. Scientific 'fine tuning' of the system offered the promise of uninterrupted prosperity.

This pinnacle of professional prestige was to be short-lived. Economists who have served as macroeconomic strategists since the mid-1960s have been less fortunate. They have been called upon to deal with an economy plagued by sluggish growth, stubborn inflation, deteriorating international payments, and energy crises. This mix of problems has not been readily susceptible to treatment with the Keynesian tools of aggregate-demand management. As Paul W. McCracken commented when taking office as President Nixon's first CEA chairman: "There is some malevolent law about the rhythm of political life that puts some of us here when it is hard to be a hero."[24]

The latter-day economic and political environment has reshaped the activities of senior macroeconomic strategists and has produced considerable mutation in the relative weight of various bodies in the shaping of policy. Members of the CEA, for example, were placed in

23. See Walter Heller, *New Dimensions of Political Economy* (Cambridge, Mass., 1966).
24. As quoted by Leonard Silk, *Nixonomics*, 2d ed. (New York, 1973), p. 3.

an unexpected and distasteful operational role in the later years of the Johnson Administration when they were instructed to intervene directly (though behind the scenes) in wage and price setting in the private sector. When their recommendation that taxes be increased to restrain an overheated economy was rejected by the President in 1966, conventional counterinflationary fiscal policy was hobbled and unconventional improvisation in 'price fighting' was invoked. It is not surprising that some of the threats directed to recalcitrant firms (e.g., possible antitrust prosecutions, denial of government contracts, etc.) were regarded as illegitimate extensions of governmental authority which were in violation of due process, nor that many economists in government were uncomfortable about such deployments of their energies.[25]

In the 1970s, the position of the CEA in the macroeconomic policy apparatus suffered further attrition. Though the Council certainly did not lack able analytic talents, the voices of its members were frequently drowned out in the clamor of the times. The U-turn of the Nixon Administration in 1971—when it imposed wage-price controls and suspended the gold convertibility of the dollar—was orchestrated more by a strong-willed Secretary of the Treasury than by the CEA (some of whose members were discomfited by features of the New Economic Policy). Jurisdictional lines have been further blurred by the creation of ad hoc bodies (such as a Cost of Living Council and a Council on Wage-Price Stability). Meanwhile the weight of the Federal Reserve Board in macroeconomic management tended to expand at the expense of the CEA. It is striking, however, that this phenomenon is coincident with the elevation of professional economists to positions as members of the Federal Reserve System's Board of Governors. Historically, these posts have been regarded primarily as the preserve of bankers. That precedent was shattered unambiguously when a former chairman of the CEA—Arthur Burns—became Chairman of the Federal Reserve Board in 1970.

Recent readjustments in the locus of 'clout' in the formulation of macroeconomic policy reflect also the widening cleavages within the profession itself on the type of model appropriate to an understanding of the economy's behavior. The era of a confident Keynesian consensus vanished in the 1970s. Monetarist doctrines acquired a heightened status and increased attention was directed to the 'supply side,' which had tended to be ignored in the heyday of Keynesian enthusiasm.[26]

25. James L. Cochrane, "The Johnson Administration: Moral Suasion Goes to War," in Goodwin, *Exhortation and Controls*, pp. 193–294.

26. It is noteworthy in this connection that the Joint Economic Committee of Congress expressed its dissatisfaction with econometric forecasting models built on Keynesian foundations and commissioned the preparation of a macro model to illuminate supply relationships in 1979.

The intellectual disarray of the past decade has also sharpened the differences between two camps within the profession: one which holds that the economic system is basically self-adjusting (and that excessive government intervention is the problem, not the solution) and another which maintains that disequilibrium is the normal condition of the system (and that more government intervention is required to correct it).

III. *Economists and Government Decisionmaking on Allocative and Distributive Questions*

The economists who serve as macroeconomic strategists tend to dominate the headlines, but their activities encompass only part of the work performed by economists in the federal establishment. Throughout the postwar years, the impact of the federal government on the economy as a spender, as a dispenser of subsidies and income transfers, as a regulator, and as a price maker massively enlarged. This trend was unambiguously observable in the absolute growth of federal budget outlays and in rising claims of government on GNP. The budget data, however, provide an incomplete measure of the role government plays in influencing the microeconomic behavior of the system. Many governmental actions crucial to the shaping of the allocation and distribution of economic resources leave little mark on the expenditure side of the public accounts: e.g., through positions adopted on such diverse matters as minimum wages, tariffs and quotas, pollution controls, and pricing policies in regulated industries.

One of the challenges to political management is the adjudication and coordination of rival claims of various sectors, regions, and groups for federal favor. While the choice of the final mix is arrived at through the process of political debate, both the executive and legislative branches have increasingly recognized that criteria of efficiency and consistency provided by economic analysis can aid in the evaluation of programs and policies.

Within the framework of the Executive Branch, a central responsibility for coordinating recommendations on expenditure has been assigned to the Office of Management and Budget (formerly the Bureau of the Budget), which, like the Council of Economic Advisers, is situated in the Executive Office of the President. Its charge is to screen the budget requests and the legislative proposals submitted by departments and agencies and to advise the President on their compatibility with the Administration's overall goals. Since 1960, six of the appointees to the directorship of this office have been professional economists. Under their leadership, use of the techniques of cost-benefit analysis has been extended, both within the office and within the departments and agencies from which programmatic proposals originate.

In the American system, a strategic situation for an economist's point of view on the budgetary process is assuredly no guarantee that this point of view will prevail. Most heads of democratic governments, one suspects, would recognize a cogency in the remark of President Johnson who once characterized his cabinet as composed of "nine salesmen and a credit manager."[27] While a dynamic of bureaucratic empire building is perhaps a universal phenomenon in modern governments, the task of containing it is institutionally more intricate in the United States than it is in parliamentary systems in which a government enjoys a majority and can enforce party discipline. Each of the major operating departments has not only developed a public constituency among the clients it serves; it has also cultivated its contacts with allies in Congress. What the President may hope to accomplish may be undone by Congressional appropriation committees.

There is thus an inherent resistance to tidiness in the U.S. system which is a natural by-product of the checks and balances imbedded in the Constitution. At times, however, the outcome may look more like the product of unchecked imbalances. Even in periods of primacy of the Executive Branch, a President's efforts to impose a more rational order may be frustrated. Roosevelt, for example, was unsuccessful in numerous attempts in the 1930s to gain statutory authority for a National Resources Board which would assign priorities to public works projects; a foot-dragging Congress, reinforced by lobbying by the Army Corps of Engineers and the Interior Department's Bureau of Reclamation (the agencies which then had the greatest stake in these programs), regarded this initiative as a threat to its pork barrel. In the early 1970s, the obstacles to coherent ordering of budgetary allocations became even more formidable. With the credibility of the White House damaged in the Watergate period, the authority of the legislative branch was asserted with renewed vigor. Many departments effectively by-passed the Executive Office of the President and dealt directly with Congressional committees. This phenomenon has been characterized by George Schultz (an economist who served as Secretary of Labor, Director of the Office of Management and Budget, and Secretary of the Treasury during this period) as "the Balkanization of bureaucracy."[28] A counterweight to this fragmentation was introduced in 1974 with the creation of the Congressional Budget Office. This body has been designed to induce Congress to take a wider view of its budgetary decisions by supplying it with studies assessing the broader impli-

27. As quoted by Cochrane, p. 198.
28. See George P. Schultz and Kenneth W. Dam, *Economic Policy Beyond the Headlines* (New York, 1977).

cations of its piecemeal actions and their consistency with aggregate fiscal targets. This office, it may be noted, has drawn a talented group of economists to its staff.[29]

The impact of government on the microeconomic functioning of the economy does not stop, of course, with decisions which have visible budgetary consequences. A wide range of policies—embodied in presidential executive orders, in administrative regulations issued by departments and agencies, and in legislation—also impinge on the economic system. Consistency in these directives can also be an elusive goal. Most organized interest groups are likely to find champions within the bureaucracy and in sympathetic congressional delegations, and the results are sometimes contradictory.[30]

Though the process has not usually been institutionally formalized, most administrations have charged their senior economists to maintain surveillance over the policy positions emanating from the executive departments and agencies. In the Eisenhower Administration, the Advisory Board on Economic Growth and Stability—which included representatives of departments with economic responsibilities and was convened by the chairman of the CEA—performed part of this function. In other cases, CEA members have been assigned to interdepartmental task forces studying particular problems. In principle, the use of economists in this way has much to recommend it. They are presumed to be the neutral parties who can transcend the constituency loyalties of departments and agencies and can bring a broader perspective of the public interest to bear on the issue in question. But this very 'neutrality' may weaken the hand of economists in the subsequent bureaucratic infighting. The unsuccessful attempt to shape a coherent national energy policy in the past three decades is a case in point. Though senior governmental economists have been involved in the deliberations, they have usually been outgunned at the point of political decision by departments with operational jurisdiction over the energy resource industries.[31]

29. In this connection, see Nancy H. Teeters, "Congress and the Economy," *Challenge* 21 (Nov.–Dec. 1978): 26–31.

30. President Ford, for example, lamented the limited success of his administration in its attempt to eliminate conflicting federal regulations, noting that "at least 50 percent of them are conflicts established by law. A President cannot do anything about them once the law is on the statute books. He may try to get Congress to take an affirmative action to resolve the conflicts, but, again, EPA [Environmental Protection Agency] has its constituencies, on the one hand, and the Department of Commerce has its constituencies on the other. And neither wants its little bailiwick interfered with." *Seminar in Economic Policy with Gerald Ford* (Washington, D.C., 1978), p. 13.

31. This phenomenon is abundantly documented in Craufurd D. Goodwin, ed., *Energy Policy in Perspective: Today's Problems and Yesterday's Solutions* (Washington, D.C., 1981).

Even so, an economist's way of thinking has still left an imprint on the official approach to a number of problems, including some which are not, strictly speaking, 'economic.' The decision to terminate military conscription in favor of a volunteer army, for example, owed much to arguments supplied by economists favoring market solutions to labor force allocation. The climate of official receptivity to a negative income tax as an alternative to an administered welfare system has also been conditioned by the work of economists on the merits of a less visible hand to guide the flow of transfer payments.

While the American political structure continues to fragment economic decisionmaking on microeconomic issues and to yield results which fall short of ideal consistency, some movement in the direction of greater coherence is detectable in the recent past. Creation of the Congressional Budget Office is one indication of recognition of the problem. Similarly, the remarkable rise of professionally trained economists to the leadership of departments and agencies can, in part, be understood as an attempt to constrain the 'balkanization' of bureaucracy. The past several administrations have chosen to appoint Ph.D.s in economics to cabinet-level posts which had historically been reserved for those who had moved up through the political ranks: e.g., as secretaries of the Treasury, Commerce, Labor, Defense, Agriculture, Energy, as well as directorship of the Office of Management and Budget. Though the economists who have occupied these positions must necessarily be particularly sensitive to problems within their department's jurisdiction, their training has presumably equipped them with a capacity to take a broader view of the requirements of consistency in government-wide decisionmaking.

IV.   *Government and the Labor Market for Economists*

The past several decades have witnessed a significant diffusion in the use of the language of economic analysis in official discourse. The appointment of economists to senior policy advisory positions has added momentum to this movement. Meanwhile, departments and agencies have increasingly recognized that persons with training in economics can make useful contributions to program formulation and evaluation and to budget preparation and defense. In parallel with these developments, the Congress has enlarged the space assigned to economists on its payrolls.

Though there can be no question about the growth in government's demand for the services of economists, its magnitude defies precise measurement. An indication of the *trend* in the Executive Branch emerges, however, in the data reported by the Civil Service Commission on the number of positions carrying the official designation of 'economist.' As may be noted in Table 1, the number of such posts has nearly doubled since the late 1950s, and their rate of growth has considerably exceeded that of other professional jobs under civil service jurisdiction.

These data are by no means satisfactory as measures of the absolute number of economists in full-time federal service. The reality is considerably understated by the omission of economists whose terms of service fall outside civil service classification: this group includes all senior policy strategists with presidential appointments (such as the members of the CEA, the director of the Office of Management and Budget, and holders of cabinet posts). Moreover, the categories of job classification used by the civil service authorities are frequently misleading. Much major analytic work is performed by persons with permanent appointments whose job titles are styled differently (e.g., as budget review officers) and is thus not captured in the reported tabulations of 'economists.' A further distortion arises from the fact that the activity of those officially described as economists is heavily statistical

Table 1. Employment of 'economists' (as classified by the Civil Service Commission) in the Executive Branch of the U.S. Federal Government

	1958	1968	1973	1976	1978
'Economists' as classified by the Civil Service Commission	3,012	4,325	4,638	5,026	5,763
Number employed in the Washington, D.C., area	1,684	2,556	2,961	3,223	3,848
Number employed in the U.S. outside the Washington, D.C., area	538	1,020	1,053	1,185	1,279
Number employed outside the U.S.	790	749	624	618	636
Index of growth in employment of economists (1958 = 100)	100	144	154	167	191
Index of growth of Civil Service employment of professionals (1958 = 100)	100	127	130	139	145

Source: U.S. Civil Service Commission, *Occupations of Federal White-Collar Workers*, Pamphlet 56-2, 1960: SM 56-08, 1968; SM 56-10, 1975; SM 56-12, 1978: U.S. Office of Personnel Management, *Occupations of Federal White-Collar Workers*, SM 56-14, 1980.

and administrative, rather than predominantly analytical.[32] These qualifications, however, do not exhaust the definitional difficulties. If, for example, the achievement of a doctorate in the discipline were to be regarded as the test of professional status, probably fewer than half of those classified as economists by the Civil Service Commission would qualify. This test—though the conventional criterion for academic appointments—is obviously too stringent when applied to governmental work.[33] It is frequently the case that career government employees have passed through all the steps of graduate training (save the preparation of a dissertation) and it is at least arguable whether the negotiation of that final hurdle would add significantly to their usefulness in government. Though data on the numbers involved are not available, note should also be made of another practice which may mislead the consumer of statistics on degrees held by official economists. It has become increasingly common for advanced graduate students to accept federal employment as a means of support—and, at times, as a research vehicle—while en route to the completion of a doctoral dissertation. Even so, it is possible to satisfy the Civil Service Commission's job specifications for 'economist' with rather modest formal background in the discipline. To qualify for the most junior posts in this category, a B.A. degree—in which only about a fifth of the curricular time over a four-year period is committed to economics—will suffice. As of 1974, it would appear that the B.A. degree was the highest academic qualification for about 29 percent of the 'economists' employed in government.[34]

Despite their imperfections, the personnel data produced by the Civil Service Commission still throw some light on the receptivity of various departments and agencies to 'economists' (as officially defined) on their payrolls (see Table 2). In view of the constituency-service functions performed by certain departments, it is not at all sur-

32. A sample survey undertaken in 1974 indicates that the activities of persons identified as economists in governmental employ are distributed functionally in roughly the following ways: management and administration—about 33 percent; research activities—more than 25 percent; reporting, statistical work, and computing—about 30 percent; activities not classified—approximately 11 percent. *Characteristics of the National Sample of Scientists and Engineers, 1974*, Part II: *Employment* (Washington, D.C., 1976).

33. As one of the pioneers of the Planning-Programming-Budgeting System in the Department of Defense has put it: "The economic theory we are using is the theory most of us learned as sophomores. The reason Ph.D.s are required is that many economists do not believe what they have learned until they have gone through graduate school and acquired a vested interest in marginal analysis." Alain C. Enthoven, "Economic Analysis in the Department of Defense," *American Economic Review* 53 (May 1963): 422.

34. *Characteristics of the National Sample of Scientists and Engineers*, 1974, part II.

Table 2. Distribution by Department or Agency of 'Economists' (as classified by the Civil Service Commission)

	1958	1968	1973	1976	1978
Totals	3,012	4,325	4,638	5,026	5,763
Department or Agency					
Agriculture	702	953	805	858	889
Commerce	249	402	504	518	589
Labor	440	684	792	891	1,111
Interior	102	232	150	166	181
State	985	927	896	958	962
Treasury	90	142	165	79	279
Defense (including Army, Navy, Air Force and other Defense activities)	65	209	269	303	327
Justice	24	42	29	47	47
Health, Education and Welfare	14	45	79	109	119
Housing and Urban Development (Housing and Home Finance in 1958)	57	144	103	125	146
Transportation	—	78	88	110	116
Environmental Protection Agency	—	—	62	48	56
Energy	—	—	—	—	259
Other	284	497	616	814	682

Source: U.S. Civil Service Commission and U.S. Office of Personnel Management, *Occcupations of Federal White-Collar Workers*, op. cit. Table 1.

prising to observe the substantial weight of Agriculture, Commerce, and Labor in the aggregate. The place of the former Department of Health, Education, and Welfare and the Department of Housing and Urban Development in the Federal labor market for 'economists' reflects growth in government's activities in transferring income between persons and between various echelons of government. In the recent past, a marked increase in the number of economists working on problems of energy, pollution, and environmental protection is notable. The place of the Department of State as an employer of economists, it should be observed, is a by-product of its absorption of the administration of overseas aid programs, as well as its concerns with the expansion of export opportunities and with the nation's balance-of-payments position more broadly. The relationship of economists to the Department of Defense is something of a special case; in addition to the analytic tasks involved in trying to maintain efficiency controls over the nation's largest procurement budget, economists have been invited to apply cost-benefit techniques to the adjudication of the competing claims of rival armed services. The Department of Justice—in view of its responsibility for the enforcement of the antitrust laws—has been relatively modest in its claims on the services of economists: this territory has historically been dominated by lawyers.

Similar growth in job opportunities for economists has occurred in the staffs and offices under the jurisdiction of the legislative branch, though the magnitudes are even less susceptible to exact documentation. The frequency of the use of the term 'economist' in the titles of congressional staff members has certainly increased. In 1959, for example, 12 staff members held this designation (3 with the Joint Economic Committee, 1 with the Joint Committee on Taxation, 5 with various committees of the House of Representatives, and 3 with committees of the Senate). By 1980, 43 staff members were so labeled (14 with the Joint Economic Committee, 11 with the Joint Committee on Taxation, 14 with various committees of the House of Representatives, and 4 with committees of the Senate).[35] Again, official categories and reality diverge. The most distinguished economists in the employ of the legislative branch (such as the director and the division heads in the Congressional Budget Office) fall outside these tabulations, as do a large number who are styled as 'professional staff members.' The most serious single omission, however, is the Federal Reserve System. Though it is a significant employer of economists, it maintains its tradition for autonomy through silence about their numbers.

Despite the growth in governmental demand for economists, academic life remains the largest claimant on the professional labor pool, engaging more than a third of the active professionals and a much higher percentage of those who have completed the doctorate.[36] The United States—in contrast with a number of countries considered in these studies—has not faced a problem of deficiency in the domestic supply of professionally trained economists. Its postgraduate educational system has been more than adequate to serve the nation's needs, while also offering training to substantial numbers of economists from

35. *Congressional Staff Directory*, 1959 and 1980.

36. Various approaches to the aggregate size of the American economics profession yield differing results. Members of the American Economic Association with addresses in the United States and Possessions numbered 14,697 in 1974 and 16,991 in 1978. The Sample Survey of Scientists and Engineers for 1974 (in which professional identification was self-declared) produced a finding that some 18,670 economists were actively employed (8,458 of whom held a doctorate). The Sample Survey's result for economists employed by the federal government was 3,538—a figure some 1,500 short of the numbers defined as 'economists' in the civil service job classifications. Roughly three-quarters of those in academic employment had achieved the doctorate (as compared with less than a third of those employed by the federal government and only about 17 percent of those employed by business and industry).

other countries. The product of the graduate training pipeline, however, is far from standardized. Though each of the academic institutions offering a Ph.D. (of which there are more than a hundred) insists on the development of competence in the tools of theoretical analysis and in quantitative techniques, they differ in their orientations and emphases. In macroeconomics, a rather whimsical distinction is occasionally drawn between 'salt water' institutions (e.g., Harvard, the Massachusetts Institute of Technology, Yale) which are predominantly neo-Keynesian in orientation and a 'fresh water' institution (e.g., the University of Chicago), where monetarism is dominant. A number of programs cultivate studies in particular specialisms (e.g., in industrial organization, public finance, agricultural economics). A few regard themselves as outposts of 'radical' economics.

In its search for economic expertise, government can and does tap talents beyond those available from the 'in-house' resources provided by economists on the full-time federal payroll. Indeed a complex network of 'inside' and 'outside' relationships has evolved. One group of economists serving government—the senior policy strategists—are 'in-and-outers' by the rules of the game; they expect to return to private life when the political guard changes. In some policy-shaping posts, turnover rates are even more accelerated. Since the inception of the Council of Economic Advisers, for example, the majority of its members have been academicians on leave from their universities for a stint of two years or so in Washington. But resignation from an official appointment does not necessarily imply detachment from major policy deliberations: consulting relationships are not infrequently maintained. The skills of the policy strategists may also be kept sharpened in other ways. Washington is the site of two research institutes (The Brookings Institution and the American Enterprise Institute), each of which has taken on some of the attributes of a shadow Council of Economic Advisers. Exit and entry of their research staffs tend to fluctuate with transfer of political power from one of the major parties to the other.

Another type of linkage between inside and outside involves a substantial number of economists who have not been in public employment, but have always been based in universities, consulting firms, or research institutes. With some frequency, departments and agencies commission studies bearing on immediate practical problems which they lack the internal resources to execute (cases in point are econometric studies of the market impacts of government stockpiling or de-stockpiling activities, modeling of the economic implications of alternative urban transport modes, general equilibrium modeling of the incidence of tax options, evaluation of income-maintenance programs). Government has also turned to outsiders for longer-term inquiries

—postmortem investigations of the effectiveness of counterinflationary strategies, projections of future international monetary arrangements, analyses of the adequacy of the government's statistical efforts, etc. A number of departments and agencies have regularly convened outsiders as commentators on proposed policy initiatives. Outsiders have been called upon to perform a further function which, in part, is prompted by the 'balkanization' of bureaucracy: that of being the 'neutral' adjudicators of conflicting analyses offered by competing departments and agencies. In addition, outsiders are regularly invited to appear as expert witnesses before congressional committees.

A crude indication of the magnitude of these informal links between the federal government and the wider body of 'laymen' can be gleaned from estimates of the number of economists receiving federal support contained in the 1974 Sample Survey of Scientists and Engineers. This inquiry indicated that some 3,840 economists outside the federal government were a part of this network. The largest single group of recipients—about 53 percent of the total—was to be found in educational institutions. About half of the academic beneficiaries were commissioned by the Department of Agriculture (a reflection of its continuing connection with agricultural economists in the nation's comprehensive system of land-grant colleges). The National Science Foundation, the former Department of Health, Education, and Welfare, and the Department of Housing and Urban Development were the other principal sponsors of academically based research. Other non-federal employees receiving some federal support as economists were found in commercial consulting firms, non-profit research institutes, and state and local governments.[37]

These data, of course, fail to capture the full sweep of 'inside' and 'outside' contacts. Nor do they provide any indication of the proportion of time committed to governmentally subsidized research and consulting by economists whose primary employment is elsewhere. If the aggregative figures are accepted, however, they would suggest that 40 to 50 percent of the active members of the economics profession had some stipendiary contact with the federal government in 1974 and that the head count of 'outsiders' was not very far short of that for 'insiders.'

V. Some Questions Outstanding

Though the American political system has made room near the top for professional economists and has recruited them in increasing num-

37. *Characteristics of the National Sample of Scientists and Engineers*, 1974.

bers to intermediate positions within the bureaucracy, these developments have been accompanied by some strains. The arrangements
which have evolved have not always been totally satisfying to the professional community, to the political management, or to the broader
public. Indeed economists may be victims of their own success. Upward mobility in the corridors of power invites questions about how far
their behavior is strictly professional (as opposed to accommodatingly
political).

In the opinion of a number of outside commentators, some economists in government have faltered in their professional integrity in being accomplices to the suppression or distortion of data which might be
awkward to the administration in power.[38] In the view of many economists who have served as senior advisers, the issue of how 'political'
their activities must be is regarded as much more complex. There is
general agreement that economists should be candid in their dealings
with their political masters, even when the tidings they bring may be
unpleasant. But it does not follow that equal candor in public statements is appropriate. As one former CEA Chairman has put it: "the
greater reconciler of loyalty and integrity is silence."[39] Some loss of in-
nocence is regarded as the price which a senior adviser must be prepared to pay if his views are to carry weight. Should the tension between professional integrity and political loyalty become too acute, the
honorable course is resignation. The absence of principled resignations
by senior economists in government—despite their occasional discom-
fort with policies adopted—is remarkable.

Among economists who have served as policy strategists, many are
ambivalent about the experience for other reasons. Life near the top
may be exhilarating, but it is also exhausting and affords little time for
analytically satisfying reflection. Many resent the time pressures which
this type of work necessarily imposes. A complex problem which deserves a year's detailed research may require a memorandum which
must reach the President's desk the following day. Pride of craftsman-
ship is compromised when such instant analyses must be generated,
even when the author is persuaded that an imperfect economic assessment of the issue is better than none at all. This theme recurs in the ob-

38. For example, an economics correspondent for the *New York Times* has leveled a
severe indictment along these lines; see Leonard Silk, "Truth vs. Partisan Political Purpose," *American Economic Review* 62 (May 1972): 376–79.

39. Remarks of Arthur Okun to the panel discussion of the American Economic Association meeting of 29 Dec. 1973 as reprinted in "How Political Must the Council of
Economic Advisers Be?" *Challenge* 17 (March–April 1974): 33. Other participants in
this discussion included Robert Stein, Henry Wallich, James Tobin, Walter Heller,
Hendrik Houthakker, Marina Whitman, and Roy Blough.

servations of the sample of policy-strategist alumni (most of whom were temporary academic sojourners in Washington) interviewed by William R. Allen.[40] The views he has recorded do not, however, tell the full story. The academic economists who have operated most effectively as policy strategists have been those who accepted that theoretically optimal solutions were unlikely to be attainable and that 'second-best' outcomes could still be improvements. Moreover they have recognized that persistence in pedagogy can shift the politician's perception and articulation of economic problems. As CEA chairmen, both Burns and Heller (neither of whom appeared in Allen's sample of interviewees) were masters of this art.

A rather different sense of frustration is to be found in the attitudes of many of the 5,000 or so economists who are a part of the bureaucratic establishment. Within this group, a feeling of 'second-class' professional status is frequently expressed. The 'in-and-outers' and their brethren in the universities who are governmentally commissioned to do the deep research studies win the kudos. Moreover, economists outside government are thought to enjoy forms of professional liberation which are not available to the permanant insiders—particularly, relief from the expectation that they will be advocates of the client department's party line. Some of these grievances have been spoken to by the Society of Government Economists. Founded in 1970, this organization sponsors monthly discussion groups in Washington and organizes sessions at the annual meetings of the American Economic Association and its various regional affiliates. The Society—with membership of about 500 in 1978—has been invited by the Civil Service Commission to submit its views on personnel procedures applicable to economists in government service. In response to this invitation, its spokesmen have taken issue with the parochial implications of practices of job classification and placement.[41] They have proposed that personnel policies should give priority to the general theoretical and quantitative skills of economists and that specialist job descriptions which presuppose specific knowledge of particular markets or institutions should be de-emphasized. Competence of the latter type is held to

40. William R. Allen, "Economics, Economists, and Economic Policy: Modern American Experiences," *History of Political Economy* 9 (1977): 48–88.

41. In the 1950s, the Civil Service Commission put economists into the following pigeonholes: general economics, business economics, international trade and development economics, fiscal and financial economics, transportation economics, labor economics, and agricultural economics. This practice has fallen into disuse, but the phenomenon of the hyphenated economist in government has not. Tables of organization continue to be drawn with slots for the fuels economists, the public utility economist, the urban economist, etc.

be best acquired 'on the job.'[42] Not only would reform along the lines suggested tend to produce greater homogeneity in the professional work of economists inside and outside government; it would also ease the transferability of economists between departments. The grievances to which this proposal speaks are real enough. Nevertheless, the economist as bureaucrat does enjoy certain non-trivial satisfactions: among them, the opportunity to work on interesting and varied problems which are of undisputed practical significance, and pay scales which, on average, are substantially higher than those in academia.

More importantly, signals that the status quo is sub-optimal have been transmitted from the political leadership. The Congress, for example, manifested its concern about the adequacy of the existing machinery when it created an Advisory Committee on National Growth Policy Processes in 1975. This group (which included in its membership a former CEA chairman and a Nobel Laureate in Economics) recommended the establishment of a new institution—a National Growth and Development Commission. This was to be an independent agency of the government with a "broad mandate to examine emerging issues of middle- to long-range growth and development, and to suggest feasible alternatives for the Congress, the President, and the public." In addition, the report called for the creation of a Center for Statistical Policy and Analysis which would be charged to develop a model of the American economy "broken down by region and sector." It was further recommended that the analytic capabilities of the CEA and the Joint Economic Committee of Congress be strengthened—most particularly their capacity to deal with "sectoral, interdepartmental, and intergovernmental problems."[43]

The institutional innovations conceived by this Advisory Committee have been stillborn, though concerns of a similar nature have been expressed from the White House. On 25 August 1977 President Carter commissioned the Office of Management and Budget to undertake a major review of the economic analysis and policy machinery within executive departments and agencies (excluding the Council of Economic Advisers and the Office of Management and Budget itself). The charge to those conducting the inquiry was to develop recommendations designed to "eliminate overlapping functions among economic agencies; repair weaknesses or gaps in the Federal government's ca-

---

42. "Recommendations of the Society of Government Economists to the Civil Service Commission," 12 July 1978. The author acknowledges with gratitude the cooperation of Donald Dalton, Secretary of the Society, in making this document available.

43. Report of the Advisory Committee on National Growth Policy Processes, *Forging America's Future*, as reprinted in *Challenge* 19 (Jan.–Feb., 1977): 11–12.

pacity to conduct economic analyses of particular regions or agencies; link foreign policy with economic decisions; and ensure that economic decisions are carried out."[44] The project staff assigned to this exercise was even more explicit on the need for searching reappraisals. As it put the issue:

> Persistent inflation, troubling shortages, and the cumulative impact of regulatory decisions have recently begun to erode confidence in the standard tools of macroeconomic policy as devices to manage the economy. As attention has turned to the need for increased sectoral and microeconomic analysis, however, it has become increasingly apparent that the government's resources in this area are peculiarly deployed, poorly focused, and not well linked to the economic policy process.[45]

The consequences of bureaucratic fragmentation were further deplored as follows:

> It has long been recognized that the Federal government has a significant impact on the inter- and intra-regional distribution of jobs and people and on the fiscal condition of state and local governments, but that this impact results more from seemingly unrelated decisions on the tax policy, conservation measures, bank regulation practices, transportation regulation decisions, and the like than from the avowed programs for community and local economic development. In fact, these implicit development policies have long worked at cross-purposes to the more explicit Federal development aids, creating deep frustration on the part of Federal program managers and local officials alike. Yet the government has so far lacked the capability to analyze these regional impacts of seemingly unrelated economic decisions or to take systematic account of what analysis is being done in the formation of economic policy.[46]

Though much thought has subsequently been given to these matters, no fundamental changes (and only a few cosmetic ones) in the apparatus of economic policymaking have yet occurred.

44. Memorandum from President Carter to the Heads of Departments and Agencies, "Review of the Economic Analysis and Policy Machinery in the Federal Government," 25 Aug. 1977, as published in the *Federal Register*, 29 Aug. 1977.
45. Work Program: Economic Analysis Study, President's Reorganization Project, Office of Management and Budget, Sept. 1977, p. 2.
46. Ibid., p. 4.

VI. *A Closing Word*

A stable equilibrium has not been reached in the relationships between American professional economists and their government. Nor, for that matter, is it likely that one will soon be established. Factors which have contributed to change in the past are likely to persist in the future. There is no assurance that tomorrow's public preferences (which will be reflected in the choice of political leadership) on the scope of government intervention in the economy will be the same as today's or yesterday's. Barring the unlikely occurrence of a major Constitutional reform, interdepartmental and intergovernmental contests over economic policy will continue. Meanwhile, it is to be expected that practitioners of the discipline will produce in the future—as they have produced in the past—arresting approaches to new problems and novel techniques for addressing older ones and that their findings will find an audience in officialdom.

It seems safe to predict that demand of government for the insights of economists will not diminish. Even administrations committed to constraining (if not reducing) the economic role of government are likely to discover that they need professional assistance in that task. Given its pluralism, the American economics profession can cater to a variety of political tastes. One forecast can be advanced with ever greater confidence: in view of the bearish prospects for the academic labor market in the decade ahead, the attractiveness of governmental employment for economists will be enhanced.

Though the terms of interaction of American economists and government may evolve in unsuspected ways in the future, at least one thread of continuity will be maintained. Whatever they may mean for government, these contacts will continue to refresh the vitality of the discipline.

Appendix A: The Organizational Locale of Major Units of the U.S. Government with Jurisdiction in Economic Affairs, 1980

Executive Branch

The President
Executive Office of the President
Council of Economic Advisers
Office of Management and Budget
(formerly Bureau of the Budget)

Domestic Policy Staff
Office of the U.S. Trade
Representative
Council on Wage and Price
Stability

Cabinet Departments
Agriculture
Commerce
Defense
Education
Energy
Health and Human Services

Housing and Urban
Development
Interior
Justice
Labor
State
Transportation
Treasury

Legislative Branch

*Central Congressional Staff
Organizations*
Congressional Budget Office
General Accounting Office
Office of Technology Assessment

*Standing Congressional
Committees*
Joint Economic Committee
Joint Committee on Taxation

House of Representatives
Agriculture
Appropriations
Armed Services
Banking, Finance, and
Urban Affairs
Budget
Education and Labor
Government Operations
Interior and Insular Affairs
Public Works and Transportation
Science and Technology
Small Business
Ways and Means

Senate
Agriculture, Nutrition, and
Forestry
Appropriations
Armed Services
Banking, Housing, and Urban
Affairs
Commerce, Science, and
Transportation
Energy and Natural Resources
Environment and Public
Works
Finance
Government Affairs
Human Resources

Independent Agencies

Federal Reserve System
Civil Aeronautics Board
Environmental Protection Agency
Export-Import Bank
Federal Communications
Commission
Federal Home Loan Bank Board
Federal Trade Commission

General Services Administration
Interstate Commerce Commission
National Labor Relations Board
Securities and Exchange
Commission
Small Business Administration
Tennessee Valley Authority
Nuclear Regulatory Commission

Bibliography

The materials bearing on this subject are vast in scope. The entries listed below identify some of the more significant published sources. The scholar concerned with detailed studies of the role of economists in the American governmental process will be rewarded by consulting the records based in the National Archives in Washington, D.C., and in the various presidential libraries. The regular publications of the United States Government yield continuing insights. The annual *Economic Report of the President* and the studies published by the Joint Economic Committee of the Congress and by the Congressional Budget Office are especially recommended.

Ackley, Gardner. "The Contribution of Economists to Policy Formation." *Journal of Finance* 21 (May 1966): 169–77.

Allen, William R. "Economics, Economists, and Economic Policy: Modern American Experience." *History of Political Economy* 9 (1977): 48–88.

Bailey, Stephen K. *Congress Makes a Law: The Story Behind the Employment Act of 1946*. New York, 1950.

Berman, Larry. *The Office of Management and Budget and the Presidency, 1921–1979*. Princeton, 1979.

Blough, Roy. "The Role of the Economist in Federal Policy Making." In *Edmund J. James Lectures on Government*, Sixth Series. Urbana, Ill., 1954.

————. "Economic Problems and Economic Advice: A Half-Century of Evolution." In *Economic Advice and Executive Policy*, ed. Werner Sichel (New York, 1978), pp. 17–44.

Burns, Arthur F. *Prosperity Without Inflation*. New York, 1957.

————. *Reflections of an Economic Policy Maker: Speeches and Congressional Statements, 1969–1978*. Washington, D.C., 1978.

————. *The Management of Prosperity*. New York, 1965.

Canterbury, E. Ray. *The President's Council of Economic Advisers*. New York, 1961.

Carson, Carol S. "The History of the United States National Income and Product Accounts: The Development of an Analytic Tool." *Review of Income and Wealth*, 1975, pp. 153–81.

Cartter, Allan M. "Whither the Market for Academic Economists?" *American Economic Review* 61 (May 1971): 305–10.

Coats, A. W. "Economists in Government: A Research Field for the Historian of Economics." *History of Political Economy* 10 (1978): 298–314.

————. "The American Economic Association, 1904–1929." *American Economic Review* 54 (June 1964): 261–85.

Colm, Gerhard, ed. *The Employment Act: Past and Future*. Washington, 1956.

Currie, Lauchlin. "Comments and Observations." *History of Political Economy* 10 (1978): 541–48.

Duesenberry, James S. "Current Policy in a Long-Term Context." In *Economic Advice and Executive Policy*, ed. Werner Sichel (New York, 1978), pp. 65–78.

Enthoven, Alain C. "Economic Analysis in the Department of Defense" *American Economic Review* 53 (May 1963): 413–23.

Fisher, Irving. "Economists in Public Service." *American Economic Review* 9 (March 1919): 5–21.

Flash, Edward S., Jr. *Economic Advice and Presidential Leadership: The Council of Economic Advisers.* New York, 1965.

Galbraith, John Kenneth. "How Keynes Came to America." In *Economics, Peace, and Laughter* (Boston, 1971), pp. 43–59.

———. "Power and the Useful Economist." *American Economic Review* 63 (March 1963): 1–11.

Goodwin, Craufurd D., ed. *Energy Policy in Perspective: Today's Problems and Yesterday's Solutions.* Washington, D.C., 1981.

———. *Exhortation and Controls: The Search for a Wage-Price Policy, 1945–1971.* Washington, D.C., 1975.

Hansen, W. L., and others. "Forecasting the Market for New Ph.D. Economists." *American Economic Review* 70 (March 1980): 49–63.

Harmon, Lindsey R. "The Supply of Economists in the 1970s." *American Economic Review* 61 (May 1971): 311–15.

Heclo, Hugh. *A Government of Strangers: Executive Politics in Washington.* Washington, D.C., 1977.

Heller, Walter W. *New Dimensions of Political Economy.* Cambridge, Mass., 1966.

Henderson, John B. "Professional Standards for the Performance of the Government Economist." *American Economic Review* 67 (Feb. 1977): 321–26.

Hitch, Charles. "The Uses of Economics." In *Research for Public Policy* (Washington, D.C., 1961).

Houthakker, Hendrik J. "The Breakdown of Bretton Woods." In *Economic Advice and Executive Policy*, ed. Werner Sichel (New York, 1978), pp. 45–66.

Jacoby, Neil H. *Can Prosperity Be Sustained?* New York, 1956.

———. "The President, the Constitution, and the Economist in Economic Stabilization." *History of Political Economy* 3 (1971): 398–414.

Joint Economic Committee. *Twentieth Anniversary of the Employment Act of 1946.* 89 Congress, 2d Session, 23 Feb. 1966.

Jones, Byrd L. "Lauchlin Currie, Pump Priming, and New Deal Fiscal Policy, 1934–1936." *History of Political Economy* 10 (1978): 509–24.

———. "The Role of Keynesians in Wartime Policy and Postwar Planning." *American Economic Review* 62 (May 1972): 125–33.

Keyserling, Leon H. "The Council of Economic Advisers Since 1946: Its Contributions and Failures." *Atlantic Economic Journal* 6 (March 1978): 17–35.

Knapp, Joseph G. *Edwin G. Nourse—Economist for the People.* Danville, Ill., 1979.

McCracken, Paul W. *Reflections on Economic Advising.* Los Angeles, March 1976.

———. "An Elder Statesman's Advice to a CEA Chairman." In *Economic Advice and Executive Policy*, ed. Werner Sichel (New York, 1978), pp. 7–16.

Norton, Hugh S. *The Council of Economic Advisers: Three Periods of Influence.* Columbia, S.C., 1973.

———. *The Employment Act, 1946–71.* Columbia, S.C., 1974.

Nourse, Edwin G. *Economics in the Public Service: Administrative Aspects of the Employment Act.* New York, 1953.

―――. "The Employment Act of 1946 and a System of National Bookkeeping." *American Economic Review* 37 (May 1947): 21–30.

Okun, Arthur M. "Conflicting National Goals." In *Jobs for Americans*, ed. Eli Ginsberg (New York, 1976), pp. 59–84.

―――. *The Political Economy of Prosperity*. Washington, D.C. 1969.

―――. and others. "How Political Must the Council of Economic Advisers Be?" *Challenge* (March–April 1974): 28–42.

Pechman, Joseph A. *Making Economic Policy: The Role of the Economist*. The Brookings Institution General Series Reprint 311. Washington, D.C., Feb. 1976.

Rivlin, Alice M. "Income Distribution: Can Economists Help?" *American Economic Review* 65 (May 1975): 1–15.

Salant, Walter S. "Some Intellectual Contributions of the Truman Council of Economic Advisers to Policy-Making." *History of Political Economy* 5 (1973): 36–49.

Samuelson, Paul A. "Policy Advising in Economics." *Challenge* 21 (March–April 1978): 37–39.

Schultz, George P., and Kenneth W. Dam. *Economic Policy Beyond the Headlines*. New York, 1977.

Schultze, Charles L. *The Politics and Economics of Public Spending*. Washington, D.C., 1968.

Scott, Charles E. "The Market for Ph.D. Economists: The Academic Sector." *American Economic Review* 69 (May 1979): 137–42.

Silk, Leonard, "Ethics in Economics." *American Economic Review* 67 (Feb. 1977): 376–79.

―――. *Nixonomics*. 2d ed. New York, 1973.

―――. "Truth vs. Partisan Political Purpose." *American Economic Review* 62 (May 1972): 376–78.

Stein, Herbert. *Economic Planning and the Improvement of National Economic Policy*. Washington, D.C., 1975.

―――. *The Fiscal Revolution in America*. Chicago, 1969.

Sweezy, Alan R. "Keynesians and Government Policy, 1933–39." *American Economic Review* 62 (May 1972): 116–24.

Teeters, Nancy A. "Congress and the Economy." *Challenge* 21 (Nov.–Dec. 1978): 26–31.

Tobin, James. "Academic Economics in Washington." In *National Economic Policy* (New Haven, 1966), pp. 201–6.

―――. "Full Recovery or Stagnation." In *Economic Advice and Executive Policy*, ed. Werner Sichel (New York, 1978), pp. 97–109.

―――. *The Intellectual Revolution in U.S. Economic Policy-Making*. Second Noel Buxton Lecture of the University of Essex. London, 1966.

―――. *The New Economics, One Decade Older*. Princeton, 1974.

Tufte, Edward R. *Political Control of the Economy*. Princeton, 1978.

Wallich, Henry C. "The American Council of Economic Advisers and the German Sachverstaendigenrat: A Study in the Economics of Advice." *Quarterly Journal of Economics* 82 (Aug. 1968): 349–79.

―――. "Economists and the Press—A Progress Report." *American Economic Review* 62 (May 1972): 384–86.

Whitman, Marina S. N. "The Search for the Grail: Economic Policy Issues of the Late 1970s." In *Economic Advice and Executive Leadership*, ed. Werner Sichel (New York, 1978), pp. 79–96.

Israel: economists in a new state

Ephraim Kleiman

I. *Historical Survey, or How Economists Came to be Employed in the Israel Government*

1. *Economists in the public sector before 1948*

Government economists are a fairly new species in Israel. The British administration which ruled the country before the establishment of the State of Israel in May 1948 pursued a rather passive economic policy. Government budgets were small, amounting to less than one tenth of national income, and were usually balanced.[1] The revenue system was based on customs, excises, and fees, and dictated the level of expenditure. The currency, pegged to the pound sterling, was fully convertible. In the absence of a central bank—currency was issued by a Currency Board situated in London—there was no place for monetary management. Most of the government's modest requirements for economic expertise were provided by the central colonial machinery of the British Empire and by an English bank which served as its financial agent. The few posts of economic management in the local administration were staffed mainly by Englishmen who were not necessarily economists. Even the more active policies required by World War II were to a great extent formulated by outside bodies, such as the Cairo-located Middle East Supply Center, and carried out with the help of personnel drafted from outside the country.

The governmental machinery of Israel evolved out of the Jewish communal institutions, which enjoyed a certain amount of semi-autonomy before 1948: the Jewish Agency, which represented the Zionist movement; the National Council of Palestinian Jews; and the centralistic labor union, the Histadrut. Though these bodies dealt with many economic matters, they did so mainly on the micro level. In the spheres where they fulfilled governmental functions, it was the relevant specialists—education, public-health, or agricultural experts—

---

1. For the economic role of the government under the Mandate, see A. L. Gaathon (Gruenbaum), *National Income and Outlay in Palestine, 1936* (Jerusalem, Bank of Israel, 1978). This is a reprint of the 1941 edition, with the addition of the originally unpublished parts and of critical comments. Also R. Nathan, O. Gass, and D. Creamer, *Palestine: Promise and Problem* (Washington, D.C., 1946).

rather than economists, whose opinions were sought. They employed economists for the preparation of macroeconomic forecasts and development plans, which, for the lack of executive powers, were used mainly to support political arguments and negotiations.[2]

The business sector, except for Histadrut-owned enterprises, consisted mainly of small, family-owned and -run firms. It followed from the government's non-interventionist attitude that insofar as this sector employed economists, their work was, again, on the micro, business-administration level.

As was then the case of all academic professions, most economists were immigrants who received their training abroad, mainly in continental Europe. At the Hebrew University of Jerusalem economics was taught only within the broader framework of Middle-East Social Studies; some evening courses, leading to a diploma, were offered by a 'School of Law and Economics,' the forerunner of Tel-Aviv University. Given this background it is not surprising that, with some notable exceptions, professional economists tended to represent the historical or institutional rather than the analytical approach to their subject. Furthermore, economics was not really a recognized profession, requiring a defined academic training. General experience in business and finance was considered to be not only a sufficient but even the preferable qualification for posts which would nowadays be occupied by trained economists.[3]

2. The changed role of government and the demand for economists after independence

The position of economists in government, and ultimately also in the private sector, underwent a rapid transformation with the establish-

2. E.g. the sections dealing with economic matters in the material submitted by the Jewish Agency for Palestine to the Anglo-American and the U.N. Committees nominated to inquire into the Palestine question: *The Jewish Case Before the Anglo-American Committee* (Jerusalem, 1946) and *The Jewish Plan for Palestine* (Jerusalem, 1947). As has been recently shown by Metzer, these institutions paid considerable attention to broad policy questions, such as that of the role of public versus private investment and ownership. J. Metzer, *National Capital for a National Home 1919–1921* (Hebrew; Jerusalem, 1979). But they viewed them, rightly, as first and foremost political decisions, to be settled on broad political principles rather than on technical economic considerations. On the role of economists in this period, see also A. L. Gaathon, "Problems of Development of an Economist," *Economic Quarterly* (Hebrew) 77 (April 1973): 58–68.

3. This was especially true of Histadrut-operated enterprises. The men who founded and ran them constituted a very special entrepreneurial-managerial type; they were neither capitalist entrepreneurs (in the sense that they were not profit-motivated) nor bureaucrats. See E. Kleiman, "From Cooperative to Industrial Empire," *Midstream* 1964, pp. 15–26; and "Solel-Boneh as Seen by Hillel Dan," *Economic Quarterly* (Hebrew), 1964, 41–42, pp. 170–83.

ment of the State. This was the outcome of a number of factors, operating on both the demand and supply sides of the market for economists. A whole government machinery had to be set up, not only to replace the local British administration, but also to deal with problems which used to lie outside the responsibility of the latter, like monetary management and exchange control. The absorption of the mass immigration which followed the declaration of independence—the population was doubled within three years—and the heavy defense burden imposed by the hostility of the neighboring states, required public spending on a scale hitherto unprecedented in the country. Relatively to national income, government expenditures rose rapidly to over 40 percent, three to four times as high as the expenditures of the British administration under the Mandate.[4] Furthermore, the Israel government was committed from the beginning to a highly interventionist economic policy. This was, in part, made unavoidable by the strains which mass immigration imposed on the economy: the necessity of providing the immigrants with some minimal nutrition and housing, and the unavailability of foreign exchange to pay for the country's increased import requirements. But direct interventionism reflected also the ideology of the Labor Party, which was to rule the country for nearly three decades, regarding both the economic role of government and the choice of its policy instruments.[5]

Table 1 provides some indicators of the *quantitative* aspects of the government's role in the Israel economy in its early years. Government expenditures, measured in real terms, increased nearly fivefold within the first ten years, doubling again in the following five. By 1964 they were ten times as high as in 1949. In the main, this reflected the rapid growth of the economy, made possible by a high rate of investment. Investment amounted to nearly a quarter of the GNP in the decade 1950–1959, more than half of it being financed by the public sector. Coupled with the *qualitative* changes—the increase in responsibilities with sovereignty, and the government's predilection for direct inter-

4. In the absence of reliable GNP or national income data for 1948–49, the figure quoted in the text is the average of the annual ratios in 1950–53, expressed relatively to national income for comparability with pre-1948 figures. The latter do not include the expenditures of the Jewish institutions, which supplemented the government in education, health, and development. However, it has been estimated that the ratio of all 'governmental' outlays to income in the Jewish sector of Palestine rarely exceeded 20 percent. N. Gross and J. Metzer, "Public Finance in the Jewish Economy in Interwar Palestine," *Research in Economic History*, III, pp. 87–159. On the other hand, some of the costs of the absorption of the mass immigration after 1948 was borne by nongovernmental agencies, such as the Jewish Agency.

5. For a critical description of the interventionist policies pursued in Israel in the State's first decade, see A. Rubner, *The Economy of Israel: A Critical Account of the First Ten Years* (London, 1960).

Table 1.   The growth of government activity, 1950–1964

Year	Govt. outlays in real terms[a] (1949 = 100)	Govt. outlays as % of GNP	Net investment as % of GNP	Govt. share of fixed investment[b]
	(1)	(2)	(3)	(4)
1950	165	30.5	27.3	42 [c]
1952	166	26.6	27.5	49
1954	307	40.0	21.3	81
1956	366	36.2	20.6	52
1958	476	38.9	21.3	53
1960	597	39.6	19.6	53
1962	822	45.3	23.7	41
1964	1,008		23.8	39

[a] Based on estimates of total government revenues from all sources, valued in constant 1955 prices.

[b] Investment financed by central government, local authorities, and the 'national institutions,' and by corporations they owned or controlled.

[c] Direct government investment only.

Sources: Columns (1) and (2)—Morag, *Government Finance in Israel*, Tables B-3 and B-4. The 1964 figures are calculated from Bank of Israel, *Annual Report 1964*, Table VII-3. Columns (3) and (4)—Halevi and Klinov-Malul, *The Economic Development of Israel*, Tables 32 and 70.

vention—these developments necessitated economic decisionmaking on a completely different scale from that required of both the Mandatory administration and the Jewish communal institutions in pre-independence days.

To staff the young State's civil service, the government had to draw upon all available sources of administrative experience: officials of the Jewish institutions and of the former administration, functionaries of political parties, managers of financial institutions and of trade union enterprises, and members of the private business community. Given the emergency conditions under which the whole governmental machinery was set up, and the accompanying enthusiasm, it is not surprising that the whole process resembled in many respects that experienced in some other countries in the early days of World War II. Service for the new government carried with it initially considerable social prestige as well as opportunities for political and personal patronage.[6] Nevertheless, in the economic sphere at least, there was a considerable lack of suitable personnel. Pre-independence Palestine

6. A popular song of the period told of the man "who had a cousin in the Kirya (seat of government offices then) and, nevertheless, behaved like any other ordinary man."

abounded in holders of university degrees who had to abandon their former occupations upon immigration. Many of them were drafted into the new civil service.[7] But theirs was usually a legal or general arts education, and few of them were economists.

Under these circumstances, the government tried to unburden itself of some of its functions by farming them out to existing financial institutions. It entrusted the issuing of currency to a commercial bank.[8] It tried to use the services of existing investment banks in allocating investment funds from its development budget. But the government's interventionist attitude resulted in the function of such outside bodies becoming very soon restricted to the purely technical carrying out of governmental orders.

In its search for economic expertise the government turned also to seek advice abroad. The list of foreign economists consulted included such luminaries as M. Kalecki, J. Mossak and H. D. White, but their opinions were often disregarded as not suiting local conditions. More successful was the establishment, in 1952, of an Economic Advisory Staff outside the regular governmental bureaucracy. Headed by Oscar Gass, formerly the Jewish Agency's economic adviser in the United States, the E.A.S. managed to recruit some top level experts from abroad, and included among its members Abba P. Lerner and M. M. Clawson, the well-known agricultural expert, as well as A. L. Gaathon, the doyen of Israel economists. A number of young economists, either newly migrated from Western countries or recently graduating in Israel, served their apprenticeships on its supporting staff. The E.A.S. had considerable influence both on current decisions and on professional standards. (Its most lasting effect, perhaps, was in the sphere of investment project evaluation, where it seems to have foreshadowed some later theoretical developments in the field.) But the government found the E.A.S.'s independence inconvenient and did not renew its contract after 1955. In the meantime, however, changes on the supply side started to be felt in the government employment of economists.

7. Out of the 75 top Treasury officials listed in the *Israel Government Yearbook* for the year 5711 (1950–51), no fewer than 19 had 'Dr.' displayed before their names. In the Ministry of Trade and Industry the proportion was even higher—18 out of 35! This reflected both the continental addiction to titles and the custom of many continental universities of not granting any degree lower than the Ph.D.

8. This bank was, however, a semi-public institution. Founded by the Zionist Organization at the turn of the century, it was by far the biggest bank in the country, and was widely expected at the time to become Israel's Central Bank after independence. The Bank of Israel was not established until late in 1954. See E. Kleiman, "The Anglo-Palestine Bank and the Establishment of Israel's Monetary System," Part III, in N. Gross, N. Halevi, E. Kleiman, and M. Sarnat, *Banker to a Renascent National* (Hebrew; Tel-Aviv, 1977), pp. 203–93; and N. Halevi et al., *Banker to an Emerging Nation*.

3. *The supply side*

The termination of the period of strife culminating in the 1948 War of Independence gave a great impetus to the development of tertiary education in Israel. Until then, undertakings of high national priority—military service in World War II, underground activity, and agricultural settlement—attracted considerable numbers of high school graduates. Released from service, the national goals now seemingly attained with independence, many of them turned to higher studies. The combined result of this pent-up supply and of the increased demand for university graduates reflected itself in a rapid increase in the number of university students. Between the spring of 1949, when hostilities ended and studies at the University were resumed, and the end of 1952 the number of students more than doubled. By 1957/58, when other universities started operation, the number of students at the Hebrew University was more than four and a half times as high as in 1949—nearly twice the growth rate of the country's population as a whole. Both the number of students and that of degrees granted nearly doubled again in the next three years.[9]

The University responded to this increased demand by introducing a three-year bachelor's degree, turning the master's degree to which students until then used to proceed directly into a two-year second degree, and by a rapid expansion of faculty and the introduction of new fields of study. Many of the new staff were recruited abroad, among Zionists to whom the establishment of the state added a further stimulus for immigration to Israel. Among them was a 27-year-old former Assistant Professor at the University of Chicago, who initiated a study program in economics along the lines accepted in English-speaking countries. The intellectual elegance and nearly mathematical precision of the new subject held considerable appeal for the day's students, who had the war veteran's abhorrence of highfalutin phrases and fuzzy thinking. An outstanding teacher, the new lecturer soon attracted a strong group of students, who upon their entrance into government service came to be known as the 'Patinkin boys.'

9. The following data on graduates from the Hebrew University in Jerusalem are derived from the *Israel Statistical Abstract* and the files of the University's Economics Department:

	Total	Economics
1950–51	46	2
1955–56	152	29
1960–61	591	49

The 1960–61 figures include graduates from the Tel-Aviv School of Law and Economics.

4. *The 'new economists' enter the government*

To finance the absorption of mass immigration, the government resorted initially to the printing press. But price controls, and the elaborate system of rationing set up to sustain them, could not withstand for
long the mounting inflationary pressures. Under the 'New Economic
Policy' announced early in 1952, inflationary financing was curtailed,
prices were raised to wipe out the public's excess purchasing power,
and—as implied by the allusion to Lenin's N.E.P.—the economy was
to be gradually liberalized. This reversal of policy required a much
tighter control of government budgets, and consequently also a more
thorough budgetary planning, than was the case until then. In autumn
1952 a separate budgets department was established in the Ministry of
Finance, which took over the preparation of the budget from the office
of the Accountant General. To head the new department, soon to be elevated into one of the ministry's four major divisions,[10] the government chose a Dutch-trained economist who came to the country
shortly before Independence and who had gained some budgeting experience in the immediate postwar reconstruction period in the
Netherlands. Dr. Yaakov Arnon, who started his government service
in Israel in the office of the controller of the diamond industry, was to
become with the years one of the country's foremost civil servants.
Successively head of the budgets division and, from 1956 to 1970, director general of the Ministry of Finance, he was the man chiefly instrumental in introducing economists into government service in
Israel.

The budgets department was established at almost exactly the same
time at which the first class of economics students graduated from the
Hebrew University. It was thus able from its beginning to recruit for its
staff some of the most promising of the 'new' economists, which it continued to do also in the following years. This fusion of what were then
for Israel a new function and a novel model of thought, turned out to be
most successful. The Budgets Division's analytical approach to economic problems ensured it a rapid ascendancy in the governmental
decisionmaking hierarchy; while the atmosphere of intellectual give
and take and the openness to new ideas which characterized it, and the
opportunity it afforded of applying theoretical tools to real-world problems, caused it to become highly regarded in the growing community of
Israeli economists. For years to come newly graduating economists

---

10. The other three being the Revenue Directorate, the Exchange Control Division,
and the Office of the Accountant General. The last-mentioned division controls actual
disbursement of funds allocated through the budget, as well as the handing out of government credits and raising of State Loans.

were to consider work with the division as offering perhaps the best professional apprenticeship available, and it was able to attract some of the best brains of successive graduating classes.[11]

The transition from the system of direct controls to that of general policy measures required a better understanding of economic processes on the part of policymakers and officials concerned. It resulted in the new economists graduating from the Hebrew University being hired in growing numbers also by other departments in the Ministry of Finance, in particular by the Foreign Exchange Division. But it was the creation of the Budgets Division, and the eminent position it soon acquired, which had, probably, the most far-reaching implications on the government's demand for economists. Each ministry had now to submit its expenditure proposals to the critical examination of the corresponding referendary in the Budgets Division. Senior civil servants, who considered themselves experts in their respective fields, found themselves cross-examined, and often browbeaten, by young men who, though lacking the formers' technical knowledge and experience, were nevertheless trained to ask the right, often embarrassing questions. Either because they genuinely realized the advantages of such training or, not less likely, because they felt that the Budgets Division's boys could only be dealt with by someone talking the same language, other ministries also hired economists. The process was then repeated, to a varying degree, within individual ministries. It was in this pattern, with supply creating demand, and vice versa, that the employment of economists spread from the Ministry of Finance, first to other ministries, then to the various agencies and government corporations associated with them and, ultimately, to the private sector.

In Table 2, we compare the increase in the number of economists employed by the government with the general development of the Israel civil service in the years 1956–1961. The total number of government employees (exclusive of manual workers) increased by one third during this period. But this expansion differed from the rapid growth of the bureaucracy which followed the establishment of the State. Table 2 distinguishes between general administrators and clerical personnel and personnel on the various 'professional' salary scales—i.e. physicians, engineers, lawyers, etc.[12] Four out of each five persons added to

11. Partly because of scarcity of suitable personnel, and partly because it could employ them at a relatively low cost, the Budgets Division used to employ students as technical assistants, some of whom later joined it upon graduation. This practice was (and still is) followed also by other government offices and agencies in Israel.

12. Teachers, though paid out of the State budget, are considered in Israel to be the employees of local authorities, and are not included. Initially, professional salary scales were provided mainly for personnel with certain types of academic education, consid-

Table 2. The growth of Israel civil service, 1955–1961

Year *a*	Total *b*	Admin. and clerical	Profes- sional *c*	Economists *d* Total	Trea- sury	Others
1955	22,020	18,289	3,731	48	20	28
1956	22,908	18,803	4,105	84	35	49
1957	23,592	19,138	4,454	95	35	60
1958	24,949	19,990	4,969	107	31	75
1959	26,850	19,849 *e*	7,001 *e*	154	53	101
1960	27,811	19,637	8,174	198	62	136
1961	29,227	20,412	8,815	217	70	147
1955–58 (1955 = 100)	113	109	133	262	155	271
1955–61 (1955 = 100)	133	112	237	452	350	525

a March 31 of each year.

b Exclusive of manual workers. (Teachers and members of the armed forces are not included in civil service.).

c Personnel on special pay scales reserved for certain groups with distinct academic or vocational training—physicians, engineers, qualified hospital nurses, etc.

d Including statisticians.

e A new professional scale was added in May 1958, resulting in a reclassification of persons already employed in the civil service.

Source: Israel Civil Service Commission, *Annual Reports*, 5 through 11.

the service in this period belonged to the latter group, its total size more than doubling between 1955 and 1961. The rise in the employment of economists was thus part of the growing general professionalization of the civil service. But it outstripped the latter by far, the relative increase in the number of economists being twice as high as that in the total number of all professional personnel employed by the government.[13] The last two columns of Table 2 reflect the diffusion

ered to constitute a distinctive profession from the point of view either of the government's requirements or of the labor market. It is, therefore, by itself significant that a separate salary scale for economists (including statisticians) was not established until 1954. (Since 1962, on the other hand, this scale has applied also to other 'social science and arts graduates'.) Over the years professional scales came to be provided also for other groups with specific vocational training, such as nurses, X-ray technicians, etc.

13. The sudden increase in the number of professional staff between 1958 and 1959 partly reflects changes in classification rather than real increases in the number of professionals employed. There was considerable pressure on the Civil Service Commission in the years 1957–60 to transfer employees from the Administrative to the professional scales, because of the higher pay in the latter in this period. See Israel Civil Service Commission, *Annual Report No. 9* (Hebrew), p. 90. But, as shown in the table, the change in the number of economists, relatively to all professional staff, was about the same between 1955 and 1958 as in the period covered as a whole.

Table 3. The growth of higher education, 1954/55–1975/76 [a]

	1954/55	1959/60	1964/65	1969/70	1975/76
Students:					
Total	4,545	9,275	18,368	36,239	52,510
Social sciences	—[b]	—	3,225	8,680	13,144
Degrees granted:					
Total	880	1,372	2,491	5,566	9,665
Social sciences	—[b]	—	391	980	2,262
Share of Social Sciences:					
Students	—[b]	—	0.18	0.24	0.25
Degrees	—[b]	—	0.16	0.18	0.23

[a] Covering all institutions acredited by the Israel Council for Higher Education. Exclusive of special programs' students. Data for 1954/55 and 1959/60 exclusive of the Tel-Aviv School of Law and Economics, which did not grant degrees.

[b] Unavailable before 1964/65.

Source: C.B.S., *Israel Statistical Abstract.*

process described earlier. Between March 1955 and March 1961, the number of qualified economists employed by the government on a regular basis increased by 169 persons. The biggest absolute addition, 50, occurred in the Ministry of Finance. But much greater, in relative terms, was the addition of 33 economists in the Ministry of Commerce and Industry and the Ministry of Agriculture: these two ministries employed between them no more than eight economists in the base year. We may regard the 38 economists added to the Prime Minister's Office to have been primarily statisticians employed at the Central Bureau of Statistics. The number of economists employed in all other government offices rose nearly sevenfold, from 10 in 1955 to 68 in 1961.

5. *Later developments*

The quantitative analysis of the spread of economists in government service after the period of their initial breakthrough is hampered by lack of data. No separate figures are available for the number of economists employed in government, nor for the total number of economists graduating from the universities, after 1961. Generally speaking, the demand for university-trained personnel continued to expand in the 1960s and 1970s. The low educational standards of the mass immigration—which trebled the country's population in the early 1950s—increased the relative scarcity of trained manpower, as did probably also the increase in the overall capital-labor ratio: relative to the average wage, the salaries of lawyers rose by 20 percent, those of engineers and of physicians by 56 and 84 percent respectively, and those of accountants by as much as 116 percent, between 1950 and 1957.[14] As a result of the rise in returns to higher education on the one hand, and of the growth of population and of incomes on the other hand, the number of students enrolled at the institutions of higher learning, shown in Table 3, doubled itself within each of the three successive five-year periods after 1954/55. It is only recently that the growth rate has started to show signs of slackening, and even so, the number of students rose by nearly one-half between 1969/70 and 1975/76.

The proportion of students taking up social sciences has increased from 18 percent of all students in 1964/65, the earliest year for which separate data on them are available, to 25 percent in 1975/76. The correspondingly lagging increase in their share of degrees granted suggests that the expansion in the social sciences started later, and continued longer, than that of higher education in general. Though part of the growth of the social sciences reflects the introduction of new fields of study, the growth in the number of graduating economists seems to have followed roughly the same trend. Thus, of the 2,870 economists 'produced' by the Hebrew University between 1949 and 1974, as many as 1,319 graduated from 1970 onwards.[15]

The vagaries of the Israel Civil Service scales make it difficult to assess the increase in the number of economists employed by it. Over the years there occurred many changes in the coverage of the 'professional' scales—new scales were created, other scales abolished and sometimes reestablished later. In particular, the separate scale for economists came to be progressively applied to other professional groups as well, until it was ultimately incorporated in a general scale encompassing most social science and arts graduates. The total numbers employed on professional scales, shown in Table 4, were adjusted, as far as possible, to conform to the same classification throughout the whole period.[16] The adjusted figures indicate that after the rapid initial expansion described earlier, the increase in the number of professionals slowed down until the end of the 1960s. This, how-

14. Adapted from R. Klinov-Malul, *The Profitability of Investment in Education in Israel* (Jerusalem, Falk Institute for Economic Research, 1966), Table D-3.

15. Inclusive of temporarily affiliated institutions, such as the Haifa University College or the H.U.'s extensions in Tel-Aviv (which later formed the nucleus of the social sciences faculty of Tel-Aviv University). Data from the Economics Department at the Hebrew University.

16. Thus the adjusted figures exclude nurses, who were incorporated into the general scale between 1966 and 1973; technicians, for whom a separate scale was introduced only in 1959; as well as some smaller groups whose classification changed over the years, such as other than university-trained social workers, or who are now outside the control of the Civil Service Commission, such as Justices.

Table 4. Professionals in the Israel civil service—selected years, 1955–1975 [a]

Years	Professional scales		Social sciences and arts graduates		
	Total	Adjusted [b]	Total	Econo-mists [c]	Ministry of Finance
1955	3,731	2,058	70	48	20
1960	8,174	3,750	247	198	62
1961	8,815	4,034	—	217	70
1962	10,804	4,393	370	294	77
1963	10,527	4,821	464	374	111
1964	11,274	5,047	509	—	102 [d]
1965	12,061	5,107	613	—	92 [d]
1970	10,809	6,432	1,366	—	127
1975	21,417	10,861	2,913	—	298
Relative growth, selected periods					
1955–1960		1.82	3.53	4.13	3.10
1960–1965		1.36	2.48	1.89 [e]	1.79 [e]
1965–1970		1.26	2.23	—	1.38
1970–1975		1.69	2.13	—	2.35
1955–63		2.34	6.63	7.79	5.55
1963–75		2.25	6.27	—	2.68

[a] March 31 of each year.

[b] Exclusive throughout of nurses, research workers, technicians, justices and one-half of the social workers employed on the social workers' scale.

[c] And statisticians. Years 1962 and 1963 include a small number of other professionals n.e.s.

[d] Reduction due to changes in the responsibilities of the Ministry of Finance (Economic Planning Authority transferred to Prime Minister's Office, etc.).

[e] 1960–1963.

Source: C.B.S., *Statistical Abstract of Israel*, and C.S.C., *Annual Report*.

ever, partly reflects a growing tendency to transfer government activities to government corporations and statutory agencies. The more rapid increase in the number of professionals between 1970 and 1975, on the other hand, was due in part to the extension of the professional scales, not all of which was netted out in the 'adjusted' column of the table. In particular there was a movement of university graduates from the general scale to the 'Social Sciences and Arts' scale.[17] Nevertheless, Table 4 suggests that the great expansion in the latter group, which includes economists, was coming to an end by the mid 1970s: despite the extension of coverage, its rate of growth between 1970 and

17. See Israel Civil Service Commission, *Annual Report No. 21* (Jerusalem, 1971), p. 24.

1975 was only one quarter higher than that of all the professional scales considered here, after being nearly twice as high in each of the three preceding five-year periods.

Separate figures on economists and statisticians are available for only part of the first of the two decades covered by Table 4.[18] It can be seen that in the early 1960s they constituted the overwhelming majority of the 'social sciences and arts,' or as it was then called, the 'miscellaneous graduates' group. Of all the social sciences, theirs were the first to be recognized as definite disciplines, insofar as employment in government was concerned. A significant demand for manpower trained in other behavioral sciences or in the arts, such as psychologists, sociologists, or orientalists, developed only later. The relative growth of these professions in the later part of the period considered here can be expected, therefore, to have outstripped that of economists. A comparison of the total number of social science and arts graduates with that employed in the Ministry of Finance, suggests that this was indeed the case. In Finance most of them are economists. Their rate of growth there was more or less equal to that of all such personnel in the civil service, until the mid 1960s, but dropped to only half of the latter between 1963–1965 and 1975.[19] Assuming total government employment of economists to have grown at the same rate as in the Ministry of Finance, their number in 1975 would be estimated at just over 1,000. However, as the Ministry of Finance preceded other government offices in employing economists, this may be a rather conservative estimate. An almost identical estimate is obtained by a rough rule of thumb classification of ministries into three groups, with economists constituting 100, 30, and 10 percent respectively of all social science and arts graduates employed by them.[20] As, with some exceptions, it was precisely the business character of certain government functions which accounted for their being gradually 'hived off,' the employment figures for all social science and arts graduates, on which our alternative estimate is based, may also be downward biased.

18. With the exception of a small number specializing in mathematical statistics, most statisticians would also have had some training in economics. Except at the Central Bureau of Statistics, most of those employed in government would be working on economic statistics.

19. The decline in the number of social science and arts graduates at the Finance Ministry between 1963 and 1965 is due to the removal from it to the Prime Minister's Office of the Economic Planning Authority and of the Civil Service Commission. The rate of growth mentioned in the text is a rough average of those calculated on the bases of these two years.

20. Included in the first group were the ministries of Agriculture, of Trade and Industry, and of Transportation, and the Central Bureau of Statistics and the head office of the Ministry of Finance; in the second group, the ministries of Housing, of Tourism and Communications, and the Internal Revenue and Customs departments of the Ministry of Finance.

The demand for economists having appeared earlier, its expansion may have subsequently lagged behind that for other social scientists. Nevertheless, the great absolute increase in their number occurred with the great expansion in the output of the social science faculties in the late 1960s and early 1970s. It has already been mentioned that until 1974 nearly half of the economists trained at the Hebrew University graduated after 1969. In the younger universities, which quantitatively have become significant only in the last decade, these recent vintages account for almost all the output. No official figures are available on the number of economists graduating from these universities in this period. But in view of their shares in enrolment and in degrees granted, it may be expected to have been between 1 and 1½ times as big as that of the Hebrew University.[21] Thus, the total number of graduates in the first half of the 1970s can be estimated at about 3,000. On our earlier assumption regarding the rate of growth in the number of economists in the civil service, the government absorbed the equivalent of one fifth of the graduating classes in this period, as compared with an average of between a third and a quarter in all preceding periods taken together, and as much as three quarters in the 1950s.[22] This supports the qualitative impression that, once the initial barriers were breached, the growth in the number of economists employed in government was for a long time restricted mainly by conditions of supply. It is only since the mid-1960s, if not later, that the expansion of the universities' output came to exceed significantly that of the government's demand for economists. By that time, however, the diffusion process described earlier generated considerable demand for them in the business sector, which began to absorb a growing proportion of economics graduates.

The expansion of supply made it possible for the government to

21. Based on the number of students and of first degrees granted in all other academic institutions, excluding the Weitzman Institute at Rehovoth, where economics is not taught, and the Haifa Technion which does not offer first degrees in economics. Informal data obtained by the courtesy of the Economics Departments at the Tel-Aviv and Bar-Illan Universities put the number of graduates there at a figure only slightly exceeding that of those graduating at the Hebrew University, suggesting a total of 2,800 graduates in this period.

22. The continuous exit of economists from the government to the business sector, discussed in a later section, means that the proportions of new graduates entering government were higher than those cited in the text, which are net figures. Thus, for example, of all economics and statistics graduates who received their degrees in the years 1964–66, as much as 86 percent were found in 1967 to work in Jerusalem, which we may regard as nearly synonymous with being employed in government. See Israel Manpower Planning Authority, *Longitudinal Study of University Graduates, 1964–1966* (Hebrew; Jerusalem, 1971). We ignored here mortality, which in view of the age structure was probably low, and emigration, which was implicitly assumed to have been offset by the immigration of economists trained abroad.

satisfy its demand for economists, insofar as sheer numbers are concerned. But unlike in the earlier years, it now had to compete for their services with the private sector. Coupled with the fact that employment in government could no longer offer the same challenges and opportunities it did when economists were few, the higher emoluments offered by business firms must have had an adverse effect on the quality of those now entering government service.

II. *The Professionalization Process*

1. *Opposition and acceptance*

The rapid advancement of economists in the Israeli civil service, described in the preceding sections, did not go unopposed. In a carry-over from the voluntary self-government frameworks of the pre-Independence period, the typical high government official in Israel's early days was, more often than not, an 'emissary' of some political party or organization.[23] Dedicated and highly motivated as such men may have been, they were nevertheless amateurs, to whom the seemingly cold, calculating approach of the economist was virtually anathema. Moreover, the whole history of the Jewish renaissance in Palestine until then was one of the triumph of vision and enthusiasm over economic considerations. These were roughly identified with private profitability. Indeed, the experience that many nation-building projects would never have been undertaken on profitability grounds alone generated the view that private profitability was in some way harmful to the national interest. As in many other newly sovereign developing countries, the political leadership viewed development mainly in physical terms. Querying the wisdom of some physically feasible but economically dubious projects was thus tantamount to putting a spanner in the wheels of progress. Finally, economists trained in the spirit of neoclassical economics tend to trust, to a considerable degree, in the efficacy of market forces. But in the early 1950s the Israeli Labor movement, like its counterparts abroad, regarded markets as essentially capitalist and therefore socially undesirable phenomena.

These attitudes towards economic considerations were reflected in the arguments raised against economists and the advice they offered, at the time their influence on the government's economic decisions was beginning to be felt. The most sweeping one was that "economics is

23. It is noteworthy that a number of future members of Israeli governments, including three of its first four finance ministers, served as civil servants in the first years after independence. Theirs was not the case, as might have been the case in later years, of bright civil servants being co-opted by political parties, but of political figures staffing important administrative positions.

not a science," implying the opinion of economists to be one among many of equal virtue.[24] Alternatively, it was argued that economic laws, even if valid elsewhere, "did not apply" to the peculiar conditions of the country. Most of the young economists may be said to have shared the left-of-center sentiments of their generation. But, as is often the case in Labor-governed countries, their views on economic policy tended to be on the right of the government's, giving rise to accusations of political partisanship. On a different, rather acrimonious level, the fact that, as related earlier, instruction in modern economic analysis was personified by a man who was the product of an American university was used to charge that the economics taught by him were alien to the spirit and the needs of Israel.

Despite this opposition, which on a diminished scale continued into the 1960s, the influence of government economists grew steadily. This can be ascribed to a number of factors. In the decade between the Sinai Campaign of 1956 and the Six Day War of 1967 defense problems were less acute than either before or after, so that more attention came to be paid to economic issues. In particular the country's main economic problem, namely its big import surplus, was realized to be not the transitory teething pain of its first years, but a chronic deficiency requiring constant and skilled attention. At the same time, economic problems became also more intricate than before. If economics concerns the allocation of restricted means among competing ends, then the scope for it in Israel was initially limited. The priority of certain ends, e.g. that of providing immigrants with a roof over their heads, was clear. The question was really more one of technological feasibility than of economics—what form of housing satisfying minimal standards of physical adequacy could be erected in the shortest possible time. In other words, the ends were few, their social rankings on the whole obvious, and the alternative ways of achieving them severely limited.[25] Gradually, as needs became less pressing and resources more plentiful, the pattern of effective allocation became less self-evident. Thus, paradox-

24. This reflected the 'there are no economic laws' stance of the Young Historical School of German economics at the turn of the century, to which many of Israel's founding fathers were exposed in their formative years. See E. Kleiman, "An Early Modern Hebrew Textbook of Economics," *History of Political Economy* 5 (1973): 339–58.

25. This should by no means be taken to imply that the decisions taken under these circumstances were inevitably the right ones, or that they could not have been improved by the application of economic analysis. But the main restriction on the economy, that of the lack of foreign exchange, was of a magnitude which no economic policy could have rectified within the time span in which the more pressing problems had to be solved, and thus had to be taken as given. An economically more rational approach, however, could have prevented some of the waste engendered by the divergence between the private and the social costs of foreign exchange.

ically enough, the easing of the economic situation generated demand for the more sophisticated economic analysis which only trained economists could provide.

A factor which contributed much to establishing the position of economists in government was the uniformity of their education and outlook. The common cultural and social background of pre-Independence society, from which most of them then stemmed, was in their case augmented by sharing the same discipline, acquired at the same university from the same teachers. They shared a common mode of thinking and used a language which, especially when they chose to employ technical terms, was virtually incomprehensible to the uninitiated.[26] Coupled with this unanimity was their broad agreement as to what the country's main economic problems were and how they should be solved, which was not shattered until the beginning of the 1970s.

This consensus was only partly the result of a common orthodoxy. Any differences of opinion which may have existed among economists paled when compared with those which separated economists from the political decisionmakers. Economists tended to emphasize the strength of market forces and the limited efficacy, and misallocative outcome, of administrative interference in the market process. They would point out that restrictions imposed on the use of certain credits would be voided by their substitution for the borrowers' own funds, which could then be used for other purposes. They also (though here their attitude became less uniform in later years) pushed the cause of efficiency as against equity, in the form in which the latter was then perceived by the political level. Arguing that the government should subsidize people, not goods, they advocated the use of direct transfer payments instead of the food subsidies then in use. More generally, it may be said that economists took a broader, macro view of the economy, as compared with that of the politicians. The latter tended to regard economic phenomena from what was, basically, a microeconomic viewpoint. Typical of this attitude was their persistence in viewing inflation as due purely to cost push, despite the fact that for most of the period before 1973, it was primarily the result of government deficits and of expansionary monetary policy. Thus successive Finance ministers refrained from raising the interest rate for fear of hiking up prices. Econ-

26. Quite literally so: the establishment of government machinery and the introduction of economics in the curriculum of the Hebrew University required, and were followed by, the development of a Hebrew economic terminology with which only economists were initially familiar. In latter years some 'economese' came into wide parlance. An extreme example is that of the Hebrew word for 'distortion,' which is now widely used to describe any unsatisfactory state of affairs.

omists, on the other hand, regarded as dominant the interest rate's effects on aggregate demand and on the efficient use of capital. A similar divergence existed for many years in attitudes towards devaluation. Thinking in general equilibrium terms, economists were more conscious than policymakers of the indirect effects of policy steps, and more aware of the time lags between cause and effect, which the latter tended to disregard.[27]

The unanimity which characterized government economists in earlier years has lately shown signs of crumbling. To some extent this reflects the growing controversy within the profession at large concerning the outstanding economic phenomena of the 1970s, stagflation and the breakdown of the fixed-exchange regime system. In Israel, this was aggravated by the weakening of the public consensus on general national goals in the wake of the October 1973 war. The diversification of the government economists' opinions may in part also be the outcome of the growth in their number and their rapid advancement in the past. Today, the more senior ones among them are older and have been in government service for much longer than their counterparts of twenty or of even ten years ago. The constant exposure to everyday practical affairs, and the dealing with a great number of special cases, took their toll in a growing tendency of at least some of them to commit the fallacy of composition through viewing economic problems and processes from the angle of the individual enterprise. Finally, with each ministry and government agency employing its own economists, their conflicting particular interests came to be reflected in correspondingly partisan opinions of the economists they employed.

The decline in unanimity must ultimately weaken the economists' position in government and lessen reliance on their judgment. Recently there has been some revival of the opposition to their influence. This comes now from social and community workers who object to economists dominating the welfare budgets, which grew very rapidly as a result of the transition to direct transfer payments, which economists had so strongly advocated in the past.

2. Rising in the corridors of power

The growth, surveyed earlier, in the number of economists employed by the government reveals only one aspect of their ascendancy

27. As late as in the autumn of 1978 the then deputy finance minister argued that the acceleration of inflation could not be ascribed to government deficit, "as in the same month in which prices rose so sharply the government was a net absorber of purchasing power from the public." For surveys of economic policy discussions in Israel, see N. Halevi, "Economic Policy Discussions and Research in Israel," *American Economic Review* 59, Part 2, suppl. (Sept. 1969); and "The Exchange Rate in Israel: Policy and Opinion," *Revue Economique*, 30 (Jan. 1979): 10–30.

in the civil service. Another one is their rise in the hierarchy. The Israel Civil Service Commission does not publish a Civil List on the U.K. lines. Though the *Israel Government Yearbook* lists the names of the top postholders in the various ministries, it does not provide biographical information, and the cut-off point for the posts included varies from one edition to another. It is thus impossible to state precisely how many of a given list of posts, or even of the posts listed in a given year, are occupied by economists. Nevertheless, the information contained in the *Yearbook* (augmented by *Who Is Who in Israel*) can be used to trace the progress of economists towards the pinnacles of the civil service.

In Table 5 we present some figures on the number of top civil service posts occupied by economists in different periods. The first group of posts examined is that of directors general of ministries. Though a civil servant, a director general in Israel is not the 'permanent head' in the U.K. sense. An incoming minister has the right to appoint his own nominee to this post, though lately this has been exercised less often than in the past.[28] And all appointments of directors general have to be approved by the Cabinet. Though the number of government ministries has varied over the years, the number of such posts was fairly stable, usually totaling 19 until the mid 1960s, and 21 since then.[29] As can be seen from the table, from 1955 onwards there was a steady increase in the number held by economists. In 1976 they headed the ministries of Finance, Defense, Trade and Industry, Housing, and Transportation as well as the National Insurance Institute. If we consider that in Israel the directors of certain ministries have, by convention, to be members of corresponding professions—e.g., a physician in the Ministry of Health and a lawyer in that of Justice—the recent proportion of economists among their total seems very high indeed. When the comparison is restricted to the 'new' economists, i.e., those who graduated after the establishment of the State and who were trained in what may be termed the Anglo-American school, the rise in hierarchy is seen to have been even more rapid.

An individual's qualifications as an economist need not necessarily

28. In particular, the new 'Likud' government established after the defeat, after nearly thirty years in power, of the Labor Party in the elections of 1977, refrained initially from any sudden mass removal of top officials nominated by its predecessors. Though some new nominations have taken place since then, it is significant that the whole upper echelon of the Ministry of Finance which began to serve before 1977, were still at their posts in 1979. (At the time of going to press, however, this is no longer true.)

29. Included in the list are also the director general of the State Comptroller's Office and that of the National Insurance Institute, whose status is that of directors general of ministries. The special case of the Bank of Israel is discussed below.

Table 5. Senior civil service posts occupied by economists, 1950–1976

	A Directors general of ministries [b]			B
Period [a]	Total economists	'New' economists	Additional qualifications	Five other senior posts [c]
1950–51	2	—	2 [d]	—
1952–55	—	—	—	1
1956–61	1	—	—	1
1962–66	3	2	2 [e]	2
1967	4	3	1 [e]	2
1968–74	5	5	2 [e]	4
1975–76	6	6	1 [f]	4

[a] Division into periods according to changes in the first column of the table.

[b] Including the director general of the National Insurance Institute. Figures show maximum number simultaneously at such posts at any given moment of time in each period.

[c] Heads of Budgets, Revenue, Accountants' General, and Foreign Exchange divisions at the Ministry of Finance, and the Banks' Comptroller at the Bank of Israel.

[d] Semi-political public figures.

[e] Retired senior army officers holding a degree in economics.

[f] Academic economist on leave of absence from his university.

Source: Israel, *Government Yearbooks*, and *Who Is Who in Israel*.

constitute the main consideration in his appointment as a director general, though they may be an advantage. The two economists who served in such posts in 1950–51 were nominated to them in virtue of their being semi-political public figures of pre-Independence days. In later years, a potential source of nominees for high government posts was senior army officers, who are retired from active service at a fairly low age.[30] Quite a number of them took a degree in economics before embarking upon a second career in government or in business. That they felt such training advantageous is, in itself, significant. But their nominations to top civil service posts should be ascribed first and foremost to their general administrative and leadership abilities. The last column of Table 5, Panel A, provides figures on the number of occupants whose nomination seems to have been dominated by factors other than an economics education. It can be seen that the rise of the 'new' economists cannot be explained in this way.

In addition to directors general, there are a number of other senior posts the staffing of which is subject to approval by the Cabinet and

30. The successive chiefs of staff of the Israel Defense Forces were in their thirties or forties when appointed to this post.

whose occupants may be regarded as policymaking officials.[31] Again, some of these posts require specific qualifications in fields other than economics, e.g. the attorney general must be a lawyer. In Panel B of Table 5 we provide data on five such posts, concerned with economic matters: those of the accountant general, the heads of the Budgets, Revenue, and Foreign Exchange divisions at the Ministry of Finance, and the comptroller of banks at the Bank of Israel. These posts came gradually to be reserved for economists: that of the Budgets Division's head since its establishment in 1953; the office of the accountant general since 1962; that of the comptroller of Foreign Exchange since 1967, and the Banks' comptroller since 1969. Of the 21 holders of these posts in the period covered in the table, 15 were economists. A similar process could be observed were we to examine changes in the staffing of lower echelons, for example of the division headships in the Ministry of Trade and Industry. It is however, noteworthy that the Revenue Division was never entrusted to economists. While the deputy head has lately usually been an economist (more often than not in charge of research), its head and the heads of its main departments of Internal Revenue and of Customs and Excise have always been general administrators, accountants, or lawyers.

The rise of economists to the governorship of the Bank of Israel deserves separate mention. According to the Bank of Israel Law passed in 1954, the governor of the Bank is also the government's economic adviser. The late Mr. David Horowitz, who occupied this post from its inception till his retirement in 1971, was certainly *sui generis* among Israeli officials. Self-educated, of considerable intellectual powers, and an early convert to Keynesianism, he was the first director general of the Ministry of Finance.[32] Fond of quoting that "the future has no constituency," Horowitz served for many years as the economic conscience of the country. The personal prestige he brought to the governorship, and his concept of the office, contributed much to the Bank's public stature as the watchdog of economic policy. The Bank's annual report is regarded as the most important critical survey of economic developments published in Israel, and the governor's pronouncements on economic policy, though often unheeded, are treated with considerable respect by both the government and the general public. The second governor was a university-trained economist who had

31. The policymaking character of these posts is acknowledged also in the pension rights attached to them. These are double the regular ones per year of service, reflecting the presumption of a shorter 'life in office' expectancy.

32. An interesting vignette of Horowitz in his role as one of the spokesmen of the Jewish community in pre-independence days is provided in Richard Crossman, *Palestine Mission* (London, 1946), pp. 48–49.

served inter alia as the head of the Budgets Division. But he seems to have owed his appointment mainly to his success as a 'generalist' in government service.[33] That the government did not as yet regard the post as the exclusive preserve of professional economists was demonstrated by its intention to succeed him by a financier-politician, the then head of the Trade Unions' Sick Fund. However, when the disclosure of some financial irregularities caused this candidature to be dropped, and the government had to play it safe, it nominated as the third governor a professional economist who has been, successively, head of the Budgets Division and director general of the Ministry of Finance. At the same time the government also nominated two economists from the Bank's staff to the posts of vice-governors, which until then had been held vacant.

3. *Where are the economists and what do they do?*

As has been explained earlier, economists in the Israel civil service are lumped together for salary purposes with some other 'social sciences and arts' graduates. Though the formal requirements demanded for many posts include a degree in economics, there exist no data on the total number of such posts or on their distribution by ministries. The following survey is, therefore, to a great extent impressionistic. Our earlier rough estimate of the number of economists in the civil service implies that only part of them can be holding policy-influencing positions. The majority of the rank and file are occupied with routine technical work. Because of the high share of total resources, and of capital formation in particular, chaneled through the government in Israel, much of their activity would consist of examining investment projects, both governmental and private, and of the costing of activities of local authorities and of non-profit institutions supported by the government. At the other end of the scale there is the relatively small number entrusted with policy responsibilities. In addition to the group of top officials surveyed in the preceding section, this includes heads of other divisions and departments in ministries dealing with economic matters, such as the Ministry of Trade and Industry or that of Agriculture. In between these two groups there is a fairly large medium echelon who, though lacking authority either to determine or implement policy, have considerable influence on its formulation. Broadly speaking, this echelon consists of:

33. As well as to his close association with the very powerful finance minister of the moment. Office maketh the man. Despite their past cooperation, the new governor soon became an outspoken critic of the finance minister's policies which he himself helped earlier to promulgate.

(i) a small number of big teams, of which the Budgets Division and the Bank of Israel's Research Department are the outstanding examples;[34]

(ii) a large number of smaller teams, such as the economic research or advisory staffs which exist in many ministries:

(iii) individual economic advisers and personal economic assistants to ministers and directors general of ministries.

The work of these economists may take different forms. They staff various departmental and interdepartmental committees charged with providing answers to questions set them by political or by higher civil-service levels. They prepare forecasts of future or hypothetical developments and examine the budgetary cost and economic implications of policy proposals raised in the Cabinet or in its Committee on Economic Affairs. They provide their chiefs with economic arguments to support the latter's political stances. They also produce—sometimes in response to demands of higher echelons and sometimes on their own initiative—the flow of memoranda, research, and position papers which often contain the nuclei of ideas which may ultimately be translated into actual policies.

It is difficult to estimate the role of this group in the formulation of policies, and it is easy to underrate it. Only occasionally does a policy proposal become widely identified with the name of its originator, mainly through its becoming attached to the committee he chaired or the memorandum prepared by him, or to his being designated by his office to expound it in the media. My own impression, however, is that it is through such channels that many fresh ideas, often raised by relatively junior economists, permeate to the top.[35] The relative success of this group as originators of new policies may be attributed to two causes: their freedom, relative to the more senior group, from time- and energy-consuming departmental responsibilities, and their age—most of them are in their twenties and their thirties.

The main economic 'think-tanks,' however, are the two large teams mentioned earlier—Budgets Division and the Research Department of the Bank of Israel. The former employed 44 full-time econo-

34. Employees of the Bank of Israel, which is an independent statutory agency, are not included in the civil service figures presented earlier.

35. The percolation process may take quite some time: see, for example, N. Halevi, "The Exchange Rate in Israel: Policy and Opinion," supra n.27, on the introduction of the crawling-peg (mini-devaluation) exchange rate regime, which was first suggested in 1966, but which was not adopted until 1975. The extent to which relatively junior levels can thus affect policy may be illustrated by the fact that the recent (1977–78) interdepartmental debate on abolishing high-school fees was conducted at the same time in a graduate seminar at the Hebrew University, of which two of the officials most directly involved were then members.

mists in 1974/75, nearly as many as did all government offices taken together twenty years earlier. Its main concern is, so to speak, *ex ante*—the raising and examination of policy proposals which will affect forthcoming government budgets. The Research Department, with an equal number of economists, is partly engaged in drawing policy conclusions *ex post*, from its evaluation of past performance in the Bank's *Annual Report*, which it prepares. However, the Department serves also as the governor's staff in his capacity of chief economic adviser to the government. Unlike their counterparts in the various ministries, its economists are not in constant conflict with the Ministry of Finance over their budgets, and they are unencumbered by any executive or administrative responsibility. For these reasons, as well as for the professional prestige they enjoy, the Ministry of Finance tends to include the Research Department senior members in the discussions leading to major policy decisions. It was partly in recognition of these services that, as mentioned earlier, the joint heads of the Research Department were lately elevated to vice-governorships in the Bank.

4. *Professional training and advancement*

The minimal formal training qualification required of a government economist is a bachelor's degree in economics.[36] This is, on the whole, also the maximum requirement. Tenders for some higher posts—unless, as is sometimes the case, especially tailored for a particular candidate—may ask for applicants with a master's degree "or, as an alternative, with two-years' work experience." As this is equal to the minimal formal period of study for the master's degree (in practice, the average is longer), the premium on it is actually negative. Apart from very few posts, e.g. an economic adviser to a minister, the holder of a Ph.D. would be regarded as overqualified.

Undergraduate studies in economics are much more specialized in Israel than, say, in the United States. Until recently, only about one third of the economics class at the Hebrew University used to combine it with another subject.[37] The rest majored in economics only, and studies are very much theory-oriented. As a result, the freshly graduated economist often complains of finding himself unprepared for government service.

One of the reasons for the relatively high specialization in undergraduate studies is, no doubt, the universities' concept of their role; an-

36. Most Israeli universities do not offer first degrees in Business Administration.

37. This proportion was even lower in the 1960s. Recently it has risen, due in part to the introduction of Accounting as a minor subject, and the higher standards now required of students wishing to major in economics only.

other is the students' age. With compulsory military service of three years for men and two years for women, the Israeli undergraduate arrives at the university considerably older and more mature than his counterpart in western Europe or the United States, and is 24 or 25 years old by the time he graduates. During his studies he will also often be called up for reserve duty. He has, therefore, on the whole, little patience for courses which are not closely associated with his main subject. The higher age of university entrants is also reflected, of course, in the age of graduates entering government service. Furthermore, it also means that many students are married and have to support families.

At the Hebrew University from which, because of its location in the capital, most economics recruits to the civil service are drawn, many second- and third-year students find employment, full- or part-time, in government offices. (Some, like the Ministry of Finance, are conveniently located just across the road from the University's main campus.) Working as technical assistants, often in the type of department which may employ them on graduation, they thus receive some of the on-the-job training which the University is both unable and unwilling to provide.

Nevertheless, most graduates on first starting in the government find it difficult to bridge the chasm between the models taught in class and the facts of the real world. Some abandon the struggle and retrogress, forgetting much of what they have learned. Others, ignoring or belittling reality's divergence from the postulates of classroom models, err into oversimplification. It requires not only some intellectual subtlety but also experience and, perhaps most important of all, the right tutelage provided by certain work milieus, for some of the latter group to strike the right balance.[38]

This importance of on-the-job training also means that in the lower rungs of the civil service, advancement is facilitated by knowledge of the department or office considered. The fresh graduate responding to the Civil Service Commission's tender for a post as an economist in some government office will, unless exceptionally and evidently gifted, find himself severely handicapped competing with someone who was employed in that office, if only as a temporary, part-time technical assistant. Grades attained at the university play only a marginal role. The importance of inside experience is officially acknowledged in the ad-

38. It has been sometimes said of government economists that the only analytical tools they have to apply are those of the introductory economics course; but that it takes a lot of brains and ten years' experience to apply them correctly.

vancement process applied to the middle and medium-high ranks. There, partly in response to the pressure of the State Employees' Union, vacated or newly created posts are put to a 'closed tender.' This means that applications are solicited first only from persons employed in the same office. Only if no suitable candidates emerge is the tender opened to other members of the civil service and ultimately to the general public. Formally, this procedure applies also to the higher echelons, except in the case of posts requiring Cabinet approval, mentioned earlier. In practice, however, the tenders for these posts are tailored to fit the measures of the candidate chosen for advancement by the department concerned.

In the highest post the factors determining advancement vary, and may be influenced by considerations of political or personal allegiance. Nevertheless, some general pattern can be discerned. Of the thirteen economists who staffed the positions considered in Panel A of Table 5 in the five-year period 1971–1976, five made their careers in the Budgets Division (three of whom headed ministries other than Finance); three were outsiders, with previous experience in the army or the academy; three others, as well as one of the outsiders, served immediately before that as heads of the advisory or research staffs of the ministries of which they became directors general; only in the Ministry of Trade and Industry did its two successive heads in this period reach the top through a progression of jobs within that ministry, and even they started their careers as personal assistants to a director general and a minister respectively. The predominance of Budgets Division's economists in this group may be ascribed both to Finance being the senior economic ministry and to the general overview of the economy which work in the Division provides. The main alternative inside path to the top seems to have been through the posts of economic adviser, or of personal economic assistant to a minister, which tends to support the impression, reported in the preceding section, of the importance of these posts in formulating policy.

These data demonstrate also the relative shortness of top official careers. Of the thirteen no more than six were in office at one and the same time between 1971 and 1976, and only five were still in office in 1978. This rapid turnover can be ascribed partly to Cabinet changes and partly to the strain of life at the top. Once retired, the holders of these, as well as of somewhat lower economic posts like that of the accountant general, can easily find comfortable slots in the private sector, where their experience and government connections constitute a considerable asset. Not unknown is also the practice by which a retiring official prepares for himself a job in a government corporation, or a statutory agency, connected with the department in which he previously held office.[39]

The rapid turnover at the top has, of course, ramifications further down the hierarchy. Coupled with the general expansion of the civil service and with the growth in the share of its posts reserved for economists, it provides a degree of mobility which would otherwise have been impossible. While it entails a cost in terms of expertise lost, it also permits the rise of new men and saves economic thinking in the government from ossification.

5. *Academy and government*

The relationship between academic economists and government in Israel has been, on the whole, an informal one. There has been hardly any in-and-out movement of economists between the universities and regular government employment. Members of the economic departments of Israeli universities did on occasion serve in various advisory capacities. But except for basically academically oriented activities, such as the supervision of research, their direct involvement was rather limited. Any influence they may have had on policy was mainly exerted either through informal consultations or through the effect which their public *ex cathedra* pronouncements had on public opinion. Their services were occasionally utilized in public inquiry committees of varying importance and effectiveness. In particular, two important committees, nominated in 1975 to recommend reforms in, respectively, the direct tax system and the salary structure in the public sector, were both chaired by economists from the universities, and had others serving on them. But there were only few cases of academic economists taking up short-term and none at all of them taking up long-term appointments in government service.

Though neither side would have openly admitted it, both had good reasons for shying away from closer cooperation. Economists in universities were no doubt reluctant to soil their hands, or rather their consciences, by the compromises required of the practitioner. No less important, probably, was their age and career structure, which reflected the rapid expansion of the student body, discussed earlier. Like their counterparts in the civil service, academic economists were relatively young. Until fairly recently, the typical university lecturer considered for a senior post in governmental service would have been in his thirties. Having chosen not to enter it in the first instance, his intellectual interest would, at this stage, still be in academic, mainly theo-

---

39. See P. J. Wiles, *Economic Institutions Compared* (Oxford, 1977) for the term *pantouflage*, by which this practice is known in France.

retical research. And his academic career could not but be hindered by the inevitable decline in his scientific output.[40] On a number of occasions when university economists were offered civil service appointments, even temporary ones, they were ready to accept them on a part-time basis only. The government, on the other hand, regarded this attitude as indicating lack of commitment and was generally reluctant to employ part-timers in other than consultative jobs. Regular civil servants may also have been expected to resent having outsiders, however eminent professionally, 'parachuted' on them from above. And both they and the political level may have been apprehensive of the prestige and independence which such temporary civil servants would have enjoyed.

Whether because of the worsening economic situation or to improve the government's public image, some university economists were drafted into government service in the late 1970s. With the notable exception of one such nominee, who went on to become the director general at the Defense Ministry, these experiments were short-lived and seem to have reinforced the prejudices with which academics and government view each other.[41]

III. *Some Further Problems*

1. *Ethics and value judgments*

A fundamental problem facing economists in government is that of making value judgments. Despite some recent soul searching, the separation of analytical from ethical considerations remains a basic principle of Western economics education. As a student, the future government economist has been trained to identify the most efficient means of achieving a given goal. As a practitioner, however, he soon finds that where government is concerned there is no single dimension by which effectiveness may be measured. What constitutes an optimal solution in terms of, say, forgone consumption, need not be such in terms of employment or of the balance of payments, not to mention in those of overall income inequality or specific distribution of income among competing groups. Assigning these considerations their relative weights involves value judgments. The political level, which is sup-

40. Furthermore, unlike in the case of the U.S. or the U.K., research based on his experience in government would be of little interest to his peers in the academic community abroad.

41. It would be beyond the scope of this study to speculate why the experience of economists differed significantly from that of other academic staff who were drafted into government service at about the same time, e.g. the two jurists who became successive attorneys general, and the political scientist who became the director general of the Ministry of Foreign Affairs.

posed to make such judgments, should presumably be provided by its economists with the whole 'menu' of alternatives to choose from. This amounts to nothing less than presenting it with the marginal rates of substitution between whatever the target variable and all other economic and social magnitudes to which the government may be sensitive. Politicians are busy men, and an economist attempting to play this game will probably have a chance to do so, if at all, only once.[42] He will, therefore, refrain from pointing out (i.e., he will assign zero weights to) the more exotic alternatives and probably also those which, in his judgment, are politically unfeasible.

Thus government economists cannot escape making not only value judgments, but also political judgments. In the upper echelons the situation is aggravated by the fact that civil servants in Israel cannot hide behind the cloak of ministerial responsibility. High-ranking and sometimes even middle-ranking government officials are expected to defend governmental policy in public, especially if they have been involved in its formulation. While some government economists may enjoy their sharing of the politicians' prerogative, and others may not be conscious of it, there is evidence that some of them, at least, are aware of the moral dilemmas entailed.[43] Their behavior under these circumstances, and the set of values implied by it, merit further investigation.

2.   What good did the economists do?

The present survey inevitably raises the question of the attainments of economists in government from the point of view of the society in which they operate. There exists, however, no accepted yardstick by which their performance can be evaluated. At most, we might have tried to trace the influence of economists on decisions relating to selected policy issues. Unfortunately, no documentation is available to allow even such a limited evaluation of their role, except in the most general terms. There seems to be little doubt that, given their terms of reference, economists have greatly improved the process of governmental decisionmaking on the micro level. This, however, raises the question of whether, if the overall policy itself is wrong, it is better for it to be carried out efficiently or inefficiently. As an economist, I can-

42. To quote R. Turvey's apt words for such a situation, "the economist will lose his job if he merely spouts highbrow agnosticism for more than the minimum period of time necessary to preserve self-respect." R. Turvey, "Present Values Versus Internal Rate of Return," *Economic Journal*, March 1963, p. 96.

43. See, for example, the statement by Beeri Hazak in the symposium "On the Role of the Economist," in N. Halevi and Y. Kopp, eds., *Issues in the Economy of Israel* (Jerusalem: Falk Institute, 1974). The author of this statement, who was at the time the Budgets Division referendary for education budgets, was killed while on active service in the October War.

not but answer this question, "Efficiently." Most broad policies are adopted by government for a wide variety of reasons. Without undue cynicism it may be assumed, therefore, that many economically 'bad' policies—say, that of excessive tariff protection—would have been pursued anyway. (Indeed, as has been shown earlier, they were pursued in Israel before economists came to be widely employed by the government.) By promoting the correct decisions (in this case, the equalization of the effective protection rates) within what is by itself, a wrong framework, economists helped to minimize its damage. And the explication of the underlying assumptions and reasoning which this required has often led to the questioning and ultimately even the revision of the basic policy.

Unlike on the micro level, where decisions—as in the evaluation of investment projects—are frequently of the yes-or-no category, on the macro level they relate more often to the degree to which a policy is to be pursued. Economists' influence on them is therefore more difficult to ascertain. Indeed, it may be questioned whether any major shifts in the Israel government's economic policies were directly initiated by its economists.[44] Once such shifts had been contemplated, however, the economists were called in not only to suggest ways and means by which they could be carried out, but also to comment upon them and point out their implications. Their effectiveness should, thus, be measured not only in terms of the policies they persuaded the government to adopt but also in terms of those which they dissuaded it from pursuing. Deliberations leading to the rejection of a policy proposal are, generally, less well documented and less publicized than those leading to its acceptance. It may well be that, as has sometimes been claimed, the government economists' most worthwhile contribution has been to have averted some of the failures which would have resulted from the decisionmakers' faulty understanding of economic processes.

Without implicating them in any way, I wish to thank N. Gross, Y. Ben-David, and A. W. Coats and participants of the Dubrovnik Conference, for helpful comments on an earlier draft.

44. Of what, in a historical perspective, may be viewed as the major policy shifts in Israel's economic history, only the 1962 devaluation may be regarded as being initiated by economists. Of the others, the 1952 N.E.P., referred to earlier, predated their ascendancy in government; the 1966–67 recession originated in a confrontation between the government and the trade unions; and the 1977 liberalization of the exchange rate regime was a quarter-of-a-century-old commitment of the political party which came to hold the Finance portfolio after the elections earlier that year.

Bibliography

Crossman, R. *Palestine Mission*. London, 1946.

Gaathon (Gruenbaum) A. L. *National Income and Outlay in Palestine*, 1936, Jerusalem, Bank of Israel, 1978. This is a reprint of the 1941 edition, with the addition of the originally unpublished parts and of critical comments.

──. "Problems of Development of an Economist," *Economic Quarterly* (Hebrew) 77 (April 1974): 58–68.

Gross, N., and J. Metzer, "Public Finance in the Jewish Economy in Inter-war Palestine." *Research in Economic History* 3 (1978): 87–159.

Halevi, N., and R. Klinov-Malul. *The Economic Development of Israel*. New York, 1968.

Halevi, N. "Economic Policy Discussion and Research in Israel." *American Economic Review*, 59, suppl. (Sept. 1969): 74–118.

──. "The Exchange Rate in Israel: Policy and Opinion." *Revue Economique* 30, no. 1 (Jan. 1979): 10–30.

──, and Y. Kopp, eds. *Issues in the Israeli Economy*. Jerusalem, Falk Institute for Economic Research, 1974.

──, et. al. *Banker to an Emerging Nation: The History of Bank Leumi Le-Israel*. Haifa, 1981.

Israel Central Bureau of Statistics. *Statistical Abstract of Israel*.

Israel Civil Service Commission. *Annual Report* (Hebrew).

Israel, Government, *Israel Government Yearbook*.

Israel, Ministry of Labor, Manpower Planning Authority. "Longitudinal Survey of University Graduates 1964–1966" (Hebrew). 1971.

Jewish Agency for Palestine. *The Jewish Case Before the Anglo-American Committee*. Jerusalem, 1946.

──. *The Jewish Plan for Palestine*. Jerusalem, 1947.

Kleiman, E. "From Cooperative to Industrial Empire." *Midstream*, 1963, pp. 15–26.

──. "Solel-Boneh as Seen by Hillel Dan." *Economic Quarterly* (Hebrew) 41–42 (May 1964): 170–83.

──. "An Early Modern Hebrew Textbook of Economics." *History of Political Economy* 5 (1973): 339–58.

──. "The Anglo-Palestine Bank and the Establishment of Israel's Monetary System," Part III. In N. Gross, N. Halevi, E. Kleiman, and M. Sarnat, *Banker to a Renascent National* (Hebrew; Tel-Aviv, Massada, 1977), pp. 203–93.

Klinov-Malul, R. *The Profitability of Investment in Education in Israel*. Jerusalem, Falk Institute for Economic Research, 1966.

Metzer, J. "The Concept of National Capital in Zionist Thought, 1918–1921." *Asian and African Studies* 11 (1977): 305–36.

──. *National Capital for a National Home 1919–1921* (Hebrew). Jerusalem, 1979.

Morag, A. *Government Finance in Israel* (Hebrew). Jerusalem, 1966.

Nathan, R., O. Gass, and D. Creamer. *Palestine: Promise and Problem*. Washington, D.C., 1946.

Rubner, A. *The Economy of Israel: A Critical Account of the First Ten Years*. London, 1960.

Turvey, R. "Present Values Versus Internal Rate of Return: An Essay on the Theory of the Third Best." *Economic Journal* 73 (March 1963): 93–98.

Wiles, P. J. *Economic Institutions Compared*. Oxford, 1977.

Hungary: economists in a socialist planning system

Egon Kemenes

I. *Historical Background*

After the Second World War various economic tasks faced the new democratic Hungarian government with the compulsive force of a struggle for survival. Following the party conflicts of the coalition period from which the Communist Party emerged as absolute victor, Hungary set out in 1949 on the path of socialist economic planning. This gave economists a greater role in government than ever before in Hungary.

However, between 1949 and 1956 many circumstances in Hungary hindered the full development of the role of economics, and thus of economists. Although the government programs primarily set targets defined in economic terms, they were based on economically imperfect and uncertain analyses, and the range of economic policy means for their implementation also proved inadequate. This is only partly explained by the fact that this change occurred in Hungary under revolutionary circumstances, and all revolutions impatiently strive to attain their ambitious goals. Revolutionaries, not economists, are the spokesmen in the revolutions of our age, as in earlier times. In discussing this period, József Bognár gave the following ideological and historical reasons for the equivocal character of economic thought:

> As early as the 19th century the founders of scientific socialism and their disciples assumed that as society took work directly into account and distributed the means of production in accordance with needs, the market would cease to exist. Distribution would take place without money, on the basis of class and social principles—in other words, through the naturalization of the centrally directed economy. As every revolution is *in se* a value-centered system, considerations of economic rationality (e.g. rational calculation, economic risk-taking and even profit) can play only a limited role.[1]

1. József Bognár, "The Qualitative Elements of Human Life," in Miklós Szántó, ed., *Ways of Life—Hungarian Sociological Studies* (Budapest, 1977), pp. 53–87.

In the emerging Hungarian postwar socialist economy there were fundamental contradictions arising from the need to find a proper place for economic rationality within the value system, and, on the other, of reconciling the forecasts and expectations —which could not, of course, be based on experience—with the existing politicoeconomic situation.

Macroeconomic research began intensively, in conjunction with planning. But some necessary disciplines were initially neglected, such as the study of the requirements for indirect methods of management, the priorities for domestic economic development and research into the foundations of microeconomics, i.e. managerial sciences.[2]

This period was characterized by an extension of the government statistical service and by a development of statistics in general as an indispensable precondition of any economic planning. The scope of activity and responsibility of the Hungarian Central Statistical Office was extended; the number of statisticians in government employment grew, and the level of their training and of expertise was raised.

Discussing the relationship between politics and economics in this period (1949–1956), Mihály Simai remarked:

A correct policy may stimulate economic development, but the political superstructure may also temporarily prevent economic development when it compels the economy through its institutions to develop in a direction opposed to the logic of economic needs, i.e. by imposing unrealistically high demands on the economy.[3]

Another factor contributing to the emergence of this voluntarist economic policy was the excessive strain imposed on the economy in an effort to attain overambitious targets. The changeover to a socialist planned economy in Hungary in 1949 and the socialization of the means of production made it possible to mobilize the potential sources for growth on a large scale. In 1951 per capita accumulation was more than double the figure for 1949. However, in the process of reinvesting this successful accumulation a large part of the results were lost, and the expected further growth was not achieved. In 1952 the national in-

2. József Bognár, "Interdependent Correlations Between Economic Research (Theory) and Economic Policy (Practice)," paper presented at the Fourth Anglo-Hungarian Economic Colloquium, Keszthely (Hungary), 20–23 Sept. 1973.

3. Mihály Simai, "On the Role of Economists," paper presented at the Fourth Anglo-Hungarian Economic Colloquium, Keszthely (Hungary), 20–23 Sept. 1973. See p. 17.

come was lower than in the previous year, and the decline in capital accumulation was even greater.[4]

The setback after the initial successes, the improvisation and muddling that followed, the unsound bases of economic policy, and the vagueness of its perspectives, contributed to a considerable extent to the serious political crisis that exploded in the country in October 1956. As a result the advocates of voluntarism were driven out of government. The year 1957 marked the beginning of the process by which the general economic objectives of the socialist system in Hungary were brought into harmony with the results of theoretical and applied economic research, and in which economists were given the leading role in the formulation and implementation of economic policy.

One of the first acts of the new government in 1957 was to convene the Economics Committee, composed not only of Communist experts but also of economists of different political persuasions and non-party-members, which was given the task of redefining the goals and means of Hungarian economic policy. In that year certain modifications were made to the system of economic guidance partly on the basis of the Economic Committee's recommendations that operated from February to July 1957, and partly on the initiative of the Hungarian Socialist Workers' Party. The planning system became more flexible; a greater role was allotted to the price mechanism; and workers were given a greater individual interest in economic activity.[5] This brought an increase in the role of economists in government, and an increased demand for highly qualified economists capable of grasping the complexities of real economic processes and guiding these processes by methods other than issuing instructions.

This economic policy, based on realistic economic foundations and more effectively coordinated, contributed to a more even growth rate and more balanced economic development. By the mid-sixties the dynamics of this economic development had altered the whole scale of Hungarian economic life, made consumer demand wider and more differentiated, and extended Hungary's international economic relations. The combined effect was to make the operation of the entire Hungarian economy more complex.[6] The scope for economic growth (e.g. by utilizing unemployed reserves of labor) since 1949 had been exhausted during the succeeding decade and a half; the stage had been reached

4. Source of data quoted: *Statistical Pocket Book of Hungary 1956* (in Hungarian; Budapest, 1956), pp. 12–13.
5. Béla Csikós-Nagy, "New Aspects of the Profit Incentive," *New Hungarian Quarterly* 6, no. 20 (1965): 15–27.
6. Egon Kemenes, "The Hungarian Economy 1945–1969," in Denis Sinor, ed., *Modern Hungary* (Bloomington, Ind., and London, 1977), pp. 120–44.

where further economic expansion was possible only through intensive growth. The task faced in the mid-sixties was thus the preparation of a comprehensive reform of the system of Hungarian economic guidance[7] and then, on this basis, the introduction of the so-called new economic mechanism in 1968.

The essence of the Hungarian economic reform of 1968 can be briefly summed up as the introduction of *indirect* guidance through economic regulators (price, credit, fiscal and wage policy) in place of *direct* guidance of economic units by *instructions*.[8] As a result, enterprises were given wider scope for decisionmaking and the responsibility of forecasting market demand. By applying various economic and political means, such as taxes, investment credits, price policy, etc., the state ensures that the enterprise's activity is in conformity with the plan targets. While the state retains the right of direct intervention, it rarely utilizes that right in practice. Consequently the enterprise managers and their staff are stimulated in their efforts to ensure the profitable functioning of the firm. Since this system of guidance calls for an expert analysis, knowledge, and responsible operation of the complex quantitative and qualitative system of interrelations among the economic agents, the reform brought an entirely new role of economists in government. This became apparent from 1965 as a by-product of the activities of the committees responsible for working out the basic concept and details of the new system of economic guidance, and forecasting its consequences. In 1968 when the reform was introduced, the economists' new role became institutionalized.[9]

The economic way of thinking, using quantitative terms and observing economic laws and interdependencies, gained ground. The former planning and statistical departments in the ministries and central state agencies have been transformed into economic departments engaged in economic studies and analyses. Their staffs, which formerly consisted mainly of statisticians, have been completed by trained economists with higher degrees in economics specializing in analysis and forecasts for policymaking.

7. József Bognár, "Towards a New System of Guidance in the Socialist Economy," and Rezsó Nyers, "Reform of the Economic Mechanism"; both in *New Hungarian Quarterly* 6, no. 20 (1965).

8. Egon Kemenes, "Three Years of the Hungarian Economic Reform," *New Hungarian Quarterly* 12, no. 42 (1971): 203–19.

9. There is an extensive international literature, including in English, on the Hungarian economic reform of 1968. The following selection has been made only from works by Hungarian authors: Béla Csikós-Nagy, *Socialist Economic Policy* (London, 1973); József Bognár, "Overall Direction and Operation of the Economy: The New Economic Mechanism in Hungary," *New Hungarian Quarterly* 7, no. 21 (1966): 3–32; István Friss, *Reform of the Economic Mechanism in Hungary* (Budapest, 1971); Ottó Gadó, *Reform of the Economic Mechanism in Hungary: Development 1968–1971* (Budapest, 1973).

The era of change in the world economy that began at the end of 1973 further extended the Hungarian economist's range of tasks and responsibilities. Since Hungary participates more extensively than any other European socialist country in the international division of labor (the value of its exports amounts to almost 50 percent of its national income, and around 40 percent of its GDP), the medium- and long-term forecasting of world economic changes has become of decisive importance in adapting to external conditions and identifying the need for structural transformation. Thus the Hungarian economists specializing in the provision of analysis and advice on international economic affairs have an especially important responsibility. Despite his slightly ironic tone, Sir Alec Cairncross's remarks could also apply to Hungary when he said that in addition to the provision and interpretation of economic intelligence, economic forecasting

> is perhaps the most important operational role in which economists are used, and one in which they are more nearly deciding than advising since they produce the forecasts and do not merely contribute to their production. The employment of economists in this way is an indication that there is presumably some scientific content to economics since it is increasingly accepted that, in some kinds of forecasting at least, economists are more likely to be right than non-economists.[10]

The attempt in the following sections to define the role of Hungarian economists in government more precisely and quantitatively is mainly concerned with the post-1968 situation.

II. *The Supply of Economists*

The definition of 'economist'

As in other countries, only a very broad definition of the concept of 'economist' can be applied in Hungary: all those who have higher qualifications in economics (obtained at a university or higher college) and/or who work in economics can be considered economists. But not all those with higher qualifications in economics can be considered economists in the Hungarian case, since according to 1970 Census data, only two-thirds of those with higher qualifications in economics were active in jobs in economics or closely related fields; the remaining third worked in entirely different areas (in 2 percent of cases they were

10. "The Employment of Economists in Government Service," paper presented by Sir Alec Cairncross at the Fourth Anglo-Hungarian Colloquium in Keszthely (Hungary), Sept. 1973.

even in blue-collar occupations or were not active earners at all—mainly mothers of young children and married women).

Moreover, many Hungarian economists have had no formal training at a university or institute but have degrees in engineering, law, education, etc. Many such graduates hold economist-type posts, and some have had postgraduate training in economics after taking a first degree in another discipline—for example, engineer-economists who have taken a two-year engineering-economist postgraduate course at the University of Technology.

The pre-1949 system of higher education in Hungary and the subsequent social changes also compound the difficulty of definition. Many people now working as economists graduated before 1949 from the University of Law and Political Science, where their course also included economic subjects. On the other hand, during the post-1945 revolutionary social transformation many workers and peasants rose directly to become economic managers and later supplemented their natural aptitude for their new careers with formal university studies in economics or were able to draw on their management experiences in their work in economics. This process still continues with the disappearance of strict barriers between the different social strata and increased social mobility. Workers and peasants continue to rise to top-level economic management posts both in the enterprises and in public service, either through their work in the political machinery or directly. In these cases too, taking advantage of the institutionalized opportunities for adult education in Hungary, they attend evening or correspondence courses in economics to acquire higher-level qualifications while continuing to work in their new posts. And finally, many persons with higher-level technical qualifications hold top guidance posts which are more economic than engineering in substance.[11]

The total number of economist posts is not statistically measurable, although by detailed monographic research such posts could be identified within a narrowly defined circle (e.g. members of the Council of Ministers, heads of major government organs, or managerial staff of larger factories). Thus for statistical purposes we are dependent on the enrolment or numbers of graduates in higher educational institutions. These statistics can also shed light on changes in the role of economists in Hungarian society and government.

11. These problems of classification frequently arise in Hungary in the course of sociological and demographic studies concerning economists: e.g. József Kepecs and András Klinger, "Demographic Data about Economists," *Gazdaság (Quarterly Review of the Hungarian Economic Association*, Budapest), 1975, no. 4, pp. 89–99 (in Hungarian, with English summary).

The nature of academic qualifications in economics

Taking into consideration that the modern conception of economics is not more than two hundred years old, it is no small achievement that the 1777 "Ratio Educationis" edict of Queen Maria Theresa reforming the Hungarian educational system, appended to the curriculum for the Faculty of Law the teaching of subjects such as Trade and Finance, Statistics, and Political Sciences.[12]

The first plan for an independent framework for teaching economics was inspired by István Széchenyi, a leading personality of the Hungarian Reform Age.[13] However, a long time was to pass before the birth of independent higher education in economics.

It was only after 1945, amid immense sociopolitical transformations, that Law 57 enacted in 1948 decreed the establishment of an independent Hungarian University of Economics in Budapest. This assumed the name of Karl Marx in 1953, and became the only higher educational institution of economics in the country.

The educational reform Act III of 1961 was the start of important developments at the Karl Marx University of Economics. Specialized studies involving organization, efficiency, and quantification were expanded; the traditional two-term mathematics studies were doubled, and the foundations of a new system of mathematics teaching were laid. A new advanced course in planning mathematics was established and previous studies designed for accountants, business mathematicians, and other routine workers were eliminated. Simultaneously a series of new technical colleges, including new higher educational institutions in economics, was established in order to provide qualifications in bookkeeping, accountancy, business correspondence, and factory management.

Further university reform, planned in 1965, launched in 1968, and designed to involve the planning and management system, brought significant changes both in research and practical economic work. To facilitate the successful conversion of State-owned companies and cooperative societies into self-management organizations, there was a vital need for knowledge of economic analysis, decisionmaking, inde-

12. The source used here and in the following on the development of training in economics in Hungary is Iván T. Berend, Antal Stark, and Ildikó Tordai, "Hungarian Higher Education in Economics," lecture delivered at the jubilee session to mark the 30th anniversary of the existence of the Karl Marx University of Economics, organized in collaboration with the Hungarian Economic Association, 11–13 April 1978; and by the same authors, "A közgazdász képzés multja és jövője" (The Past and Future of Training for Economists), *Népszabadság* (Political Daily), 7 May 1978.
13. See the section on the activity of István Széchenyi in W. O. Henderson, *The Industrialization of Europe 1780–1914* (London, 1969).

pendent marketing, selling, and organizational and manpower management activities. In place of the masses of clerks and statisticians previously required, genuine economists were needed, and at this time there was a growing public interest in economic problems and the number and quality of students at the University of Economics increased.

These conditions combined to induce a demand for changes in the content and orientation of education to emphasize functional elements and more efficient development of practical abilities. The University of Economics was enabled to produce graduates with wider intellectual horizons who could more readily think creatively, respond to new challenges, and adapt themselves to new operational needs.

As a result of the founding and expansion of higher education the number of students enrolled in colleges and universities of economics increased by 174 percent from 1961–62 to 1966–67, and by 1972–73 was 223 percent higher than in 1961–62. The percentage of economics students in the total student population also increased considerably (see Table 1) and many adults (usually between the ages of eighteen and twenty-four) took advantage of the opportunities for higher education, thereby encouraging social mobility.

At the Karl Marx University students attend courses for about two years, followed by two and a half to three years of specialized professional training. In the Faculty of General Economics, the Department for National Planning trains planning experts in econometrics, macroeconomics, methodology, and mathematical and computer techniques. The Department of Finance trains financial experts to direct enter-

Table 1. Percentage and index number of certain categories of undergraduates

| | Scholastic year | | | |
	1961/62	1966/67	1972/73	1976/77
Engineering and architecture, %	27.7	36.2	37.3	32.8
Index number	100	220	219	251
Economics, %	5.6	8.7	10.2	9.3
Index number	100	274	323	374
Law, %	7.7	4.2	4.2	4.3
Index number	100	91	90	119
Undergraduates, total, %	100	100	100	100
Index number	100	168	171	211

Source: Central Statistical Office.

prises and to provide staff for central financial institutions and banks.[14] The Faculty of Commerce of the University comprises three departments: the Department for External Economy (foreign trade and external economic relations); the Department of International Relations (economics, with courses in diplomacy, history, and law), and the Department of Commodity Trade (domestic trade). The Faculty of Production and Transport is also divided into three departments: Industry, Agriculture, and Transport. The content and specialization of university studies is directly linked to a system of postgraduate education.

The number of economists

Before 1945 Hungary was a 'nation of lawyers' but since that time the number of economists (i.e. higher-level graduates in economics) has increased rapidly. In 1949 (the first postwar year for which figures are available) there were 4,075 economists (i.e. 4.2 percent of all such graduates) as against 25,769 lawyers (26.7 percent of the total), whereas by 1970 the corresponding figures were 22,667 (7.5 percent) and 28,960 (9.6 percent).[15] By 1977 the number of economists had risen to about 35,000 (8.3 percent), and a figure around 40,000 can be estimated for 1980. For the purposes of the present study, however, the number of economists engaged in non-routine analysis, direction, decision-preparation, and policymaking is around 20,000. In 1977 they represented 4.7 percent of the total number of graduates. On this definition, according to a special survey conducted by the Hungarian Central Statistical Office, 2930 economists were employed in government organs and state administration in 1977 (i.e., 14.6 percent of all economists engaged in non-routine economic work). In Hungary, government organs include not merely the ministries but also the National Planning Office (an economics institute par excellence); the National Materials and Prices Office (which plays an important role in the elaboration and implementation of economic policy); the Central Statistical Office (which undertakes economic analysis and has special jurisdiction in supervising and implementing plans, as well as responsibility for the collection of statistical data); and the Hungarian National Bank (which is not only the bank of issue but is also the commercial and investment bank which, through its monopolistic guidance of the money flow, influences the whole of Hungarian economic life). Economists represent 26.6 percent of the personnel of government organs in this

14. Iván T. Berend, "Training of Economists," *Marketing in Hungary*, 1976, no. 2, pp. 7–9.
15. The data are shown from Kepecs and Klinger, supra n.11.

wider sense, whereas in 1938, 60 percent of government employees were lawyers and around 3 percent were economists.

It is interesting to compare the composition of members of the government, while recognizing that such a comparison is essentially qualitative rather than quantitative, since the numbers are too small to constitute a statistical sample and because a ministerial post is always political in nature, with no special qualifications stipulated. With these allowances, in 1938, 4 of the 10 Cabinet members were lawyers, and there were no economists among the ministers, whereas in 1978, of the 28 members of the government, 8 were economists and only 1 was a lawyer. It should be noted that the 28 includes 24 members of the Hungarian Council of Ministers plus the heads of four government organs which exercise jurisdiction equal to or greater than that of the ministries: i.e. the National Planning Office, Hungarian National Bank, National Materials and Prices Office, and Central Statistical Office. Since 1938 there has been a significant increase in the number of economic portfolios; for example, as against one ministry for industry in 1938 there are now three—heavy; light; metallurgical and engineering industry. In 1938 there was one portfolio for trade and transport, as against three today: home trade; foreign trade; transport and communications.

This change reflects the country's socialist nature, and with it the more intensive participation of the government in the direction of the economy as much as the increased importance of economic questions in modern government in general.

The market for economists

We have already noted that the development of Hungarian political and economic life since the mid-sixties has considerably expanded the role of economists, not only in economic life and government but in Hungarian society in general. This entailed an expansion of the market for Hungarian economists and a concomitant increase in the number of posts for economists in enterprises, universities, research institutes, government, and public administration. This market is balanced from the quantitative point of view, since manpower planning ensures that the numbers enrolled in the different higher educational institutes in economics are approximately in equilibrium with anticipated future demand. (This planning does not, of course, involve compulsory manpower placement.) The advantage of the market situation for economists lies rather in the fact that, in keeping with their aptitude and interests, and owing to the adaptability of their skills, it is relatively easier for them to change their jobs than it is for members of other professions. Economists are thus becoming the 'new generalists' in Hungarian society who find work opportunities in many areas of society and the economy.

As a result of this market equilibrium and of the Hungarian wage-policy system, there is generally no wage and income differential for those in posts on any given level, either to the benefit or detriment of economists. There are, however, income differences among the different posts that can be held by those with qualifications in economics, although these are not substantial.

At present (summer 1978) the monthly salary of a faculty head in the University of Economics is around 9,000 forints; an economist working in a ministry as a department head earns about the same. An economist working in an enterprise as a top manager may have a slightly higher average monthly income, for in addition to the regular monthly salary he also receives a share of the enterprise profits (providing, of course, that the enterprise's profit is favorable). It can therefore be said that the actual positions selected by newly graduated economists depend less on the salary offered for different types of work than on the individual bent for more hectic enterprise work or for the more reflective academic or government jobs. However, a certain propensity can be seen in young economists beginning their careers towards practical economic work in the enterprises which holds out the promise of greater material rewards.

III. *Professionalization*

In Hungary today economists are characterized by professional awareness and a healthy esprit de corps. Their corporate forum is the Hungarian Economic Association. The association's rules define its objective as the use of social means to assist the cultivation and practical application of the science of economics and of the association of Hungarian economists for this purpose. The activities of the association, which has a total membership of around 6,000, are conducted in 12 sections and 18 county branches. The association's annual scientific conference is an important event in social and intellectual life. The Fourth World Congress of the International Economic Association held in 1974 in Budapest was particularly noteworthy among the international conferences organized by the association. One of the periodic Anglo-Hungarian bilateral economic colloquia included a discussion of the role of economists in economic policy and government.[16]

If we seek a dominant economic school in Hungarian economic

16. György Varga, "A Conference of British and Hungarian Economists," *New Hungarian Quarterly* 15, no. 54 (1974): 215–19.

thinking, we can clearly point to scientific socialism as the theoretical basis on which Hungarian economists carry out their activity in theoretical and applied economics and economic policy. However, this common basis does not exclude complexity in economic thinking and lively debate. Neither does it preclude an interest in the work of the leading economists of differing views in the Western world. Indeed, the works of these authors are also published in Hungarian, and at the invitation of the Hungarian Economic Association and the Hungarian Academy of Sciences, these economists also frequently visit Hungary to give lectures and exchange ideas with their Hungarian counterparts.

Economists in government employment have the freedom to publish, and in their articles, studies, and books they often criticize economic-policy measures and formulate proposals for new approaches and solutions *de lege ferenda*.

In the competition for government jobs Hungarian economists have enjoyed exceptionally favorable conditions during the past decade and a half. At first, from the mid-sixties on, there was a demand for them in the course of the reorganization of the Hungarian system of economic guidance; and now, since the early seventies, they have been increasingly assuming the role of 'new generalists.'

The mobility of economists between government, on the one hand, and academic life and the enterprise sphere, on the other, is high. One of the reasons for this phenomenon is that in Hungary civil servants have no specific status and civil service is open (by contrast with the U.K., as described in other studies, but like the U.S.A.). Owing to the civil service recognition of their skills the economists' opportunities to exert an influence on policy decisionmaking have particularly developed since the mid-sixties.[17]

It is sufficient here to give only a symbolic indication of this influence by noting the positions held by the two representatives of Hungarian economics who are perhaps the best-known abroad. Béla Csikós-Nagy, who is also chairman of the Hungarian Economic Association, has the status of Secretary of State as chairman of an important organ of Hungarian economic policy—the Board of Materials and Prices—and

17. Here I should like to draw the attention to the fact that in several countries covered by this project it is also from the mid-sixties that a sudden expansion of the role of economists in government can be observed—namely, independently from the socioeconomic system and level of development of the countries concerned. Among others, possible reasons for this coincidence can be these: an internationalization of economic activities; the beginning of a recognition of the global character of economic problems; consequently, the increasing need for government intervention into the economic flows; and a more rapid diffusion of the results of economic thought and of the experiences in economic policy among countries (similar to the rapidity of international spread of findings in natural sciences).

thus participates directly in economic decisionmaking; while Professor József Bognár, as chairman of the National Assembly's Commission for Planning and Budget and chairman of the Hungarian Council of World Economy, is also active in decisionmaking.

Although the desire of economists to work alongside their fellow professionals is presumably a factor in Hungary, as elsewhere, in increasing the number of economists in government, a greater weight should be attached to another manifestation of this phenomenon: the relations between the government and business spheres. The dialogue between these two spheres that characterizes the Hungarian system of planning and economic guidance encourages economists in each sphere to seek out their counterparts in the other as their natural allies, since they find it easier to understand each other because of their common way of thinking and identical terms of reference—whereas communication with technological experts, i.e. engineers, is not always so simple. This is also one of the explanations for the fact (which moreover facilitates this dialogue) that since the sixties, in addition to the Hungarian university-level training in economics, there has also been a development of such training at the college level designed primarily to produce business economists who can grasp a macro-level approach to economic phenomena.

With respect to the scientific integrity of economists, Professor Bognár concludes:

A closer and more institutional connection between science and practice, as well as the coordination at the junctures of the two vectors, may impart a new impetus to economic development and may accelerate the evolution of economics. While acknowledging this possibility, we must emphasize the danger necessarily concomitant to the close cooperation between science and economic action (for there are no unequivocal things in life), that the scholar's intellectual and moral independence may be reduced. The strictly critical attitude of science with regard to practice—which, of course, has immeasurable advantages—has so far been due not only to the greater critical courage of scholars and to their perspectives (e.g. a long-term approach to the phenomena of daily life), but also to the fact that research workers have not been responsible for practice. In the intellectual sense of the term it is always easier to criticize others' mistakes than to admit our own. Now this independent position has been endangered: scholars take part in setting fundamental or concrete objectives, in forecasting world economic phenomena, in preparing decisions on enterprise development. Will the scholars—under such conditions—be able to analyze critically and to point out the errors? Or—like some prejudiced and biased economic managers—will they gloss over the troubles (as long as they can) and cover up those responsible for them (often until it is no longer possible)? It should not be forgotten that even in the course of decisionmaking concerning his behavior, a scholar is under the pressure of others; this is because the nature of bureaucracy is not altered by the fact that in elaborating various problems the scholars work together with civil servants.

It is obvious that only scholars of high moral principle and integrity will have the moral courage to admit their mistakes, and it is equally evident that the majority of research workers cannot belong in this category.

It follows that the great strides outlined above cannot be taken successfully and without major drawbacks unless the number of scholars and research workers taking part in the work is restricted; those who are left outside (and these should include also major minds) will have to be given the chance to put forth their critical remarks in some scholarly forum or some other institution in a contradictory manner. In this way the socially indispensable critical function of the 'independent scholar' may perhaps be preserved.[18]

IV. *What Do Economists Actually Do in Government?*

The prominence that the economic approach and the role of economists have gained in Hungary since the mid-sixties and especially since 1968 has in part also assumed organizational form. Each ministry has a division for economics. These divisions undertake analyses of the economic bases and contexts of future decisions, cost-benefit analyses, and the comparison of various alternatives in the search of optima. They also participate in the preparation of technical decisions through economic calculations, and weigh the economic considerations involved in the preparation of decisions by non-economic ministries. Research institutes dealing with economic analyses are also attached to a number of ministries.

On the governmental level—apart from the specialized ministries —work of a specifically economic nature is carried out in the National Planning Office, the National Materials and Prices Office, the Hungarian National Bank, and the Central Statistical Office.

In the course of the decisionmaking process, economic analyses

---

18. József Bognár, "Interdependent Correlations," supra n.2.

and evaluations (the elaboration of alternatives) are undertaken by the government and ministry organs mentioned, with the additional factor that in specifically economic government agencies (such as the National Planning Office or the economic ministries) most of the officials are themselves economists. Here questions are expressed in economic terms from the outset, and the capillaries of the process of decision preparation are firmly embedded in economics. Of course, in other ministries with non-economic functions (e.g. culture, health) the questions are brought before the economists only at a later stage of feasibility consideration.

However, in the case of Hungary we must recall the special situation where economists other than those working in the government bureaucracy participate in the preparation and adoption of economic decisions. Academic economists also participate regularly and intensively in this work. If we considered economists 'inside' the government (i.e. working in the economic units of ministries) as 'technocrats' (supplying means for a prescribed end), economists 'outside' the government (i.e. working at universities and in independent research institutes) can be regarded as 'policy advisers' (making specific recommendations or providing alternative options). The link between insiders and outsiders is generally achieved through various councils and commissions, either operating permanently or set up for special purposes. Among the permanent fora of this nature is the Council on World Economy which is composed of key figures in senior government posts responsible for external economic questions on the one hand, and of scholars and external economy experts working in universities and research institutes on the other. Experience so far in the operation of the council set up in 1969 is that the simultaneous approach and joint consideration of problems from the angle of the decisionmakers on the one hand and the researchers on the other have proved fruitful, especially since 1973, when, in the new world economic situation, the decisionmakers acknowledged a growing need for the analysts' interpretations and medium- and long-term forecasts.

Moreover, post-1973 world economic developments have encouraged closer government cooperation with academic economists. Government departments and special bodies dealing with energy questions and exploitation of Hungarian mineral resources in general have usually invited outside economists to take part in consultative and decision-preparation meetings such as were previously attended solely by technical experts (engineers and geologists). Since then, the scope of participants in seminars and scientific meetings has also been expanded to include non-government economists.

The latest (and perhaps the best) example of the ad hoc but top-level and effective participation of economists in government decisions is the intensive and, in some respects, dominant role of academic economists in the preparation of the decision adopted in October 1977 by the Hungarian Socialist Workers' Party which involved the restructuring of certain sectors and products in conformity with the changed circumstances of the world economy.

The economists' participation in all these councils and commissions largely conforms to the requirements of the independence of scholars. The academic economists involved in government decisions through these councils and commissions are independent of the government (as they are employed by non-government organs) and they are not propelled by the slow but inexorable flow of the institutionalized thinking of government bureaucracy. Moreover, they are also independent in the material sense, since they work in the councils and commissions on an honorary basis and receive no fee.

All this has produced a special symbiosis of centralization and decentralization in Hungary. Since this is a socialist planned economy, economic decisionmaking (and the organization of its preparation) is centralized, while the thinking and analysis preceding decisions are decentralized.

It can be clearly seen from the above sections that in the case of Hungary, the participation of economists in government decision-making is achieved both through formal and informal structures. The network of economists working in government jobs can be regarded as a formal structure, while the network of permanent councils and ad hoc commissions through which the government draws on the advice and suggestions of economists can be regarded as an informal (but at the same time institutionalized) structure. Two further manifestations of the government's use of economists in non-government jobs can be placed between these formal and informal structures. One is where different ministries and government organs draw up research contracts with university faculties or research institutes to carry out analyses of given current economic problems or develop proposals for their solution, financed by the ministry. These projects then enter into the flow of information for the preparation of decisions in the form of background papers or alternative decisions. In recent years the university faculties and research institutes have been commissioned by the government mainly to draw up forecasts of the evolution of world economic phenomena. This is, of course, in addition to the forecasting undertaken by the National Planning Office, which is responsible for planning foreign trade as well as domestic affairs. Most of the forecasts are published even though they may be a cause of some embarrassment to the government.

The other such intermediary form is where individual economists who work in research institutes or universities sign contracts for part-time work to participate as temporary experts or permanent advisers in the preparation of decisions and the decisionmaking activity of government organs.

V. *The Role of the Economist in Policymaking*

It can already be seen from the foregoing pages that economists play an important role in policymaking in Hungary. This is naturally related to the fact that Hungary has a planned economy, and neither planning nor implementation can be successful without qualified economists. A large number of phenomena, factors, and interdependencies have to be taken into consideration in the course of this work which can be recognized, interpreted, measured, and forecasted only with an expert knowledge of economics. Hungarian economists achieve in the area of economic analysis and policymaking what Galileo expressed in general terms: "It is the task of science to measure everything measurable and to render measurable that which could not previously be measured." In the case of Hungarian economists, this means the combination of logical and quantitative activity and at the same time the equilibrium of the two; in other words, Hungarian economists draw on the cognitive possibilities inherent in mathematical methods, but they do not rely exclusively on these methods.

Reference has already been made to the role played by Hungarian economists, both within and outside government, in the preparation, introduction, and implementation of the Hungarian economic reform of 1968. In recent years they have acquired a new role in the preparation of government decisions and policymaking. In conclusion we would like to provide a brief account of this.

Hungary is a European socialist country on a middle level of development which, because of its natural endowments, imports raw materials and exports finished products. Consequently, the rise in the world market price of raw materials (particularly crude oil) since the end of 1973 has had an unfavorable effect in Hungary too (for example, as reflected in a deterioration of the terms of trade), and this has come just as unexpectedly as in all other energy-importing countries in the world. In the case of such world economic changes government routine work based on the assumption of continuity comes to a standstill because the economic and technical experts working in government on the chain of successive decisions on the use of resources, investments, etc., are not prepared for the perception and interpretation of sudden 'discrete' changes.

In this unexpected situation only the economists dealing with research and forecasting on medium- and long-term world economic processes were able to undertake the evaluation of new phenomena and answer the questions facing the government. They were prepared for this to a certain extent, for in charting world economic processes (particularly within the framework of research initiated by the Hungarian Council on World Economy) they had already indicated in 1971 that tensions and turbulent changes could be expected in the world economy energy situation. Thus two years later, following the oil price explosion at the end of 1973, they were already well prepared to give an opinion of the new situation. Only an economic approach and analytical methods could lead, for example, to the diagnosis that the change in the price of oil was not cyclical but secular,[19] marking the beginning of a new era in the world economy.[20]

It was therefore natural that academic economists should also be invited to sessions of the special committees which attempted to draw conclusions from the new situation, at first only with respect to Hungarian energy policy and the exploitation of mineral resources. The economists' opinion was needed here, first of all because a long period of time is required for the implementation of investments in this branch, and future price and profitability relations must be estimated for years ahead when the investment decision is made. Only economists could be expected to produce the world economic forecasts needed for this. Naturally, many members of these committees questioned the validity of the forecasts, particularly engineers and experts in technology who are able to foresee the anticipated results of technical development, but whose judgment in economic questions is based on past commonplaces (in contrast to the economists, who have a tendency to project yesterday's technical standard onto the economic development they forecast). Economists are, of course fallible; but their intellectual framework provides a basis from which they make general predictions more effectively than non-economists.

Finally however, after lengthy explanations and debates, coordination of the economic and technical approach was achieved in evalua-

19. Egon Kemenes, *Impact of New Trends in World Economy on Systems Analysis of the Utilization of Mineral Raw Materials*, International Institute for Applied Systems Analysis (Laxenburg), Committee for Systems Research of the Hungarian Academy of Sciences (Budapest, 1977).

20. József Bognár, *New Forces and Currents in the International Economy* (Budapest, 1975).

tion of the new situation. (It must be admitted that a considerable time passed while these debates were being conducted, and events during this period proved the economists right.)

However, the adaptation of Hungarian economic policy to the new world economic situation could not be limited to the extractive branches. Highly respected professional economists made use of scientific forums, memoranda, and the mass media to draw attention to the need to transform the whole structure of the Hungarian economy in order to adapt it to the new situation. The government set up a network of committees to make analyses and draw up proposals, in which representatives of the science of economics played a leading role. These committees prepared the resolution "on long-term external economic policy and development of the structure of production" issued by the Central Committee of the Hungarian Socialist Workers' Party in October 1977. And since then, economists in both the government and non-government sphere have been playing just as great a role in the implementation of this resolution as they did in formulating its principles.

Concluding reflections

By contrast with the situation in some of the other countries considered in these studies there is continuing appreciation of the value of the economists' contribution to Hungarian society. Generally speaking, the economics profession has demonstrated a certain distaste for directive economic planning, and its members have consequently led the way in the introduction of market elements into the system. There has, of course, been some public criticism of their activities and influence, and certain professional jealousies have been aroused. But recent world economic events have strengthened their role in the preparation of government decisions and policymaking. Economists specializing in international affairs have been especially constructive, since the most serious recent economic problems have arisen in that sphere, rather than in connection with the domestic planning system. The analysis of international problems and trends is a less politically sensitive policy field than some others. The need to adjust to external changes as efficiently as possible is manifest, and the discussion of this process poses no ideological problems. Hungarians acknowledge the growing need for economic expertise; hence the economics profession has an assured position in the country.

Bibliography

Abstracts of Hungarian Economic Literature. Periodical of the Scientific Information Service of the Hungarian Scientific Council for World Economy. Budapest. Bimonthly, in English.

Bognár, József. "Economic Reform, Development and Stability in the Hungarian Economy." *New Hungarian Quarterly*, no. 46 (1972): 29–43.

————. *Les Nouveaux Mécanismes de l'économie socialiste en Hongrie*. Paris, 1969.

————. *Planned Economy in Hungary: Achievements and Problems*. Budapest, 1959.

Csikós-Nagy, Béla. "Perfectionnements des mécanismes économiques en Hongrie." *Economies et Sociétés*, no. 1 (Paris, 1971): 51–70.

————. "La politique économique de la Hongrie: ses objectifs et ses moyens." *Revue de l'Est*, no. 1 (Paris, 1972): 5–29.

————. *Socialist Price Theory and Price Policy*. Budapest, 1975.

Erdei, Ferenc, ed. *Information Hungary*. Oxford, 1968.

Friss, István, ed. *Essays on Economic Policy and Planning in Hungary*. Budapest, 1978.

————, ed. *Reform of the Economic Mechanism in Hungary*. Budapest, 1969.

Gadó, Ottó, ed. *Reform of the Economic Mechanism in Hungary: Development 1968–71*. Budapest, 1972.

Kemenes, Egon. "The Enterprise and the National Economy." *New Hungarian Quarterly*, no. 36 (1969): 61–76.

Kemenes, Egon. "Le fonctionnement d'une économie socialiste: la Hongrie." *Economies et Sociétés*, série G, No. 34, vol. 11, no. 5, 6–9 (June–Sept. 1977): 1504–42.

————. "The Hungarian Economy." In Zoltán Halász, ed., *Hungary* (Budapest, 1978), pp. 166–96.

Morva, Tamás. "Planning in Hungary." In Morris Bernstein, ed., *Economic Planning, East and West* (Cambridge, Mass., 1975): 271–309.

Nyers, Rezsó. *Experience of the Economic Reform in Hungary: Twenty Questions and Answers*. Budapest, 1970.

————. "Problems of Profitability and Income Distribution." *New Hungarian Quarterly*, no. 41 (1971): 21–41.

Statistical Yearbook of Hungary. Hungarian Central Statistical Office, Budapest. Published yearly; also in English.

Japan: the officer in charge of economic affairs

Ryutaro Komiya and Kozo Yamamoto

I. *Introduction*

In the Japanese case one cannot discuss the role of the economist in government, since there is not one professional economist employed by the government of Japan. The employment practices and personnel policies of the Japanese government, or any other large institutional employer in Japan, are quite different from those of countries with European traditions. Two distinctive characteristics peculiar to Japan in regard to the role of the economist in the government are, firstly, there is no profession called economists in Japanese society and, secondly, large organizations in Japan, whether government ministries, banks, or corporations, are run by generalist administrators or managers who work in most cases in one organization for their entire careers and reach the top positions after occupying many different posts in the organization.

There is no word in the Japanese language which corresponds exactly to 'economists' in English. The term *keizai-gakusha* means 'academic economist,' that is, a professor or scholar who teaches and/or does research in economics at a university or a research institute. Although a graduate from the School of Economics of a university receives a bachelor's degree of economics (*keizai-gakushi*) and is referred to as a graduate of the Economics School or 'economics graduate,' these graduates cannot be said to constitute a recognized profession. Neither in government nor business employment is a graduate from an Economics School treated as a professional economist, nor, indeed, as one significantly different from a graduate from the School of Law, Management, Commerce, or even Literature. Master's or doctor's degrees are conferred on those who have studied economics and fulfilled the requirements of the new system of graduate education started in 1949. But most of those entering the Graduate School of Economics choose to become academic economists, researchers in research institutes, or school teachers, and very few go into public service or the business world, because there is no demand from the government or business for candidates with advanced degrees in economics.[1] A Japanese ministry or agency is run by a relatively small

1. The situation is different with respect to those having M.A. and Ph.D. degrees in

number of elite generalist administrators, and there are few senior-rank positions for professional specialists of any kind in the government. The same is true of the central bank, commercial banks, and big corporations in general.

As compared with industrialized countries with European traditions there are distinctive features in the recruitment and promotion process of high-ranking officers in charge of economic affairs in the Japanese Government, such as these:

(i)   a highly competitive examination when they are first employed on their graduation from colleges;

(ii) the so-called 'lifetime employment' practice within a single ministry or agency;

(iii) extensive on-the-job training throughout their careers; and

(iv) steady promotion year by year on a seniority basis, up to positions near to the very top.

In the process of promotion according to the seniority principle the generalist administrator holds a series of different posts in a wide range of areas.

A corollary of the lifetime employment practice and the seniority principle in promotion is that government and academic society constitute two separate worlds, as far as the interchange of personnel is concerned, although academic economists and the economic policymakers interact in several ways. There is no opportunity for outsiders to enter government. The civil servant's career is completely separated from that of a professor of economics, political science, or international relations. Unlike the practice in the United States and other countries, in postwar Japan prominent academic economists have never occupied important positions in government or the central bank; nor have high-ranking officials become professors in leading universities after retiring from government service.

Because elite administrators or managers serve essentially in the same ministry or corporation for a long time—up to thirty to forty years—such an organization in Japan is a solid, independent, and cohesive body, maintaining a degree of solidarity and consistency over time. Anyone who occupies a responsible position in such an organization highly values harmony, solidarity, and consensus within the organization.

Japanese people try very hard to achieve full consensus inside an organization. Under normal conditions a decision within a tightly knit

---

Engineering or Natural Science, for whom there has recently been an increasingly brisk demand from large corporations. On the other hand, there are no schools in Japan which more or less correspond to a U.S.-type graduate school of Business Administration or Law School.

organization must be unanimous; a majority decision, however small the minority, is considered a sign of lack of solidarity. Hence a decision on a major issue by voting must be avoided as far as possible in any well-developed Japanese organization, such as a ministry, a political party, the board of directors of a corporation, or a faculty or the senate of a university.

This tendency towards consensus and solidarity among the elite administrators belonging to a ministry or agency may explain why the Japanese bureaucracy has a strong tradition of non-partisanship and political neutrality.

II. *Historical Background*

The characteristics of the Japanese bureaucracy briefly described above were already well established before World War II. Nor is government intervention in private economic affairs a new phenomenon in postwar Japan: ever since the Meiji period the government has intervened extensively in private activities for economic and other policy purposes in order to industrialize and modernize the then backward Japanese economy and society.

However, economic issues have become much more important in politics and government policy in postwar Japan. The military, which had great political influence in prewar years, collapsed at the end of the war and disappeared from the political scene. But the bureaucracy was able to maintain its broad continuity from the prewar period, despite extensive democratization measures under the American occupation immediately after the war.

In the early postwar years, the most important national objective on which the government concentrated its effort was 'economic independence,' meaning growth and balance-of-payments equilibrium without foreign aid. "Export or die" was a popular slogan in those days. Thereafter, "the high rate of economic growth" was given the top priority in government policies. Thus, economic problems and the social problems related to these objectives became the most important policy issues in postwar Japan.

About 1955, when the national economic plan was prepared and published for the first time, government officers first began to pay attention to economics and economic theory. Initially only a small group of officers in the agency (the Economic Planning Agency, EPA) responsible for national economic planning concerned themselves with economics. In practice in those early days the officers making the key economic policy decisions were not concerned with economics or the national economic plan.[2] Interestingly enough, a high percentage of the pioneers in EPA were graduates from the School of Engineering—partly, perhaps, because Marxian economics was the dominant school in economics in the leading Japanese universities during the early postwar period, with only a few exceptions, such as Hitotsubashi University. It was only after about 1960 that contemporary non-Marxist economics began to be taught on a full scale at the University of Tokyo, which continued, as in prewar years, to produce a large number of high-ranking government officers.

The Prime Minister Hayato Ikeda's Income Doubling Plan, published in 1960, was an epoch-making event in postwar Japanese economic and political history in several respects, including its impact on the role of economics in economic policymaking. This plan was based upon the original ideas of Mr. Osamu Shimomura (later Dr. Shimomura), then an officer in the Ministry of Finance, who deserves great credit for bringing economics and economic theory into politics and the bureaucracy. Since then, Keynesian macroeconomics, the Harrod-Domar theory of growth and business cycles, national income accounting and macroeconometric models have been widely discussed and rapidly disseminated in government and the business world. During the recession which began in 1965, the balanced-budget principle upheld in the postwar years was formally abandoned by a law enacted in 1966, and Keynesian fiscal policy began to play a major role as a countercyclical measure.

Throughout the latter half of the 1960s and the 1970s Japan's international economic relations with other major countries became increasingly close. The Japanese government played a much more active role in IMF, GATT, and OECD, reflecting Japan's growing importance in the world economy as a result of Japan's 'economic miracle.' The number of cooperative economic projects as well as conflicts with other countries has been increasing, and Japan's status in international conferences has been rising. Consequently the Japanese government's top officials have been obliged to take a growing interest in international economic affairs and adopt an economic approach to them.

However, despite these trends the ministries' and government agencies' demand for professional economists has not increased. As in earlier days, the prevailing Japanese bureaucratic tradition has subor-

2. On economic planning in Japan, see R. Komiya, "Planning in Japan," in Morris Bornstein, ed., *Economic Planning: East and West* (Cambridge, Mass.), 1975; reprinted in M. Bornstein, ed., *Comparative Economic Systems: Models and Cases*, 4th ed., 1979.

dinated the professional specialists, so that almost all the career officers in government are treated as general administrators rather than
specialists or professionals. As in other countries, new university graduates trained in contemporary non-Marxist economics have joined
ministries and agencies concerned with economic affairs. Older officers in those organizations have also tried to learn the subject, and incentives have been provided to encourage this re-educational process.
Nevertheless, this only means that a certain amount of economic
knowledge, especially macroeconomics, has become recognized as a
common-sense requirement for top-level officials in charge of economic affairs. It does not mean that the government has wanted to employ professional economists as such, in the European or American
sense of the term.

III.   *Economists Within the Japanese Government*

As already mentioned, there is no word in the Japanese language
corresponding to 'economists' in English, and there is no socially recognized economics profession.[3] All the government's economic affairs
are managed by elite generalist administrators.

Although the word *kancho-ekonomistuto* (economist in the government) is sometimes used in Japanese, it refers only to a very few
highly competent people who are prominent in economic forecasting,
planning, and research within the government and frequently express
their views on economic prospects and macroeconomic problems.[4]
They appear to be influential in governmental decisionmaking, both because they occupy key posts and because they display excellent judgment on macroeconomic trends and policy issues. Sometimes their
personal acquaintance with the Prime Minister, ministers, or the president or governors of the Bank of Japan may be a crucial determinant
of their influence on economic policy.

Generally speaking, however, personal specialist capability as an
'economist' is not much appreciated in Japan. In practice, an official's

3. There is no Japanese word corresponding to 'statistician' in English, nor a socially recognized profession of statistician in Japan. Socially recognized professionals
in Japan (e.g. medical doctors, lawyers, accountants) must undergo several years' postgraduate special training, are authorized or licensed by the government, are employed
or practice by themselves as professionals, and belong to coherent and influential national and regional associations.

4. Such as Mr. Hisao Kanamori (formerly EPA), Dr. Saburo Okita (formerly EPA),
Dr. Osamu Shimomura (formerly Ministry of Finance), Dr. Toshihiko Yoshino (formerly Bank of Japan) in the past, and Mr. Takao Akabane, Mr. Yasushi Kozai, Mr.
Isamu Miyazaki (all EPA), Dr. Yoshio Suzuki (Bank of Japan), and Mr. Masaru
Yoshitomi (EPA) recently. Among them Okita is a graduate of the School of Engineering, Yoshino and Kanamori the School of Law, Yoshitomi Department of Liberal Arts,
and others the School of Economics. To my knowledge only Kozai and Yoshitomi had
a formal education in economics at the graduate level.

rank or position and his ability to mobilize his staff resources are usually the decisive factors. We shall therefore focus our attention on those posts in the government which are especially important in -the economic policymaking process. These include most of the senior posts in the Ministry of Finance (MOF), the Ministry of International Trade and Industry (MITI), and the EPA, which are the three foremost among ministries and agencies in charge of economic affairs; also the Bank of Japan (BOJ), which does not belong to the government but is in charge of monetary policy; and the Ministry of Foreign Affairs,[5] which has many senior posts more or less concerned with the government's economic policy.

Most of the occupants of these posts are highly intelligent and capable men, who are generally quite knowledgeable about economic matters under their jurisdiction. In practice they often play the role of an economist. In addition, there are a few senior posts dealing primarily with economic problems in such government offices as the Ministry of Transport, the Ministry of Construction, the Ministry of Welfare, the Ministry of Labor, and the Fair Trade Commission.

Those who occupy these posts have varied backgrounds, except that almost all have at one time been what is called a 'career officer' in the ministry or agency in question. All are basically generalist administrators, diplomats, or central bank officers; none is a professional economist. They are influential in the economic policymaking process not because they apply advanced knowledge of economics or economic theory to the issues under consideration but because they have wide experience as generalist administrators and can react promptly to new problems and changing circumstances, mobilize the information, knowledge, and capabilities available among their subordinate staff, and build up a consensus among those concerned through deliberàte persuasion and skillful negotiation. In making judgments on any given issue they must take many factors into account: economic, legal and political aspects, precedents, relations with other ministries and agencies, and public opinion and sentiment. Indeed, given the existing climate of opinion in the Japanese bureaucracy any attempt on the part of a high official to parade his knowledge of advanced economic theory or to discuss current issues primarily or exclusively in economic terms, in the manner of a professional economist, will probably provoke nega-

5. In the Ministry of Foreign Affairs, some career officers, that is those who passed the senior-level diplomatic service examination, are considered as especially "strong on economic affairs", having gone through many posts dealing primarily with international economic affairs, such as posts in the Bureau of Economic Affairs, Bureau of Economic Cooperation, and Permanent Delegations to OECD and to International Organizations in Geneva, and "economic" posts in other offices of the Ministry.

tive reactions. Most of the career officers performing economist functions do not wish to be regarded as economists. They know that they may in future be transferred to non-economic work and appreciate that there are better career opportunities for generalist administrators in higher posts both within and outside the ministry or agency. There are, however, some exceptions to this generalization, for recently a few specialists have left the EPA to become university professors or join research organizations and, anticipating such a move, may have been glad to be known as economists.

IV. *The Recruitment Process*

Every year the Personnel Agency conducts National Government Officers Examinations to select candidates for government employees. The examination system, which started in 1949, includes written examinations of various categories, and each ministry or agency must select and interview its own prospective employees from one of the lists of candidates prepared by the Personnel Agency, which releases the names and records of those who passed in the respective categories. Some are employed in the main office of each ministry or agency, while others go into one of the regional branch offices.

Those wishing to become a 'career officer' (or simply 'career,' as they are known) actively involved in the process of economic policymaking in the MOF, the MITI, the EPA, or elsewhere must first pass in the senior level (*jokyūshoku-kōshu*) examination, and then be interviewed in the main office of one of these ministries or agencies. Once employed, they are promoted annually according to a given pattern, at the fastest speed permitted by the Personnel Agency Regulations, and they eventually occupy most of the key government policy decisionmaking posts.

The Ministry's other head-office staff are either hired directly after passing the medium- or junior-level examination, or are transferred from a regional branch office—in the case of the MOF, for example, a regional tax office or a regional financial office—after several years of distinguished service. Such persons are sometimes called 'non-career' officers even though they also serve on a lifetime, seniority-principle basis. Some very capable 'non-career' officers are promoted to the Division Director level in the main office.

Within the senior level there are various examinations in administration, law, economics, civil engineering, etc. (in 1978 there were 28 such examinations altogether). In each case the written examination is comparable to that set for university graduates. Most of those wishing to become career officers in economic ministries or agencies are graduates from the Schools of Law or Economics.[6]

The senior-level examination in law or economics is highly competitive, and in recent years only 1 in 40 has passed (see Table 1). Most of the successful candidates have first-class academic records in a few leading Japanese universities, so that the government can choose its career officers from among very capable graduates.

However, it is inappropriate to regard an applicant who has passed the economics examination and is eligible for interview as an economist. Under the current Japanese system, specialized undergraduate education in economics lasts only about two years (before 1953 it was three years), since the first two years of college education are devoted to general cultural education. Hence, on their employment they have only an elementary knowledge of economics. Moreover, the personnel officers of the ministry or agency in question who conduct the interviews do not expect the candidates either to possess or to acquire the advanced knowledge of economics required by a professional economist.

As Table 2 shows, recently the MOF and the MITI have annually employed about 25 administrative career officers from among the successful candidates at the senior-level examinations, and EPA about 8. They are selected mainly because of their potential ability or general personality and, second, according to the distribution of the new vintage of career officers in any given year in terms of such factors as the

Table 1: Results of the senior-level written examination for the career government officers (*jokyūshuku-kōshu*)

	Total	Law	Economics
Applicants, 1977	48,514	8,729	5,060
Those passing	1,206	240	89
Applicants, 1978	55,992	10,630	5,826
Those passing	1,311	245	89

6. There are exceptions, however; for instance, in recent years the MOF normally selects one of the new career officers employed every year from among graduates of either the School of Natural Science or the School of Engineering. The EPA also hires one or two Natural Science or Engineering graduates every year. They must first pass either the law or economics senior-level examination in order to be eligible for the interview, and quite a few do succeed! This indicates the level of knowledge in Law or Economics taught at the undergraduate level and required in the senior-level examination.

Table 2. Number of administrative career officers newly employed by the MOF, MITI, and EPA: 1960–78

Year	I. MOF Total	Econ. exam.	II. MITI Total	Econ. exam.	III. EPA Total	Econ. exam.
1960	17	1	18	6	4	2
1961	18	5	19	4	3	3
1962	21	3	23	8	4	4
1963	20	1	22	4	5	4
1964	20	5	24	8	5	5
1965	20	8	21	6	7	2
1966	22	1	18	5	9	6
1967	23	7	18	6	7	6
1968	22	10	19	9	7	4
1969	21	6	23	8	9	8
1970	22	6	19	9	10	9
1971	23	5	22	6	10	9
1972	24	8	18	6	7	5
1973	17	9	21	7	7	4
1974	27	9	21	9	9	7
1975	27	6	26	12	7	5
1976	25	7	25	11	8	7
1977	23	6	23	9	8	6
1978	26	8	26	8	7	7

Note: 'Total' refers to the number of career officers newly employed in each year and 'Econ. exam.' to those among them who passed the economics examination. Comparable figures for all kinds of officers newly employed in each year are not available. The total number of all officers in the service of the MOF, MITI or EPA is as follows:

	MOF	MITI	EPA
1970	15,895	7,755	570
1978	15,421	6,591	512

The above figures refer to the respective Ministries proper, and do not include those in the Internal Revenue Agency, Printing Bureau, and Mint Bureau under the MOF, nor those in the Agency of Industrial Science and Technology, Patent Agency, Small and Medium Enterprise Agency, and Resources and Energy Agency under the MITI. The total number of career officers in the service of the MOF, MITI, or EPA in a year is not available either, but since they normally serve twenty to thirty-five years after being employed, it would not be far from the mark if one multiplied the average figure in Table 2 for each ministry by 25.

schools from which they graduate and their backgrounds—urban, provincial, etc.

In the case of the MOF, in recent years about a fourth to a third of new career employees every year have passed the economics examination.[7] Before 1963, and especially in prewar years, most of the MOF's career officers were law graduates, and the share of economics graduates was no more than 10 percent (the prewar recruitment system was somewhat different from the present one). Apparently the MOF has recently attached greater importance to the economics examination as a source of new recruits.[8] The MITI personnel policy is similar to that of the MOF, but the share of those passing the economics examination is somewhat higher. In addition to those counted in Table 2, the MITI hires about 20 new 'engineering' career officers every year who have passed various subdivisions of the senior level engineering examination. They occupy posts in the ministry's research-oriented offices or institutes.

Besides the three government offices listed in Table 2, successful economics candidates are sought by the ministries of Construction, Transport, Home Affairs, Agriculture, Forestry and Fisheries, Labor, and Health and Welfare and by the Fair Trade Commission, Defense Agency, and Agency for Environmental Protection. However, each of these offices usually employs only from one to three recruits, sometimes none at all. An overwhelming majority of the administrative career officers of these ministries and agencies have passed the law examination.

Although the Bank of Japan is responsible for monetary policy its officers are not government officials. While its employees do not come under the National Government Officers Examination System, its personnel policy is closely parallel to that of the MOF or MITI. The BOJ hires about 25 to 30 new graduates every year as its career officers, of which the proportion of economics graduates (including a few in Commerce and Management) is approximately 60 percent, the rest being overwhelmingly law graduates. Nevertheless the BOJ does not consider economics graduates as professional economists, either actual or

7. As already mentioned, the MOF also hires about one graduate from the School of Science or Engineering every year, and he often comes out of the 'economics' examination.

8. The number of career officers who occupied the posts above the director general (*kyoku-chō*; DG) level in the MOF from 1960 through 1978 is 115, of which the number of graduates from the Schools of Economics, including the prewar commercial college, similar to the German *Handelshochschule*, is only 13. An overwhelming majority of these 115 officers are graduates from the University of Tokyo. But Mr. Masayoshi Ohira, the present Prime Minister, is a graduate from Tokyo Commercial College (now Hitotsubashi University) and was employed as a career officer in the MOF under the prewar system. Former Prime Minister Hayato Ikeda was also an MOF career officer and graduated from the School of Law of Kyoto University. They quit the MOF after filling many high posts there, became politicians, were elected as members of Parliament, and then later became minister of Finance and the Prime Minister. Thus one does not have to be a graduate of the University of Tokyo in order to be successful as a career officer in the MOF.

potential. However in recent years it has begun to foster a new breed of central-bank economists by sending a very small number of promising young career officers to graduate schools in the United States and elsewhere afterwards frequently placing them in research-oriented posts in the Research or Statistics Bureau, or the recently established Special Research Department. Roughly half of the present executive governors and directors general of the BOJ are recent economics graduates. Three out of six post-World War II presidents have been economics graduates, although none of them has ever been considered a professional economist.

V. *Promotion and Functions*

We shall now discuss how career officers in charge of economic affairs are promoted year by year within a ministry, and what kind of work or functions they perform at each stage. We shall focus on the Ministry of Finance, the office most influential on economic affairs, but mention other offices as necessary.

First years in the ministry

A freshman career officer entering MOF is usually first assigned to a division dealing with relatively generalized and/or coordinating work in a bureau such as the General Affairs Division, the Research Division, or the Archives and Documents Division in the minister's Secretariat (Kanbō). This is in order to enable him to learn about the ministry's activities and become familiar with the annual cycle of its administrative operation. Here he serves for two years as an apprentice and undergoes a basic training such as preparing documents, processing statistical data, or accompanying and helping a senior officer in negotiating with other offices within or outside of the ministry.

When a freshman is allocated to a particular division, no attention is paid to the kind of examination he passed or the school he graduated from. Thus an economics graduate may be assigned to a section dealing mainly with legal affairs, or a law graduate to a section performing economic or statistical analysis. Once a young man has succeeded in the highly competitive entrance examination and entered MOF as a career officer, he is now an integral part of the MOF family, and his academic background ceases to be a significant attribute.

In the third year, five or six out of the annual crop of about twenty-five career officers are sent abroad for two years' graduate work in Economics or Business Administration (usually two to the USA, two to France, one to England, and one to Germany). All the rest are withdrawn from administrative assignments and attached to the minister's

Secretariat as an 'economic theory (economics, as a matter of fact) trainee' for one full year's schooling in economics.[9] Thus nowadays even if a career officer is not an economics graduate, he will have had a fairly extensive basic training in economics either at home or abroad. The BOJ and MITI have similar but less extensive in-service training programs, with the main emphasis on economics.

After finishing the 'economic theory training' program or graduate study abroad, the MOF's career officer becomes a section chief (*kakari-chō*) for two years, and for the first time performs real administrative duties requiring a fair amount of judgment. This will be during his fourth and fifth years in MOF (i.e. fifth and sixth years for those who have studied abroad). However, he does not make final decisions by himself, but follows the instructions of his immediate senior officer, an assistant director (*kachō-hosa*).

Director of an Internal Revenue office

The MOF career officer is next assigned for one year as director of a local office of the Internal Revenue Agency. As the director of a small office in a local town or a city he is expected to learn how to make judgments and decisions, and above all, how to exercise leadership. At the same time he must become familiar with the reality of a local economy, and learn how the MOF administration becomes involved with the common people. He will be in charge of some fifty to sixty subordinates, many of them older, some much older than himself and with longer service in tax administration. He will also prepare himself to become a senior government officer by making formal and informal contacts with influential local personalities such as business executives, politicians, and local government administrators. This is a unique on-the-job training program for the career officer in MOF, which is an essential part of its long tradition, though it somewhat resembles the training of a French *inspecteur des finances*. Thus about 20 to 25 out of its 506 local Internal Revenue Offices (in 1978) throughout Japan are headed by such young career officers (aged 28 to 30) each year. As the result of this experience, they are said to mature greatly both personally and as administrators and leaders.

Other ministries also send their career officers to their local offices or posts in prefectural governments outside the central government. In the case of BOJ, after a year's work in its main office a freshman career employee is assigned to one of its twenty or so local branches for two years. This is considered a very useful way of enabling a young career

9. See Appendix A, below, for its content.

employee to learn how the central banking system operates on a local scale.

Assistant director

After service as a director of a local Internal Revenue Office, a career officer returns to the MOF's main office and becomes an assistant director (*kachō-hosa*) in a division, and an active participant in the policymaking process. Some of the career officers are sent or seconded to other ministries or agencies for one to three years, working there temporarily on what is called a *shukko* basis.[10]

A career officer's period of service as assistant director is usually about ten years, i.e. approximately from ages 30 to 40. During this period he changes his post approximately every two years, so as to occupy about five different assistant-director posts successively, normally in different bureaux.[11] In this phase he is expected to develop his general administrative ability, his capacity to respond promptly to a new situation, to negotiate effectively, to take leadership in reaching a consensus among those concerned, and to be knowledgeable—or to appear knowledgeable—about the matters within his jurisdiction. Needless to say, he must first be able to understand what is happening in the area in which he operates, and to make a sound judgment, whatever kind of job he is assigned to.

In the Japanese bureaucracy it is considered undesirable for the career officer to specialize in any single field or to judge a matter only from a particular point of view, whether legal or economic. In order to participate actively in the policymaking process he should form a well-balanced judgment, taking full account of both economic and non-economic aspects of a situation. Furthermore, he should use common sense, sound logic, and simple language when expressing his ideas in a group discussion, so that other career and non-career officers can understand without difficulty.

Almost all the MOF's policy plans are first prepared by an assistant director. When a certain policy decision is necessary, the assistant director in charge is called upon to prepare a basic document, which should deal, as concisely as possible, with the historical background, relevant statistical data, legal aspects of the issue under consideration,

10. See Appendix B, below.
11. The MOF's personnel policy seems to be changing somewhat in this regard. Previously, there were quite a few career officers called *shukei* (budget)-*batake* (or *bata*) or *shuzei* (taxation)-*batake*, meaning 'grown up in Budget (or Taxation) Bureau,' who have gone through many posts in the Budget or the Taxation Bureau. *Shukei-batake* officers used to be considered the mainstay of the MOF, with *shuzei-batake* coming next. But recently the MOF has tended to shift career officers around from one bureau to another, and not to foster many offficers 'grown up' in a particular bureau.

merits and demerits of possible policy changes, the arguments for and against them, and a final conclusion.

When the original draft is completed, possibly with some revisions by the director of the division, it is submitted to a formal meeting of the bureau (*kyoku-gi*). The director general and other high officers of the bureau, as well as officers of other bureaux concerned, discuss the issue and the prepared document from every conceivable point of view. The draftsman of the basic document must be able to answer promptly and clearly any question raised and to respond to opinions expressed at the meeting. If there remains any room for doubt, the document and the policy plan it embodies will not be approved at that stage. This involves a very severe test of the ability of the assistant director in charge.

When a new policy has successfully passed the 'test' of the bureau meeting, it usually becomes MOF official policy. However, if the issue is very important or, more especially, if two or more of the bureaux concerned are in disagreement, the matter will be submitted to the office of the vice-minister or minister. In such a case, the officers of the minister's Secretariat and the bureaux concerned will be called to a formal meeting of the ministry (*shō-gi*).

Division director to director general

When the period of his service as assistant director is completed, an MOF career officer either becomes the director of one of its regional offices for two to three years, which is somewhat similar to service as director of a local Internal Revenue Office in earlier years but at a higher level, or goes abroad to a Japanese embassy as a financial attaché for three to four years. Then he returns to the main office and becomes the director of a division (*ka-chō*). In the Japanese bureaucracy a division directorship in the main office is considered a post much superior to the division directorship in a regional office, although they have the same title. This is also true of the *kyoku-chō* (director general), of *kachō* and other supervisory posts. A career officer usually serves for two years as director of a particular division, and normally holds three different division-director posts successively. Beyond this he will usually become director general (DG) of a regional branch office, or occupy some equivalent post, for one to two years.

Since there is only a limited number of director-general posts in the ministry's head office, differentiated treatments start at this stage among career officers in the same class year, who have all been promoted alike up to this point. Of course, some retire from MOF after serving as DG of a regional office.

When an officer returns to the main office of MOF he ascends the final steps of the ladder to deputy DG and DG of a bureau. If a deputy DG is promoted to DG, it normally occurs within the same bureau, although a bureau DG may be transferred to an equivalent post in another bureau.

It is a tradition of the Japanese bureaucracy that only one person from a class year can become vice-minister, the highest civil service post in a ministry, since the minister is a politician. All the rest of the class must quit the ministry when one of their classmates becomes vice-minister. This is true of any ministry or agency. Thus none of the career officers of a ministry is older than its vice-minister, who has usually been around 55 years old in recent years, although the average age was considerably lower before World War II.[12]

The retirement from the MOF of career officers belonging to a particular class year usually begins when they reach the deputy DG level, or sometimes even earlier. At that stage some retire from MOF and take up a position in a government institution or a private company, particularly a commercial bank, securities company or insurance company. After having retired from the post of vice-minister or DG, or a lower post, quite a few former government officers have become politicians, especially a member of Parliament, but sometimes governor of a prefecture or mayor.

The role of non-career officers

Thus in the Japanese bureaucracy the career officer is promoted step by step for about thirty to thirty-five years, and to remain in a specific field for a long time or become a specialist in a certain area is to impair one's promotion possibilities. This does not, however, apply to non-career officers. Some posts require highly technical and/or specialized knowledge and experience in any ministry, for example, those in charge of computer work or census analysis. Such posts are usually occupied by distinguished non-career officers who are quite often treated as specialists in a particular field, and even encouraged to become such, unlike career officers.

This tendency is especially strong in MOF's budget and taxation bureaux. Indeed, the ministry has many non-career specialists who have worked in a single bureau for ten to twenty years, and their specialized knowledge and experience are very highly appreciated. It is generally recognized that no budget bill or tax law can be prepared sat-

12. An exception to the above general rule takes place in the case of the Ministry of Foreign Affairs, where the vice-minister, who is always a career diplomat, is often appointed as ambassador to the United States, Russia, or China. Quite a few other ambassadors could be older than the vice-minister of Foreign Affairs.

isfactorily without extensive work by non-career specialists. Some distinguished non-career officers have become division directors in the main office, or DG's in regional offices. Many more have become director of an Internal Revenue Office in their home town, a highly respected position in a local community, after serving fifteen to twenty years in the ministry's and/or Internal Revenue's main offices. However, none of these non-career officers ever specializes as an economist. They are experts on very specialized practical matters such as tax laws, bank inspection, financial affairs of local governments, administration of customs tariffs, and so forth. They are neither economists, statisticians, nor lawyers. Career officers have a much better knowledge of economics or economic theory, and basic documents on economic policy issues submitted to the bureau meetings are almost always prepared by career officers.

VI. *The Role of Research Divisions*

The government hires no professional economists or statisticians, for neither of these constitutes a recognized profession in Japanese society. Nor is this situation likely to change in the near future. Nevertheless, economics and economic theory are becoming increasingly important year by year in the bureaucratic economic policymaking process. One consequence is that in almost every ministry the research divisions play a more and more important role in this process.

We shall again take the MOF as an example, one where there are now five independent research divisions[13] engaged in statistical and economic analysis, forecasting, and the investigation of academic literature, and scholarly and public opinion on matters under the jurisdiction of the bureau to which they belong. They also prepare basic data, analyses, or reports on issues under the bureau at the request of senior ministry officials or members of Parliament. Such requests have substantially increased lately.

The most influential MOF research division is the Research and Planning Division of the minister's Secretariat. It is headed by a deputy-DG-level officer who is the highest ranking deputy DG in the MOF, and its staff includes a division director, two under-directors (*sanji-kan*), a couple of assistant directors, a large number of career officers, and personnel working on a temporary on-loan basis from commercial banks and other institutions. In terms of the number of its staff members it is nearly as large as a small bureau, and the functions it per-

13. The Research and Planning Division of the minister's Secretariat was established in 1952, and Research Divisions of Budget, International Finance, Taxation, and Banking Bureau in 1962, 1971, 1976, and 1977 respectively. In other Bureaux the research work is done by the General Affairs Division.

forms probably parallel those performed by economists in some other governments. Its staff analyze economic trends, compile statistics, and prepare economic forecasts. They closely follow news of economic affairs and press comments in both Japanese and foreign newspapers and economic periodicals, and collect and examine national and international economic forecasts published by private research institutes, foreign governments, and international organizations and academic studies useful in forming judgments on economic policy issues. They use their own macroeconomic model to analyze business trends and make economic forecasts. On the basis of this work they take the lead in formulating official views of the MOF on the business situation and prospects. The division frequently presents a report to the minister of Finance, vice-minister, or other top officials and holds a briefing session with them, on business prospects and economic and industrial trends. When any MOF officer needs to quote officially any figure on the economic situation he must first check it with the Secretariat's Research and Planning Division.

Every Monday economic indicators and the analysis thereof prepared by the Research and Planning Division are presented to the ministry's Executive Meeting, comprising officers at and above the DG level. This has a pedagogical value, for the high officers of the MOF learn a great deal about current macroeconomic situations. Although the division's staff perform functions essentially identical to those of economists in some other countries, they do not individually have the professional economist's ability or formal qualifications. Instead, collectively, they play the role of economists. It often happens that none of the division's top officers is an economics graduate. They have perhaps acquired their knowledge of economics partly through the Economic Theory Training program, but primarily through on-the-job training since joining the MOF. They do not simply try to apply economic theory or economics directly, but they try to analyze economic problems from an administrator's viewpoint and seek solutions which are not only economically desirable but also compatible with the logic and conventional way of thinking commonly accepted within the MOF. Their thought processes have deep roots and are derived from the MOF's long history and accumulated experience. The research divisions of other MOF bureaux are smaller than that of the minister's Secretariat, but they perform broadly similar economic functions.

However, it is difficult to evaluate the influence of these research divisions on economic policy decisions. Undoubtedly any statistics, facts, and opinions relevant to a policy issue are collected and examined carefully before making a decision, although the outcome is usually a delicate compromise between economic, legal, and political considerations.

The EPA's Research Bureau and Economic Research Institute, the MITI's Research Division of the minister's Secretariat and Research Division in the Industrial Policy Bureau, and the BOJ's Research and Statistics Bureaux and newly established Special Research Department are all performing economist-type functions in their respective organizations. The MOF's *Monthly Research Bulletin, Monthly Fiscal and Financial Statistical Bulletin*, the BOJ's *Monthly Research Bulletin*, and several other publications of these research offices are among the economic periodicals most widely read by those who closely follow current economic developments in Japan.

VII. *The Power Structure and the Bureaucracy*

The formal power structure

Viewed from a formal and short-run standpoint, the structure of authority in Japanese economic policy is highly concentrated. In principle, important economic policy decisions are made in the twice-weekly Cabinet meetings. The Cabinet has been a conservative, single-party body for thirty years and thus the Liberal Democratic Party (LDP) has the formal power, through the Prime Minister and his Cabinet members, to make all the economic policy decisions. In practice, however, frequent close contacts and negotiations take place beforehand between the ministries and agencies concerned, e.g. in vice-ministers' meetings, in order to prepare the ground for an agreement. It is no exaggeration to say that when a certain matter is placed on the Cabinet agenda the government has already made up its mind, and that these meetings merely represent a ceremonial confirmation and recording of the conclusion.

Parliament has formal authority on many important economic policy issues. The government budget must be authorized by Parliament, at least by the Lower House, and in order to implement the budget it is usually necessary to pass a number of new laws and amend even more existing ones. Such matters as tax reform, national bond policies, the prices of goods and services supplied by certain government enterprises, customs tariffs, and social-security benefits, all come under the authority of Parliament. Nevertheless in our view Parliament has not recently played an important role in formulating Japan's economic policies because the ruling LDP has held a majority in both Houses for more than thirty years. Consequently the government's budget bill and accompanying legislation have almost always received Parliamentary approval.[14]

14. As far as the budget is concerned, there have been only two exceptions. In 1972, a part of defense expenditure was subtracted from the original budget bill because it included the cost of the Fourth Defense Plan, which had not yet been approved officially

What role, then, is played by the ministries and agencies in charge of economic affairs? In our view they are quite influential in Japanese economic policymaking, since they have superior accumulated expertise and access to information. Particularly the MOF, and especially its Bureau of Budget, are the most influential bodies, for they are responsible for the government budget, and without the MOF's agreement it is virtually impossible to carry out any economic or other policy measure requiring government expenditure, regardless of the amount involved. Furthermore, the MOF often acts as a coordinator among ministries and agencies even where no direct public expenditure is involved.

The MOF is also influential on monetary policy, as the BOJ is legally under its supervision. The BOJ's president and executive governors are appointed by the minister of Finance, and any revision of the reserve requirements ratio must be approved by him. The BOJ can legally alter the official discount rate by itself, but in practice it always consults the MOF's Bureau of Banking in advance. It also has close contacts with the MOF on its lending and bond-purchase policies. On the other hand, the MOF is responsible for the foreign-exchange policy, and the BOJ is consulted by the MOF and deals in the exchange market as its agent.

The EPA is concerned primarily with economic forecasting, economic planning, and coordination of economic policies and has final responsibility for the government's annual economic prospect and for the medium-term national economic plan.[15] Its role in government is somewhat similar to that of the Research and Planning Division in the MOF's minister's Secretariat. The EPA also sometimes plays an important role as economic policy coordinator on problems involving more than one ministry or agency, such as inflation, water resources, and regional development planning. With respect to the economic prospect, it often acts as a mediator between the bullish MITI and the bearish MOF.

The role of the government party

The foregoing remarks should not be taken as implying that Japanese economic policy is entirely controlled by the bureaucracy. On the contrary, the government party, the non-government parties, various pressure groups, public opinion, and academic economists all play their roles in the process of economic policymaking.

by Parliament. In 1977, the social-welfare expenditure was increased as a result of a compromise between the government and opposition parties on a reform of the national pension system.

15. For the meaning of national economic plan and planning, see R. Komiya, "Planning in Japan", cited in the Bibliography, below.

Considering the government party, since the LDP first held the majority in Parliament in 1948, its president has always been designated as Prime Minister, and eight out of the fifteen Prime Ministers since World War II have in fact been former government career officers. Among these eight, three have been MOF graduates, including the two most recent, Mr. Masayoshi Ohira and Mr. Takeo Fukuda, who in particular kept in close contact with the 'MOF family' of present and former MOF officers and was generally regarded as 'strong on economic affairs.'

As shown in Table 3, many Members of Parliament, especially those in the LDP, are former government officers, both in the Lower House (Representatives) and the Upper House (Councillors).

Most LDP politicians are former career officers who retired from the civil service at the DG level or higher, whereas members of non-government parties include former non-career officers who have become labor union leaders.

The LDP's Political Affairs Research Committee (Seimu-Chōsa-Kai) plays an important role in the policymaking process, as it is the formal party policy-formulating organ. It has a number of subcommittees corresponding to the respective ministries or agencies, where the party's substantive policymaking decisions are made. For example, from the MOF's policy standpoint, the LDP's Fiscal Sub-committee and Tax Policy Research Committee, both under its Political Affairs Research Committee, are the two leading LDP committees. Many of its executive members are very familiar with the MOF's affairs, and some are former MOF career officers or ex-Parliamentary vice-ministers of Finance.[16] The debate in the LDP's Tax Policy Research Committee is of major importance to the MOF. The Committee's annual discussion of tax reforms parallels that in the government's Tax

Table 3.   The numbers of the members of Parliament and those who were formerly government officers (1978)

		Number of former officers	
		LDP	Non-government parties
	Total		
House of Representatives	511	69	20
House of Councillors	252	47	20

16. Each ministry or agency has two vice-ministers: the administrative vice-minister, who is the head of the ministry's career officers, and the Parliamentary vice-minister, appointed by the Prime Minister from among Parliament members. The simple word 'vice-minister' normally refers to the former of these two.

Policy Research Committee, an advisory body reporting to the Prime Minister. As the Tax Bureau has a hard job to persuade the LDP committee members every year, it has a number of experts on 'Parliamentary liaison.'

In preparing the government's annual budget the assistant directors (*shusa*; MOF career officers in their 11th to 16th year) and the Budget Bureau's Budget Examiners (*shukei-kan*, who have division-director rank) start examining requests from individual ministries and agencies in early September. The negotiations and bargaining with other ministries or agencies continue until the end of November, when the Budget Bureau holds its annual 'budget meeting.' Then the negotiations go up to higher and higher levels, first between the other ministries' DGs and the deputy DG of the Budget Bureau, and subsequently between the other ministries' vice-ministers and the Budget Bureau's DG. Eventually the government's budget bill is finalized through negotiations at the ministerial level and consultation with the three top executives of the LDP. Assistant directors and budget examiners may pay some heed to petitions and appeals from all kinds of interest groups and requests from influential members of Parliament. But they try to be as neutral and independent as possible. Sometimes the budget bill is revised in negotiations between the Finance minister and the LDP's three top executives in order to reflect the party's policy, but the budget examiners usually anticipate and prepare for this in advance.

Generally speaking, the bureaucracy outweighs the government party in the economic policy planning and decisionmaking processes and when the LDP wishes to adopt a new policy in a certain area, its implementation would be impossible without full consultation with the ministries or agencies concerned. Therefore the LDP usually consults with the bureaucracy about the feasibility of any prospective new policy at a very early stage.

The principal officers in charge of Parliamentary liaison in the MOF are the secretary general and the director of the Archives and Documents Division, both of whom are members of the minister's Secretariat. They occupy key posts, and no policy is adopted in the MOF without their consent.

Non-government parties, pressure groups, and public opinion

The non-government parties—from left to right, the Communist Party, Socialist Party, Komei Party, Democratic Socialist Party, and New Liberal Club, and a couple of other very small groups—seem not to be much interested in economic policy issues. Apart from the New Liberal Club which recently split off from the LDP, these parties have not been in power in the past thirty years, and they have little chance of being so. Their ability to collect information, analyze economic conditions, and plan policies is necessarily limited, so they tend to concentrate on criticizing the government for what it does or fails to do.

Nevertheless, these parties do exert an important influence on the government's economic policy, for they are channels, together with the LDP, whereby pressure groups and the general public participate in politics. The government's majority has recently been much reduced and some Parliamentary standing committees are chaired by non-government party members. Under present conditions the LDP government tends to avoid submitting a bill which is bound to be strongly opposed by the non-government parties. Therefore the methods of negotiating with non-government party members of Parliament (M.P.s) for the passage of each ministry's bills constitute an important part of official Parliamentary liaison work. Career officers at the division-director level and above often visit non-government party M.P.s in order to explain particular policy issues, to exchange views, and to solicit their support, or at least to ask them to refrain from strongly opposing the ministry's policy. Ministries and agencies generally assign some of their most competent career officers to this Parliamentary liaison work.

A party's policies on major current issues affect the number of votes it can collect at elections, including the general election, so that it is sensitive to popular sentiment in choosing its policy lines. Especially for the LDP, popular support from a wide range of social strata and interest groups is essential to the maintenance of its power. As a result, over the long run, pressure groups such as farmers, small enterprises, and specific industries exert considerable influence on economic policy decisions, through political parties, both non-government and LDP.

Nonpartisanship of the bureaucracy

Under the American occupation immediately after the war a large number of politicians, businessmen, scholars, journalists, and military officers were 'purged' from—that is, declared ineligible for—public or other socially prominent positions because of their active roles in World War II. But only a few civil government officials and almost no central bankers, whether in active service or in retirement, were purged then, and this may be taken as evidence of the nonpartisanship of high-ranking Japanese government officers. Although they maintain close contact with LDP politicians, and sometimes with non-government party politicians, they try to remain politically neutral as far as possible, especially as far as the LDP *habatsu* (factions) are concerned. Only in rare cases do the top civil servants lean towards any of them.[17]

But how many high officers will be asked to resign when the LDP fails to hold a majority in the Parliament and a new Cabinet is formed? If the LDP maintains a majority in a new coalition Cabinet there will probably be almost no change. If the Socialists and the Communists acquire power jointly and form a two-party Cabinet, the situation may be somewhat different, but the new Cabinet will be able only to accelerate the retirement of senior officials, exclude a few strong dissidents, and promote those sympathetic or at least neutral towards them. Even under such a drastic Cabinet change the situation in Japan would be very different from that in the United States where many top positions of the bureaucracy are filled by political appointees.

The consensus system

One of the prominent characteristics of the Japanese decision-making process lies, as already mentioned, in the high value attached to full consensus on any given decision. When a meeting is held to make a decision, it must normally be unanimous. Consequently much negotiation, discussion, and persuasion, both formal and informal, must take place before the meeting at which the final decision is made.

Within a ministry or company, there is a procedure called the *ringi* system. If a document proposing a certain policy measure is drafted by a person in charge, perhaps an assistant director, in a ministry, it goes step by step through the desks of director, deputy DG, DG and vice-minister, adding one signature at each stage. If it affects more than one bureau, the document gets numerous signatures as it goes through many desks in the bureaux concerned. In such a case, nobody knows when the decision was actually made nor who was actually responsible for it. Any attempts to circumvent this consensus procedure will mean trouble at a later stage, since some of those who should have known of the decision will complain that they have not been informed and have not yet endorsed it.

Any document sanctioned by a bureau DG goes to the Archives and Documents Division of the minister's Secretariat and, after a careful scrutiny, is sent on to the secretary general of the Secretariat and the vice-minister, and, if the matter is sufficiently important, to the minister. In this way the ministry's decision is finalized. When it is deemed necessary, the minister or other high officers will meet the Prime Min-

17. When a career officer serves as a personal (but official) secretary to or as vice-minister under a minister who is naturally a politician and belongs to a certain faction of the LDP, an intimate relationship may develop between them, and later the former may belong to the latter's faction when retiring from the civil service and going into politics.

ister to explain the ministry's view and to receive the latter's instructions or to obtain his approval. Furthermore, if the matter involves other ministries or agencies too, the responsible officers in all the divisions and bureaux concerned will endeavor to reach a consensus on it.

This consensual decisionmaking process is time-consuming, and even in Japan the system is workable only in a tightly knit organization where there are no important conflicts of interests or ideological differences, and where everyone considers himself an insider or a permanent, well-protected member of the organization. A loyal insider should always participate sincerely in the arduous process of consensus formation, although confrontation with outsiders may be unavoidable at some stage. In the process of economic policymaking, the Cabinet members, career government officers concerned, and LDP leaders are all insiders, and there should be no difference of views on important issues.

The Japanese type of consensus system appears inefficient because it takes so much time, and few dare to take active leadership when there is a sharp difference of opinion or a serious conflict of interests. But once the decision is made all those concerned are willing to accept it and to cooperate in its implementation. Thus if one looks not only at the decisionmaking process itself, but views the whole process, including implementation of a decision, it can be said to work well.

The role of academic economists

In Japan those responsible for government economic affairs and the academic economists constitute two separate worlds as far as the interchange of personnel is concerned, apart from such special cases as the EPA's Research Institute or the Ministry of Agriculture's General Research Institute.

Some academic economists are appointed by the government as members of councils or research committees, advisory bodies which discuss economic policy issues and report to the Prime Minister or some other minister. For example, among the councils and research committees related to the MOF, 2 out of 30 members in the Tax Policy Research Committee,[18] 5 out of 23 in the Public Finance System Council, 3 out of 33 in the Banking System Research Committee, and 2 out of 35 in the Customs Tariffs Council are professors (some of them emeritus) of economics. However, no academic economist participates in the Securities Exchange Council or in the Insurance Council (which have 13 and 28 members respectively). Moreover, generally speaking,

---

18. This is an advisory body to the Prime Minister, and different from the LDP's Tax Policy Research Committee mentioned earlier.

these relatively few academic economists do not appear to play an important role in the various committees or councils, nor are these bodies influential in the economic policymaking process. They merely contribute to the exchange of views and to the persuasion of certain representatives of business interests.[19]

Nevertheless it would be wrong to conclude that academic economists exert only a minimal influence on Japan's economic policy. Professors of economics express opinions and write articles in daily newspapers and non-academic weekly or monthly periodicals and appear on television discussing economic policy issues and economic prospects, much more frequently in Japan than in any other country. The government research divisions mentioned earlier, which essentially play the economist's role, always pay attention to relevant articles or the opinions of influential academic economists because these articles or opinions sometimes have an impact upon public opinion. Similarly some senior officials and ministers, and even the Prime Minister, take account of academic economists' views on important policy issues and may have private contacts with them, thereby short-circuiting the cumbersome formality of councils and research committees of the government. Indeed, these personal contacts may sometimes directly affect economic policy decisions because bureaucrats in responsible positions do not want to be criticized by well-known academics whose views may be cited in attacks on the ministry's policy in the mass media.

Admittedly there are practically no interchanges of personnel between the bureaucracy and the academic community, and only a small number each of government officers and academics meet informally and discuss economic policy issues frankly. Of course, practitioners and academics think in fundamentally different terms: politicians and civil servants tend to distrust academic economists because of their abstractness, ignorance of political factors, and unrealistic proposals; academic economists tend to look down upon practitioners because of their ignorance of economics, short-sightedness, and excessive concern with existing vested interests.

Even so, these two separate worlds still are seen to interact, when viewed in a long-run perspective. Economics and an economic way of thinking have gradually been spreading into the government offices responsible for economic policy planning and implementation in postwar Japan. Keynesian macroeconomics, economic forecasting, and planning based upon macroeconomic models and input-output analysis

19. On these councils and committees, see R. Komiya, "Planning in Japan," pp. 197–201 and 211.

have become a part of the standard equipment of civil servants in charge of economic policy. For example, academic economists have exerted a considerable influence on the government's policy in the process of liberalizing trade and direct investment. It can be said that views of professors of economics and law have had an important effect on recent developments in antitrust policy. Monetary economics also, which emphasizes the role of the money supply and a new approach to the balance of payments based upon monetary and asset balance analyses, now appears to be gradually spreading into the MOF, EPA, and BOJ.

VIII. *Concluding Remarks*

The role of the economist in government or business is merely one of many examples of the differences between Japan's culture and human relations and their counterparts in countries with European traditions. In Japan, there is no profession of economist or statistician. Government and other large organizations employ almost everybody on a so-called lifetime commitment basis, and career employees are promoted year by year according to the seniority principle. Collectively they form a hierarchical team and run the organization as generalist administrators or managers.

This does not, however, mean that the Japanese government can dispense with the functions which economists perform in other countries, for they are undertaken by teams headed by generalist administrators in the research divisions or elsewhere which are engaged in statistical and economic analysis, forecasting, and planning. As economic problems have become increasingly important among government policy issues, the research divisions and comparable offices in the Japanese government and the Bank of Japan have been playing an ever more important role in the economic policymaking process. Moreover, top government officials responsible for economic policy today have accumulated much more economic knowledge and become much more accustomed to thinking in economic terms than ten or fifteen years ago.

To outsiders the postwar performance of the Japanese economy appears to have been highly successful. Nevertheless, in comparing Japan with the other countries covered in other studies of this collection it is natural to ask whether the quality of Japan's economic policy would have been superior if the government had been able to hire good economists and had taken notice of their advice. It would obviously be unwise to answer such a large hypothetical question in dogmatic terms; but on the whole, a limited affirmative reply seems warranted. However, in order to affect economic policy even slightly such economists would have needed to be able to speak the language used by bureaucrats and politicians and to cooperate closely with generalist administrators; comparatively few Japanese academic economists are able to do this. Many academic economists are either too theoretical to be effective in government or are reluctant to leave their university posts, and there are no professional economists outside the academic community.

This study was presented at the Conference on the Role of the Economist in the Government, Dubrovnik, Yugoslavia, March 1979. The views expressed here are personal views of the authors and should in no way be taken as the views of the organizations to which they belong. Ryutaro Komiya acknowledges financial support from the Economic Research Fund of the University of Tokyo.

Appendix A. MOF's Economic Theory Training Program

The content of the program, started in 1961, is shown for 1978 in the accompanying table.

Microeconomics	25 sessions[a]
Macroeconomics	20
Mathematics for Economists	35
Statistics	20
Econometrics	20
Input-Output Analysis	20
Public Economics	15
Monetary Theory	15
Public Finance	13
International Economics	15
International Finance	10
Seminars	60
Lectures on Special Topics	32
Total	300 sessions

[a]One session consists of three hours of lecture or seminar.

The main objective is to provide a basic training in economics for young career officers who have already undertaken some administrative work. Teachers are professors and younger scholars at leading universities in Tokyo, Hitotsubashi and Keio. The course is generally considered very useful, especially for Law School graduates who have not hitherto studied economics seriously. The program obviously involves a considerable cost for the MOF, since the trainees are completely freed from administrative duties for one full year.

Appendix B. The practice of *shukkō*, on-loan service

The practice of *shukkō*, which may be translated as the 'on-loan service,' is perhaps one of the peculiar characteristics of the Japanese bureaucracy, and indeed of Japanese employment practices in general. Once a person is engaged by a ministry or a company as a permanent rather than temporary or part-time employee, whether white-collar or blue-collar, he usually serves in that organization until very near the end of his career. This is generally called the lifetime employment or lifetime commitment (from both sides) system. Sometimes, however, a career government officer may be transferred for a limited period of one to three years outside of his ministry or agency to a government institution outside of the government proper—a local government or an international organization such as the IMF, IBRD, or OECD. Private companies also send their employees on a *shukkō* basis to their subsidiaries, to joint-venture companies, or in the case of banks, to customers.

The MOF regularly lends its officials, both career and non-career personnel, at various levels to the Ministry of Foreign Affairs, MITI, Ministry of Internal Affairs, EPA, Defense Agency, Environmental Agency, Fair Trade Commission, Prime Minister's Office, and many others. Originally such relatively new institutions as the EPA, Fair Trade Commission, or Environmental Agency had to borrow senior officers because they lacked suitable high-ranking officials of their own. The MOF also sends its officials to a large number of other government institutions and local governments, and even to a few semi-government/semi-private bodies such as the Japan External Trade Organization (JETRO). In most cases, the MOF sends its officials successively to the same posts of other ministries or agencies. *Shukkō* from the MOF also includes transfers to diplomatic posts abroad, which are under the Ministry of Foreign Affairs. A *shukkō-sha* sent from the MOF then becomes a diplomat temporarily and works as a financial attaché in charge of international financial and economic affairs abroad.

Other ministries or agencies also send their officials to the MOF, but the number of posts at higher levels in the MOF occupied by the 'outsiders' (*shukkō-sha*) is very small. Some employees of commercial and long-term credit banks work in the MOF, EPA, and government financial institutions on a *shukkō* basis for a term of about two years. Because government salaries are lower than those in banking, in such cases the difference is made up by the banks who lend the *shukkō-sha*. From the banks' point of view the information, experience, and personal contacts gained during the *shukkō* period justify the cost of seconding their employees in this manner.

Bibliography

There is no work dealing directly with the role of economists in the Japanese government, since there exists no economist in the government employed as such, as explained in the text. The following are works on the contemporary Japanese bureaucracy and/or policymaking process.

Craig, A. M. "Functional and Dysfunctional Aspects of Government Bureaucracy." In E. F. Vogel, ed., *Modern Japanese Organization and Decisionmaking* (Berkeley, 1975).

Komiya, Ryutaro. "Planning in Japan." In Morris Bornstein, ed., *Economic Planning: East and West* (Cambridge, Mass.). Reprinted in M. Bornstein, ed., *Comparative Economic Systems: Models and Cases*. 4th ed. (Irwin, Calif., 1979).

Itō, Daiichi. *Gendai Nihon Kanryōsei no Bunseki* (An Analysis of Contemporary Japanese Bureaucracy), in Japanese. Tokyo, 1980.

Stockwin, J. A. A. *Japan: Divided Politics in a Growth Economy*. London, 1975.

Tsuji, Kiyoaki. *Nihon Kanryōsei no Kenkyū* (Studies on Japan's Bureaucracy), in Japanese. Tokyo, 1952; revised, 1969.

Italy: economists in a weak political system

Franco Ferraresi and Giuseppe Ferrari

I. *The Historical Background*

In order to provide an adequate background for understanding the present role of economists in Italian governmental structures it is necessary briefly to comment on the main features of public intervention in the economic field prior to World War II.

Ever since the country's unification (1860–1870) the state has repeatedly intervened in economic matters despite the fact that support for free trade and laissez-faire principles was dominant both in academic and economic circles. The newly established administrative structures were based on such principles. The state's main task was to ensure law and order, so as to permit citizens to pursue their economic activities in safety; accordingly, administration was geared to the proper implementation of formal checks and controls regarding the legality of its own and the citizens' activities. Since no interventions in the economic and social spheres were theoretically foreseen, there were no institutions to carry them out, nor any means or experts concerned with a non-formalistic (i.e. purely legal) assessment of the socioeconomic effects of public actions. Thus apart from the monetary function, with the gradual establishment of a central bank, the initial steps of government economic intervention took place in an ideologically hostile climate and utilized an administrative structure that had been set up according to non-interventionist principles. It is no wonder, then, that the economic activities of public bodies proved from the beginning to be often uncertain and contradictory.

Thereafter, a large number of interventionist tools were established pell-mell, superimposed on and substituted for each other according to circumstances without, however, altering the basic administrative structure and its operating criteria.

Within this framework, the measures adopted to deal with the economic crisis of the 1930s are especially noteworthy, because they were the product of a relatively coherent design and marked the advent of the public corporation in place of the traditional ministry as an instrument of state intervention in the economy.

Within the European context the public corporation was a new administrative model[1] designed to release public action from some of the 'guarantee state' regulations which (especially with respect to employment conditions and accountancy) had made it slow and cumbersome. Public corporations were supposed to be flexible and agile like private concerns, in order to be able to carry out 'entrepreneurial' tasks, while at the same time operating in pursuance of public goals. Thus a dual dimension was introduced in the administrative system, because the ministerial structure remained rigidly patterned after laissez-faire principles, both in its organizational and operational criteria. This also meant that it was very difficult for traditional bureaucratic organs to keep the public corporations under control; consequently they ended up by answering directly to political power, often in a personal and informal way, obviously with frequent deviations from 'correct' (and, often, lawful) administrative practices.

The contradictory nature of Italian economic policy was reaffirmed after World War II. The dominant ideology and the main line which the first important decisions were to follow (e.g. monetary stabilization in 1947, the removal of restrictions on international trade, and entry into the Common Market in 1956) were orthodox free-trade in spirit, but apart from minor alterations all the structures and tools established before the war remained in operation. However, there was no clear-cut overall design, on the part of policymakers, of setting the course of development in a different direction from the one it would spontaneously have taken. The various interventionist devices and agencies were not placed within any homogeneous framework, and there was no overall coordination of economic policy, so that all the actors, both public and private, were practically left on their own.

Concrete discussions of economic planning began only at the end of the 1950s, when the growth of the economy appeared to be solving some long-standing problems (notably unemployment) and bringing others to the forefront. At the same time the political situation was slowly moving towards the 'opening to the Left.' The economic boom had revealed structural issues hitherto concealed by the problems of recovery, such as the dual industrial structure, the distorted consumption patterns, which favored private as opposed to public expenditure, and above all, the gap between North and South. The lay and socialist sectors of the economic circles, together with some significant segments of the Christian Democrats, claimed that such imbalances could not be overcome simply through the spontaneous workings of the economy, but required a coherent and determined planning policy. Such policy began in the early 1960s amidst considerable optimism, but

1. A. Shonfield, *Modern Capitalism* (London, 1965).

was soon defeated for a variety of reasons, including the lack of a truly reformist hegemonic political force, the dramatic inefficiency of the governmental apparatus, and (one should add) the unrealism of some of the planning measures and the political isolation of the planners themselves.

Thus, owing to the weakness of the ruling bourgeois groups, the traditional fragmentation of the Italian political system persisted (see The Functions of Irrationality, in Section V, below). The political scene has continued to be characterized by innumerable pressure and interest groups, none of which has acquired a dominant position, although all or most have been able to draw some benefits from the ever-increasing state economic intervention—to the point of bringing the system close to bankruptcy. This particularistic style of policymaking has been reinforced by the fact that postwar public intervention has increasingly taken place through public corporations which, because of their quasi-private status, have been pliable vehicles for the transmission of sectoral or client-centered interests, leaving the state in the background as the proponent of the national interest.

II. *The Supply of Economists*

The definitions of 'economist'

An economist can be broadly defined as a person with an academic qualification which reveals his technical training in economics who is actively engaged in the analytical evaluation and planning of economic affairs. However it is immediately apparent that within the Italian public administration those who undertake economic activities in the governmental structure, even performing crucial roles, have rarely received an academic training in economics, while, on the other hand, economics graduates quite often hold general positions not concerned with economic affairs.

It is difficult to demonstrate this point empirically, for the management of the Italian economy is so dispersed and fragmented that it is hard to identify the *loci*, and hence the persons, who effectively influence the major economic decisions. Moreover information on the academic training of civil servants is limited and out of date.

Academic training in economics

In Italian universities several degree programs offer some economic training, although in many cases it is rather superficial and sketchy, amounting to no more than two or three courses over a period of four or five years. It would not be worth mentioning such programs were it not that many of those performing important economic tasks in government administration have had only this kind of formal academic training.

It is thus possible to identify 122 degree programs where some economics is taught, distributed in over half a dozen faculties (departments): i.e. Law, Political Science, Sociology, Statistics, Agricultural Science, and Economics and Commerce (which includes a number of programs established in the last twenty years—banking and insurance sciences, economics and social sciences, etc.).[2]

The teaching of economics is rather marginal in the faculties of Law and Agricultural Science; it is more relevant in Political Science and Sociology, where, however, economics courses are not always compulsory for all students. This leaves the twenty faculties of Economics and Commerce, which should be the main centers of economic studies. Yet, because of their peculiar history, this does not occur. Indeed, it has been authoritatively stated that "in Italy, today, there is no real advanced School in this subject" comparable to those existing elsewhere.[3] In fact until 1935 there was no specialized training in economics whatever at university level; those who cultivated the subject, though well-known and rather numerous, were generally self-taught. There were, however, some Higher Commerce Institutes, training personnel for administrative-economic positions in banks and business firms, according to a curriculum which stressed accounting, bookkeeping, industrial management, and similar matters. The present-day departments of Economics and Commerce were established only in 1935 and developed from the transformation of the older institutes which were entitled to provide university-level degrees (*laurea*). For a long time the new departments retained the business orientation of the institutes, reserving for economic courses not more than a third of their curricula (the remainder being kept for 'technical,' i.e. business and legal, disciplines). The obvious result was that such departments produced personnel mostly for business concerns, while training in macroeconomic areas, which theoretically should be of interest for governmental decisionmaking, was quite deficient.

This situation has been slowly changing in the last ten years. Officially, the curricula are still unmodified, being laid down by the Ministry of Education, and they remain the same throughout the twenty faculties. Thus, out of 19 compulsory subjects, only a handful can be broadly considered economic (Political Economy, Economic and Financial Policy, Science of Finance, and Financial Law, plus, usually,

2. F. Bartoli, P. Ciampi, V. Palanca, and I. Pierantoni, "Dove si studia economia," *Politica ed Economia*, aIX (1978).

3. A. Graziani and S. Lombardini, *Gli Studi di economia in Italia* (Milan, 1975), p. 14.

Agricultural Economics and Policy, Economical Statistics, Economic Geography).[4] In several faculties however (Modena and Ancona-Urbino being obvious examples) the optional sector of the curricula has been used to introduce strictly economic courses, altering somewhat the old balance.[5] It is difficult to generalize, because the situation varies from faculty to faculty, and often courses bearing the same title carry, in effect, quite different contents. A further complication arises from the fact that often the most interesting innovations take place outside Economics and Commerce: thus, for example, in the Faculty of Economics at the University of Turin there are only four full-tenured professors of economic subjects, as against six in the Faculty of Political Science. It seems fair to state, however, the general trend is towards a weakening of the faculties' technical-juridical character and a strengthening of their economic content.

Turning to postgraduate education, this has never been really institutionalized in Italian universities, being left mainly to the development of informal relationships between teachers and graduates—with, of course, the aid of fellowships, scholarships, grants, etc. This is true also in economics, where the existing postgraduate institutions such as SVIMEZ (Associazione per lo Sviluppo del Mezzogiorno—Association for Southern Development—Rome); ISRE (Istituto per gli Studi di Ricerca Economica—Institute for Economic Research—Turin); IPSOA (Istituto per gli Studi Ricerca Aziendale—Institute for the Study of Business Research—Padua), etc. are not university-affiliated, limit their activity to short courses, and frequently have no faculty, but utilize guest professors and lecturers. Some of the major exceptions are ISTAO (the A. Olivetti Institute for Higher Economic Studies), established in 1967 at Ancona University, and IEFE (Institute for the Economy of Energy Sources) founded in 1963 at the Bocconi University in Milan and renewed in the middle 1970s. The former is more teaching- and training-oriented; the latter more research-oriented, and in fact it constitutes a rare example of a close and positive link between the university and the industrial world.

4. The other *compulsory* subjects are Institutions of Private Law, Institutions of Public Law, Commercial Law (+), General Mathematics, Financial Mathematics, Statistics, Labor Law, Economic History, General and Applied Accountancy (+), Professional and Banking Techniques, Industrial and Commercial Techniques, Science of Merchandise, two foreign languages. All courses last for one year, except those marked with (+), which last for two, and the languages, which last for three. The students must then choose at least two optional subjects from a pool whose range varies according to the faculty. The prescribed length of the program is four years, although usually students take longer to complete it.

5. For an attempt to quantify the time allotted by two typical faculties to different subjects, see J. F. H. Roper, *The Teaching of Economics at University Level* (London, 1970), p. 210.

The practice of awarding scholarships for one or two years' study abroad is also widespread and time-honored; of course it is difficult to ascertain the numbers involved, but most academics of any standing in the younger generation have had such an experience.

Instructors, readers, and professors of economics at university level are the outcome of this rather intricate pattern of training. Data on personnel are scarce; the only reliable information is that the number of full (tenured) teachers (professors) of all economic courses (i.e. including 'technical' and 'professional' subjects) increased from 147 to 203 between 1972 and 1976. The 1980 *concorsi* have added between 150 and 170 chairs.

The university output

The official statistics on enrollments and graduations in economic subjects proper, expressed as percentages both of total enrollments and graduations, and total population, form a parabolic curve. In both cases the curve reaches its peak around 1969/70. Economics graduates rose as a percentage of the university total from 5.74 in 1949/50 to a peak of 12.06 in 1969/70, and fell thereafter to 5.53 in 1975/76. During the same period the percentage of Political Science graduates rose more or less continuously from 0.58 to 5.48 of the university total. In absolute terms the number of Economics graduates rose from 1,179 in 1949/50 to 3,987 in 1975/76; the corresponding figures for Political Science were 120 and 3,952. But as courses in economic subjects were offered in non-economics departments (especially Political Science and Sociology), there was less of a drop in the number of economists than a kind of dislocation. The curve of Economics enrollments is more like that in Political and Social Science disciplines.

The most rapid growth in Economics enrollments coincided with the so-called 'economic miracle' of the early 1960s, when there was a powerful expansion of private enterprise, and Economics departments offering training in business skills seemed to offer the best career opportunities for graduates. Similarly the 1964 depression and subsequent economic difficulties such as the oil crisis may help to explain the later decline.

Although the public sector has become increasingly important, the pattern of public administration has retained its laissez-faire character and there has been no increase in demand for economic skills. Moreover, university training focuses on business and microeconomic analysis, which is less appropriate to public offices than macroeconomics. It is therefore easier in public administration to place personnel with generalized skills, like those provided in Law and Political Science departments, which helps to explain their later growth. The fact that both provide some economics training further enhances their graduates' employment prospects.

III. *Economists and Economy in Italian Society*

Professionalization and economic theory

A rigorous interpretation of the concept of a 'professional' would probably exclude the economists, even in those countries where they have long been established.[6] In the Italian case there is no professional order or association of economists enforcing an ethical code prescribing relationships with clients, regulating admission to membership, controlling members' behavior, and defending their common interests towards society at large, whereas accountants, bookkeepers, and business consultants are all represented by professional associations carrying some weight.[7] This is all the more significant given the absence of a clearly established, highly specialized academic training. Thus there can be little doubt that the level of professionalization of economics in Italy is rather low, which means that as a group they enjoy relatively little social recognition. This may be partly due to the absence of a towering figure comparable to Jan Tinbergen in the Netherlands, Ragnar Frisch in Norway, or J. M. Keynes in Great Britain, and the fact that, at least until recently, the discussion of economic ideas has aroused very little excitement outside the academic world.

Before the First World War Italy had a school of economists including such figures as Pareto, Pantaleoni, Loria, Bresciani-Turroni, and Einaudi, whose names were well-known and highly respected in Europe. After the war, the prestige of these scholars, combined with the restrictions Fascism imposed on the freedom of scientific inquiry, inhibited economic research. Some of the best minds (e.g. Sraffa) were

6. T. Parsons, "The Professions and Social Structure," *Essays in Sociological Theory* (Glencoe, Ill., 1954); and idem, *The Social System* (Glencoe, Ill., 1951); E. C. Hughes, *Men and Their Work* (London, 1964); P. M. Blau and W. R. Scott, *Formal Organizations* (San Francisco, 1962); J. Ben David, "Professions in the Class System of Present-Day Societies," *Current Sociology*, 12, no. 3 (1963–64); H. M. Vollmer and L. D. Mills, eds., *Professionalization* (Englewood Cliffs, N.J., 1966); H. L. Wilensky, "The Professionalization of Everyone?" *American Journal of Sociology* 70 (1964); W. J. Goode, "Community Within a Community: The Professions," *American Sociological Review* 22 (April 1957). For further bibliographical information, see F. Ferraresi, "Il burocrate di fronte alla burocrazia: orientamenti politici e tecnici nella burocrazia italiana," *Archivio ISAP 1968* (Milan, 1969).

7. It is also noteworthy that, unlike the last-mentioned professions, economists do not enjoy any specific social-security program.

forced to emigrate, and Italian scholars concentrated on reworking neoclassical and laissez-faire ideas or to theorizing about the Fascist 'corporate' state, while the new issues in international economic debate
passed them by.

After the Second World War, economic studies went through a veritable rebirth, stimulated by the foreign training of scores of young
economists. Inevitably there were some intergenerational problems.
The older scholars still clung to the neoclassical framework and the
'Italian tradition,' utilizing these tools in the analysis of the country's
economic conditions, while the younger economists had absorbed
more modern theoretical approaches, first from the Keynesian, then
from the neo-Ricardian school. The effect was that for some time their
activity stood rather apart from the most urgent Italian economic issues. They took existing 'foreign' theories as their starting points, and
proceeded to review and reformulate them in the light of an often
purely formal link with Italian problems.[8] With the passing of time this
gap has tended to be filled. The two positions have come closer together as the autonomy and originality of Italian economists have increased significantly and the older generation has passed away. In fact,
there has been a massive growth of studies, researchers, and researches and a multiplication of approaches, so that at present it is difficult to discern a predominant school. The scene is very diversified,
including many brilliant scholars, with no one personality creating a
dominant pole of attraction.

Economic culture in Italian society

The predominant cultural-ideological attitude in Italy has long been
"some sort of mannered spiritualism, at times speculative, at times
only theoretical and pedagogical, which excommunicates . . . positivism, empiricism, materialism, utilitarianism, as vulgar, narrow, commercial, impure philosophies."[9] It goes without saying that in this situation economic thought belongs to the outcasts.

This fact is usually attributed, with reason, to the country's weak
economic development and the delays and distorted patterns that industrialization acquired.[10] Underlying this formulation is Max Weber's
classic hypothesis that the *rationalization* of economic impulses and
the appearance of existential attitudes *systematically* oriented on the
basis of economic rules (that is, different from the mere impulse to

8. Graziani and Lombardini, pp. 24–25.

9. N. Bobbio, "Profilo ideologico del novecento," *Storia della letteratura italiana*
(Milan, 1969), vol. IX.

10. S. Spaventa, "L'informazione economica sui mass media," *Problemi dell'
informazione* 3, no. 3 (July–Sept. 1978).

amass wealth) emerged only with the development of bourgeois capitalist society.[11] However in Italy, rationally grounded economic thought and the anti-traditional cultural model of the successful businessman, entrepreneur, or other economic actor are conspicuously absent.

When industrialization occurred towards the end of the nineteenth century its carriers were anxious to upset the existing social and cultural order as little as possible.[12] They did not claim for themselves the role of social and cultural *Vorbilder*—a role that remained with the traditional notables, the landowners, lawyers, literati. Anti-industrial feeling was channeled by intellectuals and took the form of a moralistic critique of industrial society, carried out in the name of values pertaining to an archaic social order. To be sure, this was not a uniquely Italian development; but it acquired here a vehemence unknown elsewhere,[13] being the expression of a backward culture "unable to use the conceptual tools necessary for understanding the modern world, a culture which substituted scientific analysis with anguished cries, painstaking critique with the declamation of manifestos."[14]

In fact positivism, a form of thought more congruent with modern society, did emerge, but it was quickly overwhelmed by the powerful idealist and neo-idealist reaction. As is well known, these schools of thought had little use for 'exact' sciences and held in open contempt social sciences like sociology and economics.

In the political sphere the dominant interwar ideology was not dissimilar. Fascism, in its battle against liberalism, resorted to irrational elements (race, *Sippe, Blut und Boden*, the mystic sacrifice, heroic pauperism, etc.) entailing a radical devaluation of economic rationality and open contempt towards the nineteenth-century bourgeois "merchant and shopkeeper spirit."[15] The idealization of rural living and the farmer class, with their imperviousness to industrial-urban corruption, were further elements of this *Weltanschauung*.

The postwar situation brought no significant changes. Catholic political culture, to which the ruling Christian Democrat party supposedly adhered, was also imbued with values antagonistic to liberal thought

11. M. Weber, "Die protestantische Ethik und der Geist des Kapitalismus," *Gesammelte Aufsätze zur Religionssoziologie* (Tübingen, 1922); Italian translation, Florence, 1965.
12. G. Baglioni, *L'ideologia della borghesia industriale dell'Italia liberale* (Turin, 1974).
13. A. Asor Rosa, "La cultura," in *Storia d'Italia* (Turin, 1975).
14. N. Bobbio, "Profilo ideologico."
15. H. Marcuse, "Der Kampf gegen der Liberalismus in der totalitären Staatsauffassung," in W. Abendroth, ed., *Faschismus und Kapitalismus*, EVA (1934; Frankfurt a.M., 1967).

which contained strong pre- and anti-industrial components, deep rural roots, and a condemnation of the profit motive which put them in direct opposition to "pure" economic logic.[16]

One objection might be that all these examples belong to the ideological-cultural context. After all, the anti-economic components of Fascist ideology did not prevent the regime from carrying out one of its principal historical functions, the preservation of the capitalist system. And it was Fascism that brought about an increase of governmental economic intervention unparalleled in Italian history. Similarly, the rejection of the profit motive in Catholic doctrine did not prevent the worst kind of speculation and plunder in the management of public affairs during the Christian Democrats' years. Nonetheless, the fact that the most important non-Marxist Italian political and cultural currents in this century have rejected industrialized society and the liberal economic system is very significant evidence of the deformation of this development and the bourgeoisie's limited ability to acquire an authentically hegemonic role towards the entire society. Of course, the Marxist opposition is not surprising, and is based on very different presuppositions.

In the present context the important point is that the spread of economic culture in public opinion and in society at large has been limited, even though it has been growing of late. To illustrate this point we shall consider the level of economic discussion, and the presence of economists, in two distinct institutional areas of obvious importance in contemporary society: the press and political parties.

The press and political parties

For a very long time the press released a very small quantity of information on economic matters. Only with the mid-1970s did daily papers begin carrying an economic and/or financial page giving information of this kind as a specific feature.[17] Since then the practice has mushroomed, revealing the undeniable growth of interest, but the nov-

16. G. Galli, *Il bipartitismo imperfetto* (Bologna, 1965).

17. *Il Giorno* is the main exception, having already started to publish an economic page in 1956. Most important dailies did not follow suit until 1974. *Il Corriere della Sera, La Stampa, Il Messaggero, Il Giornale Nuovo* publish at least two pages (plus, some of them, a weekly supplement), while *Il Tempo, Il Resto del Carlino*, and *La Nazione* have one. Among party organs, *L'Unità* (PCI) has a "labor and economy" page. *La Repubblica* began publication in 1976 and has four or five special economic pages. Some weeklies, like *L'Espresso* and *Panorama*, began to devote much space to the economy around 1970. There is also a specialized paper, *Il Sole-24 Ore*, generally considered to be of a good quality and with a good circulation, "especially if you consider the financial and economic cultural level of this country," as the president of the Italian Journalists Association put it eloquently. P. Murialdi, "Introduzione: perchè l'informazione economica," in *Problemi dell'informazione* 3, no. 3 (July–Sept., 1978).

elty of the experiment is still such as to influence its quality. The professional level of the economic and financial journalists is not yet high; the newspapers' files are still limited, and the search for scoops is often given precedence over systematic information.[18] Hence the maturation of public opinion proceeds rather slowly, while its low level is often used by the press as an excuse to justify the modest technical content of the articles.

As for political parties, we shall consider only the two major ones. The Christian Democrats (DC) have always either ignored or been suspicious of men of culture and their products. The expression 'culture trash,' coined by Minister Scelba in the 1950s, is an extreme but truthful summing-up of the party's attitude towards artistic and literary intelligentsia. As for 'technical' intellectuals (jurists, sociologists, economists, and the like), apart from a relatively favorable period during and immediately after the Resistance, systematic contacts with the party were destroyed,[19] and at present there are no institutionalized *loci* for economic, legal, and other forms of analysis and planning. Instead, private and personal consultancies prevail, held by individual experts for individual politicians, without any systematic frame of reference or explicit procedure. Some repercussions of this practice will be analyzed below.[20]

Though the lack of official organs for economic research in the Christian Democratic Party is not surprising, given their general diffidence towards cultural production, it is surprising in the PCI (Communist Party of Italy), where such interest has always been quite lively. Yet even in this case, the principal center for economic research, CESPE (Center for Political and Social Studies) was set up only in 1966 and has, all things considered, been less than incisive.

Perhaps the main reason for this dearth can be found in the long-standing philosophical framework of Marxist thought in Italy. Until the

18. E. Filippi, ''L'informazione dovuta dalle imprese pubbliche private''; G. Turani, ''L'infernale trappola dello scoop,'' ibid.

19. The evolution of the role of the 'technical'-type intellectual (economists, jurists, etc.) was described in 1972 by a privileged observer, G. Andreotti: ''Directly after the Liberation, important documents for the government action of DC ministers were prepared by work groups of university professors and other experts. Later, swamped by daily work, these reports were no longer requested and, except for some documents of the 'currents' the DC consultancy disappeared.'' Quoted in S. Giacomoni, *Miseria e nobiltà della ricerca in Italia* (Milan, 1979) p. 72.

20. The only known exception is AREL (Legislative and Economic Research Agency), established after 1976 by a group of Christian Democrat M.P.s, which included several economists and jurists. Its object is to undertake systematic research on political-economic themes for use in decisionmaking. It is a private association, with fifteen founding members. Because of its novelty the effects of this experiment cannot yet be assessed.

beginning of the 1960s the PCI did not participate in economic debate and was unprepared for the economic policymaking and planning discussions with the center-left governments. However, this situation is changing: the party's closer proximity to government responsibility, awareness of its accumulated delays, and the maturing of a number of young leftist scholars, have contributed to enlivening and stimulating economic discussion within the PCI. Nonetheless, the organizational structure is still inadequate. For example, the party's most prestigious cultural center, the Istituto Gramsci, has no economist of its own, but relies on outside contributions and interventions, usually on a voluntary basis. Thus it can organize meetings, conferences and seminars, often of great significance, but it has not developed a compact and continued production of its own.[21]

Even so, both parties have recognized the growing interest in and importance of economic matters and have tried to respond, especially at the parliamentary level. The PCI has a long tradition of electing 'independents' under its sponsorship, i.e. eminent personalities from several fields, in order to improve its image in terms of competence and non-partisan expertise. The Christian Democrats followed suit in the 1976 elections. As a result, several of the best-known Italian economists became members of Parliament: e.g. B. Andreatta, S. Lombardini, F. Reviglio for the DC; and C. Napoleoni (perhaps the leading Marxist) and L. Spaventa for the PCI. Economists have also been elected by other parties: e.g. F. Forte for the Socialist Party (PSI), which has always had a closer link with this group of intellectuals than the two major parties: most of the brains of the doomed planning experiment were more or less closely identified with the PSI; G. La Malfa for the Republican Party.

IV. *Economists in Public Administration*

The administrative context

Given the position of economists and economic thought in Italian society sketched in the preceding pages, public administration cannot be expected to offer a very different picture. Indeed, the literature on the subject emphasizes that the dominant culture of government administration is juridical-humanistic, and technical expertise is considered inferior.[22] "The typical bureaucrat looks down on the specialist,

21. CESPE (an offshoot of the party's Central Committee) has always been less prominent. At least until a short while ago the institute had not succeeded in becoming a central reference point in the economic research undertaken by the left. It has recently acquired new means, but the permanent staff still includes only three full-time researchers in the economic section (S. Giacomoni, *Miseria e nobiltà*).

22. F. Demarchi, *La burocrazia centrale: un'indagine sociologica* (Milan, 1965); F. Ferraresi, "Il burocrate di fronte alla burocrazia."

and tends to consider highly technical administrative work as degrading.''[23]

As noted earlier, the Italian administrative structure still feels the effects of laissez-faire, non-interventionist principles, according to which the state's main duty is to guarantee the enjoyment of citizen's rights and therefore the application of law and order (the rule-of-law state). This naturally required that its personnel should consist mainly of jurists, who are, in fact, firmly rooted in the administration.

Although the state's economic intervention has increased enormously through the years, the organizational and operational principles of the bureaucratic structure have remained unchanged. The administration is still supposed to be primarily concerned with the discharge of formal checks and controls on the legality of actions, while the economic and social effects of public interventions are ignored. Consequently, no units or posts for economic analysis (planning, cost-benefits, output budgeting, econometric model building, etc.) have been built into the ministerial structure. Some special-purpose agencies for economic analysis have in fact been established, but they have never acquired a first-rank status, probably because of their very nature as 'outsiders.'

The most important agency is the Budget Ministry, established in 1947 with the main purpose of creating a governmental post for a major Italian economist of that time, L. Einaudi (see text above n.34). Until 1967 it had no personnel of its own and worked solely with staff on loan from other ministries. Despite the 1967 reform, according to which the budget should have become the main moving force behind economic planning, the Budget Ministry still has only a marginal position vis-à-vis other ministries. Alongside the Budget Ministry one should mention the Institute for Studies of Economic Planning (ISPE) established in 1967 as the main think tank for the new Plan, and attached to the Budget and Planning Ministry, which was to provide the chief institutional support for the experiment. However planning failed, partly because the ministry was never able to assert its authority over other, more powerful ministries. Surrounded by the solid hostility of traditional bureaucratic structures and torn by internecine struggles, ISPE has never been able to carry out anything but harmless theoretical exercises.

Apart from planning, the Institute for the Study of the Economic Situation (ISCO) was set up in the mid-1950s with terms of reference relating to the survey of economic activity and short-term forecasting. ISCO is a semi-autonomous, non-ministerial body which performs a

23. J. la Palombara, ''Intervento'' alla Tavola rotonda su ''Burocrazia, potere politico e programmazione,'' *Tempi moderni* 14 (July-Sept. 1963).

useful analytical function, publishing monthly forecasts of the economic situation, but it has no power to compel decisionmaking bodies to follow its studies.

Finally, at the top government level, there is no institution comparable to the American Council of Economic Advisers, the prewar British Economic Advisory Council, or similar bodies existing in other countries which have government-appointed agencies comprising eminent scholars and experts with the responsibility of acting as the major 'observatory' and official adviser to the government in economic affairs. Such a body was actually established within the general planning structure (the Technical Scientific Committee of the Plan), but it never played a significant role in economic policymaking.[24]

The distribution of graduates

Economic tasks are of course performed within the administration, but given its framework, it is difficult to ascertain precisely where and by whom. Some insight can be obtained by looking at the distribution of academic degrees among civil servants, although the limitations of this approach are obvious. They include the low level of specialization provided by economics departments, the difficulty of establishing close ties between completed academic training and job functions, and the lack of up-to-date research materials. Nevertheless, the distribution of academic degrees provides significant indication of the development of Italian administration in the all-important area of economic management.

The data on administrative-class personnel of all ministries for 1954 and 1961 reveal three main trends (see Table 1): (a) the number and percentage of civil servants holding law degrees grows significantly; (b) economic skills grow in numbers, but their level drops; and (c) 'general' economic ministries, 'direct' economic ministries, and 'indirect' ones behave differently (cf. Table 1).

The expansion of law graduates is the most puzzling feature, considering the changes in state activity during the postwar period. Despite the evolution towards an interventionist concept of state activity, the Italian administration continues to fill its ranks with personnel appropriate to a law-and-order approach to the state. In addition, while the public administration recognizes the need to improve its ability to handle economic tasks, instead of acquiring university graduate expertise, it is satisfied with an intermediate level of staff with the accounting diploma. (This is a certificate issued by a secondary school

24. The National Council for Economy and Labor (CNEL), a quasi-legislative body established by the 1948 Constitution, has never been effective.

Table 1. Academic degrees of upper-echelon (*carriera direttiva*) civil servants by group of ministries, 1954 and 1961

	University degrees	Law	Economics
General,[a] 1954	8101	4763	1157
percent	—	58.7	14.3
1961	6472	5260	616
percent	—	81.3	9.5
General economic,[b] 1954	4925	2105	2055
percent	—	42.7	41.7
1961	6838	3428	2605
percent	—	50.1	38.1
Direct economic,[c] 1954	2534	517	414
percent	—	20.4	16.3
1961	3496	823	444
percent	—	23.5	12.7
Indirect economic,[d] 1954	1713	404	85
percent	—	23.6	4.9
1961	2934	1122	235
percent	—	41.6	8.0
Social,[e] 1954	1882	769	231
percent	—	40.8	12.3
1961	3614	1515	333
percent	—	41.9	9.2

   [a] Includes Prime Ministership, Foreign Affairs, Interior Justice and Defense.

   [b] Includes Budget, Finance, Treasury.

   [c] Includes Agriculture, Foreign Trade, Industry and Commerce, Merchant Navy, State Participation, Tourism and Entertainment.

   [d] Includes Public Works, Post and Telecommunications, Transport.

   [e] Includes Cultural Assets, Work and Social Security, Public Education, Health.

   Sources: 1954: ISTAT, Dipendenti delle administrazioni statali al 30 novembre 1954 (Roma, 1955).

   1961: Presidenza del Consiglio dei Ministri, Consiglio Superiore della Publica Administrazione, *Albo dei dipendenti civili dello stato. Carriere direttive* (Roma, 1963).

(*ragioneria*) which provides intermediate, pre-university skills in accounting and business administration. Many of its holders subsequently proceed to an Economics Department.) This stinting tendency accords with the persistent nineteenth-century conception of the state which, transferred to the economic area, manifests itself in a cautious and thrifty administation of public funds and in a Gladstonian set of expenditure procedures requiring accounting and bookkeeping skills. For such tasks secondary-school training is quite sufficient. Beyond this, in the ministries most directly concerned with economic activity, economics graduates are relatively few, while technical skills predominate (e.g. 70 percent of the senior personnel in Agriculture have a degree in Agriculture; 71 percent of those at Public Works have a degree in Engineering). Thus the administration is theoretically capable of managing the technical aspects of the sectors under its authority, but not of assessing their economic significance. (In practice, even the technical skills often remain unused, because their exponents are confined to routine administrative tasks.)[25]

V. *Economists in the Management of the Economy*

The institutional framework

Given the fact that the Italian state does intervene heavily in the economic sphere, the question remains: Do economists, however defined and placed, play a significant role in planning, deciding, and implementing such interventions? In order to answer this question it is appropriate to provide a brief overview of the structures and agencies involved in the management of the economy.

Parliament and the budget. As in most parliamentary regimes, in Italy the ultimate responsibility for control over public expenditures rests with Parliament, which has the power to reject or approve the state's budget. However, according to most observers, parliamentary examination of the budget is a "useless ritual."[26] This is due both to the general decline of Parliament's importance in the political process

25. The undervaluation of economic expertise and of economists in public administration is confirmed by the income distribution. It would have been interesting to locate income levels of all economics graduates, but the dearth of disaggregated data has made it impossible. We have instead attempted to ascertain what kind of work is performed by the highest-paid civil servants, about whom some information is available. Only the three highest ranks of the senior executive career will be considered (*carriera dirigenziale*) which, in January 1977, comprised 515 functionaries. Of these, 21 had the highest rank, ambassador; 112 the second, prefect and similar; and 382 the third, general director (*dirigente generale*). In other words, all 21 senior officers belong to the Foreign Affairs Ministry; of the next 112, 51 belong again to Foreign Affairs, 69 to Interior, 1 to Public Works, 1 to the Treasury. Only at the third rank does the scatter become proportional to the number of employees in each ministry. This distribution again seems to reflect a traditional notion of government, in which the most important functions were foreign policy (the ambassadors) and the maintenance of domestic law and order (the prefects). The only two 'exceptions' confirm the rule: namely, the chairman of the Upper Council for Public Works, and the accountant general. The former belongs to the only economic sector in which the nineteenth-century state also operated; the latter performs the role of government bookkeeper, in a traditional, laissez-faire sense. No representatives of the more modern sectors of state intervention are found at these salary levels. (It should be kept in mind, however, that only state administration proper is considered here. The picture would probably change if public corporations, parastatal agencies, and the like were taken into consideration; the dearth of information has prevented such an investigation.)

26. S. Cassese, *La formazione dello Stato amministrativo* (Milan, 1974), p. 236.

and to the content and structure of the budget. Only the latter will concern us here.

To begin with, most of the expenditures recorded in the budget have previously been authorized by Parliament in bills, called 'expenditures laws,' which cover a variety of state activities and appropriate necessary funds for one or more years. They cannot be altered during a budget discussion, but only by new laws. Thus, during recent years the proportion of expenditures actually decided by Parliament during budget discussions has not averaged above 12 percent.[27] The fact that the budget covers only a one-year period increases its rigidity. Secondly, a growing amount of public expenditures (e.g. those of local governments and other non-state agencies, which constitute almost half the total current expenditures) are excluded from the state budget. Finally, the budget approved by Parliament is only an estimate, i.e. it authorizes appropriations and revenues but does not specify actual disbursements. However, bureaucratic mechanisms are such that in recent years unspent appropriations have averaged around 25 percent of planned expenditures.

The meaning of the above limitations is clear: the public sector in Italy lacks a meaningful comprehensive statement of public revenues and expenditures which can be utilized as the necessary guideline for government economic intervention and as a reliable framework for parliamentary control over the effects of expenditures.[28]

Government and Cabinet. The difficulty in controlling expenditures is compounded by the general weakness of government as an effective controlling and coordinating agent of public policy. The reasons for this are both political and institutional. Institutionally, the governmental structure appears as a loose and disjointed swarm of ministries lacking coherence and coordination, as a result of a growth process that has taken place through the decades, with no real effort at rational-

27. Ibid., p. 237.
28. A recent (1978) Act has partially remedied this situation. It requires that the estimate and cash budgets be submitted simultaneously in order to reveal unspent authorizations. Moreover, it decrees that the yearly budget be set in a plurennial framework, by linking the estimated expenditure for the coming year with the main expenditure features for the coming three years. Together with the budget law, the government is bound to submit a so-called financial law, indicating the measures it plans to enforce in order to orient spontaneous economic dynamics towards the tendencies contained in the annual and plurennial budgets. See V. Barattieri and S. Gambale, "Il nuovo sistema della contabilità pubblica," *Bancaria*, Sept. 1978; P. de Joanna and A. Monorchio, "Le nuove procedure di contabilità ed il bilancio dello Stato," *Democrazia e diritto*, no. 3 (1978); R. Perez, "La riforma del bilancio dello Stato e la legge n. 468 del 1978," *Rivista Trimestrale di Diritto Pubblico*, 1979, no. 1. It is noteworthy that one of the most influential M.P.s working on this reform has been L. Spaventa, one of the academic economists elected to Parliament as an independent with PCI.

ization. Fragmentation, overlapping, conflicts of competence are the normal condition of affairs. For example, financial matters are apportioned among three ministries (Treasury, Finance, Budget)—a situation without parallel in modern parliamentary systems. Industrial policy is dealt with by a least four ministries (Industry, Budget, State Participations, Southern Development). Matters pertaining to energy are disputed among at least three ministries; those concerning public transportation among four; and so on. Some efforts towards coordination have been attempted by way of interministerial committees, most notably in 1967–68 through the establishment of the Interministerial Economic Planning Committee (CIPE), but the results have been disappointing. CIPE was supposed to be the mainstay of the planning process, but it was never able to acquire enough power and authority to do more than rubber-stamp decisions already taken within the single ministries; no real coordination of such decisions was achieved.

The overall coordination task should be the responsibility of the Presidency of the Council—one of the best-known victims of the system's lack of capacity or will to amend itself. For at least a century the need to rationalize the powers and means of the Presidency has been acknowledged by all political parties and groups, yet no reform of the office has been carried out (even though an article of the 1948 Constitution required it). The President is charged with the obligation to coordinate government, but is given no formal instruments (aside from those accruing from his personal political position) to do so. At present each ministry tends to go its own way and is run as a fiefdom by the politician and the small top-level oligarchy of senior administrators.[29]

The bureaucratic structure. The difficulties encountered by the Cabinet in performing a truly governing role are also due to the low efficiency of the bureaucratic structure, as revealed in various research studies.[30] Moreover, given the prevailing conception of the state and the bureaucratic structure referred to earlier, the basic legislation relating to the budget, public accounting, contracts, controls, etc., is primarily concerned with formal legality and provides no instruments for socioeconomic intervention. Likewise the provisions and regulations for personnel management and organization are concerned with

29. E. Rotelli, *La Presidenza del Consiglio dei Ministri* (Milan, 1972); S. Ristuccia et al., *L'istituzione governo* (Milan, 1977).

30. F. Ferraresi, "Some notes on the possibilities of political intervention of the Italian State Bureaucracy," *Transactions of the VII World Congress of Sociology* (Bulgarian Academy Publishing House, 1972), pp. 159–67; idem, "Burocrazia dello stato e gestione del potere", in AA. VV. *Azione sindacale e pubblica amministrazione* (Milan, 1977), pp. 81–140.

powers, obligations, spheres of competence, etc., while neglecting such matters as job content or the adequacy of available skills. The result is rigidity, fragmentation, inadequate professionalization and technical personnel skills, low morale and motivation, and strong arbitrary powers wielded by senior officials.

Many attempts have been made to reform the apparatus, but instead of comprehensive reorganization, the basic structures and principles have continued unchanged while time and again legislative bodies, agencies, institutes, etc., have been added to satisfy the demands of various political regimes. Thus, Giolitti's 'assistance state,' at the beginning of the century, nationalized railroads and established the first major social-security agencies, such as INPS (Istituto Nazionale per la Previdenza Sociale—National Institute for Social Security) and INA (Istituto Nazionale Assicurazioni—National Insurance Institute). Fascist corporatism established a score of special-purpose agencies for the assistance of a multitude of groups and categories (War Orphans, Workers' Children, etc.), while, under the pressure of the 1930s economic crisis, it initiated a massive process of state intervention in economic matters. After the Second World War, 'assistance state' agencies were expanded and multiplied to cover previously excluded categories (artisans, shopkeepers, farmers, etc.) while interventions and regulations of the economy became daily occurrences. However, the new bodies were not grafted on to the old, but suddenly introduced as partial modifications, exceptions, waivers, etc., which have undermined the old structures without creating consistent new ones.

The results are easily predictable. The arbitrary powers of the senior ranks are enhanced; and the irrationality of the system strengthens the positions of those who can provide the *interpretatio authentica* of norms and decide which regulations can be evaded with impunity and which must be enforced.

On a more general level, there are fractures in the cybernetic circuit between the administration and the outer context, as revealed by the inability to gather and process reliable and timely information, and the lack of human and technical facilities for the enforcement of plans that are drafted and for systematically monitoring their results.

There are many examples of these failures. It is sufficient to mention fiscal policy, which in many countries is a crucial instrument for the management of the economy. In Italy, however, it is nearly useless for this purpose—because of the cumbersome and inflexible laws that regulate it, because taxation is still largely indirect, and because the offices that administer it are seriously disorganized and inefficient. Under these circumstances, tax evasion has obviously been facilitated and has become a veritable plague within the system.

But some are more equal than others. The lack of effective political controls over the management of the economy, together with the general irrationality of the bureaucratic apparatus, provides opportunities for the acquisition of undue power by departments and offices which are strategically placed, or which enjoy other favorable conditions.

Probably the best-known case is that of the Treasury acting through the *Ragioneria* offices, present in each ministry but belonging to Treasury. The *Ragioneria* oversees all budgeting activities, controls all steps in the expenditure procedures, is responsible for the legality and correctness of operations, and assesses the availability of funds. In other words, Treasury is the only office with a global picture of the state's financial situation at a given moment—resources, commitments, liquidity, etc.—at the same time having the power to decide whether appropriations can be actually spent or not. The huge scale of the 'residual funds,' and the large delays in spending many appropriations (three to four years, according to a 1971 official enquiry)[31] testify to the substantial manner in which the Treasury uses its powers. However they are largely negative powers: they can delay and avoid expenditures, and can even sabotage and cripple programs; but they cannot direct, manage and effectively lead the economic system.

Perhaps more significant still is the role played by the Central Bank, especially in the 1960s. Even before then it had enjoyed a solid prestige, owing to the independence and high professional standards of its personnel. (The Bank has always had a far-sighted personnel policy, recruiting the best university graduates and giving them high-level training both through intensive home courses and, more important, by sending them abroad with generous scholarships. Nothing comparable to this occurs in the civil service.) After the boom period the importance of the Bank grew, until it became possibly the most important single public actor on the Italian economic scene, thanks to its control of monetary policy. In a context where social conflict is intense, where public administration works at a low level of efficiency, and where no institution can really influence economic policy, monetary instruments present an expedient alternative because of their apparent neutrality and the ease with which they can be employed; and this has very much strengthened the position of the Bank, which controls them. Moreover, the inefficiency of the fiscal system, and the *de facto* abdication of other authorities (such as Parliament) on financial matters, have thrust on the Bank the role of 'Grand Almoner' of the Treasury, thus again considerably reinforcing its influence.

Space does not permit an extensive discussion of public corpora-

31. Cassese, p. 238.

tions and authorities. This so-called parastatal sector has been growing and sprawling since the 1910s. Some rationalization measures were taken in 1956, with the establishment of the Ministry for State Participations, but there was no agreed doctrine concerning the use of the public sector. According to some opinions its task was to be the rationalization of capitalist development for which the old bureaucratic structures were inadequate. For others, public enterprises were to function as rivals and competitors of private monopolies, especially in the provision of cheap energy. Yet others conceived of them as devices for the 'occupation' of the state.[32]

The third position prevailed. The ruling Christian Democrats were a new party, born in 1944, fearful of left-wing parliamentary opposition, and with no links in the state apparatus. By establishing the parastatal sector and keeping managerial positions as a rigorous party monopoly, they provided themselves with a loyal network of public institutions which proved to be an invaluable source of political power and funds. However, the price paid was high. In order to keep the system outside effective parliamentary control the enterprises were granted considerable autonomy and it was not long before their huge financial power and support from their clientele made a sham of ministerial control—the more so since the Ministry for State Participations was small, new, without independent sources of strength, and altogether much weaker than the huge administrations it was supposed to control. Obviously, under such circumstances no comprehensive policy has ever been possible. On the contrary, the fragmentation of the polity has increased. When the attempt at general economic planning came about during the 1960s, the system was too deeply entrenched for change.

The functions of irrationality. The pattern described so far may appear totally irrational. However, it does possess a certain rationality of its own, albeit a perverse one, which can best be appreciated if one considers the way in which the Italian political system has been functioning in the postwar period. The dominant feature is a deep socioeconomic fragmentation due to historical factors arising from the distorted pattern of capitalist development. In order to overcome the resulting cleavages it would have been necessary to carry out structural, system-wide reforms, which would inevitably have hurt some interests belonging to the dominant groups (for example, urban speculators). This is why reform programs have never really been on the ruling classes' agenda. The dearth of really hegemonic groups has left the power block with insufficient force to cut off parasitic branches; at the

32. G. Amato, "Il ruolo dell'Esecutivo nel governo delle Partecipazioni statali," in AA. VV. *Il governo democratico dell'economia* (Bari, 1976), pp. 135–48.

same time fragmentation has made it possible to manage the system not via universalistic programs, but via particularistic allegiances, obtained through client dealings.

Within this framework the role of public administration has been crucial. If personnel, resources, and patterns of behavior had been efficient, coherent, and 'aggressive,' probably the machine would have attempted to achieve some form of rationalization of political demands or, at least, to act as a filter for the aggregation of the most sectoral and particularistic inputs. But this would have run counter to the vocation of a political class whose very power is based on the maneuvering of particularistic handouts. On the other hand, vis-à-vis such a logic, the existing irrationality turns out to be functional, because it is easily pliable to dealings with clientele. The machine itself becomes a party to such dealings, since the general inefficiency allows the senior ranks to transform into negotiable items what should be institutional duties. The short-term benefits for all those involved are considerable and obvious, but they are achieved at a very high social cost. They imply that political authority practically renounces its responsibility for performing a guiding role in the development of the country, and accepts a subordinate place vis-à-vis the demands of particularistic groups.

Economists in policymaking

Summarizing the argument so far, lower- or intermediate-level administrative units possess no specialized economic information gathering or processing agencies and no specific posts for economic advisers or analysts. The largest number of economics graduates, not all of whom are fully qualified, work in financial ministries, where they perform accounting or otherwise routine tasks.

At the upper level, the Italian government has no council of economic advisers or equivalent body of top-rank, official, highly qualified individuals concerned with the discussion, planning, and evaluation of economic policy. Such a body could presumably have helped to generate more open debate on economic issues, raising its level, and providing standards against which actual economic performance of governments could be measured. It could also have formulated broad-range, long-term, system-wide strategies, thereby imposing some constraints for policymakers. However this is exactly what the latter have studiously avoided during the last thirty years, in order to keep their hands free for sectoral, specific, day-to-day decisionmaking. And as the economists are not highly professionalized as a group (in terms of organization, common policies, defense of joint interests, etc.) there has been no professional lobby to advocate the establishment of such a council.

Nevertheless, this does not mean that there is or has been no economic expertise available to decisionmakers. For a long time, and with few exceptions, it has consisted of informal, personal relationships between economists and politicians—a pattern which is well adapted to the particularistic style of policymaking and the limited professionalization of economics.

In the absence of adequate secondary materials, the task of assessing the role of such advisers would have required direct and systematic inquiries which lie beyond the scope and possibilities of the present study, which is essentially a preliminary review of the field. Instead, a small number of crucial economic decisions has been examined in an effort to ascertain the economists' contribution. This is necessarily a cursory view of the subject, but it may provide a *toile de fond* for further, more analytical probing. A useful departure point is the set of decisions which during the economic crisis of the 1930s gave the Italian financial and credit structure its present shape (and, incidentally, in the process also substantially modified the industrial structure). This legislation included the separation of medium- and long-term from short-term credit, the concentration of powers over the direction of credit activity within a single administrative institution, the subjection of all credit enterprises to public supervision, and the reinforcement of the Central Bank, which became a public corporation. In this process a significant number of industrial concerns came under public control with the 'state participation' formula.

Some of these provisions were meant to answer the immediate needs of the world crisis. Others had a more lasting and far-reaching nature. Public administration proper, and 'regular' governmental offices were almost totally absent from the preparatory work that led to these projects: the whole operation was conducted almost privately by the chairman of two public finance corporations, A. Beneduce, a mathematics graduate, who had no formal position in government, but enjoyed Mussolini's full confidence. The preparatory work was performed outside normal administrative channels, mostly at the research center of the new-born (1935) IRI (Institute for Industrial Reconstruction).[33]

In the immediate post-reconstruction years, free trade became official Italian policy and that policy was conducted (note the exception) by economists. L. Einaudi, one of the most prestigious representatives of the older generation, was governor of the Central Bank and Budget minister, and therefore responsible for the 1947 rigid monetary stabilization measures which created the platform for the boom of the

---

33. Cassese, pp. 130, 158; A. Cianci, *La nascita dello stato imprenditore* (Milan, 1977).

1950s. Here again, however, an anomaly should be noted. Einaudi did not operate through the Budget Ministry (which had been created especially in order to give him a post in government, but had no adequate structure or personnel); instead, he utilized the Central Bank's experts, whose influence and power increased significantly at the time.[34]

Most other major decisions of the period followed the same free-trade approach, beginning with the dismantling of the Fascists' protectionist trade barriers. Such political decisions were supported by the leading academic economists; public administrators were only marginally involved, because these decisions were essentially negative, requiring neither effort nor reorientation of official functions.

Alongside this laissez-faire approach, another main current of thought was emerging which, building on Keynesian theories, strove to promote a more active role of the state in economic life. Politically, the main focus of this movement was E. Vanoni, a professor of Finance, who repeatedly held the Budget and the Finance portfolios. Several initiatives based more or less closely on this politicoeconomic philosophy were undertaken, the most enduring of which resulted in the establishment of new authorities and corporations like the Cassa per il Mezzogiorno (Southern Development Authority) or the National Hydrocarbon Corporation (ENI).[35] But although they were originally founded for economic reasons, they subsequently became the political playthings of ruthless Christian Democrat groups.[36]

When, in the mid-1950s, Vanoni attempted a comprehensive economic reform to eliminate the main imbalance and distortions in the economy, the results were ambivalent. The so-called Vanoni Plan merely set out the targets for the next decade and the efforts required to achieve them. It provided no specific interventionist measures, since it left the task of creating new employment conditions to private initiative and required the public agencies merely to increase the volume of public works. Some of the targets were reached by the spontaneous development of the economy (e.g. balance-of-payments equilibrium and the reduction of unemployment); others (e.g. the elimination of the North-South imbalance) are still far from being attained.

    34. D. Serrani, "Il ministero del Bilancio e della Programmazione economica," *Rivista Trimestrale di Diritto Pubblico*, 1973, pp. 54 ff.; P. Saraceno, *Ricostruzione e pianificazione, 1943–1948* (Bari, 1969).
    35. V. Di Cagno, *La Cassa per il Mezzogiorno. Storia, risultati, prospettive* (Rome, 1958); G. Galli, *La sfida perduta. Biografia politica di E. Mattei* (Milan, 1976).
    36. G. Galli and P. Facchi, *La sinistra democristiana. Storia e ideologia* (Milan, 1962); G. Zanetti and G. Fraquelli, *Una nazionalizzazione al buio. L'ENEL dal 1963 al 1968* (Bologna, 1980).

Moreover the public administration and general state intervention were largely unresponsive.[37]

The 1960s featured, at the political level, the center-left government coalitions, and in economic terms the attempt to initiate a fully fledged planning policy. The first step was the nationalization of the electricity companies, an action with far-reaching economic effects, implemented mainly for political reasons. The parties of the left, especially the Socialists, had advocated nationalization largely in order to test the Christian Democrats' reliability as possible partners in a reform program. The full story of the nationalization campaign has yet to be written,[38] but it appears that of the twenty or so people who prepared the program only a small minority had economic qualifications.[39] The remainder were leading figures in the parties involved. Once again, the public administrators were totally excluded.

The mid-sixties' planning experiment represents the high point of the academic economists' involvement in the management of economic policy. Its failure reveals the depth of the chasm between these professionals and the public administrators and leading politicians. The planning documents were produced by innumerable committees and boards to which, at one time or another, all the major Italian economists belonged. Several offices and bureaux were created especially for the purpose, such as the Planning Bureau at the Budget Ministry, the Institute for Studies of Economic Planning (ISPE), and the Technical-Scientific Planning Committee, where many economists (mostly with socialist leanings) undertook studies and researches for several years. The political and intellectual contribution of the planning discussions debate was massive; the technical level of the research studies was often excellent; and the experience undoubtedly helped to raise the standards of the discipline. However, the concrete results were very disappointing, for there was a failure to specify the requisite measures and policies, and none was implemented in practice.[40] This was due to both economic and political conditions, which cannot be analyzed here.[41] But it is important to note the lack of collaboration be-

37. U. La Malfa, *La politica economica in Italia, 1946–1962* (Milan, 1962); E. Vanoni, *La politica economica degli anni degasperiani* (Florence, 1977).

38. F. Di Pasquantonio, *La nazionalizzazione dell'industria elettrica* (Rome, 1962); E. Scalfari, *Storia segreta dell'industria elettrica* (Bari, 1963); E. Scalfari and G. Turani, *Razza padrona. Storia della borghesia di stato* (Milan, 1974).

39. Notably, P. Saraceno, economic consultant for IRI and for DC, and G. Carli, the governor of the Central Bank.

40. A. Graziani, "Introduzione" to A. Graziani, ed., *L'economia italiana: 1945–1970* (Bologna, 1973), p. 83.

41. G. Fua and P. Sylos Labini, *Idee per la programmazione economica* (Bari, 1963); A. Predieri, *Pianificazione e costituzione* (Milan, 1963); Ministero del Bilancio e

tween the planners (who were often unaware of the administrative implications of their projects) and a bureaucratic structure which had been conceived in laissez-faire terms and was consequently entirely incapable of undertaking the necessary planning measures.

In the 1970s the political attractions of planning gradually faded away. Initially, comprehensive five-year plans were replaced by 'sectoral' plans (for the chemical industry, textiles, etc.). Subsequently even these were discarded, and economic decisions have been undertaken with no more than token reference to any kind of general framework or plan.

In other words, the various efforts to adopt macroeconomic policy proper were unsuccessful. Instead, the familiar pattern of microeconomic dealings between the state and particular economic units has been reinforced and enlarged through the use of special concessions, credit facilities, ad hoc modification of norms, rescue operations for bankrupt industries, public contracts, direct interventions by state corporations, and so on.

In the late 1970s, in Italy as in many European countries, economic conditions markedly deteriorated: in 1978 unemployment had reached 7.0 percent of the labor force; inflation was temporarily down to 12.5 percent, but was about to increase massively in the following years; public expenditure had reached 47.7 percent of GNP, while the rate of economic growth had fallen to 2.2 percent p.a. Under these circumstances both the politicians and the general public have, naturally enough, been increasingly preoccupied with economic problems, and growing reliance on economic advice seems to be inevitable. Academic economists have become increasingly visible as experts, columnists, and commentators. Moreover, their intervention in political life has reached unprecedented levels, both indirectly, through semiregular, personal consultantships and more directly through assuming political responsibilities in Parliament (see the end of Sec. III above) and government. The 1979 Cossiga Cabinet included four well-known economists (Andreatta, Reviglio, Lombardini, Prodi, all representing the Christian Democrats); the first two of these are still in the present (December 1980) Forlani Cabinet, which also includes an economist from the Republican Party, U. La Malfa. (Needless to say, no Marxist economist has yet reached Cabinet level.)

This development certainly is characteristic of advanced industrial

della Programmazione Economica, *La programmazione economica in Italia* (Rome, 1967), 5 vols.; G. Amato, ed., *Il governo dell'industria* (Bologna, 1972); G. Ruffolo, *Rapporto sulla programmazione* (Bari, 1973); M. Carabba, *Un ventennio di programmazione 1954–1974* (Bari, 1977); G. Amato, *Economia, politica e istituzioni in Italia* (Bologna, 1976).

societies with highly complex economic systems. Still, it lends itself to ambivalent assessments: undoubtedly the presence of highly qualified economists in top-ranking decisionmaking posts[42] provides much-needed expertise in an area where it is seriously lacking. On the other hand, since, as was shown above, no middle-rank skills are available in the bureaucratic structure in order to feed the necessary analytical inputs, and since the main decisionmaking processes have remained unchanged, top-level economists run the risk of remaining prisoners in a politico-bureaucratic marshland which is quite able and willing to frustrate any efforts towards a rational management of the economy.[43] (The sneers of old-time politicians against the 'uselessness,' 'naïveté,' etc., of the 'professors' are very eloquent; so is the high turnover rate of the 'professors'—not only in the economic sphere.)

In sum: increased presence does not necessarily mean increased influence. The inertia of the administrative and governmental structures, and the network of reciprocal vetoes that entangle interest, pressure and political groups, still prevents the adoption of a flexible and modern economic policy, capable of providing the necessary governmental and public support for the country's economic recovery.

Bibliography

Allen, K. J., and B. McLennon. *Regional Problems and Politics in Italy and France*. London, 1970.

Fuà, G. *Notes on Italian Economic Growth, 1961–1964*. Milan, 1966.

———. *Problems of Late Development in Europe*. Paris, 1980.

Hansen, B. *Fiscal Policies in Seven Countries, 1955–1965*. Paris, 1968.

Holland, S., et al. *The State as Entrepreneur: New Dimensions for Public Enterprise—The I.R.I. State Shareholding Formula*. London, 1972.

Podbielsky, G. *Italy*. London/New York, 1978.

Posner, W., and S. J. Woolf. *Italian Public Enterprise*. London, 1967.

Review of the Economic Conditions of Italy (quarterly). Rome, Banca d'Italia.

42. B. Andreatta is Minister of the Treasury; F. Reviglio is Finance Minister; U. La Malfa is Budget Minister.

43. To the above one should of course add the political and economic constraints that may 'compel' economists occupying public posts to take measures that run counter to their (supposed) theoretical creeds. A case in point can be exemplified by the credit squeeze recently decreed by Treasury Minister B. Andreatta, as a reaction to the overvaluation of the U.S. dollar. Such (typically monetarist) measures were strongly disputed by the Budget Minister, G. La Malfa. Yet B. Andreatta is supposed to adhere to Keynesian theories, G. La Malfa to monetarist ones. (See *L'Espresso* 9, XXVII, 8 March 1981, p. 120).

Brazil: economists in a bureaucratic-authoritarian system

Paulo Roberto Haddad

I. *Introduction*

The Brazilian economy, which for centuries had been dependent on the exportation of a small number of primary products for its growth, has undergone important socioeconomic changes since the Great Depression of the thirties. These changes were induced basically by a process of import substitution, especially since World War II, that brought for the country, in less than three decades, a large and complex industrial sector. In the early sixties the economy stagnated and the country experienced a political crisis which culminated with the military overthrow of the government in 1964, resulting in a power redistribution between civilian technocrats and military officers.

The stagnation lasted until 1967 when the Brazilian economy entered its remarkable seven-year boom with annual real growth of gross domestic product (GDP) averaging 11 percent in the years 1968–1974. After 1974, when the effects of the oil crisis began to make themselves felt in Brazil, there was a renewed emphasis on import substitution of capital goods and basic inputs for dynamic industries. Since then the rate of inflation has increased, external indebtedness has enlarged and real growth of GDP has slackened. Growing awareness of social injustice caused by the income and wealth distribution, and international criticism of violations of human rights by military and civilian security units, brought the need for a process of redemocratization and political openness in the country. It is within these different stages of the Brazilian development process that the leading issues of the role of the economist in government will be analyzed.

In the past few years the economist profession in Brazil has won an unexpected prestige which is reflected in an increasing expansion in the number of applications and courses in Economics in all states of the country. A significant proportion of these graduates is absorbed by the public sector, which has grown rapidly during this period. From 1947 to 1969 expenditures in the public sector, even if we exclude those incurred by governmental enterprises, have grown five times in real terms, meaning that the share of these expenditures in the GDP increased from 17.1 percent in 1947 to 29.8 percent in 1969. If we consider the direct investments of the public sector and those made by public enterprises, we find that government participation in the gross fixed-capital formation in the recent period has increased to over 70 percent. Apparently, at the technical level, the economists represent the most important agents in the decisionmaking process of state intervention in Brazil's economy, through the formulation and control of overall sectoral or regional policies; and consequently the employment opportunities for economists have expanded in the different public agencies or institutions.

Unfortunately the role economists have been playing in government has not been scientifically researched so far in Brazil. Therefore the present study is not supported by other pieces of research which might serve as an initial basis. Thus it has been necessary to make full use of the limited available information. At the outset we prepared a questionnaire comprising ten open questions and interviewed more than twenty Brazilian economists working in public-sector institutions in Rio de Janeiro, Brasília, and Belo Horizonte. Most of these interviews took over two hours; they could not be greater in number owing to lack of time and financial resources. Subsequently, in May 1978, we helped the economists' professional associations in the state of Minas Gerais to organize three panels on the profession in Brazil. More than a hundred and fifty professionals and students of Economics participated in these panels, each of which had five panelists for the following topics: The Economist in Government; The Economist in Enterprises; The Economist and the Teaching of Economics. The discussions were recorded and subsequently transcribed from the tapes.

In addition to the meager bibliography available, we managed to obtain, mainly from the Brazilian Department of Agriculture and the Planning Secretariat of the Presidency, a few research reports as yet uncompleted, which had been prepared by universities and public research foundations and were indirectly related to our objectives. Also through the collaboration of the National Council for Technological and Scientific Development (CNP) and of the Department of Education and Culture, we had access to unpublished statistical reports on teaching and research in economics. Together with the former institution we organized a workshop with more than twenty knowledgeable economists in Brazil in order to prepare an evaluation and assessment of the prospects for economics teaching and research in Brazil.

The present study has been divided into three major parts: in the first we examine the problem of the academic training of Brazilian economists, emphasizing certain aspects which are mainly related to their work in the public sector; in the second we point out the recent increase in the penetration of economists in various institutions, identify the recruitment processes, the degree of professionalization, functions etc.; finally, we attempt the difficult appraisal of their role in the formulation and implementation of public policies. The reader will notice that, for the reasons mentioned above, the study is unbalanced with respect to the level of details of the information presented. In some topics a complete lack of such data is replaced by the personal impressions or intuitions of the author and the people interviewed.

II.   *The Academic Training of Economists*

Academic training of economists in Brazil dates back to the beginning of the nineteenth century. Although isolated attempts had been made by the first Brazilian economists trained in Europe before this period, it was not until the arrival of the Portuguese royal family in Rio and the consequent opening of our ports to world trade that the discipline of economics was created in Brazil. The transfer of the throne to one of the colonies thus created the need for trained personnel to deal with the problems associated with foreign trade.

From the institution of economics in Brazil as a formal discipline,[1] training proceeded along three lines: (a) Lectures on Commerce (provided since 1809); (b) Law Science schools (1827); and (c) Military schools (1810).

Law Science courses comprised the following disciplines relevant to economics: Political Economy, Public Finance, and Administrative Law. The early economics textbooks published in Portuguese were written by teachers of these disciplines, mostly at the schools of Olinda and São Paulo. Until the fifties of this century the major economic functions in Brazilian public administration were undertaken by lawyers, particularly the functions related to public finance, which were frequently approached purely from the limited standpoint of tax and administrative law. In the professional economists' subsequent rise, which clearly starts from that decade, conflicts over positions and functions in the public sector basically occurred with law-school graduates. In recent years, as the division and specialization of functions has improved, a more mature relationship has been developing between the two professions. For example, economists have recognized that in order to deal with the growing process of state intervention in the Brazilian economy, one of the most needed teaching and research areas is Law and Economics, involving as topics the role of the free market, size of the firm and market organization, regulation, investment prefer-

1. L. de F. Bueno, *A evolução de ensino de economia no Brasil* (Rio de Janeiro, 1972).

ences, etc.[2] As training at the military schools expanded, *polytechnical schools* were created where, after a certain number of reforms during the last century, Economics, Administrative Law, and Statistics were taught, with the aim of giving the engineer a background and understanding of and an ability to handle industrial and agricultural production problems. These are still relevant today, as is evident from the growing number of Economic Engineering specialized courses in the past ten years. In the public sector these specialists have performed economists' functions so effectively in the assessment of projects of sectoral programing, in situations which involve familiarity with quantitative methods of estimation and production engineering processes, that some groups of economists have reacted jealously, objecting to the organization or titles of these courses or favoring restrictions on the admission of these professionals to graduate courses in Economics.

The present-day *schools of economics* developed from commerce lectures and commerce schools. The B.S. degree in Economics was created in 1931, but its content differed significantly from the currently accepted international standards for the training of professional economists. An examination of the legislation of 1905, 1906, and 1931 (which applied until 1945) establishing undergraduate economics training in commerce schools and a classification of the number of credits in the various disciplines taught in that period, reveals how few competently trained economists there were in Brazil before 1945.

Up to the beginning of the sixties the expansion of higher education in Brazil proceeded in a gradual and controlled manner. In 1960 there were 93,000 students in institutions of higher education, and the growth rate of applications did not exceed 9 percent. From 1963 to 1967 the rate of growth rose to 15.8 percent and reached 30.7 percent in 1968, reflecting the increase of employment opportunities. In the 1970s the number of applications exceeded one million, and economics is now one of the most rapidly expanding fields. The subject was introduced as an independent discipline in Brazil under a Decree of 1945, and thereafter curricula appeared in Brazilian universities with a nucleus of specific economic techniques. In the past five years interest in the subject has grown enormously; in 1978 there were 148 courses, almost 18,000 new applications per annum, and an enrollment of 45,000 students; and about 7,000 new economists entered the labor market.

The expansion of higher education in Brazil has been explained in terms of modernization and class analysis. In the view of Echevarria,[3]

2. Conselho Nacional de Desenvolvimento Científico e Tecnológico, *Economia: avaliação e perspectivas* (Brasilia, 1978). Workshop report written by João Sayad.

3. J. M. Echevarria, *Filosofia, educación y desarrollo* (Mexico, 1967), Part 2.

it is attributable to the pressure of generalized egalitarianism in the structure of modern industrial societies spreading upwards from the high-school level to reduce social discrimination and provide the lower social strata better employment and income prospects. However, other scholars[4] attribute the expansion to economic-policy decisions which produced an intense concentration of capital and income, with correspondingly reduced opportunities to acquire capital through small businesses, crafts, and independent professions—hence the increased middle-class desire for access to and promotion within the public and private occupational hierarchies through heavy personal outlays and/or demands for publicly subsidized free tuition. It was also argued that legal requirements for entry, e.g. the traditional school entrance examination, should be reduced. However there was a conflict between public investment priorities in education and in more traditional fields, and in fact the private sector contributed a substantial share of the increased supply of higher education. Between 1960 and 1972 enrollment in isolated institutions grew (983 percent), as against 440 percent in universities, and in private (618 percent) rather than public universities (384 percent).

There was also an increase in the number of institutions providing training in economics and in the profession's social prestige as economists rose to key decisionmaking positions in the Brazilian economy. But there were deficiencies, such as the lack of an advanced training program for teachers, the difficulties of access to a specialized literature, and the absence of a research tradition in the new economics courses, resulting in an educational subsystem which binds young people to four years of technically inferior studies so that they enter the labor market without a basic professional background.

The economics graduates from our schools find it difficult to handle economic analysis because they lack the capacity for logical thinking and understanding of scientific method. Their knowledge is fragmented and their deficiencies in institutional and historical information lead them to adopt naive attitudes when faced with situations involving complex organizational or political factors.[5]

At the beginning of the sixties the only economics graduate-level training center in Brazil was the one-year program of Fundação Getúlio

4. L. A. C. R. Cunha, "A expansão do ensino superior: causas e conseqüências," *Debate e Crítica*, no. 5, pp. 27–58.

5. *Revista Brasileira de Economia* (Rio de Janeiro) 20, no. 4 (1966). This special edition includes the papers presented at the meeting of Itaipava, organized by the Ford Foundation, where a group of talented economists discussed the state of the profession in Brazil. The diagnosis of the situation of training at the undergraduate level in Economics included in the present study is based upon the consensus arrived at in this meeting.

Vargas (Rio), especially devised to prepare students to be selected for advanced studies abroad. In the preceding decade public sector economists had already felt the lack of technical background. The bachelor's-degree students possessed a variety of heterogeneous bits of knowledge with no central technical and scientific nucleus, although the 1945 reform had been designed to enable the economist to solve problems involving national economic development, and, generally speaking, the disciplines were oriented towards the analysis of public sector behavior. Therefore specialized courses were designed for Brazilian government officials (project evaluation, economic planning, budgetary planning, etc.) by the United Nations Economic Commission for Latin America (at that time, under strong influence of Prebisch's ideas and policy recommendations). Similarly the National Development Bank and the National Economic Council wanted, in a relatively short period, to supply the public sector with personnel capable of handling basic analytical tools. These courses were of fundamental importance, since they were organized during a transition period in which academic teaching was poor and the national development process insistently required economists to perform new functions.[6]

In the mid-sixties there was a widespread feeling among the intellectual elite of Brazilian economists that strong action was required to improve the preparation and training of our professionals. Through various symposia and workshops guidelines were established for medium- and long-run teaching and research policies involving: (a) the development of institutions for graduate work and research in key urban centers throughout the country; (b) the encouragement of intellectual exchanges between these centers, and the formation of a national association to bring together the nation's economists; (c) the provision of basic courses in economic theory and quantitative methods at each of the main centers, and instruction in the operation of the main economic institutions; and (d) the payment of competitive salaries in order to ensure the recruitment and effective operation of competent staff who would raise the level of undergraduate training.

6. On the evolution of graduate training in Economics in Brazil, see D. H. Graham, "The Growth, Change and Reform of Higher Education in Brazil: A Review and Commentary on Selected Problems and Issues;" in R. Roett, ed., *Brazil in the Sixties* (Nashville, Tenn., 1972), pp. 275–324; L. P. Rosenberg and P. R. Haddad, *Ensino e pesquisa em economia no Brasil: avaliação e perspectiva* (Rio de Janeiro, 1976), particularly the article by Professor Werner Baer; C. M. Castro, "A produção de economistas e o produto de economistas", *Pesquisa e Planejamento Econômico* 5 (1975): 517–69. These studies do not analyze teaching and research of Economics in the agriculture area, which presented a different evolution from the scheme elaborated in this section. The present study does not include, basically, the position of this area.

On this basis several centers were founded across Brazil and used by national and foreign institutions to develop graduate and research programs in economics during the 1970s. Financial resources from national (FUNTEC, CAPES, CNPQ) and international agencies (Ford Foundation, USAID) made an essential contribution. There are presently twelve postgraduate centers (M.S. and Ph.D. degrees) in economics in Brazil, annually offering 200 new places per annum, with different areas of concentration—regional economics, demography, public economics, industrial economics, agricultural economics, etc. In addition, a National Association was created to provide a formal mechanism for the promotion and coordination of integrated activities between the centers, such as research seminars, publications, the national selection of prospective master's-degree candidates, and the organization of visits by foreign professors. This Association provides the institutional setting for the most critical debates on Brazilian official economic policy, and the most serious consideration of alternative patterns of national economic and social development.

This new phase of developing research and teaching in economics in Brazil had a major impact on the foreign training program, mainly in the U.S.A. Although the data are incomplete, Table 1 shows the pioneering effort of Fundação Getúlio Vargas until 1965 and the growing importance of studies at the Ph.D. level in the 1970s.

Although graduate training at the above-mentioned centers is com-

Table 1.   Foreign training of Brazilian students in Economics, 1960–1974

Institutions	1960–65	1966–69	1970–74
Getúlio Vargas Foundation, Tio (EPGE)	59	6	10
University of São Paulo (IPE)	—	32	20
CAEN, Fortaleza	—	7	6
CEDEPLAR, Belo Horizonte	—	8	6
PIMES, Recife	—	5	6
CENDEC, Department of Planning	—	10	10
IPEA, Department of Planning	—	5	10
Others	—	17	—
Total	59	90	68
Number of Ph.D.s forecasted	9	50	50
Percent of Ph.D.s forecasted	15	55	75

Source: Graham, op. cit. in note 6.
Note: More recent data show that the number of Ph.D.s forecasted was almost completely fulfilled.

parable to that of the best American and European universities, and the quality of research carried out shows an improving analytical level, there is still latent dissatisfaction. Many observers and former students have complained[7] that the teaching has become rather mechanical. Besides the standard courses in theoretical and quantitative analysis there are a few 'applied' courses which add a modicum of institutional analysis and economic-policy content. Such narrowness partly reflects the minute staff in some centers, their relative inexperience, and the limited amount of institutionally oriented research so far undertaken which can provide a basis for a broader type of economic analysis. Most of the advanced texts contain generalizations based upon the institutional conditions existing in the U.S.A. and western Europe, and even there the traditional analysis is far removed from the actual economic situation. Furthermore, some economists in Brazil are raising questions, already familiar in the U.S.A. and Europe, about the adequacy of existing economic theory. On the other hand, as the graduate institutions are not yet adequately financed, there has been a growing involvement in contract-oriented research. This may restrict the opportunities for the fundamental research on which their academic reputation will depend, for some of these topics will never attract contract funds, since they involve criticism of current government economic policies.

The new generation of graduate economists has been heavily involved in federal and state technical-advisory or management functions. Despite major efforts to broaden their graduate course options and to adapt themselves to the needs of the expanding labor market, the graduate-center training is still insufficient to enable economists to be professionally capable of coping with emerging and rapidly changing public-sector problems. Thus, when they are employed by the government working with such topics as the economic aspects of urban and rural poverty (nutrition, public health, internal migrations, employment of low income groups, etc.), or involved in analyzing the control and distribution mechanisms of public resources, they recognize their limitations and produce merely descriptive reports, with, at most, naive applications of partial-equilibrium models or macroeconomic growth-rate exercises.

In attempting to account for and explain the implications of this situation we can, initially, distinguish three groups within the economics profession: the practitioners, the methodologists, and the theoreticians.[8] The practitioners concentrate mainly on solving problems

---

7. Cf. Baer, as cited in the preceding footnote.
8. R. Abler et al., *Spatial Organization* (Englewood Cliffs, N.J., 1971), ch. 1.

utilizing generally well-defined principles; the methodologists mainly devote their time to thinking about how things should be done rather than simply doing them; while the theoreticians are preoccupied with thinking about the ways people think about what they are doing. Methodologists and theoreticians are often located in academic communities, while practitioners are employed in public and private organizations.

Any discipline that concentrates its personnel in only one of these groups will advance only slowly. In Brazil, although a few major economists feel that the Anglo-Saxon analytical tools are not sufficiently relevant to the country's current stage of development, their attempts at theory construction are still largely incipient. In relation to public-sector issues, neoclassical welfare theory has been most widely taught in undergraduate and graduate courses and used to derive normative criteria for optimal resource allocation from simplified hypotheses about the behavior of consumers and firms. However, this theory assumes the absence of power and is therefore inadequate for the analysis of an essentially political decisionmaking process, particularly in the Brazilian case, where there is no interdisciplinary tradition of teaching and research applicable to typical public-sector issues. Moreover, the scope for theory building and methodological development is restricted because the research-center staff usually have to perform administrative functions and contract research as well as undergraduate and graduate teaching.

Since practitioners do not usually either question the nature of their activities or design new and improved ways of doing their jobs, it is essential that undergraduate, graduate, or specialized courses should contain substantial amounts of empirical and theoretical materials relevant to the public sector—for example, by improving the communications between academic and public-sector personnel, through individual consultancies, specialized seminars, and research contracts. Given the low professional standards of undergraduate courses in economics, the need for qualified and experienced academic staff increases as a significant proportion of the graduate program involves recycling the basic concepts of economic theory, mathematics, and statistics before the stage of more advanced studies can be attempted.

Economists employed as practitioners feel the need to specialize and update their 'tool kits' through short- and medium-term courses, generally at specialized institutions designed for this purpose. The best known of these is CENDEC, an agency of the Department of Planning of the Presidency of the Republic, which for years has trained public-sector professionals in courses on national and regional economic planning, sectoral programing, budgetary programing, project preparation and evaluation. Between 1974 and 1978, for instance, the number of professionals trained by CENDEC exceeded 1,100. The agency has close links with academic institutions, from which it recruits most of its professors, and despite its close involvement with the central bureaucracy it maintains a very independent political position in its teaching on development issues.

Recognition of the value of economics courses as a preparation for managerial or advisory positions is suggested by a survey of high-level staff at the Department of Agriculture in Brazil.[9] Of 142 directors and advisors of the different agencies of the Department (Table 2) 94 percent graduated from universities, mainly in Agricultural Departments (35.8 percent), which is natural enough, given the specialization re-

Table 2.   Brazil: university courses taken by directors and advisers, Department of Agriculture, 1977

Area		First course			Second course		
		Total	Direc- tors	Advisers	Total	Direc- tors	Advisers
Agriculture	%	35.8	46.9	25.7	3.2	10.0	—
	No.	48	30	18	1	1	—
Engineering &	%	3.7	7.8	—	3.2	10.1	—
Architecture	No.	5	5	—	1	1	—
Economics &	%	15.7	7.8	22.8	67.7	50.0	76.2
Statistics	No.	21	5	16	21	5	16
Business &	%	16.4	18.7	14.3	19.4	20.0	19.1
Accounting	No.	22	12	10	6	2	4
Human	%	6.0	1.6	10.0	6.5	10.0	4.7
sciences	No.	8	1	7	2	1	1
Law	%	19.4	15.6	22.9	—	—	—
sciences	No.	26	10	16	—	—	—
Armed	%	3.0	1.6	4.3	—	—	—
forces	No.	4	1	3	—	—	—
Total	%	100.0	100.0	100.0	100.0	100.0	100.0
	No.	134	64	70	31	10	21

Source: IUPERJ, 1978.

9. C. Sarmento, *Administradores públicos de alto nível na burocracia brasileira: o caso do Ministério da Agricultura* (Rio de Janeiro, 1978).

quirements of the public agencies in this sector. However, 23 percent had had two academic courses in Economics and/or Business Administration, and 4 percent had had three.

III. The Economists in Government: Markets, Attitudes and Influences

By comparing the remarkable growth in the number of economists coming onto the labor market every year with the fact that only a few dozen have attended the few high-level schools and are qualified for professional activities, one can see that the great majority of economics graduates do not perform professional activities as economists. Many become tired of waiting for a job compatible with their expectations and compete for positions as clerks, traveling salesmen, management assistants, etc., which do not require a higher-educational qualification. Others become business managers, performing financial management, organization and methods functions; and apart from those engaged in university teaching and research activities (in 1975 most of the 2,646 teachers of economics in Brazil were trained economists), some get public-sector employment. Unfortunately there are no statistical data on the distribution of Brazilian economists among the various professional segments. Nevertheless, some pertinent observations can be made.

In the first place many students who enroll in the schools of economics have no precise conception of the economics profession. The distinction between Economics and Business Administration is unclear, and many students enrolling for Economics are mainly interested in Business Economics and expect the conventional microeconomics curriculum to provide analytic tools for operational decisions in business enterprises. A similar confusion is apparent in a survey of graduates from one of the country's best schools of economics,[10] where the respondents provided their own job description. It is clear that only 53 percent performed economist-type functions, an impression confirmed by their comments on the readings and courses they found most useful in their present occupation. Again, a sample of economists employed in finance, commercial, industrial, and consulting companies were usually performing duties appropriate to a professional manager, mainly because the quality and content of the business administration courses in Brazil are poor. Economists have proved more adaptable and have performed better in these positions than the trained business managers; and finally, companies recruiting

10. C. M. Castro, "O que faz um economista?" *Revista Brasileira de Economia* 24 (1970): 175–96.

these specialists rarely know who does what and tend to employ economists because they have a greater public visibility.

The conditions for entry and the professional consolidation of economists in government were extremely unfavorable owing to the history of the Brazilian planning process. Since the colonial era our economists have always been interested in current economic-policy controversies, which cannot be surveyed here.[11] However, it was the planning-versus-liberalism controversy of the mid-forties that laid the foundation for the economics profession in Brazil as the source of specialists responsible for certain current public-sector themes and problems. The main actors in the debate were Roberto Simonsen, a knowledgeable intellectual and one of the outstanding business leaders in Brazil, and Eugenio Gudin, one of the leading scholars, responsible for the modern teaching of economics in the country and the training of several well-known economists. The controversies mainly centered on "the benefits of industrialization in economies which are essentially agricultural, and the advantages of a greater specialization in the international division of labor; between protectionism, aiming at industrialization *à outrance* and free exchange, imposing a severe selectiveness on possibly emerging nations; between the direct and indirect participation of the State in the economy and classical *laissez-faire*."[12]

These controversies were extended in the fifties when new participants attempted to formulate a series of economic arguments which could justify the adoption of an import-substitution model as an alternative to the primary-export model which, since colonial times, had subordinated Brazil's development to the dynamics of the foreign sector through specialization in primary-product exports: gold, sugar cane, coffee, iron ore, etc. The debates stimulated economic research and an interest in drawing on the progress of economic theory in Europe and the United States, and in organizing centers dedicated to the provision of statistical data relevant to the analysis of the questions posed. The emergence of the first nuclei of economists in newly founded institutions (Fundação Getúlio Vargas, Banco Nacional do Desenvolvimento Economico, Banco do Nordeste do Brasil, etc.) and the organized production of high-quality professional economic studies dates back to that time.

The reasons for these changes are clear. While the national economy depended upon developments in the international division of labor, the administration and allocation of scarce resources presented

11. H. F. Lima, *História do pensamento econômico no Brasil* (São Paulo, 1976).
12. C. V. Doellinger, "Introdução," in R. C. Simonsen and E. Gudin, *A controvérsia do planejamento na economia brasileira* (Rio de Janeiro, 1977).

no greater technical difficulties, since the expansion of the system basically reflected the cyclical movements of foreign-trade transactions in the three or four primary products which together accounted for almost 90 percent of Brazil's export trade. Later, when the import substitution process was triggered in a planned manner (Program of Goals under President Juscelino Kubitschek, 1957–61), the structure of the economy became more complex and diversified as dynamic interdependencies emerged among the productive sectors. It was no longer a question of eliminating bottlenecks in the economic infrastructure in order to produce and market a few exportable products, or devising an exchange policy to enhance the competitiveness of these products in international markets. On the contrary, the formulation and administration of development policies had become tasks to be performed by specialists who had to work with a network of interactive effects among independent and induced decisions by public and private agents whose functions in such a complex economic system are unclear.

The economist's participation in state and federal public administration in Brazil can be better understood if, in addition to the overall professional trend towards specialization which occurs with the nation's development process, we also examine the evolution of some public organizations, identifying their policies with respect to the employment, increase, and assimilation of economists into their structures. However, this has been possible only through interviews, data, and impressions which are presented in a summarized manner, since they are very similar to the observations reported elsewhere in this set of studies.

The criteria for the recruitment of economists into public institutions are based mainly on a public admission test, principally for the civil service. Nevertheless political cliques still exert a strong influence on the appointment of professionals to public service positions, especially within politically weak agencies and institutions. Among semi-public administrative bodies, professional rapport and personal reliability prevail as criteria for recruitment and promotion, particularly in the case of senior economists, because there is a desire to avoid mistakes, since they have a greater "power of germination within the institution," and the use of tests would be inefficient. At the senior level, less specialized knowledge is required than in junior posts (where it is crucial), whereas professional experience, political sensitivity, consensus-building capacity, and sound judgment are essential.

The expansion of the number of economists within government institutions and agencies follows a variety of patterns. In some cases other professional groups are dominant, and this obviously limits the proportion of economists on their technical staff. For instance, a major public electrical power company created in 1952 had only 5 economists until 1962. From 1965 the number of economists increased to the present total of more than 80, working on macroeconomic indicators, tariff policy, and project profitability calculations. However, when the company's engineers realized that they were losing key positions because they lacked the requisite specialized background, they began to display an interest in basic courses in financial administration, economic analysis, and economic engineering.

In other institutions where there is an active interface with administrative agencies which formulate and implement short- and long-term economic policies (e.g. in the Planning Department and Finance Department), the labor market for economists has expanded enormously and increasingly, as the State intervenes more actively in the economy. The Banco do Brasil, for example, has participated in various policy councils on food supply and monetary problems, etc., and has therefore increased its recruitment of economists familiar with the jargon and specialized affairs of such bodies. The Department of Agriculture, on the other hand, has hired more economists because they need advisers capable of formulating decisions relevant to the management of various markets (e.g. milk, meat, soybeans), pricing policies, finance, and the control of inventories.

Finally, various public agencies have recognized the value of employing economists on such matters as budgeting and budget control, project preparation, etc., because of their ability to work with the economic branches of the administration using a specialized language which has become artificially more complex and which is incomprehensible to those unfamiliar with the basic techniques of economic analysis. The recruitment of economists in these agencies is, of course, limited by and proportional to their bureaucratic growth, yet even here the demand for their services is influenced by their public prestige and by the existence of professional cliques.

There is no census of civil servants in Brazil from which to quantify this expansion, but there are some figures derived from sample surveys. Table 3 lists the number of jobs for business managers, lawyers, economists and engineers in the federal service in 1971. The figures understate the true situation, since they cover only jobs officially classified as economist posts.[13] Moreover the numbers have increased more than three or four fold during the last few years.[14]

13. O. Lima and J. F. Senna, *Mercado de trabalho de nivel superior: oferta e demanda de advogados, engenheiros, economistas e administradores* (Rio de Janeiro, 1972).
14. To cite two examples: (i) in 1978, 36 percent of the senior personnel in the Department of Planning of the Presidency had taken university courses in economics; (ii)

Table 3.   Brazil: number of existing jobs and status in federal service, 1971

Category	In public administration	In semi-public administration[a]
Managers	2,814	869
Lawyers	2,038	418
Economists	419	256
Engineers	2,857	1,330

[a] Jobs with authorities and foundations.
Source: O. Lima and J. F. Senna, op. cit. in note 13.

The relationship of economists with other professionals and the public at large has not caused insurmountable strains. In relation to journalists specializing in economic matters the major difficulties occur because, on the one hand, the journalists lack the requisite specialized training and the economists consequently complain about distortions of fact or technical errors in presentation; on the other hand, journalists frequently complain that the political situation has led the government economists to adopt a form of self-censorship and unwillingness to discuss controversial issues. Even so, a content analysis of economic material in our leading newspapers and magazines—which are devoting increasing space to national and international economic issues—indicates that the quality has improved substantially, and a number of economists are contributing articles.

In relation to the academic community, government economists maintain permanent programs designed to support educational institutions and research contracts with research centers or directly with the researchers themselves. Experience with these contracts is very uneven, and there are complaints about their poor technical quality, inadequate approach, delays in delivering reports, irrelevant results, ignorance of what is going on in the economic realm, etc. During the interviews we noticed that public-sector economists agree that the best way to support academic centers is through research contracts which require slower development results capable of anticipating issues so that, as a respondent put it: "when the decisionmaking moment comes, the results should be at hand . . . to make this possible, the universities should conduct basic multipurpose research, since the routine decisionmaking process in the public sector demands a choice between alternatives made available from inaccurate information re-

in the same year the 109 positions held by economists in the State Secretariat of Finances (Minas Gerais) were classified as follows: leadership, coordination, supervisory or control, 19 percent; advisory (intra- or interorganizational relations), 21 percent; executive or operating, 60 percent.

quiring a permanent development of creativity and the capacity to
pick up what is really important."

Relations with politicians have presented great difficulties during
the past few years. The economists' language is becoming more and
more self-contained and specialized, thus creating an insurmountable
barrier to communication with the uninitiated. The intellectual arro-
gance of the economists who took over the top echelon of public administration, as the political power of the military grew and the officers
became increasingly dissatisfied with businessmen and politicians in
decisionmaking capacities, has caused a growing uneasiness among the
politicians. On the other hand, there are built-in control mechanisms in
public organizations which withdraw the technicians from contacts
with politicians for fear of a reaction at higher administrative levels.
According to one respondent, "in the decisionmaking process, the
economist contributes his technical equipment, but the politician's intuitions and experience are essential . . . departments in economic
areas should be filled by politicians who can listen to experts' opinion
. . . these experts should always go through the exercise of learning
continually how to affect the political view of problems . . . this rather
radical position is justifiable, because economists in government lack
the feeling of compassion, since they act as businessmen, in an
incrementalist perspective, without a fundamental questioning of
structural problems."

Finally, it is worth noting the good relationship between economists
and statistical experts owing to the fact that many outstanding Brazilian economists began as statisticians, for example in the National Accounts Group of Fundação Getúlio Vargas, after World War II. During
the controversy of the 1940s about the need for economic planning, it
was also insistently maintained that statistical information about the
balance of payments, economic aggregates, price indexes, etc., was an
indispensable basis for national decisionmaking. Yet despite this tradition, the national census bureau (FIBGE) has only recently begun to
hire economists (now more than 40). Since the beginning of the 1970s
recruitment has mainly consisted of cartographers, geographers, and
statisticians. This is a definite step forward, since the traditional idea
that the FIBGE should produce only primary or basic statistics was
abandoned in favor of the generation of derived statistics, thereby
creating a demand for other specialists, such as economists, sociologists, and anthropologists.

IV. *What Role Do Economists Play in Governmental Planning?*

The Brazilian postwar economic planning experience has comprised two different types: rational-comprehensive planning and prag-

matic planning.[15] The former reflects the planners' obsession with rational action, the interdependence of decisions, and the assessment of the overall sectoral and spatial impact of any given change on the economic system; the latter embodies the practical element in public policy, speed in decisionmaking, and concern with immediate and visible public-sector problems.

The use of general equilibrium models in analyzing is almost invariably associated with rational-comprehensive planning. Thus, in order to analyze the impact of a decision affecting the allocation of resources the planner may want an enormous quantity of information, revealing the many interdependencies, on which to base his assessment of the effects of the decision upon the the economy. This may entail the preparation of planning models which are far too sophisticated in terms of the available data, and given the problems of implementation, especially the requisite political power and administrative feasibility, the resulting recommendations become merely rhetorical. There is consequently a growing wave of pragmatism in the public-sector decisionmaking centers. It is based on the assumption that governmental agencies usually have the requisite knowledge and experience to enable them to act without the usual delays. The emphasis on the 'practical utility' of planning reflects not only the decisionmakers' impatience at the delays occurring while the technicians produce research reports and studies, which in fact often lack relevance to the problems for which solutions are required; it also reflects the anti-intellectual attitude of some public managers who are impervious to the conceptual and abstract world of theoretical formulation, and the pressure of economic agents who can take advantage of gaps in the public-sector decisionmaking process.

What do economists do in government? Firstly, there is a group of economists in the planning divisions in federal and state governments, or in the planning superintendencies of sectoral development agencies, who concentrate their technical resources on medium- and long-run economic problems by means of analytical diagnosis, projections and prognoses, discussions of development alternatives, surveys oriented towards policy evaluations, etc. They favor a rational-comprehensive approach and are quite removed from the final stage of decisionmaking; they derive their prestige and power in the preparatory phases of general or sectoral government plans or economic crisis debates and, despite their importance in the bureaucracy, tend to be critical of the prevailing development model and the political establishment.

15. P. R. Haddad, "As políticas de desenvolvimento regional no Brasil: notas para uma avaliação," In W. Baer et al., eds., *Dimensões do desenvolvimento brasileiro* (Rio de Janeiro, 1978).

A second group of professional economists tends to be more pragmatic, working on short-term movements of macroeconomic variables and adopting a more conservative attitude towards the economic system. This group is better known by the entrepreneurial community and the public in general, since they deal with current economic affairs and produce reports oriented towards decisions embodied in decrees, regulations, and norms which are usually issued by the Finance Department, the Central Bank, or the Advisory Staff of the Secretaries. Their work tends to be implemented in a piecemeal, incremental manner by specific measures designed to meet immediate needs. Yet in tackling one problem others are created, and the process can continue almost indefinitely.

This kind of action is criticized by the first group of economists who contend that a succession of marginal or incremental changes in an underdeveloped economy can generate perverse dynamics and a timid conception of what is possible, whereas there is a need for programs and projects which will restructure the prevailing growth process. The factors favoring the dominance of one style rather than the other in the policy process can be illustrated through the recent course of events.

After the military coup of 1964 the decisionmakers were primarily concerned to reactivate the national economy, which was performing well below its potential owing to the serious inflation and balance of payments deficit. The spectacular recovery after 1967 (when the GNP growth rate reached 11 percent per annum) was ensured by an intelligent application of fiscal, exchange, and monetary policies, coupled with the reorganization of the relevant policymaking institutions. Decisionmaking was concentrated in a few public agencies controlled by groups of economists well trained in the neoclassical tradition. There was a general tendency toward both vertical and horizontal centralization of the economic-policy instruments.[16]

This outcome reflected the political rationale of the 1964 military revolution. Given the state bureaucracy's inexperience in the preparation and conduct of macroeconomic policies, and the urgent need to stimulate economic activity, it was impossible to adopt a slow-moving decentralized procedure. Given the scarcity of experienced personnel, they had to be concentrated in key decisionmaking centers within the state machinery. In view of the conflicting policy objectives, open disagreement among social groups or regions might have threatened the new political regime; consequently it was essential to establish a technical staff with the power to define the conditions of 'stability' of the

16. P. R. Haddad, "Os economistas e a concentração de poder—notas preliminares," *Fundação JP; análise e conjuntura*, 8 (1978), pp. 2–7.

economic system. The two leading Brazilian economists at this time were Roberto Campos (1964–67) and Delfim Netto (1967–74).

Between 1965 and 1974, the formulation and management of the country's economic policies were so much under the control of high-level technocrats, especially economists, that they became part of a leading political echelon, constituting a kind of oligarchy able to make decisions that used conventional bureaucratic instruments for their own benefit, so that their power base no longer solely consisted of their technical-scientific skills. In this period the economists cooperated in the rational organization of several legal and institutional control mechanisms on the personal income distribution process, of which the most important involved an undesirable restriction of union collective bargaining and political expression. These mechanisms were designed to regulate the distribution of national income among social groups and classes in order to promote monetary stabilization and capital accumulation policies. As the recovery and accelerated expansion of the GNP appeared to demonstrate the success of the policies, the economists' professional prestige rose rapidly in the public sector and especially among the administrative elite.

However, after 1973/74 the national and international economic scenery changed. Internal inflation repressed by official price controls led to a general scarcity of those wage goods whose prices were fixed. The idle capacity in manufacturing was exhausted, and there was great pressure on the balance of payments (quite apart from the fourfold increase in oil prices) owing to the import of machinery, equipment, and basic inputs. There was a recession coexisting with inflation in the main industrialized countries, and a contraction of the international capital markets. There were intolerable inequalities in the distribution of income and wealth, which were aggravated by the accelerated expansion of the economy in the 1967–74 period.

The economists' traditional analysis on which policy had hitherto been based proved incapable of coping with these adverse conditions. There were wrong decisions and conditional predictions were falsified. The prestige of the technocracy was shaken to such an extent that one of the major national newspapers claimed that the economists, in proposing their policies, "were like Christopher Columbus, who sailed off without knowing where, arrived at a place he did not know, and was all the time financed by public funds."

From this moment other economists started to reveal, with greater insistence and penetration, their ideas about the country's development alternatives. They considered that the key problems were not merely to eliminate the economic gap between actual and potential

GNP, nor to provide anticyclical measures, but much deeper questions, such as the elimination of absolute poverty levels in the rural and urban areas, the discovery of economically feasible energy alternatives, the restructuring of supply in favor of a greater production of public goods and wage goods, maintenance of the per capita GNP growth rate and price stability in face of the unfavorable international economic situation, and so on. They attempted to show that these new challenges could be met by a decisionmaking process which assumes the concentration of power within the technocracy, but which was fundamentally opposed to the dynamics of political re-democratization in the country.

The economists' role in policymaking

The economists' role in the formulation, implementation, and control of public policies in Brazil can be considered either in terms of their methodological approach to the question of the nature and scope of government intervention in the economy or, more directly, by examining the range and variety of functions they perform in changing political and institutional conditions.

In methodological terms two different positions can be identified: the neoclassical and structural-historical approaches. According to Lionel Robbins' famous definition of economics[17] a clear-cut distinction must be made between Economic Science, which is concerned with the formal relationship between given ends and scarce means, and Economic History, which is concerned with the actual manifestations of such relationships over time. Critics contend that this dichotomy is too rigid, and that existing social institutions are assumed to be given and unchanging; and proponents of the alternative, Political Economy, approach emphasize the need to take account of the dynamics of institutional change, thereby bringing economics back into contact with Sociology, History, and Political Science. Political economy includes the analysis of short- and long-run adaptations, and the phenomena of evolution and revolution, whereas static Economic Theory abstracts from institutions and structures, thereby becoming merely a rationalization of the status quo.

What are the implications of these two approaches for the professional economist in government? Robbins' view, subsequently formalized by Milton Friedman, starts with a conceptual distinction between positive and normative statements,[18] and the impossibility of deriving

---

17. L. Robbins, *An Essay on the Nature and Significance of Economic Science* (New York, 1969), ch. 2; and J. Marchal, *Cours d'économie politique* (Paris, 1959).

18. M. Friedman, *Essays in Positive Economics* (Chicago, 1953), pp. 3–43.

the one category from the other, and accordingly prescribes the economist's task as taking as given the ends, objectives, or priorities of different policies established in the political system and derived from ideological preferences, and utilizing his positive knowledge in order to explain or predict the consequences of any change in circumstances or events. He can make an important contribution to policy discussions by producing probabilistic statements about the consequences of specific economic policies or social legislation. The choice of policies will, however, be determined by the values and objectives of the individuals and groups participating in the decisionmaking process.

In Brazil many professional economists in government have confined themselves to 'intelligence' problems[19]—that is, the "gathering, processing, interpretation and communication of the technical and political information required by the decisionmaking process." In our interviews we observed that executive managers and advisers in public agencies (especially those in the National Departments of Finances and Agriculture) strongly favored this Robbinsian conception of the economist as a person who investigates the conditions for the optimum allocation of scarce resources in situations where the goals have been exogenously determined. Thus they become bureaucrats, accepting the "specific duty of loyalty to the prescriptions which are inherent to their job, placing themselves at the service of an objective and impersonal purpose, constituting an efficient and subservient instrument at the service of a centralized and supreme command."[20]

Turning to empirical studies of the economist's role in the policymaking process in Brazil, there are three sources of information: (1) surveys and panels with public managers in high administrative positions; (2) personal reports by key actors; and (3) the institutional analysis of public bureaucracies. In a survey of top-level managers and advisers from the Department of Agriculture, in which the questions were designed to identify the limits of their decisionmaking capacity, the results revealed that:

(a) 66.7 percent of executive managers and 65.8 percent of advisers considered themselves to have little influence on major government decisions and policies;

(b) 83.6 percent of executive managers and 87.7 percent of advisers denied that public administration was so complex that it was incapable of improvement;

19. H. L. Wilensky, *Organizational Intelligence* (New York, 1967), ch. 1.
20. C. Sarmento, *Administradores públicos de alto nível na burocracia brasileira: o caso do Ministério da Agricultura* (Rio de Janeiro, 1978), ch. 3: C. E. Martins, "Tecnocracia e burocracia," in C. E. Martins, *Tecnocracia e capitalismo; a política dos técnicos no Brasil* (São Paulo, 1974), ch. 2, pp. 28–48.

(c) 87.9 percent of executive managers and 69.9 percent of advisers denied that the interdependence of issues made it difficult to make decisions on specific matters;

(d) both groups considered that the lack of information about the activities of other public agencies constituted a source of difficulties;

(e) opinions were divided as to whether the size and diversity of the Department's activities constituted a serious obstacle to decisionmaking.

The relevance of this questionnaire is unquestionable since it included almost 80 percent of top-level managers and advisers in a department which has dealt systematically with economic policy for more than fifteen years. Almost half its personnel are agricultural economists, and it should be noted that in Brazil there is no marked gap between them and other economists.

From our interviews and panels it appears that, on the whole, public sector economists consider themselves to have a broad degree of freedom to formulate and implement decisions on economic policies. But they lack the freedom to deal with such basic matters affecting the accumulation and distribution of wealth as the role of foreign capital in the economy, the institutional relationship of wealth ownership, and the extent of state intervention in productive activities. These matters are determined not by the technical staff but by the 'system'—i.e., the military establishment, national economic pressure groups, and multinational corporations. Finally, an increasing number of economists feel that their professional associations, which enjoy greater freedom of expression than the public agencies in which economists are employed, should exert more influence on national economic decisions. Hitherto these associations have avoided party political issues, but have been timidly starting discussions about such current political issues as civil liberties and political amnesty.

Among the personal reports, one of the most representative was that by Celso Furtado, who during the 1950s and early '60s exerted a great intellectual influence upon a number of government economists through his academic work and professional activities in various high-level federal positions.[21] In a testimony to the Institute of Economists of Rio de Janeiro, Furtado stated that in his day economists did not feel inhibited by their involvement in the machinery of government:

> although, in our group, there were conflicting ideological lines in various respects, we all had the characteristic of considering our-

21. W. Baer, "Furtado on Development: A Review Essay," *Journal of Developing Areas*, Jan. 1969. The testimony of Furtado to the IERJ was in August 1978.

selves, first of all, as politically responsible citizens towards the community . . . and because of this, we discussed economic problems as extensions of the political debate and from a political point of view; this caused our debate to have an immediate external impact on the political field.

He was convinced that the economists were the professional group best equipped to deal with the central problems of Brazilian society and was consequently surprised that in the current discussion of institutional reconstruction and the definition of general national objectives, fifteen years after the military movement of 1964, economic problems were being assigned a subordinate position as though "they were not the fundamental issues to consider and those which will ultimately define the level of the political discussion in the medium run."

Furtado observed that during the past twenty years there had been a considerable advance in the economist's professional training. Yet the highest-quality training had generated some rigidity, for the economist had been relegated to the background of the present debates as though "transformed, in fact, into a supertechnician, and not into a man who is capable of approaching general problems." For Furtado, therefore, the great risk for the present generation of economists, with their non-political behavior, was that of becoming a technocratic instrument of other social groups within the political system. Thus "the reduction to formal rationality decreases the effectiveness of economic thinking and really limits the economist's inventive capability."

Another reliable source of empirical data on the economist's role in policymaking is the institutional analysis of public bureaucracies undertaken by Brazilian political scientists during the past five years as a method of assessing national public policies. Starting from the principle that traditional economic theory presupposes that public organizations which design, prepare, and execute or control policies possess a purely instrumental or neutral character, they examine the influence of institutions as "recalcitrant instruments" or obstacles to the implementation of objectives, possessing "different histories, different decision and centralization levels, serving different customers and developing crystallized interests and objectives of their own."[22] On the other hand, private-interest associations, in mobilizing their representation, attempt to become meshed in with the public agencies in order to strengthen their bargaining power. Such agencies tend to stimulate such relationships in order to demonstrate their administrative legitimacy and efficiency, thereby increasing their interdependence with the

22. Fundação João Pinheiro, *Plano nacional de pecuária* (Belo Horizonte, 1978), vol. 4, ch. 9.

private sector. These interdependencies result from the weakness of private associations in mobilizing actions in favor of their interests, which results in the increase of decisionmaking by public institutions, and the oligopolization or cartelization of private interests in organizations with politically powerful enough 'anti-planning' actions. In the former case, depressed areas, low-income farmers, groups of consumers, or small and medium-size entrepreneurs are politically fragmented and disconnected. Some economists increasingly sympathize with these areas or groups by advocating planning and devising special development programs to promote their interests. In the latter case, the increased capacity to control economic groups has led them to articulate their interest with the political subsystem without the mediation of the technical level. In such cases, the economists and other experts in policymaking have been put in the uncomfortable position of rationalizing ex-post decisions which have been exogenously determined for them.

Concluding remarks

There has been no systematic research in Brazil on the role of economists in government and related issues. Although most of our graduates work in the public sector, which has dominated the country's economic growth and development, the available bibliography is only indirectly relevant to this subject.

While the quality of teaching and research in Economics has improved greatly during the past two decades, since the university political crisis of 1968 the number of Economics students and courses has increased exponentially, leading to an excess supply of technically unqualified economists in the market. Those who entered government service have brought with them many ideological prejudices about the role of government in economic development and are quite incapable of dealing with the Brazilian economy's current problems.

However many professional economists—both in the top echelon of the public bureaucracy and among those critical of official policies—are in touch with the frontiers of economic analysis and with current European and United States theories on the formulation and evaluation of public policies. In the 1980s these economists will have to play a crucial role in laying the basis of a new pattern of economic growth and development for Brazil which may reinforce the process of political redemocratization.

Bibliography

The following items constitute a basic bibliography on the development of the Brazilian economy.

Baer, W. *The Brazilian Economy: Its Growth and Development*. Columbus, Ohio, 1979.

Furtado, C. *The Economic Growth of Brazil*. Berkeley, Calif., 1963.

Malan, Pedro S., and R. Bonelli. "The Brazilian Economy in the Seventies: Old and New Developments." *World Development*, Jan.-Feb. 1977.

Roett, R., ed. *Brazil in the Seventies*. Washington, D.C., 1976.

Stepan, A., ed. *Authoritarian Brazil: Origins, Policy and Future*. New Haven, 1973.

Conclusions

A. W. Coats

The preceding studies contain valuable new evidence on the historical circumstances and institutional arrangements under which professional economists, as practitioners of a distinctively modern branch of specialised knowledge, have come to play an increasingly important role in the processes of government since World War II. Admittedly, none of the individual country studies in this collection can claim to be complete or definitive; and taken as a whole, the collection is neither large nor representative enough to serve as a basis for confident generalisations about the nature and significance of the subject. Nevertheless it is appropriate to conclude this exercise by drawing attention to some of the tentative findings of our investigations. These are presented under two broad headings: (a) common features and trends, and (b) reflections on the current state of knowledge of the field, and the need for further research.

In the interests of brevity, and in order to avoid unnecessary repetition, no attempt will be made here to cover all the topics referred to in the introductory essay. In some instances there is nothing significant to add to the general remarks therein; in others the experience of the various countries is so varied and complex that no simple generalisations can apply to all cases.

Common features and trends

The employment of professional economists is now generally accepted by governments throughout the world, and also by a wide variety of private and public, national and international institutions. Despite considerable variations in the timing and pace of this movement, economists have, in a number of cases, been in the vanguard of the process of professionalisation in modern government (as, for example, in the cases of Brazil, Hungary, and India described above).

The demand for professional economists is both an integral part and a by-product of the seemingly inexorable twentieth-century expansion in the range and variety of government economic and social activities and responsibilities. In this process ideas and events have interacted in subtle and complex ways. Political regimes of all colourations have called upon professionals and technical experts to solve current problems and promote economic growth and social welfare, and they have been spurred on by rising expectations derived from the dissemination of general education, the mass media, and doctrinal developments such as Keynesian ideas of macroeconomic management and various species of economic planning. Important, too, has been the global spread of economic and military competition and international measures to promote economic development stabilisation, and political, financial, and commercial cooperation.

The increased employment of government economists would obviously have been impossible without the rapid, sometimes dramatic, growth and transformation of higher educational institutions largely, but not exclusively, financed by public funds. In the early postwar years many of these institutions were ill-equipped to provide an adequate supply of qualified economists and other trained personnel for the public service, and in some countries considerable cultural barriers and resistance had to be overcome. Nevertheless, postwar experience reveals that given sufficient pressure of perceived demand, backed by adequate pecuniary and non-pecuniary inducements, there has usually been a rapid and substantial response on the supply side. Needless to say, an increased output of trained 'economists,' a category exceedingly difficult to define unambiguously, is no guarantee of quality, and many of the new recruits to the profession have doubtless been deficient in knowledge and technique when judged by the standards applicable in leading countries. Moreover, the studies in this volume reveal the absence of any exact correlation between the quantity and quality of educational facilities, the state of development of economics as a discipline, and the growth in the numbers and importance of economists in any country.

During the period under review there have, of course, been very substantial changes in the content of economists' academic training. The average level of technique and analytical rigour has risen markedly, and American methods and standards of graduate education have exerted a disproportionate influence in this process, at least in Western nations. Innumerable foreign students have been trained in North America and Europe, many of whom have returned to their homeland or have obtained employment in other governments and international agencies. In addition to the global diffusion of new ideas and techniques there have also been direct national and international political and financial pressures and inducements to raise the quality of economic expertise and performance. Not only are there many more economists, but those available now can generally be said to have more to offer potential employers in the form of concepts, tools, models, and quantitative skills than their prewar or early postwar precursors. It is therefore hardly surprising that they are now engaged on a much wider range of activities and in a much wider variety of government department and agencies than two or three decades ago.

This state of affairs constitutes strong prima facie evidence of the value of the economists' services. However, there is some danger of accepting too complacent and simplistic an explanation of recent trends. For one thing, fashion as well as demonstrable effectiveness has played a significant part in the demand for ever more sophisticated analysis and techniques, e.g. in econometric forecasting and model building, and in the utilisation of cost-benefit analysis, planned programme budgeting systems, and more elaborate attempts at public-expenditure controls. There has been a subtle combination of pressures from politicians anxious to fulfil overambitious election promises; rising public expectations, fueled by the press and the academic community; the demand for economic techniques from those ministers, party members, and senior officials who have either been trained in the subject or have become persuaded of its value; and, last but by no means least, from the internal demand generated by government economists anxious to work with their own kind. No doubt many civil-servant administrators genuinely recognise the value of economists, provided of course that their own position is not threatened by the professionals. Indeed, this largely explains the well known urge to keep economists and other experts 'on tap, not on top.'

Another reason why the autonomous scientific and technical development of the discipline is not the sole reason for the increased demand for economists in government is that many, if not most, of them are not regularly utilising the more advanced and esoteric parts of their professional equipment. The growth of modern government has not merely generated a demand for economic specialists, it has also transformed the character of public administration. Hence many trained economists are now engaged on tasks similar or identical to those previously performed by generalist administrators. Economists' training gives them a comparative advantage in handling the enormously expanded volume of quantitative data generated nowadays in public and private life. But this may of course be too slender a basis on which to establish claims to professional recognition. As noted earlier, economics is a vocationally non-specific subject; there is no neatly demarcatable range of tasks for which economists are ideally and exclusively equipped. Moreover, the greatly enlarged opportunities for in-service training in economics and statistics provided for non-specialists, and the increased employment of other professionals with numerate skills may be reducing the number of problems and subjects on which economists have clear differential advantages over other categories of officials. Here too, circumstances vary greatly over time, and from one part of the machinery of government to another. But having once been in the vanguard, economists, like jurists in an earlier epoch, may occasionally look over their shoulders to view the catching-up process with some misgivings.

As the preceding essays abundantly confirm, the value of an economist's contribution to government does not depend on his professional competence alone. In addition to analytical ability and technical skill a variety of other qualities are essential, such as

> tact; patience; adaptability; the capacity to work quickly under pressure; the ability to communicate with non-specialists; skill in the arts of persuasion; a sense of timing; grasp of bureaucratic procedures and conventions, or more colloquially, the capacity to 'play the machine'; appreciation of the problems of administrative feasibility and political practicality; recognition of the limits of one's professional expertise; and sheer stamina.

Of course, not all these desirable qualities are required in equal measure in every government post. Unfortunately many of them cannot be taught in educational institutions, and the relevance of the economists' academic training to their experience in government is a matter referred to below, item (3). But while there is clearly a role in government for 'thinkers' as well as 'doers,' it is easy to appreciate why 'academic,' when applied to a government economist, is not necessarily to be taken as a commendation.

The preceding contributions provide clear evidence of the wide variety of functions performed by professional economists in government. Generalisations about these functions are liable to be either unreliable or banal, but there has usually been a spread of functions downwards through the hierarchy, beginning with the occasional or permanent high-level adviser, who is often the first professional to be appointed.

While there has been a growth in the number of high-level advisers, and a tendency for economists to capture an increasing proportion of top posts previously occupied by traditional administrators, the most striking recent developments have been in the middle and upper ranks of the hierarchy. This has been a direct by-product of the increasingly technical and quantitative content of modern economics, and has led to an expansion of the size of research and other specialised divisions or units, often directly connected with central economic management (i.e. macroeconomics) or the budgetary process. One exception to this generalisation is agriculture, which has often been a pioneering branch of government economics, followed at a later stage by specialist groups of microeconomists concerned with other specific fields—trade, transport, industry, labour, etc. Employment of economists in social departments usually occurs well after they have been established in economic departments. With the growth of numbers there is also eventually a need for administrative and personnel management of the professionals, a matter to be considered below in connection with the professionalisation process.

With respect to the market for economists there is a serious dearth of relevant information and analysis apart from the United States, where there has been considerable research on this matter, and a provisional study of the British situation. During most of the period under review academic economists have been in great demand both within and outside educational institutions, but the end of the long postwar university boom, which is apparently a general phenomenon, will undoubtedly bring major changes. Several of the preceding studies contain impressionistic evidence of changes over time in the relative attractiveness of government, academic, and other employment opportunities, and there are obviously great differences between countries like the United Kingdom and the United States, where significant numbers of professional economists have entered government service for short periods, and those like Japan and Italy, where regular exchanges between academic and official posts are either unknown or very unusual. The other cases covered in this series fall somewhere between these extremes, and it is worth noting the absence of significant salary differentials between government and other economists in Hungary, and the fact that in Israel significant numbers of professional economists have moved on from official life to other posts with no intention of returning to public service. In India, as in many other countries with widespread poverty, economists find government employment attractive as a permanent career, and it is noteworthy that in Britain, where alternative employment opportunities have deteriorated sharply in recent years, the Government Economic Service has now become almost entirely a permanent cadre. It is too early to gauge the effects of this change from early postwar decades, when regular interchanges between government and universities were generally regarded as beneficial to both sides.

The preceding studies provide considerable if uneven evidence of the professional economists' rise to positions of prestige and influence within the bureaucracy; but while this has undoubtedly enhanced their opportunities for professional autonomy and self-control, there is much less evidence on these matters. Despite widespread recognition of the risks of professional obsolescence and the potentially damaging effects of prolonged immersion in immediate problems and day-to-day bureaucratic routines, there has been comparatively little collective interest in the provision of organisational safeguards. These are, of course, less essential in situations where there are regular exchanges between academic and government personnel, and where close relations have been maintained between the two categories. Even without regular exchanges, government economists have tried to secure rights to attend conferences, publish uncontroversial research papers, and even have periodic leaves of absence—which are, of course, difficult to institutionalise, especially for key personnel. More surprising, perhaps, is the apparent lack of formal concern for professional ethics, possibly because economists as a whole are less organisation-minded than some other categories of social scientists (e.g. psychologists and sociologists). In the preceding cases the one significant exception is the United States, where professional issues are usually more conscious and open among academics than in many other countries. Apart from the interest in market conditions referred to earlier, problems of professional ethics and politicisation have figured prominently in public discussion largely owing to the special delicacy of the professional economists' position on the Council of Economic Advisers.

The contributors to this collection have no confidence in efforts to provide formal measures of 'influence.' Nevertheless, the preceding contributions provide abundant, if somewhat impressionistic, evidence of the impact of professional economists on governmental processes and policies. Even in Japan, where there are no recognised professional economists in the government, the influence of occasional advisers and consultants, academic opinion, and the views of other outsiders are not to be entirely discounted. Elsewhere, making due allowances for variations in the individual authors' emphases and approaches, it appears that economists have exerted comparatively little influence in Italy, largely owing to the weak and inefficient bureaucratic system and to disagreements within the economics profession itself; while at the other end of the spectrum, they seem to have had the greatest impact in Norway, Brazil (since 1965), and Hungary (since 1968). Their influence has also been considerable in Australia, Israel, and—possibly to a somewhat lesser extent—in India. In the United States the situation is complicated by the present countervailing forces within the political, executive, and bureaucratic structures. Few observers would deny that economists have been prominent and important, especially in recent years, but attempts to implement policies have often been thwarted or significantly modified by Congress, which has frequently been overexposed to a babel of voices, including many conflicting professional opinions. In Britain the small number of professionals in Whitehall prior to the mid-1960s, their effective integration into the higher civil service, and the combination of a consensual style of government and an effective Official Secrets Act make it peculiarly difficult to form any precise judgement. However, the growth in the numbers and rise in status of professionals in government since the mid-1960s is powerful prima facie evidence of the increase in their influence in Whitehall, as elsewhere.

Needless to say, any attempt to construct a league table of 'influence' must necessarily be suspect and potentially misleading. Limitations of evidence apart, it is seldom possible to identify and evaluate all the operative conditions in complex policymaking processes. The preceding studies do, however, provide general indications of the factors conducive to the influence of economists in government. These include a stable and effective government committed to consistent and feasible policies,[1] willing to provide the resources necessary to achieve its objectives, and ready to recognise and provide suitable opportunities for economic experts and advisers to formulate, decide, and implement appropriate measures. This is more likely to occur where the bureaucracy is well-organised and efficient, and where senior officials are eager to cooperate with economists and provide them with necessary information, supporting staff, and channels of communication. (The bureaucracy need not be politically committed to the government's programme, for an efficient but neutral bureaucracy can be a powerful source of support.) Economists are more likely to be effective where their profession is well-developed and unified (without, of course, being dominated by a single group or doctrine) and where its leaders command respect, are professionally competent, and willing to work within the constraints of political and bureaucratic life. The existence of an ideological rapport, or at least mutual confidence between politicians, senior civil servants, and professional economists is also a strong positive factor, if not indeed a *sine qua non*.

These broad generalities seem somewhat empty, even obvious, when set against the complex and varied conditions portrayed in the

---

1. In the postwar period the predominant tendency has been towards interventionism of various kinds. But there is no reason in principle why economists cannot or should not assist in formulating and implementing non-interventionist policies. If the government's policy is one of inaction or neglect, whether benign or otherwise, there is no need for professionals of any kind. Whether economists in government should help to implement or even subvert policies they believe to be ineffective or harmful is a delicate question of professional ethics. See the discussion under Professional Ethics and Standards in the "Introduction" to these studies.

preceding studies. Contrary to Weber's ideal type, orderly bureau-cratic routines are constantly being disrupted by emergencies derived from the irrationality, irregularity, and inconsistencies of political life. As Cairncross has remarked, the normal atmosphere of a large govern-ment department is frequently akin to that of the "loony bin," and W. R. Allen's fascinating interviews with American government econo-mists have revealed some of the inescapable compromises, and sudden and erratic changes of intention and direction in high official places.[2] In government there is an almost irresistible tendency to resort to short-run expediency rather than well-considered long-run strategies; for—as the familiar phrase has it—in official life the important must of-ten give way to the urgent. In such circumstances economists are liable to find not merely that optimal solutions to problems cannot be specified, but also that second-best or even third-best solutions may be viewed as too costly or painful to be acceptable in practice.

Given our limited knowledge of the role of economists in govern-ment, the highly interdisciplinary character of this field, and the lack of previous systematic research, it is hardly surprising that there is no readily available model or framework of analysis that will accommo-date the relevant variables, which seem to interact in an unsystematic but non-random manner. The studies presented here provide valuable raw materials for such a construct, even some explicit typologies. But none of the authors has seen fit to attempt such an undertaking, though some have gently suggested that this should form part of the editor's responsibilities!

To economists, the most obvious model is that advanced by Jan Tinbergen and his associates, couched in terms of general "aims," pre-cisely defined "objectives," and specific "instruments" or "mea-sures" to achieve these objectives.[3] However, attempts to apply this type of model to past experience have encountered severe difficulties. According to one authoritative recent commentator on British policy:

> Policy makers were uncertain about their objectives; they often pursued intermediate objectives, tended to concentrate on one thing at a time, and found that differences in political philosophy often revealed themselves in choices of instruments rather than objectives. Partly because knowledge of the economic system was imperfect, policies were liable to considerable instability; as one

2. Cf. Coats, "Britain: The Rise of the Specialists," above, at n.68, and Allen, "Economics, Economists, and Economic Policy: Modern American Experiences," *History of Political Economy* 9 (1977): 48–88.

3. See, for example, Jan Tinbergen, *Economic Policy: Principles and Design* (Amsterdam, 1956); E. S. Kirschen et al., *Economic Policy in Our Time*, vol. 1: *General Theory* (Amsterdam, 1964).

set of policies appeared unsuccessful, another set, which implied a different view of the working of the economy, was ready and waiting in the wings.[4]

Non-economist students of policy processes have noted that economists—especially those lacking firsthand experience of official life—tend to exaggerate the rationality of government decision-making.[5] The interaction of political, social, and economic conditions, ideas, individuals, and institutions is in practice so complex that there is, at least at present, "no unified perspective and no one overriding scheme for rational interpretation and explanation." Public policy may, indeed, be inseparable from the policy processes themselves, and it is therefore necessary to emphasise "the uncertainty, complexity, and intermittent activity of policymaking, the diversity of influences making it, and the fragmentation of institutions."[6] These words are intended neither as a counsel of despair nor as a ban on efforts to construct systematic approaches to our subject. They are merely an indication of the reasons why such an undertaking is considered to be beyond the scope of the present symposium.

Reflections on the current state of knowledge and
the need for further research

No attempt will be made to list all the significant questions and potentially fruitful topics for investigation arising from the researches undertaken for this collection. What follows is simply an enumeration of some of the most glaring gaps in our knowledge and stimulating opportunities available to future researchers.

(1) First and foremost, on a purely practical level, is the urgent need for access to relevant documentation in government archives, for this has been the main obstacle to the research undertaken for most of the country studies. Given official restrictions, it will not be easy to open up the archives, but the task may be facilitated if this set of studies demonstrates the potential usefulness of the subject to politicians and public officials, as well as to academics. However, even without government archives it is apparent that considerable progress can be made by utilising official publications, the great variety of secondary

---

4. Blackaby, *British Economic Policy 1960–74* (Cambridge, 1978), p. 10.
5. See, for example, Hugh Heclo, review article, "Policy Analysis," *British Journal of Political Science* 2 (1972): 104. For a sympathetic but critical treatment by an economist of the 'economistic' approach adopted in recent public-choice literature see Peacock, *The Economic Analysis of Government, and Related Themes* (Oxford, 1979), Part IV.
6. G. Hawker, R. F. I. Smith, and P. Weller, *Politics and Policy in Australia* (St. Lucia, 1979), pp. 22–23.

sources, interviews with leading participants in governmental processes, and, in some cases, the unpublished papers and correspondence of ex-government economists.

(2) The central issue of interest to most economists, as to many
other scholars and members of the public, is this: What light does this
research shed on the professional economists' contributions to government, and more particularly, their influence on policymaking? For the
reasons already stated, any direct and simple answers to these questions must be regarded with suspicion. Even so, our studies fully justify the claim that substantial progress has been made, and that the
promise for future research is clear. A major desideratum is the abandonment of the previous practice of posing the relevant questions in
too crude and simplistic terms. 'Influence' needs to be specified more
precisely; more systematic attempts must be made to distinguish between areas, issues, and periods in which economists have played a
significant role (even though it is not exactly measurable) and those
where they have been ignored, by-passed, or overruled. It may also
help to answer such questions as these: Do professional economists, in
general, exercise restraint on interventionist regimes (the supposed
'conservatism,' both political and professional, of economists and
other social scientists),[7] or do they function mainly as innovators and
irritants within the bureaucracy, possibly encouraging politicians and
senior civil servants to be overambitious? And, more generally, does
this research shed any light on J. M. Keynes' oft-quoted remark that
the world is ruled by "little else" than the "ideas of economists," a
suggestion dangerously attractive to students of the history of ideas.

(3) Given the available evidence on the functions performed by
government economists, it is appropriate to consider the level and content of training most suitable for this type of employment. For example, what are the respective merits of an initial general degree, which
includes an economics component, of a specialist first degree in economics, of an initial degree in another subject, or combination of subjects, plus a postgraduate or in-service 'topping up' in economics? Of
course the answers will depend partly, if not mainly, on the type of job
to which the appointee is posted; and unless the job is a temporary one,
his long-run career prospects will also need to be taken into account. In
some contexts an advanced postgraduate degree in economics is regarded as a prerequisite for professional status; but more generally the
requirement may be that of an ABD—i.e. 'all but dissertation'—since
an academic piece of research is viewed as less relevant to government

7. A significant recent example is described in Henry J. Aaron, *Politics and the Professors: The Great Society in Perspective* (Washington, 1978).

employment than the preparatory training itself. Doubtless there is no single optimal answer, certainly not without an examination of the curriculum content and the relevant job specifications. Nevertheless a study of these matters would be fruitful, especially in view of the widespread contention that the training of economists nowadays overemphasises theoretical sophistication and command of technique at the expense of other qualities, such as the ability to grasp the relevance of theory to practice, knowledge of the workings of the economic system, and historical understanding. These qualities may be especially important to the economist working in government.

(4) There is, of course, a need to examine the role of economists in government in a number of other countries—for example, in eastern Europe, Latin America, Asia, and the Middle East.[8] Studies of Russia and some of the less-developed countries would also be revealing, as would studies of the work of economists in supranational bodies like Comecon and the EEC. The results of such enquiries would be of great interest to students of development economics and of comparative politics and economic systems.

(5) There is also a need for more intensive and systematic research on a large number of topics that have been passed over briefly in the preceding chapters. The most promising include these:

(a) The feedback effects of government employment on academic economics by means of interviews with ex-government economists, and by an analysis of their teachings and/or writings before and after their official service. It would also be instructive to compare situations where there are or have been regular exchanges between civil-service and academic personnel with those where such changes have been rare or lacking. How far, for example, has the experience of government work affected the content and progress of knowledge, especially the relationship between 'pure' and 'applied' research?

(b) The 'effectiveness' of economists in different types of work and organisational settings—e.g., as advisors, technicians, or quasi-administrators; as occasional consultants, temporary insiders (whether or not political appointees), or as permanent officials; as individuals or in groups (whether in specialist units or mixed divisions); in central economic as against peripheral social departments or agencies; as between bureaucracies of different 'styles'; and in central, state, or municipal government. The re-

8. Research on lines somewhat similar to that undertaken for these studies is already advanced in Belgium and the Netherlands, and there was an unpublished Ford Foundation survey of a number of Arab countries in 1966.

sults of such studies should be of interest to economists and also to students of bureaucracy, occupational psychology and sociology.

(c) The relations between economists and politicians, generalist administrators, and other professionals and specialists in government (e.g. statisticians). Research here would shed new light on old questions, such as 'specialists' vs. 'generalists' (for example, by statistical studies of the changing position of economists in civil service hierarchies) and the relations between politicians and 'experts.' It would also provide new insights into public administration and the sociology of the professions and could lead to studies of the role of economists in legislatures and in the press.

(d) The professionalisation of economics, both within and outside government. In the former context this topic would include such matters as professional autonomy, recognition, and self-control (e.g. over recruitment, placement, and promotion); the growth of trade-union mindedness as the proportion of full-time officials increases; and problems of job satisfaction, research and publication opportunities, methods of countering professional obsolescence, politicisation, and questions of professional ethics and standards.

(e) The market for economists, of which government work constitutes a highly variable component both with respect to period and time.

(6) Two other topics, indirectly related to the preceding studies, deserve mention by way of conclusion:

(a) The role of economists in government during and before World War II—a field with rich promise for historians of various types.

(b) The role of economists in international agencies, such as the League of Nations and the International Labour Organisation during the interwar years; and, since 1945, such bodies as the United Nations, World Bank, International Monetary Fund, Organisation for European Economic Co-operation, etc. The list is potentially endless; but the subject is especially promising as an example of the international diffusion and influence of a single important profession. It would provide a stimulating new perspective on the development of the postwar world.

Additional bibliography

General

Dogan, Mattei, ed. *The Mandarins of Western Europe: The Political Role of Top Civil Servants*. New York, 1975.
Jöhr, W. A., and Singer, H.W. *The Role of the Economist as Official Adviser*. London, 1955.
Schaffer, B. B., ed. *Administrative Training and Development*. New York, 1974.

Belgium

Steinlet, Georges. *Economists and the Civil Service System: The Belgian Case*. Louvain, 1978.

Malawi

Giles, B. D. "Economists in Government: The Case of Malawi." *Journal of Development Studies* 15 (Jan. 1979): 216–32.

Mexico

Camp, Roger Ai. *The Role of Economists in Policy-Making: A Comparative Case Study of Mexico and the United States*. Tucson, Ariz., 1977.
Solis, Leopoldo. "Mexican Economic Policy in the Post-War Period: The Views of Mexican Economists." *American Economic Review*, Suppl. *Surveys of National Economic Policy Issues and Policy Research* 61 (June 1971).

The Netherlands (supplied by Drs. M. L. Bemelmans-Videc)

Albert, J. G. *Economic Policy and Planning in the Netherlands, 1950–1965*. New Haven, 1969.
Baehr, P. "The Netherlands," In *European Political Parties*, ed. S. Henig and J. Pinder. London, 1969.
Centraal Planbureau, The Hague. Regular publications in English.
Eldersveld, S. J., et al. "Elite Perceptions of the Political Process in the Netherlands, Looked at in Comparative Perspective." In M. Dogan, *The Mandarins of Western Europe* (New York, 1975).
Goudsblom, J. *Dutch Society*. New York, 1967.
Hasenberg-Butter, Irene. *Academic Economics in Holland, 1800–1870*. The Hague, 1969.
Marris, Robert. "The Position of Economics and Economists in the Government Machine: A Comparative Critique of the U.K. and the Netherlands." *Economic Journal*, Dec. 1954.
Schneider, Hans K. *Grundsatzprobleme Wirtschaftspolitischer Beratung. Das Beispiel der Stabilisierungspolitik*. Schriften des Vereins für Sozialpolitik. Berlin, 1968.

356   Economists in Government

Singh, W. *Policy Development: A Study of the Social and Economic Council of the Netherlands*, U.P.R., 1972.
Verrijn Stuart, C. A. "The History and Development of Statistics in the Netherlands." In *The History of Statistics; Their Development and Progress in Many Countries*, ed. J. Koren (New York, 1918), pp. 429–44.
Westrate, C. *Economic Policy in Practice: The Netherlands, 1950–1957.* Leiden, 1959.
Wolff, P. de. "Die Beratung der Stabilisierungspolitik in den Niederlanden." In *Grundsatzprobleme Wirtschaftspolitischer Beratung*. Schriften des Vereins für Sozialpolitik. Berlin, 1968.

Zaire

Rimlinger, G. V. "Administrative Training and Modernization in Zaire." *Journal of Development Studies* 12 (1976): 364–82.

Index